FR MORAN OF KATHMANDU

Dedication

In memory of my mother,
Amey Ellen (Bates) Messerschmidt

And remembering three friends in Kathmandu,
James Donnelly, SJ, John Locke, SJ, and Fr Ludwig Stiller, SJ,
each of whom died in 2009 as this second edition was being prepared.

FR MORAN OF KATHMANDU

Pioneer Priest, Educator
and Ham Radio Voice of the Himalayas

The Biography of Fr Marshall D. Moran, SJ
(1906-1992)
2ND EDITION, REVISED

Don Messerschmidt

Orchid Press

Don Messerschmidt
FR MORAN OF KATHMANDU: Pioneer Priest, Educator and Ham Radio Voice of the Himalayas

2nd Edition, 2012

ORCHID PRESS
PO Box 1046,
Silom Post Office,
Bangkok 10504, Thailand
www.orchidbooks.com

Copyright © Orchid Press 1997, 2012

Protected by copyright under the terms of the International Copyright Union: all rights reserved. Except for fair use in book reviews, no part of this publication may be reproduced in any form or by any means, electronic or mechanical, including photocopying, recording, or by any information storage or retrieval system without prior permission in writing from the copyright holder.

ISBN 978-974-524-140-4

Contents

Illustrations	vi
Foreword	vii
Introduction to the First Edition, with Acknowledgments	xi
Preface to the Second Edition	xv

THE YOUNG MORAN
1.	Youth	3
2	Scholar	27
3	Passage to India	48

EARLY CHRISTIAN MISSIONARIES IN INDIA, TIBET & NEPAL
4	Jesuits in India and Tibet	64
5.	Early Christian Missions in Nepal	85

MORAN IN NORTH INDIA
6	Two Years in Bettiah	105
7	Ordination Studies at Kurseong	126
8	The Patna Years	147

MORAN IN NEPAL
9	Into Nepal	175
10	Opening Godavari School	198
11	Affairs of State and High Society	227
12	Men to Serve Others	263

HAM PRIEST OF THE HIMALAYAS
13	On the Air	289
14	First Radio	306
15	Voice of Nepal	318
16	Friends Around the World	334

Epilogue	347
Bibliography	352
Index	360

Illustrations

1. Marshall Denis Moran, St. Louis, Missouri 1929. (Sid Whiting, Photographer) — 2

2. Fr Thomas M. Downing and Fr Marshall D. Moran, at Godavari School. — 26

3. Fr Moran with students. — 49

4. The Nepalese, as depicted in Kircher, *China Illustrata*, Amsterdam 1663. — 65

5. The Nepalese, as depicted in Kircher, *China Illustrata*, Amsterdam 1663. — 87

6. Fr Moran at his ham rig. — 106

7. Fr Moran's 9M1MM QSL Card, at his rig with school boys. — 126

8. Xavier Hall, Godavari School, with Fr Moran's ham radio antenna on the roof. — 149

9. Young priests on board the ship to India, 1920. L-R: Frs. George Dertinger, Charles Bonnot, Marshall Moran, Richard Welfle, Dick Mehren, John Morrison. — 176

10. Fr Moran in a Godavari School classroom. — 199

11. Fr Moran in front of Xavier Hall, Godavari School, with his Ham radio antennas on the roof. — 228

12. Fr Moran operating his ham radio rig. — 264

13. Fr Moran talking to students during the 40th anniversary celebration of the founding of Godavari School, 1991. — 288

14. Fr Moran with students. — 307

15. Fr Moran with students. — 319

Foreword

By Jolene Unsoeld, Member
U.S. House of Representatives
Washington DC, 1994

Even then he was mythical. It was 1962 and we had just arrived in Nepal—Willi and I and our four children, along with seventy-eight volunteers in the first wave of American Peace Corps Volunteers. Willi was Peace Corps Nepal's new Deputy Director. Our intensive training in the USA in Nepali language, culture, and history had included a chapter on Fr Moran of Kathmandu. Now, on arrival, it seemed that everyone who was anyone in that mountain kingdom had been educated by him at the St Xavier's Schools of Godavari and Jawalakhel.

He was a Jesuit priest from Chicago, a bit quixotic perhaps for giving up his US citizenship, but that was fitting for our group of PCVs; many of them were as inspired by the high Himalayan peaks and the forbidden Tibetan border as Moran was by a life of educational development in this remote corner of the world. Rumor had it that he kept his 'Western' outlook through his amateur 'Ham' radio contacts, a passion begun as a teenager.

Whether or not it was actually 'his' school, we all learned that 'Father Moran's School' was the ultimate in education for outstanding Nepalese boys, regardless of money or social status. His contribution to these lovely people was outstanding and consistent with his notions of service to God and service to those to whom the earth had been entrusted.

With our four small children, all of them feverish, coughing, or having their bouts with intestinal complaints, I missed meeting Fr Moran at the welcoming party for the Volunteers. He was one of several Western Jesuits in the country, and I wondered if I would be able to recognize him.

Then, one crisp, dry winter day as our family headed out of Kathmandu for a Sunday picnic, our jeep was barely creeping as we tried to gently maneuver through a flock of goats being herded by a couple of eight- or nine-year olds. As we safely pulled ahead of the herd, the sudden revving of a motor startled me. I looked out the side window to see a vintage motor cycle careening past us. (How did it get by the goats?) The rider was wearing a beret perched jauntily on his head, white cassock streaming in the wind, and a delighted little Nepalese schoolboy clinging to the back. Who else, but Father Moran?

It was not until Willi left to go climb Mt Everest with the 1963 American Expedition, however, that I really got to know him. Willi was part of the expedition, temporarily on leave from the Peace Corps. Fr Moran was the main radio contact for the team throughout much of the expedition.

I had married Willi not least because of his love for adventure and my desire for more of it. But with four small children, this was the closest I would come. Now Fr Moran became the direct link between those of us left behind in Kathmandu and those climbing the mountain. I, along with the official expedition historian and writer, James Ramsey Ullman, and several other expedition wives, haunted 'Kathmandu Base Camp' –the ham radio shack where daily contact was made with the men on the mountain. Fr Moran was usually at the 'mike', especially during the days Willi was on the West Ridge and the day of his summit attempt.

Each evening, either Fr Moran or the American Embassy Attaché, Col William 'Bill' Gresham, would contact Mt Everest Base Camp to keep us up to date with the progress of the climb. Each contact brought us news from the mountain. One time we were told of a smallpox epidemic in a village along the expedition route, for which the team requested an emergency supply of vaccine. Another time it brought us the terrible news of the accidental death in the Khumbu Icefall of our friend, Jake Breitenbach. One of the brighter messages we sent to the mountain was the news of the birth of climber Lute Jerstad's baby daughter. On May 2nd, we were told of the team's first summit success via the South Col route by Jim Whittaker and Nawang Gombu Sherpa. This particular news freed up the West Ridge team, Willi and his partner Tom Hornbein, to begin their pioneering assault.

Three weeks after the first summit, on May 22, 1963, while Fr Moran was at the mike talking through the static with Base Camp, we listened to the news that Tom and Willi had radioed from high on the mountain, but no other word of either them or of Barry Bishop and Lute Jerstad who were climbing from the South Col. The four had hoped to rendezvous on the summit. There followed a night of silence and numbing fear of not knowing where they were on the mountain. As a climber, I knew that however high they might have reached, the descent would be harder than the climb up.

The next morning we were back at it, apprehensively listening to the news coming down from the mountain through Fr Moran's radio receiver. Willi and Tom had radioed from just below the summit, telling Base Camp of their success just as evening shadows were overcoming the mountain. And then, more silence. No one knew whether any of the climbers had made it down off the summit.

Not until 5 pm on May 23 did the call '9N1-ME calling 9N1-MM'—Mount Everest to 'Mickey Mouse' (Marshall Moran) —bring word of tremendous events: success on the peak followed by a night out in the intense cold and, not least, of the miraculous stilling of the normally ferocious mountain winds. The men had not only climbed the peak via the previously untested West Ridge but they had survived the world's highest mountain bivouac. Now, we were told, they were descending with help to the safety of Base Camp...

And Fr Moran? He had handled it all in his inimitable way—with profound grace and faith, and not least a strong-worded prayer to still the Mt Everest wind just this once for their protection.

Fr Moran became our good friend, and over the next few years he was a frequent guest at our table. There he entertained many a diplomat, climber, PCV, and family friend with his stories of life in the Himalayan Kingdom and of long hours at his ham radio (when he wasn't teaching), transmitting emergency messages around the world and (at least that once, quite beyond this world), saving lives.

We left Nepal in 1967, but kept up with Fr Moran's career as a pioneer priest, educator, and ham radio 'Voice of the Himalayas' through mutual friends, his occasional visits back to Chicago, and even relayed through other ham operators with whom he made radio contact in my part of the world.

The story of Fr Moran's life is an important one for this time in world history, when real heroes are too few. He was one among the handful of truly inspired individuals, dedicated to helping people improve their lives, working diligently amongst some of the poorest of the world's poor. He did a splendid job of it, with sincere motivations and supported by the strict and self-effacing discipline of the Jesuit order. We admired him for that, and will never forget this man of God who dedicated his long and active life to the peoples of Nepal and India.

...And somewhere out of range of our own radio, he's impatiently revving his motor cycle, still inspiring, and always ready to leap forward into adventure in some other lifetime.

Note: In 1994, when Jolene Unsoeld wrote the Foreword to the first edition (well ahead of its publication) she was a Member of the U.S. House of Representatives (1989-95) from Washington State. Prior to that, during the early 1960s, the Unsoeld family—Jolene, Willi and their four children—knew Fr Moran well when they lived in Kathmandu while Willi served first as Deputy Director (1962) then Director (1963-65) of the American Peace Corps to Nepal. During those years, Fr Moran was a good friend of the Unsoeld family and of many American Peace Corps volunteers, including the author.

In 1963, Willi was on Mount Everest with the American Mount Everest Expedition (as described in Chapter 14). In 1979, he was killed in an avalanche on Mt. Rainier, in America's Pacific Northwest. Jolene Unsoeld lives near Olympia, Washington.

Introduction to the First Edition, with Acknowledgments

A great many people and institutions have helped in the preparation of this book. Not least among them was Father Marshall Denis Moran, SJ.

I first met Fr Moran in 1963, when I came out to Nepal as a young American Peace Corps Volunteer. In preparing for that adventure, I heard tales of the famous 'Moran of Kathmandu' from my trainers and language teachers. I met him soon after I arrived and we reacquainted time and again as I returned to Nepal over the years (often), and sometimes "on the air" by ham radio or in person when he visited the United States.

During the early 1980s, when my family and I were living in Nepal, Father Moran used to visit our house—always around coffee time. He loved our dark, fresh-brewed coffee and home-made cookies! On those occasions he would chat about his life in the Kingdom. He told many stories and anecdotes about historic events, places, and people he had known over the years, many of which are recalled in this book.

After one such visit in 1984, I suggested tape recording the events of his fascinating life. Someone, I said, should record it. Then, when I said that I would like to try my hand at writing his biography, he pondered the notion only for a moment, broke into a broad grin and said, quietly, "That would be wonderful, Don."

"But you know that I am not a Catholic," I remarked.

"That is all the better," he candidly replied. "I wouldn't want anyone to write a narrowly Catholic sort of book. And since you have lived here so long and you know so much about Nepal, you can put it all into proper perspective."

The task took over a decade to complete. At first I interviewed Fr Moran directly, sitting with him in his room upstairs in Xavier Hall at Godavari School. That did not work very well. The story line was inevitably broken when I interrupted his thoughts to tease out some detail to better understand a particular incident in his life, or asked how to spell a name, or to establish a specific date. Often we were interrupted by a priest or a school boy who needed Fr Moran's help or advice. He never refused them.

Eventually, I left a tape recorder and blank cassettes with him, and a list of topics that I updated frequently. When I listened to the first tape, I discovered that Marshall Moran had a remarkable ability to remember facts and places and whole conversations dating all the way back to his youth in Chicago. I also discovered that he was taking this all very seriously, setting aside an hour or two each day in the privacy of his room to respond to my questions. I filled in a great deal around his account by intensive library research, and other interviews. Much of this book is based on Moran's own nostalgic recorded reminiscences, with some details filled in by his friends and associates.

"Nostalgia," writes one of Fr Moran's former students from St Xavier's High School in Patna, India, "can be very destructive in that it makes one live in the past, but when one is in the autumn of one's life it is ever so delectable to go back occasionally to one's memorable archives" (see Chapter 8). In this case, Moran's personal memory archives proved very fruitful and delectable indeed.

In 1987 I visited Nepal to live near Fr Moran for a month at Godavari School in the Nepal countryside outside of Kathmandu. While there I shared in his daily life and in the lives and activities of the other priests, brothers, lay teachers and students. That experience put me in touch with the simple but incredibly rich and busy affairs of this remarkable man, his associates, and the school.

In 1989 I moved back to Nepal on a work assignment (international development assistance). I had already written several chapters of the book, but now I had the opportunity to make corrections and additions, and to continue the detailed exercise as time allowed. I plied Fr Moran with many questions to clarify details small and large. Every chapter was read and corrected by him (except the Epilogue), making this book mostly his with my help. By the end of 1991, the bulk of the manuscript was complete. The final details were written within weeks after his death on April 14, 1992.

Over the years, I corresponded with dozens of Marshall's friends and acquaintances around the world. Fr Moran knew many people—hundreds attended his funeral, hundreds were informed by mail of his death, and hundreds more heard of it "on the air" [by amateur radio]. His friends included Nepalese "old boys" [former students] and their families, government officials and peasant farmers, kings and queens and lesser royalty, ambassadors, journalists and researchers, movie stars and movie-makers, foreign aid officials and Peace Corps volunteers, fellow priests and colleagues and, not least, thousands of ham radio buddies. Most of the latter knew him only by voice and as a face in the picture on his QSL card. 9N1-"Mickey

Mouse," as he was fondly known the world around, was one of the most sought after amateur radio DX (long distance) operators ever, the original "Voice of the Himalayas." Other people knew him more personally, some of whom worked closely with him over a great many years in the Jesuit missions of Nepal and North India.

Most of the people to whom I wrote responded immediately and with enthusiasm to my requests for information about their friendship. Some replied with very detailed accounts about the points where their lives and his intersected. They wrote letters, sent cassettes, or answered my inquiries by phone or in personal interviews. A number of them recounted some remarkable coincidences and connections, as Fr Moran himself often did. Like the time he was asked to repair a broken radio receiver in Patna, an event that put him squarely back in touch with the hobby of his youth. Or the link in time between a young boy enrolling in Moran's Patna school as a war refugee in 1942, then visited Moran at his death bed fifty years later as the Archbishop of Delhi. Or, like that between a sickly premature baby born to a young Indian couple employed at St Xavier's School in Kathmandu in 1966, who was Marshall's last attending physician and signed his death certificate that last evening in Delhi, in April 1992 (described in the Epilogue).

I am thankful to all who have helped with the book. They include many of his amateur radio friends, some of whom knew him only by voice and reputation "on the air," certain librarians and academic colleagues in the USA. Mary K. Shaw of the Library of Congress in Washington, DC; and my friends Alice Spitzer and [Professor] Fritz Blackwell of Washington State University in Pullman, Washington. Special acknowledgment must also go to the director and staff of the Jesuit Missouri Province Archives in St Louis, Missouri. The archive librarian, Nancy Merz, was especially resourceful and supportive. She helped find a great deal of historical information about life the Jesuit mission in Bihar, India, where Father Moran began his career.

Many of the fathers and lay brothers associated with the Jesuit Mission in Nepal, and many of the "old boys" of St Xavier Godavari and Jawalakhel schools there, also helped in very specific and important ways. I particularly want to think Frs James Donnelly, SJ and John K. Locke, SJ of Kathmandu for their considerable energies correcting and improving drafts of the book.

Several people read the manuscript at crucial stages in its evolution, scrutinizing it from various perspectives. They all made important observations, suggestions, and corrections. Special thanks go to Bonnie Darsie, Kareen and Liesl Messerschmidt, Bruce Morrison, and Richard Kingston..

There were certainly many others who helped, but it is impossible to name them all—the list is far too long. They each know who they are, and I have thanked each of them personally already. Nonetheless, they deserve yet one more sign of my deep gratitude, from my heart and in the spirit of Father Moran: *Thank you, and God Bless!...*

Don Messerschmidt
Spring 1996

Preface to the Second Edition

The first edition of this book has had a short and interesting history. The book was originally entitled *Moran of Kathmandu: Priest, Educator & Ham Radio 'Voice of the Himalayas'* (amended slightly now to: *Fr Moran of Kathmandu*). After it was published by Orchid Press in 1997 (ISBN 9748927164), it met with enough popular interest, apparently, to attract a pirate publishing firm, State Mutual Book & Periodical Services Ltd., to print and market it illegally over the Internet, at an inflated price, under a false ISBN number. When this deceit came to our attention, the publisher and original owner of Orchid Press, H.K. Kuløy, quickly posted the following Customer Review comment on Amazon.com:

> *This is a pirate edition breaking copyright laws!*
> Poor old Father Moran would turn in his grave if he knew that State Mutual Book & Periodical Services Ltd. had illegally published his memoirs under ISBN 0785574387! The legal publisher is Orchid Press in Bangkok, and we trust amazon.com customers will buy the Orchid Press edition of the book, at less than half the price of this pirate edition! H K Kuloy, editor and publisher, Orchid Press

As author, I followed up on Amazon by clearly stating "*I am not flattered.*" And an independent reader posted this plea to prospective buyers:

> *Great man, good book, and despicable counterfeit edition*
> I knew Father Moran in Kathmandu and the author does a wonderful job of accurately portraying this colorful character and his significant achievements in Nepal and influence world wide.
>
> Readers should only buy the edition by Orchid Press, the original publisher. The other edition with greatly inflated price is an unauthorized edition by well-known publishing pirates. Please avoid and buy the Orchid Press edition only. (Edgar Metzler)

Meanwhile, the book was reviewed in several journals. One for students of Himalayan studies was written by a St Xavier's Nepal "old boy", Kumar Pandey, and posted on *The Nepal Digest* (1998). The following excerpt rather gracefully sums up the purpose for writing it:

> Very few people are able to create possibilities and persevere for success in the face of unimaginable odds. Fewer leave behind lasting

legacies which future generations will remember and admire. And there are not many with the diversity to be priest, teacher, radio operator, social worker, sports enthusiast and more, in one. Fr Moran was endowed with all these skills and abilities, and his is a life worth remembering and celebrating. [...]

Overall, this book is a worthy token of appreciation for the life and work of Fr. Moran. No book, however, could do entire justice to his achievements. It is not an easy task to bring forth a character so diverse, so intense and driven to achieve the high standards he set for himself. As a former student of Fr. Moran, I read these pages with full admiration for its protagonist, his courage and accomplishments. Fr. Moran's life should inspire many others.

Early in 2009, the current publisher/owner of Orchid Press, Chris Frape, suggested reissuing the book with necessary corrections, additions and updates. For this second edition, therefore, I have made numerous small adjustments to the phraseology and grammar, have added a little more information in a few places, and have made other improvements. I have also divided the book into five parts and have reordered several chapters. See the new Table of Contents.

Acknowledgments

In addition to those named in the Introduction to the first edition, I wish to add the following persons to the list of those who have helped with the second edition:

- Harold Christensen, who read the newly edited manuscript in its entirety and made important corrections and suggestions;

- Reverends Gregory Sharkey, SJ (New England Province), Jomon Jose, SJ (Nepal Region) and John Kenealy, SJ (Archivist, Patna Province);

- My son, Hans Messerschmidt (http://themodcorp.com), who has greatly improved the cover image over his original first edition cover; and

- My publisher, editor and friend Chris Frape of Orchid Press, who has patiently seen this second (revised) edition through to publication.

Thank you, one and all.

Don Messerschmidt
Vancouver, Washington
Spring 2011

THE YOUNG MORAN

1. Marshall Denis Moran, St. Louis, Missouri 1929. (Sid Whiting, Photographer)

1

Youth

> *We shall not cease from exploration,*
> *And the end of all our exploring*
> *Will be to arrive where we started*
> *And know the place for the first time.*
> T.S. Eliot, from 'Little Gidding' in the *Four Quartets*

Fr Marshall Moran once encountered these lines from T.S. Eliot's poem in the autobiography of Sir Alec Guinness, the British actor. They aptly sum up a life that Guinness described as a "Great adventure... a spiritual journey." They inspired Fr Moran as he recorded for this book the events of his own long journey of exploration and self discovery. "We need more simplicity," he told me, "more faith, more hope, more trust in the way of God hidden very often from us, but ceaselessly working with infinite wisdom and gentle loving power."

His own life of simplicity and spiritual search began one spring day, May 29, 1906, in Chicago Heights, Illinois.

The Frank Morans of Chicago

Marshall Denis (Marsh) Moran was the first son of Frank and Bertha Moran. His first brother, Francis James (Frank), was born in 1908, and his second brother, John Richard (Jack), in 1921. They had no sisters. Shortly after birth, Marshall was christened a Catholic at Our Lady of Sorrows Church. These were simple and, for an Irish Catholic family in America, unexceptional beginnings.

It was always with a certain pride, that Marshall pointed out some of the famous people born on May 29: The American patriot Patrick Henry (1736), the British writer G.K. Chesterton (1874), the comedian Bob Hope (1903), and President John F. Kennedy (1917). May 29 was also the date, in 1953, when Sherpa Tenzing Norgay and the New Zealander, Edmund Hillary, became the first to stand atop Mount Everest. Marshall turned forty-seven that year and was one of the first Westerners to meet the Everest summiteers on their return trek to Kathmandu from Base Camp. During his sojourn in Asia,

Fr Moran met many famous people. His pride in recounting those events never flagged.

Fr Moran is often remembered for his silly puns (which belied his much more serious nature). Of his birthplace, Marshall joked that he and his brothers were born in the shadow of one of Chicago's great contributions to American business, the "male" (mail) order firm of Sears, Roebuck and Company.

The Morans of Chicago were devout, serious and hard working people. Despite the usual sibling rivalries and differences in talent and interest among the three brothers, they cherished their bonds of closeness and affection, and their dedication to the Roman Catholic Church. Later, in the tradition of so many Irish Catholic families, Marshall, as eldest son, became a priest. It was not a family decision, however, but was entirely his own. Later, as a missionary to India and Nepal, he rivaled only his grandfather, Denis O'Keefe, as the most well-traveled member of the family. His brothers, meanwhile, lived lives of public service in and around Chicago.

While growing up, Marshall never really got to know his youngest brother very well. Jack was barely three years old when Marshall left home for the seminary in 1924. But as Jack grew up, he exchanged occasional letters with Marshall in India. It was many years, however, before Marsh and Jack met as adults. It happened soon after World War II, during Marshall's first home leave from the India mission. Jack had already retired as an officer in the U.S. Navy, after a career punctuated by war service in both Europe and the Pacific. He had earned several decorations for bravery during the Normandy invasion and for his dedicated service to General MacArthur in the Philippines, at Leyte and Okinawa.

In contrast to Jack's distance as the youngest sibling, brother Frank, only two years his junior, grew up with Marsh. They knew each other well, but they were not much alike and therefore did not share many of the same ideas, activities and goals, nor their boyhood aspirations or ambitions. Remembering Frank, Marshall said, "We were of completely different temperaments, but that never led to quarrel or misunderstandings. Because of our talents, our different gifts, we had different friends and enjoyed different entertainments. We were never close chums in what we did."

Frank Moran liked sports. But Marshall preferred music and immersed himself in good books and amateur radio, and had an innate curiosity for science. Frank went to Saint Mel's High School, run by the Christian Brothers, while Marshall attended Saint Ignatius Academy, run by the Jesuits.

After high school, Frank studied at the University of Wisconsin, then found a job with the telephone company at a time, during the Great Depression, when jobs were scarce. He did well at his work and was eventually promoted to a high office in AT&T, the American Telephone and Telegraph Company, in Chicago. In contrast, Marshall joined the Jesuits and set off across the world as a missionary to India. These were the sort of life choices that separated the brothers, both intellectually and physically.

Looking back on his youth, Marshall expressed a deep appreciation and respect for his brothers. "I have a debt to them for the help they gave to my work in India and Nepal," he said, "by their encouragement, their prayers, and their financial donations to mission work."

Marshall's paternal grandfather, James Moran, was the son of Irish immigrants who had settled in Wisconsin in the early nineteenth century. In his youth, Grandfather Moran served in the American Civil War with the famous Wisconsin Volunteers Brigade, led by General William Tecumseh Sherman. He traveled with Sherman's Union Army of the West through Tennessee and Georgia. He was present at the capture and burning of Atlanta, and participated in Sherman's historic 1854 March to the Sea. After the war, James Moran married Marry Anne Prendergast and settled in Chicago, where he worked as a mechanic for the Chicago Streetcar Company. Grandfather Moran died in 1921; his wife died in 1927.

Marshall remembers little about his paternal grandparents, however, other than some old war stories that his grandfather told. He was much closer to his mother's side of the family and particularly to his mother's Irish stepfather, Denis O'Keefe, and his wife Catharine.

Grandmother and Grandfather O'Keefe
Grandmother Catharine O'Keefe was a very strong willed German woman. "Her appearance, her manners were those of a girl from the farm. But she was always with a book, always reading," it seemed to young Marshall. "She did not have the benefit of a high school education, but she was well informed and open minded." Marshall learned a great deal from her about books and music. She often took him to concerts and plays and bought him any book that he dared mention, especially classics by Robert Louis Stevenson, Sir Walter Scott, Charles Dickens, and others.

Catharine O'Keefe was also an active member of the Chicago Art Institute and the Field Museum of Natural History (formerly the Columbian Museum), both of which were founded by Chicago's famous entrepreneur philanthropist (and Marshall's namesake) Marshall Field.

The O'Keefes loved to travel and because they had the financial means they could afford luxury trips to South America, Europe and other places around the world. Catharine wrote travelogues, which were printed in serial form in the newspaper.

Grandmother O'Keefe's influence on Marshall during the formative years of his youth was immense. She endeared him early to books, the arts, science and travel.

She also influenced his religious life. Besides a great uncle, who was German Lutheran, Catharine O'Keefe was the only close relative of Marshall's who was not Catholic. Her upbringing was in the strict tradition of Anabaptist Protestantism. Her German-speaking ancestors were among the early eighteenth century settlers of Lancaster County, Pennsylvania, the followers of the Swiss Mennonite leader, Jacob Ammann. Catharine remained a Mennonite throughout most of her life, but consented to the conversion of her twelve-year-old daughter, Bertha, who became Marshall's mother. Bertha later told Marshall that she was attracted to Catholicism by her Catholic playmates and their joyful church school. She saw to it that her sons were raised in the same religious environment.

As a boy, whenever young Marshall visited the O'Keefes, which was often, his grandmother insisted that he attend church regularly. He took instruction in the catechism and was taught prayers and respect for the church by his parents. Even during summer holidays at the O'Keefes, he never missed Sunday mass. "Whenever I stayed with them, Grandmother O'Keefe always took me to church on Sundays and sat there next to me week after week. She used to say, "It's your duty if you are a good Catholic." She was a most tolerant and sympathetic woman in this regard and avoided religious arguments. Grandmother O'Keefe eventually converted to Catholicism, much later, in 1948.

His grandmother's respect for Marshall's religious conscience and Catholic tradition helped influence Marshall to dedicate himself to ecumenical brotherhood between people of many faiths. It became a major theme of his life work. Her sympathetic understanding and respect for distinctly different religious views was a significant factor in Marshall's own tolerant and enlightened approach to persons of Christian expression, as well as to those of Hindu, Muslim and Buddhist faiths whom he later encountered in Asia.

Grandfather Denis O'Keefe, from whom Marshall takes his middle name—Denis, with one 'n'—was a highly successful salesman with the National Candy Company. His business accounts included such large scale buyers as the mail house firms of Montgomery Ward, and Sears, Roebuck. In time, O'Keefe bought shares and eventually became a partner in the candy company, enlarging his personal fortune by speculating in sugar futures. Marshall remembered that "he was especially good at 'playing the market,' as grandfather called it. He knew when to buy and when to sell. His most unique contribution to the business was the Zanzibar candy bar, which tickled the sweet tooth of Americans at the turn of the century."

Marshall thought of his grandparents as very generous people. "Over the years, after I came out to India, they sent me thousands of dollars for different projects, such as the beginning of the high school in Patna and the purchase of school land and buildings in Nepal. Grandfather O'Keefe left a trust fund, which, since I cannot accept any fixed income as a Jesuit, is managed by my brothers. I owe them all a great deal for their support."

Bertha Inez Moran, Marshall's mother, was Grandmother O'Keefe's only child. Her father was Isaac Riley, Catharine's first husband. By the time Denis O'Keefe met and married Catharine in 1894, she had already been divorced from Riley for several years. As she had no other children, Denis's fatherly affections were spent on his grandchildren, especially Marshall, whom he treated like a son. They were very close during Marshall's youth and remained in constant touch by letters until O'Keefe's death in 1952, at the age of eighty-eight.

The elder O'Keefe doted on the young Marshall, as an adoptive grandfather can do, forging man-boy ties that lasted many years. One of their closest relationships developed around automobiles. "As a child, I remember my grandfather spending hours servicing his motor car. He taught me at the same time. And, of course, I was eager to help. I learned to drive at an early age and to know what was wrong if the engine stopped. Whenever there was car trouble, I could usually analyze it, find out what was wrong, and do simple repairs. It was a Kissel, a car unheard of today, manufactured in Hartford, Wisconsin."

When Marshall was fourteen, he surprised a small town garage mechanic with his knowledge and adeptness at car repair. The family was spending the summer at their holiday house in Lake Geneva, Wisconsin. One day when his father was away at work in the city and Marshall was left behind with his mother, an aunt, his brother and cousins, one of the leaf springs on the family car broke. Marshall took over immediately, diagnosed the problem, raised the chassis with a jack, fitted a block of wood under the spring so that it would not rub on the tire, then drove the car for a more permanent repair at the mechanic's garage, six miles away. When the mechanic asked how he had known what to do, Marshall proudly replied, "My grandfather taught me all about cars."

Positive, ego-reinforcing experiences like this one, instilled in young Marshall a strong self pride that he often exuded when relating these anecdotal accounts, unabashedly, about himself. His talent in car mechanics, and later in radio electronics, stayed with him from youth to the maturity of his old age.

Marshall's Father and Mother

The boy's relationship with his father, Frank James Moran, was also close, but in ways much less demonstrative than with his grandfather. His father was a "typical Irishman," as Marshall once put it, "except in one aspect. Papa was not forward nor bold nor brash. Rather, he was a reserved and studious man, retiring and bookish."

Frank Moran was a member of two fraternal clubs, the Elks and the Knights of Columbus, a Catholic benevolent society, and was elected secretary in local chapters of both. But while very active in club affairs, the elder Moran was outwardly reserved and otherwise socially inconspicuous.

"One of my earliest memories of papa was at a semi-pro baseball game in Chicago. I was very small, and my father was a catcher on the team. Of course I didn't know what a 'semi-pro' was then, and I had never seen my father play baseball. I don't remember him ever talking about it at home. My mother took me to the game, and when father stepped up to bat in the first inning, my immediate reaction caused great amusement in the grandstand. Apparently, I shouted out quite loudly to mama, sitting beside me, 'I didn't know papa knew how to play baseball!' The spectators around us got quite a laugh out of it."

Marshall's gregarious, self-assured nature was undoubtedly inherited from his mother. "My mother was much bolder and outgoing than papa. She was very musical and during my childhood I saw her often on the stage at church functions. Like the first time I saw my father playing ball, you can imagine my surprise and excitement when—I was about five years old—I first saw mama on stage singing a solo in a musical comedy."

His mother was socially active. She participated as a volunteer in parish work, in various school and neighborhood activities, and with the Red Cross Society. Later, after Marshall had become a priest, she founded and was president of the Jesuit Mothers' Club. "After I left for the missions in India, she worked in Chicago to build up the mission society that helped support us in Patna. Mama and I were very close. She was always concerned about me."

Grammar School Days

At age five, Marshall was enrolled in first grade at McKinley Public School, a block away from home in Chicago Heights. His teacher, Miss Anne Coveny, wrote to him years later (in 1935), describing those first school days. She was amused at his way with words and recalled the time he arrived in class wearing a rather gaudy shirt. "This is my Methodist shirt," he said proudly. "Mama bought it at a Method church bazaar." His sense of humor developed early and endeared him to many of the people he would meet over the years. One casual acquaintance was heard to remark dryly some seventy-five years later that for as long as she had known Moran, he was quite adept with "his dreadful puns."

Marshall's childhood from first through eighth grade was a happy time, except for the inevitable measles, mumps and chicken pox. To him the neighbors were especially warm and wonderful people. "They belonged to various churches, Catholic, Methodist, Presbyterian, Episcopalian, Lutheran, and the like. Three of my schoolmates in grammar school were the sons of Protestant ministers. I was often the only Catholic in my class, yet I had nothing to complain about, as they respected my faith, which I by no means kept hidden. There was never any bitterness. I remember misplacing my rosary once, and when it was found by a Protestant boy it was graciously returned. I'd often attend weddings and funerals at their churches. These were intimate and dear life-long friends."

The memory of his old school chums stayed with him into old age, including Lucille Mulhern who later became a nun, and Eleanor Bailey, Walter Krebs, William Hilderman, Francis Shanks, and many more. They shared the sorts of experiences common to children of that time, with neither the ubiquitous television of today nor the mobility that the modern automobile and other technologies provide. As he remembered it, "In those days, there were very few cars on the streets; horses and buggies were still going about. We made up much of our own entertainment. One of my greatest joys was my bicycle. I rode it for many hours, many miles, for many years. I was a great enthusiast in riding bicycles." He never lost that youthful enthusiasm, and later transferred it to driving a motorcycle at breakneck speed along dusty lanes in India and Nepal.

While still a young boy in grammar school, Marshall took a small job on weekends at the Model Bakery. He used to go there on his coaster wagon Saturday mornings to buy fresh coffee cake and rolls for the family. One morning the baker asked him, "Would you like to come back after an hour and take pies around to the restaurants?" Of course he would, and although the baker didn't say much about the nature of some of the establishments he served, Marshall soon found out that they included certain saloons, establishments where liquor was served. His responsibility was to stock their lunch counters. This was his first job, although it wasn't very hard work. He did it "for fun and a few dollars." Back home, his parents raised their eyebrows a bit when they found out what he was up to. His mother said to him, "Your very strict grandmother might not like to hear about some of these places where you deliver pies." They never told her.

In time, Marshall became aware of The Great War (World War I), partly because of the shortage of butter and the rationing of sugar, and partly from radio broadcasts. Radio was just beginning to be popular in America. During the last years of the war, after 1917, when the Americans had entered on the side of the European Allies, he read books about the campaigns in Europe. One of them, *Over the Top*, by Arthur Guy Empey, described the incredible suffering and tragic loss of life in the trenches on the Western Front, in battles between the allied French and British against the Central Powers, the Germans. Marsh had a good atlas and followed the progress of the war on maps, thus learning some of the geography of France and Belgium. He also kept track of famous battles, such as at Marne, Somme and Verdun. The war's staggering death toll shocked him. He remembered all his life the great numbers of men who died in the trenches, six hundred thousand among the Allies alone in the Battle of Somme in France, five million lives altogether (half of them French and Russian), against three million Germans and Austro-Hungarians. Another twenty-one million soldiers were wounded by what he long remembered as "that terrible war that left such a great impression on me as a boy."

There were also happier times, of course, including singing all the war songs of the day: Irving Berlin's 'Over There' and 'I'm a Yankee Doodle Dandy', and others like 'Smile Awhile' and 'Keep the Home Fires Burning.' Marshall learned them by ear and played them on his mother's piano without the benefit of formal lessons. He had a good memory and could sing the words of at least twenty or thirty popular songs even decades later (if anyone was inclined to ask; few were). Sometimes he hung around Woolworth's five-and-dime store "where they played popular tunes on the piano and sold sheet music. Then I'd go home and play the melodies back from memory and teach them to my friends."

His mother always had a stack of sheet music on the piano bench, some semi-classics of Victorian vintage and many that were romantic or sentimental. "She never took to the modern music of the time.

Musicals and dance shows did not appeal to her. From her I learned to sing 'I'm Forever Blowing Bubbles' and 'When Eyes of Blue Come Smiling Through.' He was also fond of such tunes as Tosti's 'Goodbye' in the Italian style, 'O Solo Mio' made popular by the Italian tenor Enrico Caruso, and ballads by the Irish tenor John McCormack. "I'd sit there at the piano with all these songs and entertain myself hour after hour, perhaps more than I entertained others."

When Marshall was eleven and in seventh grade, a neighbor boy named Ralph introduced him to yet another wonder: radio. Already, in grammar school, Marshall was developing a fascination with the sciences. In Ralph he found someone who knew all about radio, a phenomenon that excited Marshall's inquiring mind and rapacious imagination. Ralph was at least five years older than Marsh and was preparing to enter college; but they struck up a close friendship nonetheless. Ralph shared his radio magazines and taught his young acquaintance all he knew of the subject, giving Marshall lessons (rather formal, he thought) in radio theory and electricity. The two boys stretched a wire between their homes and communicated with one another by simple telegraphic code, using the Morse alphabet. It was also about this time that the first public radio stations began broadcasting and Marshall became fascinated with listening. These were exciting times for Marshall and with the invention and growth of radio broadcasting his interest grew into a lifelong infatuation.

First Communion
The first time Marshall celebrated Holy Communion in church was a great event to him. As a boy he often sang in the church choir and was a member of the Sodality, a Catholic youth club that engaged in devotional and charitable activities. During the spring of 1918, as he approached his twelfth birthday, he began formal studies of the church catechism or, as he called it, "our dogma." He took lessons with other youngsters in the church under the tutelage of the parish priest who drilled them in the sacraments, the commandments and how to make confession. He had to study many months before he could receive his first Holy Communion. "As a boy, church meant a great deal to me," he once said.

Thereafter, following the Catholic tradition, Marshall went faithfully to mass each week. In those days it was the practice to go to confession prior to communion. For Marshall, this meant confession on Saturdays, in the afternoon, so that he could receive communion at mass on Sunday morning. Later, as a Jesuit, communion was daily, and confession was a weekly occurrence.

By Touring Car to New York

In honor of his twelfth birthday and his first Holy Communion, Grandfather O'Keefe offered Marshall a motor car trip to New York City. "I was delighted" (an understatement). "We started out in June, the three of us—my grandmother, grandfather and I—in grandfather's Kissel motor car. I remember vividly the various places we stopped along the way and the reactions to the comments we heard the farther we got from Chicago. Our first stop was Goshen, Indiana, where grandmother was born. People there thought it was very daring of us to come so far on gravel roads. We never saw an asphalt or tarmac or concrete highway. Paved roads came later."

One evening in northern Ohio, the trio pitched their tent in an empty school yard. They asked the farmer across the road if they could draw water at his pump. He replied, "Yes, on this condition—that you bring your tent over here to my orchard and have dinner tonight with us in the farmhouse." That's how the travelers made friends along the way. "The farmer and his family were very kind to us," Marshall remembered, "but they thought it strange to see a motor car with an Illinois license so far from home."

The travelers stayed two days in the city of Cleveland, then drove on through Pennsylvania to Buffalo, New York. They saw Niagara Falls, then drove along the Erie Canal to Ithaca and on through the New York lake country to Sleepy Hollow. That was Marshall's introduction to the story of Rip van Winkle by Washington Irving, a writer whom he later read with great interest, having visited his home place. They also passed through Tarrytown and saw West Point Military Academy.

Of New York City he remembers the impressive gothic architecture of Saint Patrick's Cathedral and the Episcopalian Cathedral of Saint John, which was still under construction. They visited Coney Island and even went to a few baseball games in the New York polo grounds. And he remembers the Woolworth building, highest in the world at the time. Years later, when Marshall returned to New York, he could still find his way around the subway, Central Park and along the main streets and avenues.

In Washington DC they stayed in the Mayflower Hotel and visited historic sites in and around the capital. A two-day tour of Gettysburg aroused in Marshall a great interest in the Civil War. He and his grandfather used maps to recreate the history of the place and later, in high school, he impressed the history teacher, Fr Sam Knox Wilson, SJ, by answering far more about the war on the final examination than the textbook provided.

Several times during the trip they went to the movies. One was 'Hearts of the World' with Lillian Gish, directed by D.W. Griffeth, who made fame by bringing historical novels to the screen. World War I was still on and as a patriotic gesture one time they invited two sailor boys, strangers, to accompany them to the movies. "I remember that we first took them out to dinner, then to a "first run" as it was called, a premiere showing. We never heard of them again, but I am sure they remembered us from time to time, as we remembered them."

Influenza, the War and a Job
Marshall was back home in Chicago Heights in time to enter the eighth grade in September. During that winter of 1918-19, about the time the Armistice was signed in Germany (November 11), an influenza epidemic swept across North America and thousands took ill. Marshall remembered it vividly: "The war, which we'd almost lost the year before, was finally drawing to its bitter end. The American public was tired of war and panicked over the epidemic. Thousands were dying and the government ordered schools and movie houses closed. There were no assemblies, the only exception being that we could go to church. Many in our neighborhood died from pneumonia contracted after the flu; there were no antibiotics in those days and no medicine at all for treating pneumonia."

During the school closure, which lasted for eight or nine weeks, the eighteen year old boy next door took ill. He was diagnosed as consumptive, with tuberculosis of the lungs, and was put to bed, unable to work with his father, Johnny Maier, a tinsmith. Maier's factory produced skylights, window and door frames, stove pipes, racks and drain pipes out of galvanized sheet metal. "There were many government orders to fill and with his son sick, in addition to the general shortage of labor created by the war emergency and worsened by the epidemic, Johnny was in trouble." Marshall was only twelve years old but had often visited the shop to watch the men work. He occasionally helped with little things and had learned to solder and rivet. With nothing else to do while school was closed, and knowing that Johnny was short of help, Marshall bravely asked for a job.

"Johnny was reluctant to take me on, since the child labor laws those days did not allow children to work until they were fourteen; but he needed all the help he could get. 'No,' he said at first. 'I know you can rivet, but I don't want you working at the bench.' Then, reconsidering, he said, 'But you can take my son's place driving the delivery truck.' He knew I had learned to drive from my grandfather."

As a driver, Marshall was responsible to pick up sheet metal from the freight house and to deliver the finished products to factories and stores. "Johnny had a Model-T Ford, what we would now call a pickup truck. It had old-fashioned solid tires, so you can guess how we bounced around on the brick streets of those days. I earned all of twenty cents an hour at that job."

"I even got to drive Johnny's Buick, a very high-class motor car," he said, remembering one of the most exciting times of his youth. He was very proud of himself and very self-confident. "I'd chauffeur Johnny's wife when she wanted to go into Chicago to shop. There were few motor cars on the road in those days and the roads were not usually paved. Even in Cook County, on the edge of Chicago, none of the roads were paved. So it was slow driving; accidents were almost unknown."

High School Days

The following spring, in May 1919, as Marshall turned thirteen, his father took a new job and moved the family into the city, to the west side of Chicago. Their new house was at 4400 West End Avenue. Before, when they lived in nearby Chicago Heights, Marshall's father worked for the Chicago Heights Belt Railroad. But he had also studied nights and after qualifying as a certified public accountant, he found better paying work as an auditor and tax expert with a large real estate company in Chicago proper. The company bought up tracts of land and built housing projects. There was a great shortage of housing after the war and both the real estate and building industries were booming. Frank Moran earned much more, now, in Chicago than he had while working in Chicago Heights; and while they were never really wealthy, the Moran family lived quite comfortably on the increased income.

After grammar school, Marshall enrolled for fall classes at Saint Ignatius Academy, run by the Jesuit Fathers. The school was on Roosevelt Road (formerly 12th Street) in the heart of the city. (Later the name of the school was changed to St Ignatius High School, and more recently to St Ignatius College Preparatory School.) St Ignatius was noted in those days, and still today, as having one of the highest academic and pre-college entrance standards in the American Midwest. It is located in what used to be a very poor neighborhood, but that changed over time. Today Ignatius Prep is situated in a considerably more prestigious surrounding adjacent to the University of Chicago's city campus.

Marshall's father had attended St Ignatius Academy from 1896 to 1898, and he was pleased that his son would be taught by the Jesuit Fathers, some of whom were his own former classmates. He was proud of his Class of '98. Sixteen of his classmates went into the priesthood, and one became Archbishop of Cleveland, Ohio (Reverend Edward F. Hoban, SJ). Most of the others went out into the world as doctors, lawyers, businessmen, accountants, and in other professions. The Moran family expected that young Marshall would do the same. The family physician, Doctor W. Murphy, was one of them. Dr Murphy encouraged Marshall's scientific inclinations towards biology, physiology and medicine.

Over the years, Marshall met many teachers and priests who had graduated from St Ignatius with his father. He remembered the teachers among them at the academy as "very strict and perhaps even a little hard on me. I got no special favors from them. Those who were friends of my father tried to be so neutral that they were almost hostile towards me at times."

In high school, Marshall became greatly attracted to the Jesuit Fathers. He admired their work, their character, their abilities, their general cheerfulness and happiness. Gradually he learned of their high regard as a group, their skill in arts and science, philosophy and theology. It was at St Ignatius that a notion about his future life began to grow in his mind and heart. Almost unawares, an idea emerged of doing something special for God and Man. At first he considered going into medicine, but in the back of his mind another vision was gradually emerging, of dedicating himself to work for humanity through the church itself, with the Jesuits. It would be awhile before he made a firm commitment to join the Jesuits, but looking back on that formative time in his youth, he said, "It never entered my mind to think of another order. I think it was God's good providence that led me in His own mysterious ways to have a father who admired the Jesuits so much and put me into their school."

His teacher that first year was Fr Hormes, an elderly Belgian priest who was nearing retirement. He had a bit of an accent and a quiet, wry sense of humor. At the time, Marshall could not tell if his accent was French or Waloon or German, but he often imitated the priest's manner of speech, without any intent at malice.

Another teaching priest who impressed him was Fr Jim Preuss from St. Louis, Missouri. Preuss took a special interest in young Marshall. He taught in the room next to Marshall's class that first year and he often observed the boy coming early to school. Marshall was never late, although he lived quite far across the city and had to make two transfers, riding three different street cars to get there. Fr Preuss also noticed Marshall in the school library, virtually devouring books and magazines, especially those about radio. One day Fr Preuss asked Marshall if he would be a volunteer on the library staff. The boy agreed and soon learned how to accession new books, make index cards and take books from the shelves for rebinding and repair. In 1921, during his third year at the school, Marshall was elected to lead the library volunteers. He remembers the day of his appointment clearly, but for another reason: word came that day that his grandfather and Civil War veteran, James Moran, had died.

"Every noon hour and after school, I worked in the library. It had thousands of volumes and multiple copies of the works of Sir Walter Scott and Charles Dickens and other English classics for classroom assignments and homework. Jesuit schools had a reputation for stimulating interest in good books, so the library was one of the places most frequented by the students. It was my favorite place." In his spare time he'd go there to read books and magazines, especially good literature and poetry, and books on physics (especially about radio), biology and physiology (especially regarding medicine). All along, his mother encouraged him towards medicine as a fitting profession for a young man of his day. She was especially pleased whenever he spoke of his interest in the subject.

One day Fr Preuss asked Marshall if he would join the school's elocution contest. Each boy would recite a poem and there were prizes for the best three, he explained. At first Marshall said no, but Preuss encouraged him by offering to help. "I'll give you some training and advice, Marsh, and I'll choose a suitable piece for you," he said. Marshall had great respect for Fr Preuss, but not the courage to refuse. So he joined and was given 'Little Orphan Annie', a popular poem by James Whitcomb Riley, to memorize. At the elocution contest some weeks later, he impressed the audience by mimicking the little girl Annie seeing ghosts. And, "For years after that," said Marshall, "the students teased and called me 'Little Orphan Annie.' That annoyed me."[1]

He also joined the school choir to sing at Friday services and often at high mass. His thirteen-year-old voice was a very loud soprano. "I enjoyed singing in the choir and never missed a single practice. We performed Palestrina, the Gregorian chant and melodies of the masses that were written in a somewhat Victorian, almost operatic, style." Later, while studying theology and performing the music of the mass at Kurseong, in the hills of north India, he would remember his first introduction to these old church masters.

One time the high school boys performed in a musical drama, dressed up like bell hops in very gaudy uniforms with brass buttons and little caps perched on the corner of their heads and fastened under their chins. He felt slightly silly in that getup. He had already been singing and performing in parent-teacher shows during the eight years of his public schooling and with a bit of practice he learned to read music.

According to Marshall, he had what he thought was "a deep appreciation of music. I could carry a melody quite well," he said. "I was given a part in a play, singing a duet with another boy named Moran, no relation. It was a musical comedy called 'Let's Go' written by two young Jesuit scholastics, not yet priests, Daniel Lord and Frank Quinn. There were some rich melodies, although a few were rather ridiculous travesties, with versified comic words sung to popular operatic arias of the day, like 'Aida' and 'Madame Butterfly'. One of them went like this: '*Say lusty Aida / oh baby, how I need a / black soprano to sing this scene / your Rha-da-mes is waiting / music his lungs dia-lating. / Oh, my coloratura / Colorado Madura. / Oh Aida / my opera queen.*' All the school boys' parents, and my own family, were astounded at this surprising and colorful entertainment. It was entirely a show by boys, some of whom had to perform as female Egyptian dancers."

Soon after starting his second year of high school, Marshall began the study of *The Gallic Wars* by Julius Caesar, dating from 58 to 51 BC. "We read it in Latin class. It was very monotonous. The vocabulary bored me, with its tiring mixture of tenses and moods and clauses. Oh, I was all disturbed by the grammar. Instead of reading by pages, we would read a paragraph, then pull it to pieces using all the rules of Latin grammar. Boring. All those rules. I preferred to learn by usage, as I had learned English, not by all the rules by which we studied Latin. That year it was Caesar; the next year it was Cicero." Marshall was miserable. Later, however, in training to become a Jesuit, he learned Latin fluently, and enjoyed it.

The assigned readings in his English literature class, however, more than made up for his early distaste for Latin. He read two or three English literature books each week during all four years of high school. Marshall was a good, fast reader. He greatly enjoyed books, no doubt a reflection of his Grandmother O'Keefe's influence. He was rather selective in his choices and was especially fond of historical novels, biography and poetry. Long before he had a poetry course, he knew many of the works of Tennyson and Browning, and of Francis Thompson, whose long religious poem, 'The hound of heaven', was one of his favorites.

He read Charles Dickens' *David Copperfield* and Sir Walter Scott's *Ivanhoe*, books by Robert Louis Stevenson, and many others, some of which he already knew well. The English teachers required a book report every month, following a fixed format. It took four pages of writing, in which each young scholar had to describe the major and minor characters, plots and sub-plots, and write an exposition on which chapters were most interesting and why. Marshall favored the historical novels of England and America, describing the French Revolution and the Civil War. In that way he learned a great deal about history. It became one of his favorite subjects and good preparation for teaching in the mission schools of India and Nepal, later.

At home, the family kept a small library of short stories. His father had purchased several sets of classics in their English translations by French, Russian and German authors. There were also stories by modern English and American authors, like O'Henry and Richard Harding Davis. He got a good grounding from them in the structure of writing, and he learned the characteristics of their style. Later, when he was assigned short stories in college, most were already familiar to him.

In 1923, during his senior year of high school, Marshall had a very inspiring English literature teacher named Fr Louis F. Doyle. That year Tennyson's writings attracted him, as well as Edward Fitzgerald's translation of the *Rubiyat of Omar Khayyam*. He also read H.G. Wells, well known for *The War of the Worlds* (science fiction), his many novels and novellas, and a recently published theoretical work, *The Outline of History*. Marshall also tried what he calls "the more than serious writings" of G.K. Chesterton. Chesterton wrote dozens of novels, as well as poetry, short stories, plays and essays. But Marshall found Chesterton's often paradoxical style uninviting with all its references to modern philosophers.

Early in the second year at St Ignatius, Marshall joined the school debate society. He was too small for athletics, he thought, except for tennis, which he enjoyed playing with his school chums. And, he didn't want to stay after school each day for the physical training that most athletic activities required. Debate, however, was a different matter. It challenged and enthused him and provided an early outlet for his erudition. Most of the preparation was in writing speeches. The St Ignatius debate team periodically participated in meets with other of Chicago's Catholic and public high schools. Marshall never made the first team, but he was appointed as team chairman and whenever visiting teams came to campus he introduced the topics and the speakers and served as time keeper. He did this for three years until graduation in 1923.

During his junior year, he passed a major milestone in social maturity, graduating from short pants to trousers. "But I only felt at ease in them in the fourth year, my senior year," he said, when remembering this long abandoned social custom.

Marshall's best chum in high school was Bill Connelly. Bill had a great facility with poetry and was an expert at turning out humorous verse. Once a month he entered a limerick contest featured in one of the Chicago evening papers. He sometimes took first prize, earning a hundred dollars for his talent. "In those days, winning a hundred dollars was a great incentive to try. But the only limerick of his that I ever remembered was one about me: 'Marshall Denis McSweeny Moran / went to call on his girl Mabel McCann. / With a yell and a whoop / he cleared the front stoop / just ahead of her father's brogan.'"[2]

Every Sunday during his senior year, Marshall was up early to attend mass at St Mel's Church. On many Sundays, after mass and a quick breakfast, he joined his friend Bill on "the El," Chicago's elevated railway. They rode down to the center of the city together to take in a show or a concert or some special lecture, whatever was on. They preferred movies that had something more than mystery to them, like musicals, or those based on history. Rudolph Valentino, the Italian actor and early pop icon, was popular at the time, but Marshall did not care for his romantic style of acting. He much preferred the great comedians of the day, like Harold Lloyd, Charlie Chaplin and Fatty Arbuckle. Some Sundays they listened to Jessie Crawford sing. In the evening, they would sometimes go to the orchestra hall where great preachers and speakers and famous people came to lecture, often from as far away as Europe.

Early Radio
Marshall's growing passion for radio saved him from too much school work and study. "It was a very healthy distraction. I was constantly listening to early programs and I even experimented with making simple receivers and selling them to the neighbors for a few dollars profit." He especially liked to listen to grand opera and other classical music broadcasts from the Chicago's early radio station, WGN, operated by the Chicago *Tribune* newspaper company. "Every night as soon as I finished my homework, I would tune in on the airwaves, listening with a receiver that I had constructed myself. Each week during the winter, from 8 p.m. until 10:30 or 11 o'clock, I listened faithfully to the Chicago Grand Opera Company broadcasts. My mother sometimes came to my room to hear a little, a half hour or an hour's worth. But I was the most serious opera listener in the family, by far."

He was an avid listener to broadcasts from other cities, also, and was encouraged by his science teacher to practice what came to be known in radio jargon as 'DX', or long-distance tuning.

Summer Jobs
Marshall took employment each summer from 1920 to 1924. His

various work experiences left an indelible mark on his personality, and influenced his outlook on life and his approach to other people.

His first summer job came after his first year of high school. "Well, now," he remembered telling himself, "I have part of June and all of July and August ahead of me. I'll try to get work and make a little pocket money." So he trudged from Lake Street to Randolph, one after the other, up and down Washington, Madison, Monroe and Adams. He stopped at all the big sky scrapers and large buildings looking for work, but found nothing. Then he came to a little street called Quincy, off South State Street, just before Jackson Boulevard. There he asked a doorkeeper if he thought there was anyone in this building who needed an office boy. "Go up to the office on the top floor and inquire," was the doorman's advice. He did and was offered a position at the mail desk in the headquarters of the Carnation Milk Company.

Thereafter, for the rest of the summer of 1920, young Marshall Moran, mail boy, opened and sorted letters each morning, then distributed them to the company's various departments—letters of complaint to Finance, job inquiries to Personnel, and others to the officers of the company. Afternoons, he gathered up the letters typed during the day by the secretaries, and sealed and stamped them for mailing. He was among the last to leave each evening, well after 5 o'clock. On his way home he delivered the letters to the Central Post Office, a block away at Clark Street and Jackson Boulevard.

Looking Back
A Raise, and Tickets to the Opera
Fr Moran

One day, after a few weeks on the job, the office manager called me in. "Are you satisfied with your work, Marshall?" he asked. "Are there any improvements you want to suggest?"

I thought a moment, then told him: "Yes, I am very happy with the job. But I am uncomfortable with the system I was taught for purchasing more postage stamps."

I explained that whenever the stamp supply was getting low, I would ask for five hundred dollars to go out and buy more. This was a temptation and a risk, I said. I recalled a young bank clerk I'd heard about who worked on LaSalle Street, not far away. He had been caught cheating under circumstances very similar to my own. I told the office manager that I always asked one of the office people to check on the stamps I was buying and to count the letters occasionally to see that everything was proper.

The office manager was pleased to hear this, so pleased in fact that he gave me a raise. It was only a few dollars, but it sure made me feel good. Then he said that the following Saturday was the company picnic. It was being held at the Carnation Creamery near Oconomowoc, Wisconsin, about twenty miles west of Milwaukee. "Bring a friend," he said. "We'll go by chartered train. There'll be fried chicken for lunch, and boating and swimming in the lake, and we'll see the company dairy and cheese factory. You'll be home by 8 o'clock in the evening," he promised.

When I went home that evening, I told my parents the good news. "I got a pay raise today," I said, "and I'm going to take a friend to Wisconsin for a Saturday holiday." When mama asked who that friend was, I smiled. "You, mama!" I said, and gave her a hug.

A similar thing happened again later that summer. Moving around the office each day, as I went back and forth delivering and collecting letters to mail, putting on the stamps and so forth, I'd often hum or sing or whistle a melody. As I've said, I knew many different kinds of tunes, popular hits of the day as well as opera themes. I'd whistle them all.

One afternoon a man said to me, "Do you really like music? It sounds like it."

"Yes, I do," I replied.

"Have you ever been to grand opera?" he asked.

"No, but I've heard it on the radio."

"Well, then," he said, "'Madame Butterfly' is being performed tonight at the Auditorium Theater. I can't go, but I've got two tickets for the main floor. Here, you take them and enjoy the evening."

The Auditorium Theater was Chicago's largest in those days. It attracted the best opera companies, with singers like Enrico Caruso, the Irish tenor John McCormack, and Amelita Galli-Curci, the renowned coloratura soprano. Tickets to see them were expensive and I was more than delighted at the offer. I was astounded. I went home that evening in especially high spirits.

At home, I very calmly put the tickets on the table. When my mother saw them, she said, "What are you spending your money like that for?"

I said, "No, mama. Guess my luck! These are complimentary tickets. A man from the office gave them to me. They're choice seats." Then I told her that the man had asked me which girl I would take. I told him I would take "the best one." And when he asked "which one do you consider is best?" I told him "Bertha Moran, my mother, of course!"

I knew she'd enjoy the opera more than anyone else I knew.

Towards the end of summer, Marshall went off to visit his Uncle George Olenroth and Aunt Margaret, his father's sister, at their summer home at Lake Geneva, Wisconsin. He remembered Margaret as "a wonderful aunt. My favorite. The perfect cook, a marvelous baker. I stayed with them for several weeks that summer. In fact," he recalled wistfully years later, "I visited them every summer from 1912 until 1924 when I left Chicago for the Jesuit novitiate in Missouri."

Those were great times for Marshall, on summer holiday at the lake.

Back in Chicago, during his second summer of high school, in 1921, Marshall worked for two months for Babcock-Rushton, a bond house on LaSalle Street in the banking district. It was across the street from the C& C, the large Continental and Commercial Bank of Chicago. Banking and financial transactions fascinated him, an interest brought on no doubt by his father's occupation as an accountant and auditor, combined with the impressive success of Grandfather O'Keefe at financial speculation and, not least, by the influence of his Uncle Olenroth who worked only a few blocks away at the Chicago Board of Trade.

Marshall's work at Babcock-Rushton had only an indirect relation to the money side of the business. His job was running an Addressograph machine in the mail room, and posting monthly investment reports to customers who followed the stock transactions on Wall Street in New York City and the Chicago grain market. He learned a great deal about the stocks and bonds business, about how people chose preferred and common stocks, and how to invest in bonds and mortgages and grain futures.

During the summer of 1922, Marshall persuaded two of his school buddies, Michael English and John Paul Downey, to join him working at Sears, Roebuck & Company, the big department store. Boys his age were impressed by the size of Sears, Roebuck, especially its thick mail order catalog. There were hundreds of pages, with almost anything one could possibly wish to buy, like motorcycles and bicycles, guns and toys, dry goods and hardware, ready-made clothes, shoes, boots, and so forth. The three boys worked in the dry goods summer sale department and had a great deal of fun together. They rode their bicycles to work and home together each day, as it was only a short way from where they lived. In this way they avoided the hectic traffic of the city center. Being so near home also gave them more time for tennis, one of the few sports that Marshall enjoyed playing.

In June, 1923, Marshall graduated from St Ignatius Academy, in a class of eighty boys, many of whom went on into the elite professions. One became a prominent politician. Others studied medicine or law, or took up journalism, or became realtors. And although a number of them joined the Jesuits, Marshall's own decision that way has not yet solidified. He thought, at first, that he would try medicine, so he applied and was accepted into the fall class for pre-med studies at Loyola University of Chicago.

And, again, that summer before college, he went looking for employment close to home so he could avoid the hassle of commuting downtown and back by streetcar and elevated railway. He preferred to come home each noon for a quick lunch with his mother, while still having a good experience and a little pocket money to spend. He found what he was looking for at the nearby Garfield Park Trust and Savings Bank.

At the bank, Marshall was responsible for handling all the checks that were cashed on other banks in the city or the nation. He prepared them for the clearing agency.

He did good work, made many friends in the office, and was even offered a permanent job with double the pay if he would come back the following summer, after his first year in college. He did go back the next year, but it was his last summer job, for by then he had made up his mind to join the Jesuits, a decision that molded the course of the rest of his life. Meanwhile, he used his summer experience at GPT&S to save a little money and learn a bit more about human nature.

Looking Back
Observing Human Nature
Fr Moran

That last summer at the bank, when work was finished in my section, I would go down to the main floor behind the tellers' cages and watch the people come in to make deposits and withdrawals. I didn't know it at the time, but I was observing the psychology of people on both sides of the cage, the customers and the bank employees, the tellers. And although I had not been trained in any way, I could see at times that simple common sense and courtesy were violated.

One time a man came in with a very large check to cash, many thousands of dollars. The customer had failed to notice that the check was unsigned. The teller was a sly fellow who showed me the check, pointing to where the signature was missing. When he was about to turn the customer away, about to say that the check was useless, I stopped him. I recognized the name printed on the check as that of Walter Powers, one of our bank's directors. I suggested that the teller hold up the transaction for a moment, while I went to the phone and called the vice president of the bank, the man who had hired me in the first place. I asked for Mr Powers' phone number. Then, when Powers answered my call, I said politely, "Mr Powers, this is Marshall Moran. There is a check here at the bank for such-and-such an amount that you've forgotten to sign. Will you come over and sigh it, or shall I send the man back to you?"

He said, "No, I'll come at once to sign it. Meanwhile, please pay the man and let him go so he won't know my mistake. He probably didn't notice."

When the vice president heard to whom I was speaking, he asked me sternly, "What business, Marshall, do you have with Walter Powers?"

"He happens to be a friend of my father," I said, a little nervously. "I knew he was a director of this bank, and I knew he would be embarrassed to have the man delayed when he really wanted to pay the check. That formality is now taken care of; he's coming over to sign it."

When Mr Powers arrived, he asked me, "Marshall, how did you get this job without my recommendation?" To which I said: "Well, I know other people around in the banking business, friends of my grandfather on the other side of the city. I used their names so that you wouldn't be responsible for all of my crimes."

We had a good laugh.

His second summer at the bank was a bit melancholy for Marshall, knowing that he was about to dedicate the rest of his life to something far different and far away from home. Nonetheless, he enjoyed his last days at work.

Early that summer he convinced his grandfather to buy a fancy new automobile, a Packard. He gave his advice out of a concern that, as he had always serviced the stalwart old Kissel, he would not be around anymore to help with its upkeep. The new Packard was an automobile that O'Keefe could easily afford and could easily maintain by himself. "I showed my grandfather that on the new Packard of that day there was one little grease box with a plunger on it, so he could grease the whole car himself and save a lot of trouble."

He also hoped that his grandfather would give him the old Kissel to drive himself grandly to and from work each day. He did, and "I drove it proudly," he said, "wearing a beautiful Panama hat that my grandfather had brought back from a recent trip to the Philippines. It amused the other bank employees that I, the lowest paid employee in the firm, showed up each day in a fancy car with an equally fancy hat on my head."

Marshall loved motor vehicles almost as much as he loved radio. His showmanship and frisky daring, capped with a touch of humor, came through whenever he drove the classic Kissel through the heart of Chicago. Years later, reminiscent of those days of his carefree youth, he amused the townspeople and his acquaintances in Nepal, roaring down the crowded streets and alleyways of Kathmandu on a souped-up motorcycle looking like the Red Baron with a white scarf streaming from his neck or, as often, in a rustic Land Rover while dressed in priestly black and Roman collar, with a French beret perched jauntily on his head and a load of Godavari School boys hanging on for dear life in the back.

Notes to Chapter 1: Youth
1. We can imagine the boy Marshall reciting this ghostly verse from 'Little Orphan Annie': "*When the night is dark and scary, / and the moon is full and creatures are a flying and the wind goes Whoooooooooo, / you better mind your parents and your teachers fond and dear, / and cherish them that loves ya, and dry the orphans tears / and help the poor and needy ones that cluster all about, / or the goblins will get ya if ya don't watch out!!!*"

    James Whitcomb Riley originally entitled his 1895 poem 'Little Orphant Annie' (the spelling was "corrected" later), and in 1924, a cartoonist named Harold Gray created the immensely popular 'Little Orphan Annie' comic strip for the Chicago *Tribune*.
2. A brogan was a style of men's shoe popular during the early twentieth century. It is derived from the Scottish or Irish Gaelic word *bróg*, meaning 'shoe'; plural *brògan*. A brogan is also known as a 'wingtip'.

2. Fr Thomas M. Downing and Fr Marshall D. Moran, at Godavari School.

2

Scholar

I fled Him, down the nights and down the days;
I fled Him, down the arches of the years;
I fled Him, down the labyrinthine ways
Of my own mind...
Ah, fondest, blindest, weakest,
I am He Whom thou sleekest!...
   Francis Thompson, from 'The hound of heaven'

The school year of 1923-24 was a decisive one for the seventeen year old Marshall. He graduated from St Ignatius Academy in June, and after his summer job at Garfield Park Trust and Saving Bank, he enrolled at Loyola University in Chicago, on the shore of Lake Michigan. He arrived at college as an impressionable young freshman, skinny, proud, keen on tennis and fond of debate and theater. But he was still undecided about his future and, at first, he did not take it all very seriously. His academic grades were mediocre.

During the year, through the slow cold months of the Chicago winter and on into a vigorous Midwest spring, he gave considerable thought to his future, weighing the counsel of family and friends, but especially the wishes of his mother. She would see her eldest son as a successful medical doctor; and he agreed to prepare himself in that direction, partly on her account and partly from his own genuine fascination with the sciences of biology and healing. But, like the man in one of Marshall's favorite poems, Francis Thompson's 'The hound of heaven', his contemplation on life's direction and meaning was in direct response to a God who was, he thought, somehow testing and pursuing him for a special purpose that was not yet fully revealed. That is how, with the hindsight of age and experience, he later interpreted his youthful indecision and contemplations on life in 1924, and the personal and spiritual deliberations that led to his decision to become a priest.

Finally, during the Easter holidays of 1924, he made up his mind to abandon medical studies and join the Society of Jesus, the Jesuits. This thoughtful young man, among the very youngest in his class, had made a choice that he later considered quite mature beyond his age (although several other boys in his class were on the verge of making similar decisions about the priesthood). And, while his pursuit of a life's work may have seemed over, it had only just begun. "Can someone so young as I make such a momentous and life-long decision so readily?" he asked himself. He thought so; and on the advice of his priest counselor, and influenced by the example of his Jesuit teachers at St Ignatius Academy and Loyola University, he applied and was accepted at St Stanislaus, a well known Jesuit novitiate in Florissant, Missouri. Once there, perhaps he would be selected for a foreign mission, he thought. Travel was in his blood, so to speak, thanks to the influences of his world traveling grandparents, Denis and Catharine O'Keefe.

Marshall's life calling to the priesthood did not come as easily, nor as suddenly as this brief account implies. During his high school years, and especially during the year at Loyola, he found himself pulled in two directions. His mother was determined that he would become a physician, but the priesthood also held a strong attraction and challenge for him.

A gregarious woman by nature, Bertha Moran sought closeness in her family and needed friends and company, distractions and high goals to keep her busy. As a mother, she wanted only the best that society could offer for her family, especially her sons and particularly for Marshall, her first born. She had often spoken to him about the medical profession, praising it as a good career, socially respectable, an important vocation, just right, she said, for him. She cherished the noble hope that he would one day become a noted doctor. That, she thought, would keep Marshall close to her. She silently feared his other option, the priesthood, though it was always a ready option for a son in an Irish Catholic family. His becoming a *missionary* priest was her greatest unspoken concern, for surely, she thought, it would take him far away from home, away from her.

Therefore, she impressed upon him that a medical career was best. And, in truth, it was unquestionably attractive to Marshall. "When I enrolled at Loyola to study pre-medicine, mama was very pleased." Marshall rose quickly to the new challenges of university life, although it was not until towards the end of the year that he took his studies seriously.

The freshman class at Loyola that year had over two hundred students, fifty or more of whom were graduates of Chicago's St Ignatius Academy. The Ignatians were a close and active group. They set about, with Marshall's involvement, to organize debating and drama societies. Drama was one of the highlights of his youth and, for awhile at Loyola, acting and not academics occupied much of his time.

Looking Back
On Stage at Loyola
Fr Moran

During the 1923 fall term at Loyola, I participated in a dramatic production called 'The Pageant of Youth,' written by Fr Daniel Lord, SJ, a well known and popular author and Catholic youth leader in high schools and colleges across America. At the tryouts I recited a few lines from 'Little Orphan Annie', which I'd memorized in high school. I proceeded in the best voice I could muster, an effort so full of power and clarity that even those in the back of the hall said they could hear every syllable. It must have been convincing, for I was assigned not one but three parts in the play. In the Introduction I played St Michael at the gates of heaven, sounding the keynote for the entire affair. In the middle of the play, I highlighted a particular crisis, and at the end, I recited the concluding lines, all in blank verse.

The pageant was directed by Reverend Charles Meehan, SJ, a Loyola University professor who had been one of my father's high school classmates twenty-five years earlier. It was all very pretentious, I thought, even extravagant. Large groups of actors moving across the stage in bright costumes, sometimes dancing, playing parts of crusaders, angels and fallen angels. There was even a scene from hell. A small ensemble from the Chicago Symphony Orchestra was engaged to play the background music.

The production was held during Thanksgiving week, eight performances in all, to audiences totaling over twelve thousand people. My mother and father attended the first night, watching anxiously for me to appear on stage. At the end of the first act, mama turned to papa and asked, "When is Marshall coming? He was supposed to be in the first act, I thought."

"Well, he was," said my father. "You just didn't know him in his costume and stage voice."

I had been there, of course, but she didn't recognize me. We had a good laugh. It became one of those small family jokes. But whether the joke was on my father who didn't tell my mother when I appeared, or on my mother who didn't recognize me, or on me, or on all of us, I'm not sure.

In the spring, after Easter, our group performed Shakespeare's 'The Merchant of Venice'. The choice was mine, although at first there were protests from the other players in the club. "It's too familiar," they said. "It's beyond the talents of the group. Shakespeare's language is too antiquated." And so forth.

But, I prevailed. I challenged the group not to make a decision one way or the other until they had seen a good performance by a professional English troupe that happened to be in Chicago at the time. A week later we met again to decide. In the meantime, many had seen the British Shakespearean performance and were convinced that we, too, could put on a good show and make it interesting, despite earlier reservations.

I took the part of Lorenzo, the romantic youngster who eloped with the daughter of Shylock the Jew. My opposite was played by a good-looking Swedish girl with flaming red hair. As I had by that time already announced to my friends that I was going into the priesthood, I suffered some lighthearted teasing. How could I be so romantic with the girl on stage, they asked, while at the same time I was planning to forsake marriage to become, as they put it, "locked up like a monk for the rest of your life"? I took it all in good spirit.

During the first performance, in one of the early acts of the play, Seignior Antonio declares: "Here comes Seignior Bassanio." But Bassanio was nowhere to be seen; he was still in the dressing room. I was on stage and immediately saw the problem. As Lorenzo, I blurted out *ad lib* to save the scene—"Oh, forsooth, he tarrieth. I go to fetch him!" I said it in good Shakespearean style and rushed off stage to pull the curtain until the missing character was found.

Years later, when I returned home to Chicago on my first furlough from the India mission, I looked up some of my old friends and classmates from Loyola. One was Robert Hartnett, SJ, who had become editor of the Catholic weekly magazine *America*. When we met at his office after all these years, he recalled my famous line. "Oh, forsooth, he tarrieth. I go to fetch him!", Hartnett said when he saw me enter his office. It surprised the others in the room, and we all had a good laugh before launching into other remembrances of those college days so long before.

Marshall lived at home and commuted daily to classes at Loyola that year, taking "the El" train, first to the center of the city, then transferring to the line that took him north to campus. His studies included the usual freshman courses in preparation for a science degree, including biology and physics, and German to satisfy the foreign language requirement. During his daily commute he became acquainted with one of the train attendants, a German immigrant from Berlin. On impulse one day, while exiting the train, he said to the man, "*Guten Tag. Ich werde Sie morgan sehen.*" (Good day. I'll see you in the morning.) To which the man responded, "*Jawohl, Ins morgan.*"

Every day after that Marshall met his new found German friend on the train and practiced his lessons during the ride. As his skills at German improved, Fr Froebes, the German Jesuit who taught the college class, was impressed by how well and how quickly Marshall was learning. He asked one day if Marshall's family spoke German at home. "Not at all," Marshall replied. "But thank you for the compliment, Father. My grandmother was raised speaking German, but no longer does so; and neither my mother nor my father knows a word of it. That just shows," he went on, tongue in cheek, "that you are a very good teacher." Then he smiled and confessed to the flattery, telling Fr Froebes the truth about his daily lessons on the train.

Despite the direction of his studies and his college interests, an awareness grew in Marshall's mind all that year that he wanted to do something special for others, for God, and for his church, perhaps with the Jesuits whom he admired so greatly. He felt it had been God's good providence that allowed him in some mysterious way to have a father who admired Jesuit education and a mother who encouraged him to persevere in his studies.

It was in part his deep-felt concerns about improving the welfare of others and promoting tolerance for other ways of thinking and doing that played key roles in Marshall's choice of the Jesuit priesthood. These concerns fueled two of the major themes in Marshall's long life—teaching, and ecumenism (religious unity and equality).

He remembers vividly his first encounter with the prejudice and malice of others towards disadvantaged people. Awareness began when he was ten years old.

Looking Back
For Whites Only
Fr Moran

When I was still a boy I began to see that there were great inequalities and injustices practiced by some groups and nationalities. As a Catholic, of course, I saw some of the subtle, and sometimes not so subtle prejudices that existed even between religious groups. All this bothered me, as it has bothered so many people for so long.

I was once riding with my father on a railway train from Chicago to Chicago Heights when I noticed a sign on one coach: "Whites Only," and on another: "Negroes Only." In those days you didn't say "Blacks"; it was considered a bad word. Things have changed since then.

"What does that mean, papa?" I asked, unaware of such distinctions.

He explained that those coaches must have come off the Dixie Flyer, a train that ran regularly between Chicago and Jacksonville, Florida, in the deep South. "The Negroes," he said, "have to stay in a special coach, use special restrooms, stay in their own hotels and eat in their own restaurants. They even attend their own churches, or worship in specially segregated parts of churches."

Call it my innocence or ignorance, or a high ethical sense, but whatever it was, I was annoyed and upset. As I began to question and to learn, I thought less of the great American quests for human freedom.

I also remember the summer of 1919, when race riots between Blacks and Whites broke out in Chicago's stockyard area, down at 35th South and along Western Avenue and in those neighborhoods, I asked my father to explain it. He told me how the Negroes had come up from the South during the war, around 1916 and 1917, to work in the stockyards. It was not a very high-class type of work. The trouble started when white soldiers came back from Europe, also looking for work. Jobs were hard to find. They blamed the Negroes and took out their frustrations in the form of riots and arson to drive the Negroes out.

I remember very well my deep anger that men should behave like that. I had been taught, and firmly believed, that law and order, good legislation and good government would make such a thing impossible.

A few years later, I witnessed a disgusting event in Goshen, Indiana, something that I have never forgotten. While visiting relatives, I went for a walk one evening and came across the Ku Klux Klan holding a meeting on the courthouse steps. They all had their hoods on and were verbally abusing both Catholics and Negroes. I stood on the sidelines and did some heckling. When a couple of local boys came up and talked rough to me, I suggested that we all go to the sheriff and see what he said. They left me alone.

It made me angry, and I felt strongly that in view of the American Constitution and my feelings about human rights and decency and freedom, these men were a menace. I was learning fast that sadness of what we call "civilization", when it is not controlled by good ethics, morality and a little self-sacrifice, patience and, mostly, tolerance for other people and other beliefs, other ways of thinking and living.

Those memories stayed with me.

I saw much worse years later in India, the terrible poverty and the economic and social discriminations of caste, especially, during the ugly violence and rioting between Hindus and Muslims in the 1940s in north India. From the start, it encouraged me to do something useful for people, through the church.

By the spring of 1924, Marshall's notion to join the priesthood was too strong to ignore or further resist. Marshall made up his mind during Holy Week while on a three-day retreat, a triduum.

Looking Back
The Final Decision
Fr Moran

As I look back on that threshold to my adult life of dedication to the church, I remember being afraid that I might miss my true "vocation" or "calling" by following the easy way, by following the crowd. I must say that I had a certain distrust for what we call "the crowd". Following the crowd, I thought, did not provide a very clear test of my ideals, nor did it lead me very clearly toward the pursuit of a life based on the deep eternal values and religious convictions that I strongly felt.

It dawned on me, rather suddenly it seemed at the time, that I would soon have to make a firm and perhaps final choice. While I had once thought that medicine was a good direction for me, I was not so very sure any more. I had certainly been encouraged and had the strong backing of my mother for that profession. Yet, I asked myself and God, "Should I become a doctor, or something else?" I had thought a long time about becoming a medical person, a doctor or surgeon. But there were many young men trying to get into medical school and I wanted to perform my life's work where there was not such a crowd already gathered.

"Is there some other vocation for me?" I asked, "something rather more special that I could, or should do?" And almost instantly, I answered my own question: the priesthood, the Jesuit missions, perhaps in India. I had always been fascinated by travel, having grown up on the stories of my grandparents' world travels and having read the Catholic mission magazines.

Up to that time, I knew only what I had read in mission magazines, the accounts of Catholic clergy abroad whose work and devotion stirred my imagination. There was a lot of talk in the early 1920s about new missions in India. I had read about St Frances Xavier, the first Jesuit to travel to Asia, the first to establish the India mission in the sixteenth century. It aroused my interest, my admiration, my resolve. I, too, would become a missionary priest; and, I decided, I would simply volunteer for India, certain that I would be chosen to go.

It sounded easy. And to some people, perhaps, it may seem like a form of escapism. But as Fulton Sheen once said, "Those who think that religion is an escape should try the Cross."

I was also worried, to some extent, that any personal lack of courage in this matter, or any postponement of the choice, might mean that I would soon be too old. Impetuous youth, you know, often think such things!

Would I be suitable and able to meet the requirements? Could I adequately prepare, through my studies, for the inevitable change of personal habits that a life of poverty, chastity and obedience in the solitary pursuit of the priesthood required and demanded? I asked. Yet, at the same time, I felt confident that if God wanted it, He would give me the help, grace, assistance, inspiration and consolation necessary to persevere.

"I have only one chance to pass this way," I told myself. "Let's try it," I said in my meditation and prayer.

Still, there were nagging doubts. And some of my friends openly voiced the opinion that I wasn't the type, not serious enough. After all, they reasoned, I had had so many experiences and opportunities, good jobs, so many friends, a close family, summer holidays with my relatives in Wisconsin, and so much travel. How could I suddenly become so serious to join the priesthood?

Admittedly, it seemed even to me to be a bit impulsive. Until that time, I had not been very serious in my college studies. I did not try very hard to get good marks. But, once I made up my mind, all that changed and, by the end of my last term at Loyola, my usually mediocre grades had risen to A's and A+'s.

On Easter Sunday, 1924, I told the family of my resolve.

Marshall's mother cried, although she tried not to show it in front of him. She was upset at the thought of her son living a life single-mindedly devoted to a lonely mission, physically deprived and isolated in some unheard of place half way around the world. She thought he was too young and immature. "After all, Marshall," she told him, "you are not yet even eighteen years old. What terrible things will you have to endure living a solitary life in some far off mission?" But, she didn't press him too hard.

His father, on the other hand, was rather more neutral about it, wishing neither to oppose nor to push nor encourage his son too strongly in any direction. "Papa's relative silence in the matter seemed to imply that it was, after all, my life and my decision to make. I respected him for that. He was quite proud of me."

Marshall's Mennonite grandmother, Catharine O'Keefe, said little except "I am not surprised. It is in my family that we have so many ministers and good serious Christians."

Marshall's very serious German Lutheran uncle, George Olenroth, took him aside for a talk. It was a conversation that Marshall never forgot. "I am proud of you, Marshall," he said to me, "and proud to be your uncle. But don't expect encouragement from those around you. I would also be so proud if one of my own sons would do what you are doing in joining the Jesuits."

Unfortunately, one of his sons, an elder cousin of mine, suffered through a bad divorce and a lot of unhappiness in his life.

Uncle Olenroth's remarks left a strong impression on Marshall. But in the end, it was probably his father's influence, in his quiet way, that gave young Marshall the greatest strength and resolve to abandon his studies at Loyola and apply to join the Jesuits.

Meanwhile, Marshall took his second and last summer job at the Garfield Bank. He played tennis on weekends and on most evenings was home pursuing his beloved radio hobby, knowing now that he would soon have to leave it behind.

The last week of August was a time of contemplation and sad good-byes, as Marshall packed and prepared to leave Chicago and begin his new life. He shipped his belongings off to the novitiate in Florissant, Missouri, in a well-traveled steamer trunk his grandfather had given him. Then, together with Grandfather and Grandmother O'Keefe, his mother and his younger brother, he started out for Florissant in O'Keefe's shiny new Packard automobile. They stopped first in South Bend, Indiana, to see Notre Dame University, then went on to nearby Goshen to visit relatives he had never met and whom his grandmother had not seen in almost forty years. Some of her relatives were German speakers. Marshall translated. They found it strange that she had so completely forgotten the language she had spoken as a little girl and were amused that her grandson Marshall, the young city-slicker, could translate so well.

From Goshen they drove to Terra Haute, Indiana, to see St Mary's of the Wood College, where Bertha Moran had gone to school and where several of Marshall's church friends and acquaintances were enrolled to become nuns. Bertha was proud to introduce her son to the teachers.

They reached St Louis on a Sunday and drove directly on out to rural Florissant, a few miles north of the city. Marshall checked into the seminary's House of Studies where he recovered the trunk that had arrived earlier.

That old trunk had gone everywhere that Marshall's well-traveled grandparents had been—to Europe, Asia, and South America. It was plastered over with stickers from the best hotels in London, Paris, Rome, Rio, Honolulu, Manila, Tokyo, Bangkok, Delhi and even the Taj Mahal. When it arrived (he heard later), there were mutterings about who the "pretentious whipper-snapper" might be who owned such a thing with all the labels. It went unmentioned for several days until someone said, "Marsh, you seem to be quite a traveler."

"Yes, some," he replied, innocently, not realizing the source of their curiosity. "I've been to Canada once, and to New York, Washington DC, and Gettysburg, Pennsylvania. I went with my grandfather and grandmother. But I haven't crossed the Atlantic or the Pacific. Not yet."

"Then where did you get all those stickers on your steamer trunk?" someone asked.

"Oh," he replied, "that's my grandfather's trunk!", at which the bubbles of his pride and of their envy burst. Nothing more was ever said of it.

A Novice at Florissant

Marshall's novitiate studies began formally on September 1, 1924. St Stanislaus Novitiate was part of St Louis University, a Catholic institution. In time, he hoped, he would also study at the main campus. For the first time in his life he was away from home, cut off from family and friends in Chicago. But, he was immediately busy and had little time to contemplate on what he had left behind. As time and the rules of the novitiate allowed, he occasionally went into St Louis to use the library at the university. Good libraries were always an attraction, and he was in awe of the size of this one.

He pursued classical studies at Florissant for four years. It was the standard track in preparation for the Jesuit priesthood. The first two years were taken up with spiritual training, reading, prayer and a thirty-day retreat. More academic studies followed, including church history, theology, philosophy, English, German, some science, and Latin and Greek. His disdain for Latin was soon forgotten and he became fluent and able to give theological discourses in this ancient language of the Roman Church. His real aptitude for it proved invaluable later, during his advanced studies of philosophy and theology in India.

One focal point of the novice course is studying the life of the sixteenth century founder of the Jesuit Society, St Ignatius of Loyola (Ignacio López de Loyola in Spanish, Loyola's mother tongue). Church historians have long credited Loyola with a singularly remarkable achievement in crafting the deceptively simple but remarkably flexible *Constitutions* of the Jesuit Order. The *Constitutions* specifies very clearly how the Society of Jesus should be governed. Marshall always marveled at how adaptable *Constitutions* has been over the centuries, in the face of a changing church and a changing world. So well does it work that the Society's governing system has been emulated by several other religious orders.

Years later, in Nepal, Marshall read the works of George E. Ganss, SJ, a prominent American Jesuit historian and scholar. Ganss has noted that Loyola's writing of the Jesuit *Constitutions* was a gradual, distinctive and impressive process. Had St Ignatius expressed more literary abilities and charm, he might have rivaled St Augustine[1] among the church literati. Ignatius is the model for young Jesuits, and during the novitiate they are well schooled in his life and times, and thoroughly immersed in the *Constitutions* and the *Spiritual Exercises*.[2]

According to Jesuit sources, "The *Spiritual Exercises* of St. Ignatius of Loyola are a month-long program of meditations, prayers, considerations, and contemplative practices that help Catholic faith become more fully alive in the everyday life of contemporary people. It is set out in a brief manual or handbook: sparse, taciturn, and practical. It presents a formulation of Ignatius' spirituality in a series of prayer exercises, thought experiments, and examinations of consciousness—designed to help a retreatant (usually with the aid of a spiritual director) to experience a deeper conversion into life with God in Christ, to allow our personal stories to be interpreted by being subsumed in a Story of God."

"These Exercises are usually made in one of three different ways: first, extended over approximately thirty days in a silent retreat away from home, which was its original form; or second, as condensed into a weekend or an eight-day retreat based on Ignatian themes; or third, in the midst of daily life, while living at home, over a period of several months."[3]

Looking Back
On Spirituality and the Inspiration of St Ignatius
George E. Ganss, SJ[4]

Christian spirituality is the application of relevant elements in the deposit of faith to the guidance of men toward spiritual perfection, that rich development of their persons which flowers into correspondingly greater insight and joy in beatific vision... Because of the need to come to grips with varying needs and opportunities in different eras; because of the varying personalities and temperaments of men or women; because of varying levels of education in diverse epochs or places; because, above all, of the formative influence which the Holy Spirit exerts through the distribution of His graces, one person or group has drawn more inspiration from one aspect of God's revelation and another from another. Thus it arose that, in age after age, it was God who took a cooperative man or woman and molded him into the personality of a Benedict, a Francis of Assisi, a Dominic, an Ignatius, a Therese, or a Francis de Sales, and gave him a message of value for his own age and for later eras...

(Ignatius) lived for God, to such an extent that St Thomas's beautiful words were fully verified in him: "Charity makes us tend to God, by uniting our affections to Him, so that we live, not for ourselves, but for God"... God was the center and preoccupation of Ignatius's thoughts, and the object of his special love, and the beloved Person for whom he wanted to do all the little acts which make up daily living. He wanted to be bound irrevocably to God, with the bridges burnt which might lead back to another way of living in which he might have interests other than God... One spontaneous expression of his spirit of total dedication rolled off his pen many years later: "To bind oneself more to God our Lord and to show oneself generous toward Him is to consecrate oneself completely and irrevocably to His service, as those do who dedicate themselves to Him by vow..."

The end result of his God-given natural character and temperament, his infused contemplation, his university studies, and his experiences in founding and organizing the Society was a mysticism which impelled him not merely toward love of God in contemplative solitude but also toward service through love... In meeting the needs of his times, he gave a new orientation to religious life and developed a fresh concept of spirituality oriented toward apostolic service... (Ignatius) always attributed a primacy of importance to grace and supernatural means which unite the human instrument with God; but he also valued natural gifts, carefully cultivated and skillfully used. As a result, he habitually employed a balanced union of natural and supernatural means to his objectives...

Ignatius inspired his followers by the ceaseless repetition of his inspiring ends—glory, praise, honor, and service to God... At the summit of his world view was the stimulating thought of bringing greater glory to God from himself and his fellow men, both in this life and the next; and he saw everything else as means to this end...

To produce such genuine men of the church was the central objective for which he devised his *Exercises*, mobilized his Society, and composed his *Constitutions*...

Through his study of the *Constitutions* and his observations of the functioning of the Society about him, Marshall quickly learned its hierarchical structure, descending from the superior generalships in Rome to the lowliest priests and brothers in Jesuit houses, village parishes and mission schools around the globe. As a novice, he was a mere beginner, not yet a Jesuit in anything but aspiration. He knew it would be years, following a great deal of concentrated study and personal testing, before he could attain the priesthood he sought.

Traditionally, there are four categories or levels of Jesuits, beginning, after the novitiate, with scholastics and including lay brothers, spiritual coadjutors and, finally, at the pinnacle of achievement, the professed priests. In Ignatius' time, these distinctions were thought to be important due to the low level of education of some individuals who sought to join the Society. Ignatius encouraged a high level of academic attainment in his priests, and only those of highest achievement could reach the top. Others were assigned to lower levels in the hierarchy according to their abilities. In modern times, however, and especially following the liberalizing force of the ecumenical council known as Vatican II (1962-65), the traditional roles and particularly the distinctions between levels of priesthood (coadjutor and professed) have become blurred.

Scholastics are young Jesuit trainees who have completed their preparations as novices and have taken their first vows. Jesuit scholastic training begins at the level of novitiate, a two year period of mostly spiritual exercises, followed by the juniorate, which focuses on the study of classical humanities. Marshall completed these first four years at Florissant, then moved into St Louis to the Jesuit college associated with St Louis University. There, he began the next phase, the philosophate, which concentrates on philosophical training. The philosophate typically lasts three years, followed by four more years of concentrated theological studies in the theologate. Only after all this preparation, sometimes spread out over a period of ten years or more and usually including a teaching assignment at one of the Society's many schools, is that Jesuit candidate finally ordained as a priest. In Marshall's case, the period as a scholastic was shortened slightly under circumstances of ill health during his first few years in India, and by his personal drive to excel and proceed.

Jesuits who stand out both spiritually and academically and complete the full rigors of the theologate continue on to become professed priests. In modern times, the vast majority are professed, but in the past, men of lesser drive, ability or inclination, became spiritual coadjutors, priests who have not achieved the level of learning or degrees required of professed priests. They also abide by the three principal vows of priestly life—poverty, chastity (celibacy), and obedience—and are assigned to ministerial, pastoral or educational duties, or to help supervise or manage Jesuit houses. These days only a tiny minority of Jesuits are coadjutors.

Professed priests are men of high achievement, selected for their demonstrated spirit of learning, after thorough testing and various other proofs of their virtue and self-abnegation. Several years after completing the theologate and ordination, and after a period of tertianship, a year-long time of contemplative probation and thorough self-examination, they profess again the three solemn vows of poverty, chastity, and obedience, followed by the uniquely Jesuit fourth vow of obedience to the Pope. Among the professed priests, the practice of poverty is to be as perfect as possible.

Marshall Moran's career followed the normal path, albeit slightly speeded up. In 1926, he became a vowed scholastic in Missouri. In 1935 he was ordained in India, only nine years after entering the novitiate. In 1942 he became a fully professed priest.

Men not interested in becoming priests may join as lay brothers, and many do. Traditionally, lay brothers helped in the operation and upkeep of Jesuit houses, some as manual laborers and others as highly skilled technicians. In India, and later in Nepal, Marshall worked alongside lay brothers who managed the gardens or kitchens, or served as librarians, carpenters, or printing press operators. Today, however, they are given many more responsibilities in the operation of Jesuit houses, schools and social programs. Marshall spoke highly of those with whom he was privileged to work, like Brother Pais in Bettiah and Brothers Louis and Karpinski in Kathmandu. Like all priests, lay brothers also abide by the three principal vows of poverty, chastity and obedience.

During his first four years of study, while Marshall pursued his novitiate and juniorate phases at Florissant, missionaries would sometimes come to lecture and speak to interested students. Marshall was one of the most interested. He had read about foreign missions in Catholic magazines, like *Far East, Maryknoll* and *Jesuit Missions*, and he was especially attentive when visitors arrived from India.

In 1926, Bishop Louis Van Hoeck, SJ, of the new Jesuit Diocese of Patna, the capital of Bihar in North India, visited the St Stanislaus Novitiate in Florissant. He spoke to the novices about the Indian mission. After hearing the bishop's lecture, Marshall went to him to learn more about the missionary's life and work in Patna. The Patna Diocese was especially in need of dedicated, strong young men, he was told. It was the Society's most recent undertaking in India, and while it was historically quite old, the Jesuits had only recently taken it over in a somewhat neglected condition from the Capuchins.[5]

With his interest aroused, Marshall began corresponding with several priests in India. He also asked friends in Chicago to send donations to them. The students of Providence High School, for example, the school that his mother had attended on Chicago's west side, responded with enough money to finance roof repairs to a village chapel in a tiny place called Chainpatia, north of Patna, outside of the town of Bettiah and quite near the southern border of Nepal. Nearby Bettiah was the site of his first teaching appointment and a few years later, after he was assigned there, he personally visited Chainpatia and reported to the school in Chicago how their contributions had been spent.

Marshall and several of his companions formed a mission study group at Florissant. They collected photographs of different mission stations in India and prepared a traveling display to send around to Jesuit high schools and colleges. It described social and educational works in India and included photographs of children, priests and nuns in the schools and village parishes. Several of his friends from the mission club were eventually posted with Marshall to India. They included Joseph Mann, John Morrison, and Felix Farrell. One friend, Calvert Alexander, devoted his entire life to editing the *Jesuit Missions* magazine. Another, Robert Hartnett, became editor of the prominent Catholic magazine, *America*, through which the missions also attracted financial support.

Annual contemplative retreats are the custom at Jesuit schools and seminaries. For Marshall, these month-long events "greatly stimulated my thinking and orientation towards the priesthood. I became very familiar with the works of the early Jesuit co-founders and saints, as far back as the 16th century—men such as Ignatius Loyola, Francis Xavier, Aloysius Gonzaga, Stanislaus Kostka, Robert Bellarmine, Peter Canisius, and others. They were on my mind and in my thoughts constantly, punctuated, of course, by their feast days and other commemoratives. I could not help but grow in admiration and wish to emulate them."

Marshall kept many memories of Florissant, not all of them related to his classical and theological studies. For example, "In May 1927—it was May 20th, I remember well from the newspaper headlines—we became excited about the flight of Charles A. Lindbergh across the Atlantic Ocean in his monoplane, 'Spirit of St Louis'. Of course," he explains, "living so close to St Louis accounts for much of our interest and attention to this event. Lindbergh's take-off had our prayers and blessings; and when he landed thirty-three hours later in Paris, we were elated. We talked about it around the seminary for days."

"I was fascinated by this relative new thing called 'flight', and one of the best things I did before leaving Chicago to join the seminary was to convince my grandparents that I should have a trial flight in an airplane, thinking that it might be my last chance before I die." Marshall saw his entry into training for the priesthood as a huge step away from everyday life and mundane pursuits. "One day I did fly for fifteen or twenty minutes at Hines Field, in Maywood, just outside of Chicago. Later, when I learned about Lindbergh's feat, all those lonely hours over the Atlantic with so few navigational aids and no radio, I could identify a tiny bit with him. When the details of his flight were described, I almost memorized them, I was so interested."

Preparing for India

In 1926, Marshall completed the two-year novitiate and entered the juniorate. Then, in 1927, at the age of 21, the young scholastic Moran was recommended by his provincial, Francis X. McMenamy, SJ, to work in the mission schools of the Jesuit Diocese of Patna, India. While he had volunteered himself to the India mission, strictly speaking it was not his choice, but that of his superiors. Confirmation of his assignment to India was the answer to Marshall's prayers, and not the least to a little determined (though largely silent) pleading on his part. Before departure, however, his Jesuit superiors expected him to complete at least one more year of academic preparation.

While he continued his intense studies of Latin, Greek and philosophy at Florissant, from the moment his assignment was announced, India occupied much of his attention and curiosity. He read everything he could about India and the new Jesuit mission at Patna in the north.

In those days, the church did not readily send one so young to the Asian missions and, once they were overseas, missionaries were not expected to return home. The sea voyage was long and expensive and it was not the custom of priests to return, except under circumstances of ill health, special duties or reassignment. Even knowing this, Marshall was no less enthusiastic. He felt both physically and spiritually prepared to dedicate the rest of his life to the difficult, isolated existence of a missionary priest and teacher.

Family Obligations

His plan was to depart for the India mission at the end of the 1928 academic year, in the company of three other young scholastics, his classmates Marion Batson, Felix Farrell and Augustine Wildermuth, and one priest, Fr Leon Foster. In October, however, barely into his final year of study, Marshall received sudden and unwelcome news from home—his father was gravely ill with appendicitis.

Before the coming of modern antibiotics, appendicitis was greatly feared and with any complications very serious, potentially life threatening. The penicillin antibiotic that we take for granted for the treatment of appendicitis and similar infections today was not yet known.[6] Marshall rushed to Chicago with a certain dread in his heart. Within hours of his arrival, his father died, leaving a widow and three sons to mourn.

After the funeral, Marshall returned to Florissant and reported to his provincial, Fr McMenamy. On hearing of the family tragedy and knowing of the extended responsibilities that the young man, as eldest son, would have over the next few months, Fr McMenamy postponed his departure to India by one year, until 1929.

Marshall was told to continue his studies to complete the Bachelor's degree. At the same time, he would be available to help his mother and brothers through their time of adjustment. It was both an opportunity and a disappointing setback, about which he had little choice. Instead of sailing to India with his friends, Marshall bid them farewell, Godspeed, and safe passage instead. He was sad at their departure, but confident that he would join them the following year.

In September, 1928, he transferred to St Louis University for further studies in philosophy. He took a room on Lindel Boulevard, next to the university offices.

He remembers it as "an interesting but serious year, concentrating on the study of logic, epistemology and ontology. Ontology is the study of reality and the nature of being. I found it very interesting," he later said, reminiscing. "For awhile I was a Platonist, enamored with Plato's theory of ideas, or forms. Later, I delved into St Augustine's writings about truth, simplicity and beauty—*Omne ens est unum, bonum, et verum*, in Latin. I enjoyed St Augustine, but sometimes found him very abstract and abstruse."

During the year at St Louis University, Marshall matured in emotional, intellectual and practical ways, all of which prepared him even better for the work ahead in India. In addition to attending rigorous lectures on philosophy, all in Latin, he also spent two days a week studying biology, comparative anatomy and embryology at the School of Medicine. He was excited by this brief return to medical studies, knowing that it would be invaluable to him as a missionary.

Marshall was an excellent student and graduated in the spring of 1929 with a Bachelor of Arts degree in Latin and Greek, but with enough credits in science for a Bachelor Science degree as well. At graduation he was the pride of all his family. The only sorrow was that his father was not present to share the moment. Following graduation he received final instructions on his posting to India. He had until the following October to prepare.

Bertha Moran's Pilgrimage

That extra year at the university after the death of his father allowed Marshall to help his mother through her time of mourning and adjustment to widowhood. To salve her widow's grief, he urged her to sail to Europe for an extended overland pilgrimage to Catholic holy sites. It was a sacred journey he, too, hoped to make someday. He set about planning her travel itinerary with the youthful enthusiasm, imagination and attention to detail that were the hallmark of all his serious endeavors.

After she arrived in Europe, Marshall received letters and postcards from his mother describing the wonders of France, Germany, and the holy sites of Rome.

In France she visited Notre Dame de Lourdes in southwestern France, near the Pyrenees mountains. She was one among the six hundred thousand pilgrims that year. Lourdes is the most famous Catholic holy site in all of France, and perhaps in all of Europe, with the possible exception of St Peter's Basilica in Rome. It was at Lourdes in 1858, in the grotto of Massabielle, that a young peasant girl saw a series of visions of the Virgin Mother of Jesus and heard the apparition speak. News of her vision spread throughout Europe, and Our Lady of Lourdes and the little spring that flows from the grotto became famous for miraculous cures among the ill and infirm.

Bertha also visited the French shrine of St Therese of Lisieux, known affectionately to the devout as the "Little Flower of Jesus" and as "St Therese of the Child Jesus". St Therese's childhood name was Marie Francoise Therese Martin. As a girl, Marie Martin entered the austere order of Carmelite Sisters at Lisieux where, it is said, she lived her brief life in humility, simplicity and patience, while suffering terribly from an acute lung ailment that eventually caused her death at the age of twenty-four. Marshall's mother was especially attracted to this particular saint, in part by their closeness in their birth years. (And later, like Marie Martin, Bertha Moran also suffered from a lung ailment, tuberculosis.)

The fame associated with Marie Martin's life and suffering spread rapidly, and she was frequently invoked to obtain favors from heaven. After 1925, when she was canonized, her shrine became a popular retreat. Devotion to Marie Martin as St Therese became particularly strong among priests and missionaries, one reason why Marshall encouraged his mother to go there.

The pilgrimage to the shrines of France had a strong effect on his mother. As a child, she was raised as a Mennonite before converting, at age twelve, to the Catholicism of her stepfather and some of her closest school friends. She had always been a strong family person and while unquestioningly serious about her Catholic faith and convictions, she was, nonetheless, understandably concerned and worried about her eldest son's resolve to become a missionary.

During her travels through Europe, she thought frequently about him and his missionary calling.

Her solitary pilgrimage left a strong spiritual impression on Bertha, deepening her religious convictions. Importantly for Marshall, it also provided her with the strength needed to give him her full blessing; although, as he recollected later, not without a twinge of maternal reluctance. Hers' was the blessing Marshall most cherished as the day of his departure for India approached.

Vacation in the Canadian Rockies

Following his mother's return from Europe and Marshall's graduation, and with only a few months left in America, Marshall left St Louis to join her on a brief holiday in Canada. It was a family gift to him. They insisted that he and Bertha visit the resort at Banff and see the beauties of the Rocky Mountains, out of a concern that in his future life on the flat, dusty plains of north India he might never see mountains again.

Those summer days at Banff were pleasant ones, rich in the shared affection between mother and son. They strolled the forest paths around the Chateau Lake Louise, savored rich coffee and sweets in the chateau's famous restaurant, and stood in awe on the blue-green lake shore viewing one of Nature's most spectacular geologic wonders. The glacial lake backed on the west by Victoria Glacier was every bit the "Pearl of the Canadian Rockies," as Canadian Pacific Railway travel posters of the day described it.

Their time together allowed mother and son to reminisce on his childhood, to talk about the family back in Chicago, and to consider the future. And, not least, they pondered God's intent and what might lie ahead for Marshall, so far away, perhaps never to return. The memory of those moments of closeness with his mother remained with Marshall all his life.

With the coming of autumn, he was back in St Louis. The day of his departure was set. He would sail first to Europe from New York harbor on October 12, 1929. As he made final preparations for the journey, he had much on his mind, a great deal to occupy his thoughts. Beneath his typically cheerful and determined demeanor, he felt a certain sadness at the thought that he might never again see his mother and brothers, his grandparents, and his aunts and uncles; nor his Chicago home and the Wisconsin lake cottage that he loved to visit as a boy.

He was once asked if he ever had any doubts about his calling to the priesthood—especially at this time of ultimate departure from home. He changed the subject. It was only natural that he must have thought about it more than once. But Marshall Moran's convictions were strong and his pride was fierce. He had made a choice, and wavering was not his style.

Alone with his thoughts, prayers and aspirations, and doubtless wondering what lay in store for him across the ocean, his imminent departure was also a time of hope and excitement. Marshall had high expectations for a life of promise and accomplishment in the service of the Society of Jesus. In his small way this young Jesuit scholastic felt quite self-assured despite his youth and inexperience. He often said that he felt privileged to be following in the footsteps of no less than St Francis Xavier who, four centuries earlier, had founded the first Jesuit mission in India. Marshall prayed to the saints, especially Ignatius of Loyola, Francis Xavier and Therese of Lisieux, asking for a measure of their patience and humility in the face of the difficulties and uncertainties that surely lay ahead of him in a strange and foreign place.

Notes to Chapter 2: Scholar

1. St Augustine (354-430 AD) wrote *Confessions* and *City of God* over fifteen hundred years ago, in the late fourth and early fifth centuries AD. According to Catholic scholars, St Augustine "is the most important of the Latin Church Fathers. His work formed the foundation for much of what would become Western Christendom." Augustine was born in North Africa and rose in the church hierarchy to become Bishop of Hippo, a north African port city on the Mediterranean Sea" (Paul Halsall, ed., *Internet Medieval Sourcebook*, 2009). Augustine's *Confessions*, were written in 397-398 AD and are considered by some to be the first autobiography in the West; or, if not a complete autobiography, then the earliest form of it in Western literature. *The Confessions of St Augustine* (an alternative title) traces a dialogue between Augustine and his God and represents "a journey toward rising above one's self" (Albert C. Outler, translator and editor. 'Introduction' to *Augustine: Confessions*, 1955).
2. On the *Constitutions* see George E. Ganss, SJ (1970).
3. See Society of Jesus/Oregon Province, 'The Spiritual Exercises of St Ignatius' (2009).
4. Ganss (1970, p.23).
5. On March 6, 1921, Fr Louis Van Hoeck, SJ (1870-1933) was consecrated as the first Jesuit bishop of Patna in a ceremony held at Ranchi, Bihar. When Bishop Van Hoeck took charge he found a poor and largely rural diocese with a population of twenty-five million people covering a vast region of India's Gangetic plain. Five thousand of them were Catholics served by six priests. His first challenge was to recruit Jesuit scholastics

and priests from America. On his visit to Florissant, Missouri, in 1926, the bishop whetted the imaginations and challenged the spirits of young Marshall Moran and a number of his seminary friends.

6. The antibiotic properties of penicillin were first discovered in 1928 by the British microbiologist Alexander Fleming. It was not until the 1940s, however, that penicillin became widely used, virtually eliminating the fear of a ruptured appendix and other previously deadly ailments.

3

Passage to India

*He was sailing that day, Marshall said, to discover India—
with all due respect to Columbus.*

As the October date of his departure for the mission in India approached, Marshall Moran planned his travels to arrive in New York City well enough ahead of schedule, in order to briefly visit Wall Street to see the world famous (about to become infamous) New York Stock Exchange. Only a few years before, while working at the Garfield Bank in Chicago, he had visited the Chicago Board of Trade with his uncle. Watching the action of the world's largest commodities exchange, he was impressed seeing wheat, corn and other agricultural "futures" being bartered loudly in "the pit" on the commodities exchange house floor. Now, on the eve of his departure from America, he wanted to observe how stocks changed hands on Wall Street. He knew he would never speculate in stocks, but he was curious, nonetheless.

During those first days of October, 1929, Wall Street was a flurry of activity, a blur of financial dealings, as buyers and sellers reacted to rumors and counter-rumors. The newspapers were full of speculations about market conditions. Neither Marshall nor anyone else imagined that in little more than two weeks this great fiscal center would be reeling under the effects of the world's most spectacular financial crash, tumbling America and the world into the Great Depression. Some joker once told Marshall that it was because he left America that the stock market had collapsed and the Depression began. Some humor—a rather grim joke, Marshall thought.

On Columbus Day, Marshall bid his last farewells and, not without tears, boarded the twenty-thousand ton Anchor Line steamer *Samaria*. He was sailing that day, Marshall said, to discover India— with all due respect to Columbus. Brochures touted the Anchor Line Fleet as having the "Fastest Passenger and Freight Steamers in the World." Their motto was: "There is no Better Way."

Marshall shared the passage to India via Europe with five other Jesuits. One was his former teacher, Reverend George Dertinger, SJ.

3. Fr Moran with students.

The others were fellow scholastics Richard Welfle, Richard Mehren, John Morrison, and Charles Bonnot.[1] Marshall shared a cabin with Dertinger and Bonnot. On their long voyage he got to know them all well.

Looking Back
About Moran
John A. Morrison, SJ[2]

About Moran. I have known him since 1924. I joined the Jesuits in 1923, and when the next year's batch of recruits came to Florissant, my novice master appointed me their "guardian angel"; i.e., to take care of them during their first week of novitiate. About that time I remember only that I had to tell him, "We don't play tennis wearing sleeveless underwear." During the novitiate and later, in the juniorate, he was one of many, and much the same during our time together in philosophy at St Louis University.

We came to India together by ship—there was no aviation in those days—and the ships across the Atlantic and Mediterranean, Red Sea and across to Bombay took one month. There were six of us, three in one cabin and three in another. Moran did not share my cabin.

Moran was a friend, never what you would call a best friend, and one of the facts of his character was a sort of "aloofness" towards so many of his fellow Jesuits. I do not want to denigrate in any way the outstanding work that Moran has accomplished as a Jesuit. His superiors in Rome held him in high esteem for the work he accomplished. But it is safe to say I am not the only one who had some close association with him in the earlier times who saw a certain aloofness, maybe call it a superiority complex.

On reaching Plymouth, England, the six young men boarded an overnight train for London. While he saw very little of Plymouth, Marshall was quite aware of its historic significance as the port from which the Puritans had set sail for religious freedom in America on the *Mayflower* in 1620.

The Sights of London
Their travel schedule allowed four days for sightseeing in London. Marshall was excited, ready to see all that he could. While at sea he whiled away the hours studying maps and guidebooks of the city. He knew England's secular and church history from his high school and college studies, and he wanted particularly to see places associated with the difficult early years of the Jesuit establishment in London. He quickly oriented himself to the street names and landmarks, sure that once he saw the river Thames and the Houses of Parliament he would know where to go for all the other places on his list.

London was a test of young Marshall's tenacious memory for detail. He was proud of it, a pride that sometimes put other people off and could be interpreted, as John Morrison did, as "a certain aloofness" or superiority. It was this facet of his character, however, that ingratiated him to his superiors and led him in time to become a leader and to strive for accomplishments that were sometimes beyond what others felt were strictly necessary. Today he might have been called a youthful over-achiever.

On their first morning in London, Marshall startled his older companions by announcing that he would take them on a tour.

"I will be your guide," he said confidently.

"What do you know about London?" they asked, a little taken aback at the determination of their youngest companion to lead.

"Well," he said, "do you see all those trees there, down the street?

That happens to be Hyde Park. Come on, now, let's walk down there and I'll show you a few things."

Marshall had done his homework and resolved that they would share in his enthusiasm and unabashed curiosity. "I can't be bothered with taxis; instead we should walk," he said. He had a long list of famous places to see and was determined that they join him afoot.

So his companions set off with him, perplexed and a little put off by his insistence; but, nonetheless, they followed. First they visited Hyde Park, then walked down along the Thames, admiring the London and Tower bridges and the sweeping view of the Parliament building.

In the next few days they toured the British Museum and Westminster Abbey. At the museum they were impressed with the legacy of colonialism in the displays from Egypt and India. At Westminster Abbey they absorbed a bit of British secular history among the crypts of past heroes and monarchs, entombed within and beneath the cold stony majesty of the abbey's eleventh century architecture.

At the Tower of London and the Marble Arch they contemplated the persecution of the martyrs of the church in England. There, during the reign of Queen Elizabeth I (1558-1603), such notable early English Jesuits as Edmund Campion, Alexander Briant, Robert Southwell, and Henry Walpole were publicly hanged, drawn and quartered. It is said that well-dressed Protestant gentlemen stood by and shouted encouragement to the executioners in their fervent butchery. Thereafter, throughout much of the rest of the seventeenth century, especially during the reigns of Kings James I and Charles I and II, many more Catholic activists were executed for preaching the faith. It was the stuff of legends, and of saints.

Marshall Moran had a good memory for Roman Catholic history in the England of that bygone time. He recalled that the mid-seventeenth century was a time of great religious strife and civil war. Altogether, more than ninety priests and Catholic laymen suffered martyrdom at the hands of the Protestants during those difficult years. Conditions for Roman Catholics began to improve only after 1660, when Charles II ascended the throne. A decade later, in a secret clause to a treaty with France's King Louis XIV, Charles II declared himself a Roman Catholic (although he did not openly acknowledge his conversion until shortly before his death fifteen years later). Within two years of the treaty, in 1672, however, Charles's Catholic sympathies became clear with his Declaration of Indulgence, whereupon the Protestants in Parliament expressed their fury by passing the Test Act (1673), which summarily excluded Roman Catholics from public office.

Meanwhile, in 1660, Charles's younger brother and potential successor to the throne, James, the Duke of York, had also converted to Roman Catholicism. He had previously fled to Holland, in 1648, out of fear for his safety. The Protestant parliament continued to rail against Catholicism and tried unsuccessfully to exclude James from succession to the throne. But Charles and James prevailed, and on Charles II's death in 1685, James II was crowned King of England, Scotland and Ireland. Once in power, the Protestant rebellion against him was suppressed and James acted swiftly to assure religious tolerance and freedom for all denominations throughout the land. From the time of James II onward, Roman Catholics were allowed to take up public office.

This rich, eventful, but sorry chapter in the religious history of Britain inspired Marshall's brief tour in 1929. Years later, in Kathmandu, he was reminded of his London pilgrimage when, in 1970, word came from Rome that forty seventeenth century English Catholic martyrs, nine of them Jesuits, were being canonized for their faith. Marshall had read the gripping accounts of their persecution and death, and had seen the sights of their martyrdom. He felt proud that they had achieved the ultimate recognition that the Catholic Church bestows upon its heroes.

On their last full day in London, a Sunday, Marshall and the small company of Jesuit colleagues celebrated high mass together at Westminster Cathedral.[3] This cathedral is dedicated to the "Precious Blood of Jesus" and, as such, is especially favored among Catholics. Compared with many other historical sites they visited in London, this magnificent Catholic cathedral was of relatively recent construction. It was built between 1895 and 1903, covering fifty-four thousand square feet. At the time Marshall saw it, the cathedral was only twenty-six years old.

He was impressed by the cathedral's architecture and sacred appointments, the Byzantine sanctuary, the Romanesque style of the retro-choir behind the main altar, topped by a great baldacchino brocade canopy and the central crucifix—large, commanding, but not imposing—suspended from the sanctuary arch. And, not least, he was deeply moved by the singing of the cathedral choir. He wondered if, once settled in India, he would ever see and hear such beauty again.

Lunch after mass was also Marshall's idea. He took his companions to the Lyon Restaurant, where the food, he recalls, was not unlike that of the Childs or the old Thompson chain of restaurants he had frequented in Chicago.

Before leaving England, he attended to one last errand, unassociated with either his religious or touristic ambitions. Earlier that summer, before departing Chicago while saying his final goodbyes to the family, Grandfather O'Keefe had asked Marshall to stop at Selfridge's, one of England's oldest and largest department stores, to buy a dozen of the very highest quality fine silk neckties. They would make grand Christmas presents, his grandfather said. Grandfather O'Keefe knew precisely what to buy from his own earlier visits to London, and Marshall carefully noted the brand name, colors and designs.

When the cheerful young cleric, dressed in a black suit and stiffly starched Roman collar, approached the counter to pay for his selection of ties, the sales girls giggled and whispered to each other. "What are they thinking," Marshall said to himself, "that I am preparing to leave the order?" Why else, they must have wondered, would he need all this fancy neckwear?

He described the scene in a hastily written note to his grandfather and tucked it in with the ties as they were wrapped for mailing to Chicago.

A Pilgrim in France

On Monday morning, October 18, the six pilgrims began the second leg of their journey. Upon departing England they divided into two groups, then set out across the English Channel to see the holy places of France. They agreed to rendezvous in four days' time at Marseilles, the seaport on the Mediterranean coast from which they were scheduled to embark on the final portion of their long sea passage to India. Welfe, Morrison and Mehren set off to visit Lourdes, while Moran, Dertinger and Bonnot opted to tour the shrines of St Therese at Lisieux and of St Margaret Mary near Lyons. At last, Marshall was following some of the pilgrimage route he had so carefully and reverently planned a year earlier for his mother.

Lisieux was all that he had imagined it to be, and more. This agricultural trading town in northern France is known for its dairy products and, among the devout, for its shrine of St Therese, the "Little Flower of Jesus". By this visit, Marshall's faith was greatly strengthened. The three missionary pilgrims prayed together for the necessary determination to persevere in service to the Little Company of Jesus, the Jesuits.

After only a few hours in Lisieux, they continued on to Paris where they spent the night of Tuesday, October 29th. It was there that they first learned of the events of "Black Tuesday" back on Wall Street in New York City.

Looking Back
The Stock Market Crash
Fr Moran

It was in Paris, between trains, that we first saw the headlines in London and New York newspapers. They screamed financial disaster—the Stock Market had crashed.[4]

I bought a paper and read that over sixteen million shares changed hands in quick succession the day before on Wall Street. This triggered billions of dollars in losses. As one after another bank closed its doors and its assets were liquidated, the panic spread from America to Europe and around the world. It was the end of post-World War I prosperity and the beginning of dark financial times. The Great Depression had begun. I was concerned, of course, and fascinated at the same time.

Looking back on it over the years as a history teacher in the Jesuit schools of Patna and Kathmandu, I told my students how conservative President Hoover's solutions to the crisis were ineffectual. It is my feeling that only with the selection of Franklin Delano Roosevelt to the presidency of the United States in 1932 were strong enough measures finally taken to restore financial confidence in the U.S., and to provide employment. Only Roosevelt's strong social welfare programs of the New Deal brought help to millions in despair.

I have long been fascinated by this example of the seeming failure of modern capitalism. At the time I tried as best I could, at such a distance across the world, to understand what caused the Crash and how it could be solved or avoided in future. As the Depression unfolded, I could only read about it occasionally in the Indian weeklies and later in books published by the Brookings Institution of Washington DC. I also probed the writings of Karl Marx, trying to understand the turgid, difficult and long-winded prose of that nineteenth century dialectal materialist. In years to come, I turned again to the teachings of socialism in an attempt to understand better, and to interpret for myself and my students, the unfolding events of Europe of the 1930s and '40s that so ineptly wrapped men's hearts and souls in such a cold and misguided doctrine.

The events of 1929, and the Depression that followed, focused my attention on the need for social welfare and economic reforms in U.S. society and around the globe. And although I was a long ways away from feeling the direct impact of circumstances back home in America, living as I was in the isolation of village India, I felt, nonetheless, the long arm of the world-wide financial reshufflings in their effect on the colonial British pound and the Indian rupee.

In one sense, the Wall Street crash was a boon to missionaries. Our expenses in India were very low. Devaluation actually helped us. It conveniently gave us more rupees to live on after converting the American dollars donated by supporters back home in places like Chicago, Detroit, Cleveland and Cincinnati.

All that was still ahead of me at the time of the Crash, however. Meanwhile, the France of Catholic saints and pilgrim shrines occupied my attention.

From Paris, Marshall and his companions caught a train to Paray-le-Monial, near Lyons in Burgundy, not far from the Swiss border. At Paray they spent two days admiring and praying at the shrine of St Margaret Mary Alacoque. It was there, especially, that they sought solace in the memory of this frail but noble saint, seeking the self-assurance necessary to withstand the physical rigors of their calling.

St Margaret Mary, who lived in the seventeenth century, was canonized in 1920. She was known especially for leading others in devotion to the Sacred Heart of Jesus, described by Catholics as the adoration of the humanity of Christ. In her youth, Margaret Mary saw visions of the Christ. Later, while suffering from paralysis, it is believed that she was miraculously cured by the Virgin Mary, whereupon she consecrated herself to the religious life at the Visitation Convent in Paray. By the mid-nineteenth century, remembrance of Margaret Mary and devotion to the Sacred Heart were common among Roman Catholics worldwide.

The three young Jesuit pilgrims had missed the recent Feast of St Margaret Mary by less than two weeks (October 17). But their two-day stay at Paray was moving and memorable, nonetheless. Margaret Mary had only recently been canonized, and devotion to the Sacred Heart of Jesus had been raised that very year, 1929, to the highest rank in the Roman Catholic Church.[5] For Marshall, this holy person had special meaning as his own patroness saint, to whom he had personally devoted himself at the time of his rite of Confirmation in the church, as a Catholic youth in 1918. He addressed her now, as he had St Therese in Lisieux, seeking humility, guidance and inspiration in the face of the unknown trials and opportunities ahead in India. He would not be disappointed.

After completing their visit to Paray, Dertinger, Bonnot and Moran proceeded back through Lyons to Marseilles. During a morning wait between trains, Marshall ordered breakfast and was served hot chocolate and some dried rolls. So much for French cuisine, he thought. An American breakfast of eggs, bacon, toast, jam, juice and coffee—especially coffee—was what he craved; but that was unheard of there; it was quite unknown. When he described it to the waiter, the man was astonished and laughed at the thought that people would eat so much so early in the morning.

The Onward Journey

After rejoining their friends at Marseilles, the six young Jesuits boarded the large single-class cabin cruiser *S.S. California*, bound for Bombay. Marshall was eager now to continue, and could not hide his excitement at the prospect of the final sea voyage to India. The ship was crowded, near full to capacity with four thousand passengers. But their accommodations were comfortable enough. The six of them shared two cabins of four bunks each.

Sailing the Mediterranean was uneventful. They used the time to get acquainted with some of their fellow travelers. As they strolled the decks and lounges, they met proper young British civil servants setting out on careers with the colonial Raj, British soldiers returning to India from home leave in the English countryside, wealthy Indian gentlemen and their wives in flowing saris returning from business tours of Europe and America, a few students, and others who, like themselves, were bound for a new life in the East. The weather was fair, the seas calm, and Marshall made himself comfortable reading, playing a few games of deck shuffleboard, and talking with the others about what lay ahead for them at the mission in Patna.

On November 1, All Saints' Day on the church calendar, they were in the Suez Canal. While ashore for a few hours at Port Said they got a tantalizing glimpse of Egypt, although they would have liked to have gone farther to view the pyramids and the Great Sphinx. Following the advice of fellow passengers, they each brought a sun helmet in the bazaar, in the commonly held belief that everyone going to the tropics must wear such a *sahib*'s topi, or risk death by sun stroke. None of them was willing to dispute the claim, no matter how ridiculous they might look wearing a helmet atop their flowing cassocks in the dusty villages of the subcontinent. Even as missionaries, they were about to join all the other "white *sahibs*" and were expected to look and act their parts in the colonial style of life, as part of the British Raj.

In contrast to the cool breezes of the Atlantic and the Mediterranean Sea, the trip down the Suez Canal and across the Red Sea was hot and steamy. In those days before air conditioning, the fans seemed only to blow the hot air on them all the more intensely. The more experienced of the ship's travelers had booked the more expensive staterooms on the shaded side of the ship, following the dictum, "Port Out, Starboard Home," which gave rise to the term "POSH" for traveling in luxury. Such luxury, however, was not an option for these budget-conscious novices to the seas, and they suffered with the heat along with the majority of their shipmates. This was their first introduction to the tropics. They patiently endured it by swilling cool drinks and favoring the shady port side decks each day. They suffered stoically in the heat for the rest of their way across the Arabian Sea to the port of Bombay.

Bombay, First Impressions
On November 11, the eleventh Armistice Day since the end of the Great War to end all wars, they disembarked at Bombay, today's Mumbai. Suddenly immersed in a new culture and society, the Europe and America they had left behind were far from their minds. Passing beneath the Gateway to India Arch, which was erected in 1911, and standing now on the threshold of the Asian subcontinent, their first experience with the sights, sounds and rich smells of India were intoxicating.

Looking Back
On Arriving in Bombay
Richard A. Welfle, SJ[6]

> November 11, 1929, is a date I will always remember. That was the day the *S.S. California* docked in Bombay, and I came down the gangway to take India for better or for worse, until death do us part. On that same day I met a venerable missionary who had had many years of experience in India. Appraising me with a critical eye and reckoning that he was old enough to be my grandfather, he said: "Young man, since this is your very first day in India, you are going to need two things: a good stomach and a good sense of humor—in reverse order. A sense of humor comes first."

To the neophyte Jesuits, Bombay teemed with a ceaseless, sweating humanity. Scantily clad men hauled freight and passengers through the crowded streets and alleys. Others hawked hot spicy treats and sticky sweetmeats, or peddled trinkets and bright cloth, or sold themselves, their talents, their wares, for a few rupees or for some *chai* to drink and *chapattis* to eat. They saw every form of dress and costume, from the simple loin clothes, *dhotis* and rags of the poor, to European suits and fine silk saris of the rich. Bare backs, bare feet, torn trousers and shorts were the garb of many men and countless children, and threadbare saris on the poorer women, the few they saw. From every corner they watched the horse-drawn *tongas* and *ekkas*, along with modern motor cars, carriages and bicycles crowding the streets, horns tooting raucously, competing with the furiously tinkling bicycle rickshaw bells, like an untuned symphony.

Funeral processions seemed to pass at all hours of the day and night, accompanied by brass bands playing tunes sometimes familiar to the Western ear—like 'Marching through Georgia'—on the way to the burning ghats. Occasionally, Marshall caught a glimpse of some notable personage being jogged along in a palanquin on the shoulders of sweating servants, curtained from sight, as if a gauze veil could cut out the view and the sounds and smells of so many others of lowly status. Pariah dogs and naked street urchins scuttled underfoot, and bullocks and cows seemed to flow stodgily and endlessly about them in a sea of human exotica and dung and flowers and filth.

The days were hot and sticky, but the nights were pleasantly warm. Balmy sea breezes wafted about and mixed the fragrance of flower gardens with the stench of urine and coal smoke and smoldering joss sticks, attacking the nostrils and besieging the senses. Above it all they heard the din and cry of hawkers and fakirs, priests and beggars, simultaneously shouting, praying, beseeching, babbling and bantering in Marathi, Hindi, Gujarati, Parsi, pidgin English, Goan Portuguese, and various tribal tongues, some of which languages Marshall and his little company of priests had yet to learn as strangers in that strange land.

For Marshall, as for all who first enter India from the relative serenity and comforts of the West, it was simultaneously magnificent, depressing and overpowering, an attack on the ears, an assault on the senses that would take years to sort out and appreciate. He couldn't help but admire other Catholic priests he met there who had spent almost their entire lives in this exotic place and who mostly appeared comfortable and conversant with it all. And he wondered what he, among these millions, could possibly do with and for them.

Their host in Bombay was a jolly Spanish priest named Heras, who put them up in the guest rooms at St Xavier's College. Fr Heras had also studied in the United States at St Louis University and was eager to catch up on news of mutual friends and teachers. His hospitality was generous and he impressed Marshall with his knowledge of Indian prehistory, the lore and legend of ancient Harappan civilization in the Indus river valley, and of the Aryan invasion, of which he was a specialist.

They stayed at the college for two days, trying to absorb and sort out and learn a little of Indian life and custom before continuing on to Patna, their ultimate destination. Fr Heras filled them with advice on how best to ride the trains, what to say (a few phrases), what to see, to eat, and to avoid eating. From the college kitchen Marshall tasted his first hot curries and suffered his first bout of stomach cramps. A bad stomach plagued him off and on for years whenever he overindulged in the hot, rich spicy fare common to the subcontinent.

By Train to Patna

At the Bombay railway station on the day they departed for Patna, as on every day in other stations along the route, they were assailed by the unaccustomed and earthy expressions of the human condition. They saw maimed and crippled children and homeless women clutching crying, dirty babies, begging with outstretched hands at the train car windows. They saw vendors of sweets, peanuts and *bidi* cigarettes, and others selling oranges from open baskets. Those sweet oranges saved Marshall during the first days in India, he recalls. They were among the few things he could eat without suffering gastronomic grief.

The trains were surprisingly well kept and once underway the ride was quite comfortable. The railroads ran on time and were clean and comfortable, reflecting the indulgence and preeminence of British punctuality and perfection. But Marshall was constantly surprised and a little depressed at what he saw out the windows—cities and villages and farmsteads, all looking shabby, poor and grimy to his eyes. There were people of all types, dressed in all colors, all styles, some hatless, some in turbans, wearing leather shoes or sandals or barefoot, fat (a few, the rich) and thin (most, the poor). Some of the women in saris looked extremely regal and bright, but the majority of dress seen in the passing villages was faded, torn, ragged and dirty. At first sight, all the poverty and dirt overwhelmed him.

A decade later, he would remark while traveling by train to South India that the social atmosphere had changed. The people seemed more polite and did not talk in such loud voices. They appeared neater and cleaner, and looked better. There seemed, by comparison, to be less pushing and shoving to get on and off the train cars. And the food seemed better, less spicy. Or were these feelings simply the result of his becoming an "India hand," acclimated and less sensitive to the dire circumstances one grows quickly to take for granted in Asia?

The train from Bombay that November 1929 took the six priests inland from the Arabian Sea coast in a northeasterly direction through the Central Provinces to the town of Bhopal, then north to Agra in the United Provinces and, finally, east past Allahabad and down along the river Ganges to Patna in Bihar Province.

At Bhopal they disembarked briefly, at the insistence of Fr Heras, to visit the nearby historic site of Sanchi. There, Heras had told them, they must see the pillar edict of King Ashoka dating to over two centuries before Christ. It was one of several such inscriptions across North India proclaiming his reign and praising the peaceful morality of Buddhism.

Marshall had learned from his studies of Indian history that Ashoka ruled from approximately 269 to 232 BC. According to contemporary accounts, he usurped the Mauryan throne from his father, initiating what began as a bloody and tyrannical reign. In a few years, however, the young king had a change of heart, espoused Buddhist pacifism, and proclaimed a reign of peaceful reform, abandoning aggression and war. More than one historian has described the converted Ashoka as a benevolent king, part dreamer and quite ahead of his time. Surely he ranks among the noblest leaders India has ever known, perhaps even one of the great kings of the world.

All this impressed Marshall, who was beginning to get a feel for the variety of Indian experience and expression. Learning about Ashoka for the first time provided him with an introduction to the richness of the subcontinent's culture, society and history, subjects that he later pursued with fascination in Indian literature, art and architecture. In a few years he would become well versed in Hindu and Buddhist philosophy and theology, which enabled him to expound and explore it further with many of the educated pundits and scholars of his new chosen home. And later, whenever possible, he would seek out other Ashokan sites near Patna. Eventually, he visited Lumbini, in southern Nepal, where Siddhartha Gautama, the Buddha, was born, and where Ashoka had erected another of his famous inscribed pillars.[7]

At Agra, Marshall viewed the sixteenth century Taj Mahal under a bright moon, marveling at the devotion of the Mogul emperor, Shah Jahan, who had built this marvelous edifice out of pure white Makrana marble as a mausoleum for his wife Mumtaz-i-mahal. Poor Shah Jahan; deposed by Aurangezab, his jealous son, he spent his last days, it is said, denied even a view of his wife's marvelous tomb, except by reflection through a tiny mirror mounted on the wall of his barren cell in the nearby Red Fort.

On November 17, Marshall Moran and his colleagues reached Patna. His passage *to* India was over. He was now beginning his life-long passage *through* the subcontinent, building upon the work of many others during the long history of Jesuit exploration and missions in South and Central Asia.

Notes to Chapter 3: Passage to India

1. Of the group, John Morrison was assigned to work among the poor Santals of Bihar, where he became something of a tribal rights activist. When he came into conflict with the civil authorities the church reassigned him to a mission on Truk Atoll in the Pacific Ocean. Richard Mehren spent only a few years in India, then returned to the USA to become a layman after receiving dispensation from his vows. George Dertinger died in India in 1938, within a decade of his arrival. Charles Bonnot stayed for some twenty years before returning home due to illness. Richard Welfle remained with the Patna Jesuits for fifty-eight years. He died in 1987.
2. John A. Morrison, SJ, personal communication (1987).
3. Westminster Cathedral is a Catholic edifice and sanctuary, not to be confused with Westminster Abbey, a center point of the Protestant Church of England. Both have rich significance in the history of England.
4. Marshall read about the Stock Market Crash in the newspapers of Paris, though for the most part the French press virtually ignored it. Instead, the front pages were preoccupied with France's own political crisis. The cabinet of French President Aristide Briand had fallen the week before, and the government was in turmoil.
5. Margaret Mary's spiritual adviser, Claude La Colombière, SJ (1641-82), was also beatified in 1929. He was with Margaret Mary in 1675, when she saw the visions and later when she was cured. Claude La Colombière was canonized a saint in 1992.

    Canonization is defined as a decree regarding the universal public veneration of an individual by the worldwide church. *Beatification* also permits public worship, but on a more narrow scale or local level. Typically, the importance of an individual man or woman in Church history is first recognized and decreed through beatification, and only later by the more formal decree and rites of canonization.
6. Richard Welfle, SJ, in his Preface to *Pieces of India* (1963).
7. For an interesting discussion of the discovery of the Buddha's birthplace and the Ashoka pillar in Nepal (at Lumbini) and the site of the Buddha's upbringing as a youth (in nearby Kapilvastu) see Charles Allen, *The Buddha and Dr Fuhrer: An Archaeological Scandal* (2008).

EARLY CHRISTIAN MISSIONARIES IN INDIA, TIBET & NEPAL

4

Jesuits in India and Tibet

...we are to be obliged by a special vow... to go without subterfuge or excuse, as far as in us lies, to whatever provinces they may choose to send us... even (to) those who live in the region called the Indies...
        St Ignatius Loyola, *Constitutions*

Francis Xavier founded the Jesuit India Mission over 460 years ago, in 1542. At first located among the Hindus settled around the Portuguese colonial west coast port of Goa, it eventually spread along the southwest coast, called the "Fisher Coast," and inland in the south of India. By 1590, the Jesuits had also moved north to the Moghul court of Akbar, at Fatepur Sikri (and later at Agra), to within sight of the snowcapped peaks of the Himalayas. It was there, in the north, that the Jesuits opened the Moghul Mission, hoping to gain a foothold among the people of the Gangetic plain. They did not do very well among the Moghuls, however (if success is measured in numbers of conversions), but were more active in using the Moghul center as a springboard for exploration and early mission endeavors through the Himalayas to Tibet, and ultimately to Nepal.

Although the Jesuits were the first in these northern reaches of India near the Himalayas, in time responsibility for missions in north India (including Nepal, or "Little Tibet" as it was called) was changed from the Holy See in Rome to the Capuchin order. Not until the early twentieth century did the Jesuits return. Then Jesuit adventures in north India at Patna (Bihar) took up where the old Moghul Mission and the Capuchins of the seventeenth to nineteenth centuries left off. The Jesuit's Patna Mission was only ten years old when Marshall Moran arrived in 1929.

The Patna Mission included the neighboring but inaccessible jurisdiction of Nepal. That Hindu kingdom was closed tight to virtually all Europeans, however, as it had been since the Capuchins departed one hundred and sixty years earlier. It would be two decades more before missionaries and other Europeans and Americans were allowed to return.

4. The Nepalese, as depicted in Kircher, *China Illustrata*, Amsterdam 1663.

Meanwhile, Marshall took up his assigned work in Bihar, within clear view of the Himalayas, the "Abode of Snow" that form the backbone of Nepal and north India. From the first time he saw the snows, Marshall's imagination was fired. Nepal was all the more tantalizing by its physical, social and political isolation. But it was many years of energy and enterprise, and not a little perseverance and prayer, before he was able to reintroduce a Catholic presence to the kingdom.

In considering his long life and talents as a modern but very real pioneer Jesuit leader, Fr Moran's ultimate successes on the subcontinent rest solidly on the already firm foundation established by others. They included the Catholic missionaries of the past in both India and Tibet, and on the work of his gifted and dedicated fellow Jesuit contemporaries. He was especially fortunate to be assigned to Bihar with good friends and confreres from many countries, including some who eventually followed him into Nepal. At the time of his arrival in India, however, becoming "Fr Moran of Kathmandu" was still years away.

The Society of Jesus is well known for its educational apostolate, its spirit of intellectualism and reform, and its worldwide mission efforts. Contemporary Jesuits feel great pride in the vision and actions of their founders and predecessors, especially Francis Xavier and Ignatius of Loyola. Many mission schools in India and eventually in Nepal, and widely around the world, are named for these honored saints of the church. Their memory and accomplishments are enshrined in church and world history.

Xavier and Loyola

Francis Xavier (1506-52) and Ignatius of Loyola (1491?-1556) were contemporaries, and their two lives were closely intertwined personally and in the history of development of the Catholic Church. They studied together, vowed lifelong service to their church together, and together with several other confreres founded the Jesuit order. The lives of these two saints of the church reveal a great deal about the nature of the Jesuits and the motivations of its clerical and lay missionaries.

Ignatius of Loyola was born Iñigo de Loyola in the 1490s. Scholars debate the precise birth year, somewhere between 1491 and 1495.[1] His aristocratic parents were Spanish Basques, settled near Azpeitia, in the north. He was raised in the foothills of the Pirineos (the Spanish Pyrenees) not far from the Bay of Biscay and the French border.

As a youth, Ignatius entered the service of the Duke of Najera as a soldier fighting against the French. At the Battle of Pamplona in 1521, he suffered severe wounds from which he carried strong memories and a permanent limp the rest of his life. His brief encounter with battlefield horror and heroism left a profound impact on him, eventually providing inspiration for developing what came to be known as a company, or society, of soldiers for Christ.

While recovering from his injuries, Ignatius read religious accounts of the life of Christ and of the saints. They moved him greatly, so much so that he decided to abandon a worldly life of frivolity and privilege to dedicate himself to the church. He was especially impressed by members of the Benedictine order and their dedicated search for spiritual fulfillment. As a follow-up to his physical recovery he began a spiritual recovery as well, traveling through the Spanish countryside on a mule and even living for awhile in a cave near Manresa. While there he subjected himself to many physical discomforts and had mystical experiences. All this moved him to write his famous *Spiritual Exercises*, the little book that has guided the Jesuits in daily prayer and self-discipline to this day.

In time, Ignatius went to study theology in Paris where he met the fellow Spaniard, Francisco de Xavier. The two young men became close friends, studying together and jointly planning a life of dedication to the church. In 1537, they were both ordained as Catholic priests.

As early as 1534, Ignatius and Xavier and four other companions met in the Chapel of the Martyrs atop the hill of Montmartre, in Paris, and vowed a simple life of poverty and chastity, devoting themselves in the service of others. They also began planning a pilgrimage to Jerusalem, but had to abandon that quest in 1537 in the face of war in the Holy Lands. Instead, they took up various works in Italy. By then their group numbered ten men who, when asked, identified themselves simply as *la compañua de Jesús*—the Company of Jesus, or Society of Jesus. These were the first Jesuits, though at first they had no strong notion of formally creating a religious order. Within two years, however, the need for some sort of stable, organized group was evident, so Ignatius set about to draft a charter. The Jesuit charter was presented to Pope Paul III and was accepted in 1540. Ignatius was appointed its first superior general.

1540 was a pivotal year for the Jesuits. Not only were they formally recognized as a priestly order by the Pope in Rome, but they set out that year to establish the Jesuit name in world history as a society of intellectuals, educators, and explorers. Since the beginning, the Society of Jesus has drawn strength and fame from great explorations, closely associated with global missionary efforts on every continent. Some of the world's most ambitious explorers from the sixteenth century onward were Jesuit priests.

The Society's foreign missions were all the more remarkable "because of the difficulties, met and overcome, arising from staggering distances, unfamiliar cultures, strange languages, and even Christian perfidy."[2] Within fifteen years of the Society's founding, dedicated Jesuits were established in South America, Africa, and East and South Asia, generously supported by Portugal's far-sighted and adventurous monarch, King John III.

The Jesuits' missionary zeal is usually traced to Francis Xavier who, several months before the society's formal recognition, set out for India as its first missionary. The choice of Xavier to go was something of an accident. Originally, King John asked Ignatius to assign two other men to undertake the mission. Their preparations were to begin in Portugal. Simon Rodrigues and Nicolas Bobadilla agreed to go, but when Bobadilla took ill, Xavier was sent in his stead. Before long, however, Rodrigues was reassigned back to Portugal and Xavier set off alone.

His charge was to spread Christianity in the Portuguese possessions along India's Malabar coast, operating from the port of Goa. Arriving after the long sea voyage, Xavier founded the Jesuit Province of Goa, from which all other Jesuit missions in South Asia are descended.

His missionary endeavors were far reaching and highly successful, and he and his contemporaries are credited with converting hundreds of thousands of people. Xavier's first mission work provided the foundation for today's international Jesuit activities. The Jesuits, however, were not the first Christian missionaries to India. Others had already been established there for several decades, including Franciscans, Dominicans and Augustinians.[3]

Among the first activities of the Jesuits in India was the operation of St Paul's School, founded in 1542 in the hope of training at least some of the boys attending it for service in the church. St Paul's was the first school ever run by Jesuits, and the early Jesuits were known for a long time in India as "Paulistas." Xavier eventually moved out of Goa proper, however, after finding many of the Portuguese, especially the seamen, to be bad examples for the Indian Christian converts. It is said that "Few Indians were attracted to Christianity when they saw the lives of these soldiers of fortune and riff raff that drifted into the Portuguese colony."[4]

Francis Xavier remained in India for over two years. After establishing the Jesuit headquarters at Goa, he moved on to minister in fishing villages along the coast. Then, leaving India, he sailed east to Malaya, where he opened another mission and stayed four years. He returned to Goa in 1548, and in 1549 sailed to Japan. Three years later, in 1552, he died on a small island off the coast of south China. As it was his final wish to be buried in Goa, his body was returned to the sight of his first mission where it still lies today, enshrined for the faithful to see. The Chapel and Tomb of St. Francis Xavier in Goa is a popular pilgrimage destination for Indian Catholics. It is simple structure with plastered walls, wooden rafters and a tiled roof.

In Rome, meanwhile, Ignatius continued to recruit young men to the new order, sending them after Xavier's example to the far corners of the earth, to India, Malaya and Japan, as well as to Brazil and the African Congo. (Later, Jesuits also became prominent in the opening of North America to European culture and Christianity.)

Ignatius wrote the Society's *Constitutions* at this time, firmly establishing an organizational structure and a distinctly Jesuit way of life. The Jesuit life style remains virtually unchanged today and the *Constitutions* persist as the central document of the order and a model to which other Catholic orders look for inspiration. (Even some non-religious institutions have turned to the Jesuit *Constitutions* for an organizational model.)

Among the fundamental principles of the Society of Jesus is the charge to promote religious education and preach the gospel in Asia and the New World. The church historian, W.V. Bangert, SJ, extols the wisdom of Ignatius's vision of the Jesuits as an educational order when he writes that "once it became clear in his mind what excellent service to the church could be rendered in the field of education, he applied to this new enterprise all his talents for organization, and on December 1, 1551, he recommended to the Society in a circular letter the inauguration of colleges throughout Europe. Guided in great measure by reflection on his own personal experience, he advanced the cultivation of the intellectual life through the study of literature in the form of the ancient classics, of philosophy as developed primarily by Aristotle, and of theology in which St Thomas was the master. With independence of judgment, he envisaged an educational structure for which he took the stones of the ancient world of the classical authors, the medieval world of the great universities, and his contemporary world of Renaissance passion for humanism."[5]

The Jesuits also helped reform the Roman Catholic Church in Europe during the Counter Reformation. "Ignatius's ideal was clear. From its inception the Jesuit school became one of the more influential exponents of the spirit of Catholic reform..."[6]

Francis Xavier died in 1552, followed by Ignatius in 1556. On March 12, 1622, both men were canonized as saints. St Ignatius Loyola's feast day is July 31, and St Francis Xavier's is December 3.

Jesuit Missions to North India

Not many years after their start in India, Jesuits from the Province of Goa accepted an invitation to visit the Moghul court of Akbar, in the north. In a short time a new mission was started there under the leadership of Fr Jerome Xavier, a nephew to Francis Xavier. By the early seventeenth century, the Jesuits were well enough established at Agra, the capital of Akbar's domain, to spread the faith even farther afield. From Agra the Jesuits ventured more widely across northern India, especially into the kingdom of Bihar, along the broad middle course of the Ganges River. It was also from Agra that they mounted their first exploratory missions across the Himalayas into western Tibet.

It wasn't many years, however, before they were ordered by the Sacred Congregation of the Propaganda in Rome (the office in charge of foreign missions) to abandon Tibet, the Himalayas and Bihar, and turn mission work there over to priests of the Capuchin order. Only much later would they regain their hold in north India, building on the diligent and inspired but often poorly supported work of the Capuchin priests.

The Capuchins in Bihar

Following the Jesuit departure from the north, two Capuchin Fathers, Joachin da Loreto and Pietro da Petrona, took up mission work in Bihar. They arrived in 1713. Little is known of their activities or the early history of the mission, for the simple reason that virtually all local records were destroyed in a thorough sacking of the Capuchin Mission in 1763. On June 24 of that year, the English residents of Patna were massacred by Muslim soldiers who, leading an infuriated mob, also broke into the Mission House and destroyed much of what they found. Three priests praying in the sanctuary at the time barely escaped with their lives after being stripped naked and beaten.

By 1772, the Capuchins had regrouped and were restrengthened enough to begin building the famous Patna Cathedral. (This was the church at which, in 1782, three years after the sanctuary was completed, a member of the royal family of Nepal dedicated a large bell.) The Patna Cathedral has served many needs of the church, the city, and greater Bihar ever since.[7]

Within half a century of their arrival, however, the Capuchin Mission was suffering a lack of support from headquarters in Italy and was forced to maintain and outfit the cathedral with mostly local donations. The health of the mission generally and, not least, the upkeep of the Patna Cathedral, the central symbol of Catholic efforts in Bihar, fell on hard times. A 1921-22 account in *Catholicus*, an official publication of the Allahabad Diocese, described the situation when Bishop Anastasius Hartmann took up the Vicariate of Patna in 1846. One of his first tasks was restoration and renewal of the cathedral edifice: "On account of the removal of the missionary in charge of Patna, in 1841, this magnificent church, which cost its founders so many trials and difficulties, on account of which for several years he travelled barefoot all over his extensive Mission to collect the necessary funds and endowed it with so many riches, became the habitation of birds."[8]

Bishop Hartmann's biographer describes the scene when he first entered Patna and walked its narrow streets looking for the cathedral: "...what a terrible sight met his eyes! The magnificent Church was in a state of sad and pathetic ruins... 'I began to weep like a child,' (the Bishop) records in a letter, 'at the sight of such desolation. Everything had to be done. The Cathedral was falling into ruins, doors and windows were broken, the roof was caving in, and the whole presented a most sad spectacle of desolation.'"[9] With considerable effort, Bishop Hartmann was able to restore the cathedral to its original beauty and splendor and to renew the vast mission operations to a new level of strength and activity.

For awhile the fortunes of the church in Bihar went up, but after Bishop Hartmann died in 1866, hard times returned, epitomized by further decline of the Patna Cathedral. Later, it was repaired and refurbished under the leadership of Fr Gregory of Bankipur and the Capuchin Bishop of Allahabad, Reverend P. Gramaigna. It then remained in generally good repair until the arrival of the Jesuits in 1919.

By the turn of the nineteenth century, all the European Capuchins in Patna were of Austrian nationality. At the outbreak of the First World War, India's British colonial leaders, being suspicious of all Austro-Germans, restricted the Capuchins in their work and later repatriated them to their homeland. That left the mission without a staff or assistance. It languished leaderless and unsupported from abroad for several years.

In September 1919, in an apostolic letter from Rome, a new Diocese of Patna was created within the Ecclesiastical Province of Calcutta and placed under Jesuit jurisdiction. It was formed out of the Prefecture Apostolic of Bettiah and Nepal, in the eastern part of the Diocese of Allahabad. The new diocese encompassed most of the districts of north and south Bihar including Darjeeling (now part of West Bengal state). Administrative responsibility to staff, rebuild and support the mission was assigned to the church's Missouri Province in America (later transferred to the Chicago Province).

In 1919, the Patna Diocese encompassed 26 million people over a vast territory of Bihar, and tiny Nepal. There had been no church activity in Nepal, however, since the original Capuchin missionaries departed in 1769 (described in the following chapter). Bisecting this vast mission territory was the Ganges River, known to devout Hindus as sacred Mother Ganga. Patna stands on its south bank, near the site of ancient Pataliputra, whose archaeological ruins date to the sixth century BC. It was from Pataliputra that the teachings of the Nepal born Gautama Buddha were spread throughout Asia. And it was there, in the early twentieth century city of Patna, that the Jesuits established their diocesan headquarters and took charge of the renewed Bihar Catholic Mission.

The Jesuits of Bihar

The first few Jesuits from the American-based Missouri Province arrived in Patna in 1921, led initially by Fr William Eline as superior, followed shortly by the first Bishop of Patna, the Right Reverend Louis Van Hoeck. The American mission to Patna started small but after aggressively advertising the need for young priests from America many responded, including young Marshall Moran along with several of his companions from Florissant and St Louis University.

In 1929, American mission jurisdiction for Patna was changed from the Missouri Province to the newly established Chicago Province, and Bishop Van Hoeck was succeeded by Reverend Bernard J. Sullivan, SJ. It was Bishop Sullivan to whom Marshall reported on his arrival in Patna by train on a cool, dry winter day in 1929.

The Patna Mission steadily grew under Bishop Sullivan's charge. By 1936, there were thirty-five priests, thirty-six scholastics and five lay brothers. Mission headquarters and the Bishop's House were established in a suburb of the city called Bankipur, where the British housed their local colonial administration. From the Bankipur offices the Missouri Jesuits, followed by priests from the new Chicago Province, looked after another thirteen district residences across their vast jurisdiction.

One of the outlying mission stations was at Bettiah, in the north of Bihar near the southern border of Nepal. In 1931, after his introduction to Patna and a year's special study in the south of India, Marshall was sent out to Bettiah to begin his teaching apostolate. There he joined a long line of missionaries working in the rural districts of India, all building on a legacy of missionary teaching (and exploration) that stretched back many centuries. And there, near Bettiah, Marshall met for the first time ethnic Nepalese residing in the tiny farming village of Chuhari. The Chuharis were descendants of the Christian converts who had fled Kathmandu in 1769 with the Capuchin Fathers of the first Christian mission to Nepal.[10]

In a small way, Marshall's introduction to the early history of the church in the Himalayas was one of several events that encouraged him years later to go to Nepal. The extreme difficulties of the Capuchin establishment and early Jesuit explorations in the Himalayas and Tibet, dating all the way back to the seventh century, taught Marshall a great deal and helped him prepare for his future life and work in the Kathmandu Valley after 1951.

Desideri's Influence on Fr Moran

When asked what inspired him and eventually led him to launch a new mission in the Himalayas, Marshall once said: "There is no single, simple answer." He described some of it as spiritual, some personal, some historical chance, and all "the work of God." Then, reaching for a book on his shelf, Fr Ippolito Desideri's *An Account of Tibet* published in 1932, he said "And some of it is in here, in this account of exploration by the last Jesuit to visit Nepal over two hundred years ago."

Desideri's account, originally written in the 1700s, provides a foundation history of early Christian missionary-exploration in high Asia. It is a vivid and inspiring description of perseverance and hardship virtually unparalleled in the annals of the early explorers of the church. As the Jesuit historian Fr Cornelius Wessels wrote in 1932, in eloquent understatement, "Danger and hardship are the appendage of every mission."[11]

Desideri's life work in Asia provides a basis for our own understanding and appreciation of those brave, dedicated men and their time. Reading Desideri also gives us a glimpse of Moran's most immediate Jesuit predecessor in the Himalayas; and it describes some of the almost unimaginable physical hardships that early church explorers endured. Desideri's account, and the published journals of several other of his contemporaries and predecessors, gave Marshall and fellow Jesuits a lesson, warning of the dangers of the past and of the trials and tribulations that missionaries faced in seventeenth and eighteenth century Tibet and Little Tibet (Nepal), lands that were then (and until relatively recently) quite unknown to Europeans and Americans. In the 1930s, when Marshall first read the accounts by Frs Desideri, L'Abbé Huc and others, he experienced a premonition of sorts.[12]

Marshall's copy of the Desideri book was old, well worn and well read. It meant so much to him that he carried it with him for over half a century, since he first discovered it in the seminary library at Kurseong. The cover is stamped with three accession marks from the Library of St Mary's Academy in Kurseong, from the Fathers' Library at St Xavier's in Patna, and from the St Xavier's Godavari School Library in Nepal. The book remains today with the Jesuit Nepal Mission.

If history sets the stage for the present and the future, then what Marshall read and learned about his predecessors helped prepare him for his work both in India and, especially, Nepal. That same history provides us with a preparatory interlude to the story of Fr Moran and the modern Jesuits of Kathmandu.

The Lost Christians of High Asia

Desideri wrote that "in all this discomfort and suffering we were much comforted by the loving kindness and paternal assistance of God, in whose service alone we had undertaken this journey and exposed ourselves willingly to whatever might happen. Thus we hardly felt the hardships, but with courage, good health, and contented minds we conversed together, and with others, as though we were travelling for amusement and pleasure."[13]

Fr Cornelius Wessels' 1932 introduction to Desideri's writings describes what attracted and drove the early Jesuits and their Catholic predecessors to explore Tibet and Little Tibet in the first place. "It was a rumour constantly cropping up... that the unknown and inaccessible regions beyond the Himalaya mountains sheltered Christian communities, the scattered remains of evangelization in centuries long past.... (W)hat could be more natural than a wish to inquire on the spot, and, in case the rumours should prove to be true, a desire to assist those neglected brethren of the faith?"[14]

The seventeenth and eighteenth centuries were a time of expansion of the Jesuit India missions northward up and out of the hot plains of India, through the Himalaya and on to the "roof of the world." Interest was fueled by a fascination for exploration of the unknown—unsaved heathens in the unmapped, hostile regions—strengthened by rumors of "neglected brethren of the faith" in communities somewhere in inner Asia, or in the vast high valleys of Tibet and greater Himalayas. To some, these lost Christians were thought to be remnants of refugee groups that had earlier fled from the Muslim invasion of the subcontinent. More likely, if they existed (and there is some evidence that they did), they may have been remnants of Nestorian Christian outposts in Asia dating to the early centuries of the Christian era.

Part of the documentation of the Church's search for the missing Christians is thin and incomplete, based on fragmentary church records and scattered accounts and descriptions in letters and travelers' accounts. We know that Jesuits were quite active as missionary-explorers, as were their Franciscan, Dominican and Capuchin brothers. The rumors they heard and responded to were spread by merchants and other travelers returning to India and Europe from Central Asia. Those tales were thought credible enough to lead devout churchmen to set out searching on foot through the world's highest and most impenetrable mountains.

Jesuit and Capuchin historians have pieced together the various travel accounts of the time. Some of them describe a religious fervor, stony resolve and incredible strength of physical and mental character that is simply horrendous, especially knowing what travel conditions were like for these European clerics in the strange and inhospitable Asian hinterlands.

In 1602, Jesuits responsible for the Goa Province, residing in Akbar's court at Agra, decided to send a mission of search and exploration north across the mountains. They chose the Portuguese Brother Bento (Benedict de Goes) for the task. Br Bento first crossed Turkestan where, from Yarkand, he wrote of his failure to locate the lost Christians. He suggested that they might be found somewhere in Tibet proper. Although Br Bento died in China before he could return, the mission dispatched a second expedition on his advice. It was turned back at the snowbound passes into western Tibet above Kashmir.

In 1624, another attempt was launched, this one led by the Portuguese Jesuit Fr Anthony Andrade (sometimes written Antonio D'Andrada). He was accompanied by a Portuguese lay brother named Manuel Marques and two Christian servants. Charles Allen describes the forty-four year old Andrade as "a tough, battle-hardened veteran of the mission field."[15] Only a man of remarkable courage, bravery and dedication to duty could have survived the rigors of the trip. For their travels were not without trouble. On the way, Fr Andrade and his companions were arrested. When they were about to be bound in chains, they revealed their mission and were set free and allowed to continue.

High in the Himalayan foothills in Garhwal, just west of the present western border of Nepal, they joined a large party of Hindu pilgrims. Disguised as fellow Hindus, the Jesuit party ascended up the dangerous path along the banks of the roaring Alaknanda River to the sacred headwaters of the Ganges at Badrinath. There they slipped away from the Hindus (who apparently never discovered their true identities) and struck out alone towards Tibet across the perilous Mana pass at nearly 18,400 feet (5,605 meters). Such high Himalayan passes are free from snow and open to passage only for a short season each year, often not before late July. Fr Andrade and his party persevered under trying conditions, and eventually crossed into the Tibetan valley of the Langtchen-Kambo, the upper Sutlej River.

Can we imagine their suffering?—struggling along sick and weak from the poor pilgrim fare, clinging perilously to the canyon walls, ill clad to cross the snow and ice fields, shivering against the intense cold, their feet and hands blistered and frostbitten, braving the thin air and enduring the inevitable headaches encountered at those heights.

One of the best accounts of Fr Andrade's travels and the perils he and his companions faced was written by L'Abbe Huc in 1873.[16] "We then began, says D'Andrada, to climb these lofty mountains, which have not their like perhaps on the surface of the globe... In some places the passage between them is so narrow, that we could only just put one foot before the other, and for a long way we had to go first on one side and then on the other, climbing to the rocks with our hands, and at a single false step we should have been dashed to pieces... We were several times obliged to turn round and go backwards, as if we had been going down a ladder, and to step with the greatest possible caution; but we had constantly before our eyes the example of pagans (Hindu pilgrims) who were braving all these difficulties to honour their gods..."

Continuing on, ascending even higher into the mountains, Fr Huc relates Andrade's astonishment at "...the unfortunate traveler [who] can never assure himself of the solidity of the snow on which he steps, but runs constant risk of being swallowed up and buried alive in some of these abysses." After some weeks, they encountered the high Tibetan desert, "intersected by a vast range of mountains... where there are neither human habitations, nor trees, nor grass; nothing, in fact, but rocks covered with snow... travelers are obliged to live on the roasted corn and snow they bring with them, and only people in robust health can possibly endure such a journey, even under its most favourable circumstances."

Then, says Andrade, "we plunged into the desert and struggled on with difficulty, sometimes up to our waists in snow, sometimes up to our shoulders, and never less than knee deep, and occasionally dragging ourselves at full length along the surface of it, as if we were swimming... The cold was so severe, that we had lost all feeling in various parts of the body,—principally the hands, feet, and face... Once when I tried to hold something, a bone came out of one of my fingers, but I was not aware of it till I saw the blood on my hand; while our feet were so swelled and numbed, that if a hot iron had touched them we should not have felt it... We had almost lost our sight, but I myself had suffered less than my two servants... though for five and twenty days I could not read a letter of my breviary."

L'Abbe Huc concludes this account of Andrade's difficulties with understatement: "The reader may possibly think there is some exaggeration in this account; but as we have traversed the same regions ourselves, and undergone the hardships of a similar journey, we know by experience that the narrative of Father D'Andrade is rather below the reality."[17] Andrade's sufferings serve as an example of some of what the Jesuit and Capuchin explorer-priests endured during this period of Tibetan exploration, the "reality" of which was by no means unique.

Fr Andrade at Tsaparang

In the fourth month of his arduous travels, in early August 1624, Andrade and his companions arrived at the medieval Tibetan citadel of Tsaparang, royal residence of the King of Gugé (pronounced "gu-gay"). There they encountered a rough-hewn people who had survived centuries of feudalism and bitter warring among local kingdoms with such tongue-twisting names as Gugé and Gunthang, Jumla and Ladakh, Ngari and Zhang-zhung. In a time and under conditions virtually unimaginable to Western travelers and scholars then or now, local warlords and kings rose and fell as frequently as the wind, vying for control of limited resources, long distance trade routes, and the allegiance of a poor and sparsely scattered population of yak herders, hunters, miners, merchant traders, caravaneers, Bönpo shamans, and Buddhist monks.

Buddhism was introduced to Tibet from India in the seventh century AD, but appears to have done little, at first, to unify the local populace. Among the colorful legends that surround the arrival and survival of Buddhism are accounts of its sages and teachers personally waging battles of stealth, wit and trickery over powerfully demonic spirits, and the black magic of the locally popular shamans of a loosely defined religion called Bön. Some colorful accouterments of Bön remain today in Tibetan Buddhism (Lamaism) as legacies of those archaic times, the origins of some of its rich tantric symbolism.[18] It would be many years, however, before these remote and isolated parts of Tibet were unified under the Fifth Dalai Lama, Tibet's spiritual and temporal leader at Lhasa, in 1642 AD.[19]

Meanwhile, although Fr Andrade's search for lost Christians failed, his unexpected arrival at Tsaparang in 1624 made history. He was the first European to visit the kingdom of Gugé, and he made perhaps the first European reference to Nepal. The early twentieth century French Indologist, Sylvain Levi, interprets one incident recorded by Andrade as possibly the first reference to the valley of Kathmandu. As Levi recounts it, Fr Andrade described giving silver to some goldsmiths residing in Tsaparang, asking them to make a cross. To his surprise, they said that in their country of birth, some two months' walk distant, there were religious symbols quite like the Christian cross, made of both wood and metal.

While Nepal is not directly mentioned in Andrade's account,

Levi was convinced that it could be no other. The distance (measured in months of travel) is about right, and the artisans' profession as goldsmiths further indicates their probable Nepalese origins (as Kathmandu Newars), Levi says. The three Newar ethnic cities of the valley of Nepal—Kantipur (Kathmandu), Lalitpur (Patan) and Bhatgaon (or Bhaktapur)—were already widely known as sources of Tibetan religious craftsmanship and art.[20]

Later, during the eighteenth century, Capuchin missionaries in Nepal corroborated Andrade's seventeenth century account, describing similar crosses that they found on display in Hindu temples, a fact that greatly amazed and impressed them and gave rise to further speculation about early Christian origins.

Similarities between Christian and Buddhist symbols convinced many early explorers that they had found evidence of early Nestorian or other Christian influences in high Asia. Catholic priests were especially impressed by similarities in the structure of clerical orders and various behaviors and symbols common to the order of worship in both religions. L'Abbe Huc, who traveled extensively in Tibet during the nineteenth century, described "their resemblance to Catholicism, ...(and the) striking analogy between the government of the Grand Lama (Dalai Lama) and that of the State of the Church. During our residence among the Buddhists of Thibet, we remarked, besides the cross, the mitre (headdress), the dalmatic, and the chasuble (both are vestments), that the superior lamas carry with them, when travelling, or performing some ceremony out of the temple, the choral service, the exorcisms, the censers (for burning incense) supported by gold chains, and made to open and shut, the blessings which the lamas bestow on the faithful, laying the hands upon the head of the supplicant, the rosary, the practice of ecclesiastical celibacy, or spiritual retreats, of worship of saints, fasts, processions, holy water, litanies, and many other details of ceremonial, which are in use among the Buddhists, precisely as in our own Church, are evidently of Christian origin,"[21]

Some of the artifacts of Tibetan Buddhist worship that Fr Huc saw in the nineteenth century and attributed to Christian influence could have been of more recent origin, passed along through the hands of Newar craftsmen from Nepal who resided in Tibet and produced the vast majority of Tibetan Buddhist religious arts and crafts. They could easily have learned to make them from the Capuchin priests who resided in Kathmandu Valley in the early eighteenth century. This does not explain, however, the astonishment of both Fr Andrade in Tibet in the seventeenth century and of the Capuchin Fathers in Nepal in the eighteenth century at finding what they (and, later,

Sylvain Levi) interpreted to be evidence of the Christian symbol of the cross. In Kathmandu valley, the Capuchins were also impressed by the image of the Hindu deity Indra who, in one pose, is depicted with his arms outstretched like a crucified figure. Many if not all of these similarities can probably be traced to indigenous elements within Indian Hindu and Tibetan Buddhist cultures.

The Tsaparang Mission and Its Demise

Fr Andrade describes his experiences at Tsaparang in terms of the harsh realities, physical deprivations, and political vagaries and intrigues with which virtually all visitors to those isolated, feudalistic societies had to contend. His arrival caused considerable interest and commotion for the King of Gugé and his retainers. Here is how Cornelius Wessels has reconstructed the scene: "At first, the king, unable to believe that a man, not a trader, could undertake such a journey, was somewhat displeased; but after the first interview, at which the missionary explained the reason of his coming, both he and the queen showed themselves quite pleased. A religious conviction prompting such deeds of daring did not fail to impress him. Andrade availed himself of this favourable disposition to further the object of his journey of exploration. He became aware that there were no forlorn Christians to be assisted, but a new mission field might be opened among the pagan population of these remote regions."[22]

The king was so impressed, in fact, that he dispatched Andrade back to India with a letter that read (in translation): "We earnestly desire the great Padre (the Provincial of Goa) to send us at once the said Padre Antonio (Andrade) that he may be of assistance to our peoples." The king promised that the Fathers would be allowed to teach the holy law, to appoint one among them as "child lama" of the place, and that he would protect them from any malicious accusations by the local Muslim minority (he called them "Moors").[23]

The following year Andrade returned to formally open the first Tibetan Mission at Tsaparang. In time an outpost mission was also established at a place called Rodok, a hundred miles distant in the land of a vassal to the King of Gugé. Much of the work of these missions is undocumented, however, and reasons for the outpost at Rodok are unclear. It is known that Andrade travelled extensively during his first years in Tibet, as far as the western reaches of China proper. Tsaparang was a small place, described in a 1635 Jesuit account as having barely five hundred inhabitants, a fact that may have encouraged them to reach out to other population centers.

Church authorities back in India were unaware that, despite a valiant start, the Jesuits in Gugé were in danger. A series of unpredictable and uncontrollable political and natural events conspired against them (events the likes of which later missionaries in these and similar locales were to experience time and again). For one, the king's interest in the Christians alienated the chief Buddhist lama of Gugé, the king's own brother. The king's financial support to the Christians took away from the revenues traditionally promised to the lamas. For another, in 1630, church officials in India called Andrade back, to appoint him to govern the Jesuits' entire province of Goa, which now included both Agra and Tsaparang. He was apparently too good a man to keep isolated in far off Tibet. The result for the Tibet Mission was the loss of its energetic founder and leader at a most inopportune time.

The final misfortune occurred when the sympathetic King of Gugé took ill. Seizing on all these weaknesses, the lamas conspired with the king of neighboring Ladakh to raise a popular revolt in Gugé. The King of Gugé lost, the Buddhist lamas won, and the Jesuit Mission presence was threatened, and rapidly collapsed.

When word of these troubles reached Andrade back in Goa, he sent a relief party. It arrived, barely, in 1638, after four of its six members had either died on the way or had turned back too incapacitated to carry on. Two priests reached Tsaparang, Frs Francisco de Azevedo and João de Oliveira. The conditions they found were discouraging. The five remaining Jesuit missionaries were surviving precariously at the mercy of an uncompromising military commander who forced them to live as virtual prisoners in their own house, unable to carry on. In their ten years in Tibet, the Fathers had not administered even a hundred baptisms. Local support was weak. The Buddhists had campaigned actively and successfully against them. And the local people were considered difficult to convert and not prepared to understand the Christian faith. Even the landscape was described by the Jesuits as extremely poor and inhospitable.

The relief party was not well received by the local authorities, and shortly after arriving, the Tibetans summarily banished all missionaries. Within the year the Tsaparang Jesuits were all back in India.

Five years later, Br Manuel Marques, who had been with Fr Andrade in 1624 and 1625, attempted to reopen the Tibet Mission. But western Tibet was now firmly closed to European outsiders. When they arrived back in Tibet, Br Marques and a companion, Fr Stanislao Malpichi, were captured and held for ransom. Although they both managed to escape, Marques had the misfortune of being recaptured and was never seen alive again by his companions. One final mention of him is found in a document dated 1641. It states only that he was languishing in bonds, badly treated, a prisoner at

Tsaparang. After that no more appears in the official record. The last word from Br Marques was silence.

The only physical evidence ever found testifying to the Jesuit Mission at Tsaparang was a weathered wooden cross found lying on top of a large stone chorten that a British civil servant saw in 1912 and reported to the Jesuits in India.[24]

The Ütsang (Shigatse) Mission

Andrade's interests did not stop at the borders of Gugé. Rather, he had a wider vision of his mission to Tibet and set about to find out as much about the place as he could. "When Father de Andrade... was actively engaged in gathering more accurate and detailed information about the extent and the state of Tibet, he learned from merchants coming from China of the existence of a great country, Ütsang, situated, it was said, at one and half months' journey east of Tsaparang. To him this meant a possible new mission field..."[25]

On Andrade's suggestion, a second Tibetan Mission set out in the year 1628 for Ütsang. Three Jesuits were sent: Fr. João (John) Cabral, Fr Estivão Cacella, and Br Bartolomeo Fonteboa. They departed from Cocho in eastern India north of which "Their road took them across the unknown territory of Bhutan, on which no European had set foot." Lhasa was the goal, but after struggling for almost two years enroute, the trio had only reached Shigatse west of Lhasa, a religious and trade center. It wasn't long before Cacella sent Cabral back to India on mission business, and Cacella, himself, attempted unsuccessfully to go to Tsaparang. After a long wait, Cabral did not return, so Cacella set out for India, only to return a few months later to Shigatse, where he soon died. Finally, in 1631, Cabral returned briefly to Shigatse, but seeing no prospect to continue, he abandoned the church's efforts there, and in this manner Ütsang Mission was closed.

Meanwhile, back in 1628, when Fr Cabral left Tibet the first time, he sought a shorter, more accessible route over the Himalayas to India. On advice of a Tibetan guide, he took the hitherto unexplored (by Europeans) trade route via Kuti (today's Nyalam) down the Bhote Kosi River gorge to Kodari and on across the Himalayan foothills to Kathmandu in the Nepal Valley. He is the first known European to have visited the kingdom of Nepal. The going must have been difficult, but Cabral wrote little about it. It is known only that he carried a letter addressed to the King of Nepal, requesting whatever help the traveler might need.

It is Cornelius Wessels who ultimately put Cabral's accomplishment into perspective. "In reading his account of this journey we are scarcely, or perhaps not at all, impressed when coming across the name of Nepal; but in 1628, this mountain state was still absolutely unknown to the West, so that, as far as can be ascertained, Cabral was the first European to visit and traverse it... The reader is left to imagine those paths and passes buried under deep snow at an altitude of many thousand feet, and in the midst of these the lonely traveller with his one or two guides whose language he hardly understands, and thence to form his judgment of the grit and intrepidity required to undertake it and carry it through."

By 1640, it was clear that the Jesuits' first two energetic attempts at establishing missions in Tibet had failed. "Brother Marques remained in bonds at Tsaparang and at far-away Shigatse there was no one to take up Cacella's work and pray over his lonely grave." But the fabled "neglected brethren of the faith" in high Asia still attracted attention until past mid-century.

In the 1660s, two more Jesuits, Frs John Grueber and Albert d'Orville, also trekked across Tibet, searching. They visited Lhasa in 1661, then in January 1662 they followed Cabral's new route and passed through the Kathmandu valley on their return to India. After these last brief encounters, the Jesuits abandoned their quest for the "lost," and perhaps non-existent, Christian communities. For some years in the 1700s, the Jesuit presence in Tibet was renewed primarily under the leadership of the Italian Fr Ippolito Desideri. Unfortunately, however, the Jesuits were ultimately forced to quit Tibet altogether on orders of the church in Rome, at the same time that their mission in north India was given over exclusively to the Capuchins.

Despite all these wanderings over a century of early Christian exploration in Tibet and the Himalayas, no lost Christian communities were ever found and no permanent new ones were established.

Notes to Chapter 4: Jesuits in India and Tibet

1. When Loyola died in 1556, his age was given as 65, so 1491 is generally accepted as his date of birth.
2. William V. Bangert, *A History of the Society of Jesus* (1972, p.29).
3. The very earliest presence of Christianity in India is said to date to a few years AD, when legend and some archaeological evidence on the Indian west coast supports a belief in the establishment of a Syrian Christian Mission led by Saint Thomas, one of the disciples of Christ. Nestorian Christians were also known to have traveled widely in Asia, especially in Tartary and "High Asia" (Turkestan, Tibet and China), where they are thought to have influenced various expressive forms of ecclesiastical Buddhism. For an early and richly descriptive account of the legacy of

St Thomas in India and the Nestorians in Tibet, see M. L'Abbé Huc, *Christianity in China, Tartary and Thibet* (1873).
4. Bangert, *History...* (p.27).
5. *Ibid.*
6. *Ibid.*
7. The Patna Cathedral was built by the Capuchin Fr Giuseppe of Roveto, Prefect Apostolic of the Nepal Mission. Construction was begun in 1772 and took seven years to complete. It was officially opened in December 1779. The cathedral was renovated on several occasions, and completely rebuilt after the devastating earthquake of 1934. Its two hundredth anniversary was celebrated in 1979. Henry Pascual Oiz described it in his 1991 book *History of the Patna Jesuits* (pp.240-241): "The cathedral has a lofty and imposing façade of Ionian style, the interior being Corinthian. Over the altar there is a large picture of the Visitation of Our Lady to St Elizabeth, to which mystery the church is dedicated. This building is usually considered to be the oldest European building in Patna."
8. Gilbert J. Garraghan, *The Jesuits of the Middle United States* (1938, v.3, p.532).
9. Fulgentius Vannini, *Bishop Hartmann* (1966, p.40).
10. See Theodore Riccardi, 'The Nevars of Chuhari' (1990).
11. Cornelius Wessels, in his Introduction to Ippolito Desideri, *An Account of Tibet* (1932, p.16). See also Wessels' *Early Jesuit Travellers in Central Asia, 1603-1722* (1924); Father Giuseppe's 'An account of the Kingdom of Nepal' (1801); and Huc's *Christianity in China, Tartary and Thibet* (1873). It was mostly Desideri's and Huc's accounts that attracted Moran's attention and drew his imagination into the history of early Catholic adventures in high Asia.
12. This chapter draws directly from several important works of exploration history, including Desideri and Huc, previously mentioned. Another invaluable and more recent account is by the Capuchin historian, Fulgentius Vannini, entitled *Christian Settlements in Nepal During the Eighteenth Century* (1977). The Italian historian of Nepal, Luciano Petech, has accumulated the most complete record of the Capuchins in Nepal in four volumes of letters and documentation, published as *I Missionari Italiani nel Tibet e nel Nepal* (1952-56), in Italian.

    For a brief but slightly exaggerated overview of Catholic (Capuchin) beginnings in Nepal, see also Jonathan Lindell's *Nepal and the Gospel of God* (1979, Ch.1: 'Men in beards, hoods and robes'). And, on the relationship between the Capuchins and the authorities in Kathmandu at the time of the Gorkha Conquest of the Nepal Valley (Kathmandu), see Ludwig Stiller, *The Rise of the House of Gorkha* (1973). Frs Ludwig Stiller and John Locke have also provided invaluable comments (personal communications) to the author on the history of early missionaries to Nepal.
13. Desideri, *An Account of Tibet* (1932, p.88).
14. Quoted by Wessels in Desideri, *ibid.* (p.3).

15. Charles Allen, *A Mountain in Tibet* (1983, p.35).

    Fr Andrade wrote of his expedition in two letters published in Portugal in 1626. These letters were rather grandly entitled 'Novo Descobrimento do Gram Cathay, ou Reinos de Tibet' (A New Discovery from Grand Cathay, or the Kingdom of Tibet). Allen describes them as revealing "an extraordinary faith and stamina on the part of Andrade and Marques," but also as "understandably vague on geographical details. The result was that their claims to have entered Tibet came to be regarded as exaggerated and unreliable. Later generations of European travelers who crossed into Tibet by the same route were quite unaware that the Jesuits had been there before them—nearly two centuries earlier" (*ibid.*).

16. The description in the next few paragraphs, quoting Andrade on his perilous travels to Tibet, is from L'Abbé Huc, *Christianity in China...* (1873, v.2, pp.217-233 *passim*).

17. *Ibid.*

18. For recent accounts of Tsaparang and its little-known history, see Frits Staal, 'In the realm of the Buddha' (1986), and Lama Anagarika Govinda, *The Way of the White Clouds* (1956). Another excellent and superbly illustrated study about this part of Tibet is *Sacred Landscape and Pilgrimage in Tibet: In Search of the Lost Kingdom of Bön* by Geshi Gelek Jinpa, *et al* (2005). Situated between Kashmir and Central Tibet on a minor southern branch of the famous Silk Road across Central Asia, Tsaparang (Tse-pu-rung in Staal's description) lies today in ruins and neglect. Staal's photographs, however, provide a rare glimpse of the rich art and religious architecture that Fr Andrade saw in 1624-25. Tsaparang is also briefly described from a recent visit by Manosi Lahiri in *Here Be Yaks: Travels in Far West Tibet* (2007).

19. The current Dalai Lama, Tenzin Gyatso, is the fourteenth in this line of venerated Tibetan leaders. He resides in exile at Dharamsala, in the mountains of north India's Himachal Pradesh state.

20. Sylvain Levi, *Le Nepal: Etude Historique d'un Royaume Hindou* (1905, v.1, p.80).

    The straight-line distance from Tsaparang to Kathmandu is four hundred miles. The long time it took travelers in those days to make the trip is attributed to the style of travel, in large yak caravans that were frequently delayed by the necessity to pasture the beasts, and by the often difficult and circuitous routes through the mountains.

21. L'Abbé Huc, *Christianity in China...* (1873, p.19-20).

22. Wessels in Desideri, *An Account of Tibet* (1932, pp.4-5).

23. *Ibid.*

24. *Ibid.* (pp.18-19).

25. *Ibid.* This entire description of the Jesuit attempt to establish a mission in Ütsang is informed by Wessels' account in Desideri's book, and all quotations are from that source (pp.19-26).

5

Early Christian Missions in Nepal

> *A small group of travelers has been moving for 35 days across the northern Gangetic plain of Hindustan... through the jungles and up over the middle Himalayas and has entered the Nepal Valley. ...it has been reported that there are strange European people among the travelers... men in beards, hoods and robes.*
> Jonathan Lindell, *Nepal and the Gospel of God* (1979)

Shortly after the turn of the eighteenth century, priests of the Capuchin order took up where the Jesuits had left off in Tibet proper and soon in Nepal (Little Tibet), as well. For awhile, they shared life in Lhasa with the dedicated Jesuit explorer-scholar, Fr Ippolito Desideri, SJ, before the Jesuits were ordered completely away and the Capuchins were given exclusive rights by Rome to missionize this remote area.

The Capuchin Order was established in 1525 as a reformed order of the Franciscans. Their founder was a disenchanted Franciscan monk named Matthew of Bascio. It took almost a hundred years, however, before Bascio's group was formally recognized as an independent branch of the Franciscans, in 1619. It is said that Italian children gave the Capuchins their name. When they first saw these friars they cried "Cappucini, Cappucini!" pointing to their hooded cowls (*capuche*). The brown robe and cowl were adopted in emulation of the thirteenth century saint, Francis of Assisi. This form of dress became one of their identifying characteristics. Another was their popularity as missionaries noted for dedication, practicality and sensitivity.[1]

The first Capuchin expedition to Tibet was mounted from Europe in 1704. It was, as Fr Desideri of Pistola later described it, "an immense journey through Turkey, Babylonia, Arabia and other countries" to India. After passing onward through Nepal and across the Himalaya, they arrived in Lhasa in 1707.

The Capuchin success in reaching Lhasa was a great accomplishment, but otherwise the trip was a disaster. Four of the six missionaries had either died or turned back enroute. These early missionaries paid a high toll to spread the faith in remote places.

From 1707 to 1712, the Capuchins lingered tentatively in Lhasa and later at an outpost called Takpo. In time, illness and death added to their toll and only a few replacements were sent to carry on. The priests in Tibet fully expected to receive subsidies from Rome to allow them to continue, but "subsidies having failed to arrive, the last two Capuchins still working in Lhasa had to be recalled to avoid starvation... Indeed, by all human standards the first phase of the Tibetan Mission ended in a disheartening failure."[2]

The renowned historian and scholar of Tibet, Sir Charles Bell, described the first Capuchin mission to Lhasa: "In 1707 Capuchin Fathers arrived, coming from the mission station at Kathmandu in Nepal. They were received without marked disfavour by the rulers and people, who were fully occupied in their own political upheavals. The missionaries on their side worked quietly. From the authorities and colleagues of their own Mission came but scanty support..., in spite of the appeals for assistance that they circulated to their brethren at other stations. One of them, Da Fano, soon returned and in 1711 the others left both Tibet and Nepal and came to Chandernagore in Bengal. During ten years, fifteen Fathers had gone out to Bengal, Nepal and Tibet but had made only two converts to Christian faith. We may with some safety assume that neither of these two were Tibetans."[3]

A cursory examination of the Capuchin failure suggests a simple formula for potential failure of any missionary endeavor to this part of the world: lack of funds + shortage of personnel + poor lines of communication. These conditions have plagued many far-flung missions over the centuries. The lesson of the Capuchins, and earlier of the Jesuits to Tsaparang and Ütsang, were not lost on Fr Moran and his colleagues in Patna in the 1930s, nor in Nepal in the 1950s.

Determined to try again, in 1714, Capuchin leaders in Rome drew up a reorganization plan with which to renew the Himalayan enterprise. In 1716, after a lapse of four years, they returned to Lhasa to open their second mission to Tibet. This time they were better organized and better prepared. And this time, Nepal figured prominently in the plans.

Inauguration of the new plan led directly to the opening of the first mission outpost in Nepal as an intermediate station in support of the all-important Tibet Mission in Lhasa. Three other stations were also established—at Chandernagore, a French settlement and port town in Bengal on the lower course of the Ganges River; at Patna, a center of commerce in the Kingdom of Bihar along the middle course of the Ganges; and at Tron-gne in the province of Takpo in southeast Tibet, near Sikkim.

5. The Nepalese, as depicted in Kircher, *China Illustrata*, Amsterdam 1663.

A "key position, enroute to Lhasa, was occupied by Kathmandu," writes the Capuchin historian, Fulgentius Vannini. "It was indeed, a good resting place for the weary traveler who had just crossed the unhealthy, marshy land of the Tarai, abounding in tigers and other wild animals and was about to face the formidable challenge of the Himalayan solitudes. The Valley of Nepal was a compulsory passage for caravans, plying between India and Tibet. Looking back at the length of the journey which had already been left far behind, one of the first missionaries wrote to Rome: 'We cannot hope to put the mission on a sound basis unless we get a foothold in Nepal.' If Tibet was the statue, Nepal was the pedestal, the bloodstream in the life of the whole undertaking... With the opening of Kathmandu..., they preferred the Patna-Nepal route, which was more conveniently spaced and offered more facilities to the traveller."[4,5]

Meanwhile, the Jesuits had sent their last mission to Tibet in the person of the stalwart Italian scholar-priest, Desideri of Pistola. It was a half century since the failure of the Tsaparang and Ütsang Jesuit missions. He had little hope of finding any remaining Tibetan Christians, but he wanted to visit Tsaparang. He set out in 1714 accompanied by a Fr Freyre, but they were misdirected and failed to reach the old mission. Instead, they traveled for two years, eventually crossing central Tibet in winter, finally arriving exhausted at Lhasa in March 1716. Fr Freyre left soon after, but Desideri stayed on for five years, at first quite alone as the only European in Lhasa, but soon joined by member of the second Capuchin mission.

In Lhasa, Desideri was befriended by the regent, the *de facto* "King" of Tibet, in place of the still juvenile Seventh Dalai Lama. Desideri was allowed to preach and to reside for a time at both Ramo-che and Sera monasteries, where he studied Tibetan language, culture and religion. His ambitious goal was to write a formal refutation of Tibetan Buddhism along with a defense of Christianity, in the Tibetan language.

He personally got on well with the Capuchins after they arrived, but jurisdictional rivalries in Rome ended his sojourn. Like north India, Tibet was declared an exclusively Capuchin territory and the Jesuit scholar was ordered out. In 1721, Fr Desideri resigned himself to the judgment of his superiors, abandoned his energetic studies and left via Nepal for India, and ultimately to Rome.

Looking back on these events with the hindsight of history, the Sylvain Levi noted in 1905 that "Events themselves are sometimes intelligent. Condemned in the Roman court, the Jesuits, in disgrace, give way to rival orders. The will of the Holy Father assigns Tibet to the Capuchins. The church has made its choice... Heirs of an outmoded tradition, the Capuchins waste sixty years in the Himalayas..."[6]

On leaving Tibet, Desideri passed through Kathmandu, following in the tracks of his Jesuit predecessors, Fr John Cabral (in 1628) and Frs John Grueber and Albert d'Orville (in 1662). He stayed in the Nepal Valley for nearly a month as a guest of the Capuchins living there.

Meanwhile, up in Lhasa, the second Capuchin mission to Tibet began well. The priests were treated politely by their hosts, at first. In 1724, an official proclamation of the young Seventh Dalai Lama who had begun exercising limited power from the Potala by then, declared them free to build a small convent and church because, as the official document states, "they came to Tibet and remain here simply for the good of their fellow-creatures and to help them; not, like so many others, for their own gain and benefit."[7]

It was not long, though, until they felt the familiar sting of local resistance. Sir Charles Bell later wrote that hostility "soon developed among the Tibetan monks and the populace, always ready to follow the lead of their priestly advisers. During the following year (1725) the river burst its embankment and flooded Lhasa, a sign that the gods who dwelt in the ground were angry at this desecration of the Holy City. A mob assembled at their door and was restrained only by being shown the edicts of the Dalai Lama and of the Regent stamped on yellow satin and supported by the Emperor's seal. But the mobs returned and if they ventured into the streets the missionaries were molested. At length the Regent issued a proclamation affirming that he had consulted the Oracle at Sam-ye, on the Tsang-po (river), south-east of Lhasa, and its god had declared that the flood was due to the sins of the people themselves... molestation accordingly ceased for a time."[8]

The missionaries then set about to reestablish good will by pursuing medical work among the inhabitants. But ultimately, all too familiar troubles overwhelmed the Capuchin efforts—wars, illness, deprivation, death and, not least, lack of support from outside. Replacement priests were not coming. By the mid-1730s only three Capuchins remained in Lhasa, surviving under increasingly trying circumstances. The formula for failure was being reapplied. By the end of 1734, the Tibet Mission was closed, followed by the Nepal Mission.

Only after prolonged lobbying in Rome was a third Capuchin Mission to Tibet and Nepal opened, in 1741. The Tibetan Buddhist authorities seemed open and amenable to their return. But again, and only within a year, the little church in Lhasa was in trouble and had to go underground. Envious lamas had mounted open demonstrations against them, and the Tibetan regent, acting on behalf of the young Dalai Lama, was forced to withdraw the government's nominal support, declaring the missionaries and their local converts out of favor. In April 1745, the Capuchin Mission to Tibet was finally abandoned for the third and last time.

History had repeated itself. The events in Lhasa were quite similar to those under which the Jesuit Tsaparang Mission had collapsed just a few years earlier. Before it was over, a similar story would be repeated among the Capuchins in Nepal.

The Capuchins in Nepal

The first Nepal Mission was opened by the Capuchins in January 1715, in preparation for and in direct support of the second mission to Tibet. The Valley of Nepal was dominated at the time by three city-states, known then as Kantipur, Lalitpur and Bhatgaon (today's Kathmandu, Patan and Bhaktapur). The Capuchins chose to settle first in Kathmandu, where the *raja* (king) seemed friendly and supportive. Later, they also established hospices in Lalitpur and Bhatgaon.

The first three Capuchin priests to Nepal were the Italian Frs Joseph Felix of Morro, Francis Horace of Pernabilli and John Francis of Fossombrone. They set up house in a building donated by Raja Jagat Jaya Malla. It had living quarters, a small chapel room, and a dispensary at which the priests gave free treatment to the local people. The residents of the city apparently spent much time observing the novelty of these hooded, bearded strangers and frequently came to them with various health problems. Even the raja admired their simple life style and dedication, so much so that he invited them to the palace to sit and converse with him and his *Raj Guru*, the Hindu high priest. The Raj Guru, a Brahmin, was spiritual advisor to the king and a member of the Royal Council. By all accounts he was tolerant and generally sympathetic towards the Capuchins.

The following year the main force of Capuchins trekking towards the mission in Tibet passed through Kathmandu. At that time the Nepal contingent was changed, leaving Fr Felix of Morro in charge of two new and younger men. Later, Fr Felix sought favor from the Raja of Bhatgaon with the thought of opening a second outpost in the valley. The overall objective of the Nepal Mission was to support the greater effort in Tibet, and it was the most important physical link to the outside in the whole of the mission reorganization scheme. Thus, Bhatgaon was an excellent location for a mission outpost, a central node on the India-Nepal-Tibet trade route.

Trouble started almost immediately, however, and plagued the mission throughout its brief existence. Some of it appears analogous to events that precipitated the collapse of the Jesuit Tsaparang Mission and, later, the Capuchin Lhasa Mission. On the one hand, there were various political intrigues, confounded by rising jealousies and revenge against the Europeans by the local Hindu religious establishment. On the other hand, even after a strong beginning and promises of full support from India and Rome, the entire Nepal-Tibet Mission effort soon suffered from the all-too-familiar lack of support—priests were not replaced and communications and funding from Rome were neglected.

The priests could not have been unaware of hidden dangers in the life they pursued in Kathmandu, but some of the manifestations of trouble must have surprised them. They were accused of being spies in the vanguard of foreign conquest. They were identified by some as Mohammedans (Muslims), highly despised at that time by Nepalese Hindus. The raja had to intercede to protect the Capuchins. During a terrible plague that devastated the populace, Nepalese Brahmins spread rumors that the brown habit these Christian strangers wore was an inauspicious color, a bad omen that offended the deities of the land. When the Brahmins took their complaints to the raja, he acquiesced. His power was not strong and he was forced to stop giving patronage to the Christians, declaring his neutrality in the matter.

In 1722, unable even to walk safely in Kathmandu, the Capuchins moved across the valley to Bhatgaon, where they were more cordially hosted by a royal rival, Raja Jaya Ranajit Malla. On his suggestion they donned white habits to avoid continuation of the troubles associated with their traditional brown garb. Beyond that small fact, virtually nothing else is known of their life in Bhatgaon. The record is blank, except for brief mention in Desideri's written account of his visit to Nepal.

Desideri's Visit
During the winter of 1721-22, the Capuchins briefly hosted Fr Ippolito Desideri on his final journey out of Tibet and back to Rome. Fr Desideri was much impressed with Nepal, although he was quite disparaging of the moral character of some of the local inhabitants. He wrote little about the troubles that plagued the Capuchins, but described in some detail a plot by Newars, the indigenous inhabitants of the valley, and by local Mohammedans, against the Raja of Kathmandu. He also described the clothing, food, drink, and religious customs of the common people.

Looking Back
A View of Nepal in 1721-22
Ippolito Desideri, SJ[9]

We arrived at Kathmandu on the twenty-seventh of December, where the Very Reverend Capuchin Fathers received me with much charity, and kept me in their hospice with great kindness for nearly a month. The Kingdom of Nepal owes no allegiance to any foreign power, but is divided among three Kinglets who reside in the three principal cities; the first at Kattmandu; the second at Badgao [Bhatgaon], the third at Patan....

The chief people in Nepal, after the petty Kings are the Guru and the Pardan [Pradhana]. The former are priests and spiritual directors, but are allowed to marry and are not numerous. Every Kinglet has his special Guru, to whom he turns for advice. The Pardan are ministers, officers of the law and nobles. The rest are merchants whose business is in Nepal, or who have dealings with Thibet or Mogol. These Neuars are acetive, intelligent, and very industrious, clever at engraving and melting metal, but unstable, turbulent and traitorous... They wear a woollen or cotton jacket reaching to the knees and long trousers down to their ankles, a red cap on their head, and slippers on their feet; when it rains men and women go barefoot. Nobles, and even the king himself, make no use of saddles, but sit on the horse's bare back with their legs hanging down, or at most have a horse-rug. Rice is their principal food, either cooked, or crushed and roasted; the latter serves as bread and as a relish. If they eat meat it is generally buffalo. They drink water and a nasty liquor made of a certain millet which grows in this country and is the staple food of the very poor. A kind of beer is also made from wheat or rice, and some drink *arac* distilled from raw sugar. Much rice is grown as well as wheat, sugar cane, vegetables, and fruit. The houses, of several floors, are well built, and the streets in the town are well laid out and paved with baked bricks set on end. They are very superstitious in all things, futile observers, and utter heathens... They write on paper with an iron style and know nothing of printing, but have numerous manuscript books. False Gods are worshipped by them, such as Ram, Mahadeo [Mahadev]. Brumma [Brahmah], Viscnu [Vishnu], Bod [Buddha], Bavani [Bhavani],[10] and many more. At a certain quarter of the moon they offer an infinite number of sacrifices to the Goddess Bavani of sheep, goats, and buffaloes, which they allow to rot, and then eat with great devotion as precious relics. On that day the number of animals slaughtered in the whole Kingdom amounts to many millions. The many temples to their idols are generally small, save the magnificent ones to Bavani at Kattmandu and at Sangu, a town not very far from Kattmandu. They believe in metempsychosis[11] to an even greater extent than the Thibettans, as they hold that souls not only migrate into animals, but into plants and other vegetables. Corpses are not buried, but burnt, and wives often elect to be burnt with the dead body of their husbands. The common people have an intense dislike of persons belonging to a different religion, especially of Christians, on account of the severity with which Pagans are treated at Goa. Although so many animals of all kinds are killed for sacrifices and food, yet the people treat them with the greatest consideration; they are not made to work, as everything is carried by men. To their false Gods they offer horses and oxen; but instead of killing them they let them loose to go where they will. The beasts wander about the fields and do much damage to rice, wheat, and other cereals; for they belong to the Deuta (as the Gods are called) and may not be driven off or disturbed; also this people have a most superstitious veneration for cows....

As to their marriages the law is that every man must marry a woman of his own caste or tribe for instance, a Bramman must wed a Bramman girl; a swineherd, a girl who tends pigs, and so on. Otherwise they lose grade and caste. They are not restricted to one wife, but have as many as they can afford to maintain. For a widow to remarry is considered disgraceful and almost infamous... The Kingdom of Nepal is not large, and one can go from one end to the other in a few days; part of it is flat, open country, but the principal part is mountainous; the mountains however are well wooded and pleasant. The chief products are wheat, rice, a certain black millet, vegetables, and various kinds of fruit such as prickly pears, pineapples, lemons, and oranges.

The city of Kattmandu, situated on a plain, is large, and it contains many hundred thousand inhabitants, and has a few handsome buildings. There is much commerce in this place, as many Thibettans and heathens from Hindustan come there to trade, and merchants from Cascimir [Kashmir] have offices and shops in the town...

The city of Patan is about three miles from Kattmandu, also standing on a plain, and has several hundred thousand inhabitants. Badgao stands on a hill some six or seven miles from Kattmandu, the air is much better, and with its fine houses and well laid out streets it is a much gayer and more beautiful city than the other two; it has several hundred thousand inhabitants who are engaged in trade...

At Bhatgaon, Desideri was graciously received by the Capuchins, and by the local king whom, he writes, "twice sent for me, showed me much honour, and when I left, gave me a letter to the King of Bitia (Bettiah), whose kingdom I was to traverse; he also gave me an escort to protect me until I had crossed the uninhabited mountains."[12]

Desideri left the Kathmandu valley on January 22, 1722, continuing on to India via Bettiah. He worked in the Indian mission for five years before being ordered, finally, to return to Rome.[13]

Capuchin Comings and Goings

Little else is known of the Capuchin Mission until it was suddenly abandoned in 1731. It is assumed that the Capuchin presence in Bhatgaon was not so strongly contested and that the mission's ultimate failure at this time rested, instead, on the lack of new priests to replace those who fell to illness and death over the years.

In 1735, the Sacred Congregation of Propaganda in Rome decided at last to send reinforcements. They dispatched three young

Capuchins as the vanguard of a second Nepal Mission. The three priests had just reached India when, on hearing of their arrival, the Rajas of both Kathmandu and Bhatgaon dispatched delegations to Patna to formally invite them back. Even the high priest, the Raj Guru of Kathmandu, wrote in support of his king's renewed interest. For their own reasons, the rival rajas were apparently eager to see the Capuchins return to their territories.

In Patna, Capuchin church officials were apprehensive and suspicious of the new Raja of Kathmandu, Jaya Prakash Malla, whose father had ruled during the previous times of trouble. Inquiring about the new king's character, they were assured that he displayed none of the erratic behavior of his father and that he would be both generous and understanding in his approach to these outsiders. Church authorities had less concern about the Raja of Bhatgaon, for he was better known to be sincere and sympathetic towards the priests and good to his word.

The Capuchins' dilemma was now that they might create trouble for themselves if they rejected one king's request by accepting the other's. Still undecided, a delegation was sent to Nepal to discuss the conditions under which a renewed mission might be undertaken. Both kings promised ample housing and each offered a special Decree of Liberty of Conscience permitting the Christian clergy to practice in an atmosphere of religious tolerance and to minister to the needs of their Nepalese converts. Satisfied that all was well, the Nepal Mission was reopened late in 1740, almost simultaneously with, and ostensibly in support of, the third Capuchin Mission to Tibet.

The Capuchins resettled in Bhatgaon, where their welcome had been assured by the king in an exchange of formal letters with Pope Benedict XIV in Rome. Later, near the beginning of 1742, a second mission house was opened in Kathmandu, and in 1744 yet another was dedicated for the first time in neighboring Patan (Lalitpur). Patan's Raja Prakash Malla eventually awarded them a Decree of Liberty of Conscience and a land grant, recorded on copperplate. It was done following the example of his rivals in the other valley kingdoms. Thus reestablished, they proceeded with considerable confidence in the future.

Trouble came soon enough, however. It began in 1745 with the collapse of the third Capuchin Mission to Tibet and the death of the Apostle of Tibet, Fr Francis Horace of Pennabilli. With the Tibetan Mission closed, Nepal became an isolated outpost without its original motive as a stopover on the supply route to Lhasa. Problems continued to plague the tiny Capuchin community in Nepal over the next twenty-four years until, in 1769, they were forced to depart once again, for the last time.

The years 1745 to 1769 were filled with high points and low. On the positive side the priests opened several churches and attracted a sizable following among the indigenous Newars of the valley. Yet, all the while some of the ill feeling they had encountered earlier was rebuilding, and new and more dangerous accusations were heard, making life difficult and sometimes dangerous.

The Conquest of Kathmandu Valley
The event that ultimately led to their final departure from Nepal was the conquest of Kathmandu Valley by Prithvi Narayan Shah, an ambitious warrior-king from nearby Gorkha, a tiny mountainous principality located a week's walk west of the valley in the central hills. In 1762, recognizing that trans-Himalayan trade was the life blood of the valley, the Gorkhalis blockaded Kathmandu Valley from the south, halting all commerce and communications with India. By 1764, the blockade also included trade routes north to Tibet. Prithvi Narayan's goal was to topple the Malla rulers of all three of the valley's weak city-states.

But the Kathmandu Valley states did not fall easily nor quickly, and for several years the valley was ringed by the Gorkhali army. On at least one occasion, Prithvi Narayan, exercising his military power and jealous of the attentions that the missionaries were receiving from the valley kings, sent for some priests to join him at Nuwakot, his stronghold on the valley's western rim. There he insisted that they provide medical treatment to a Brahmin, as well as to the elder of his two sons, Pratap Singh Shah. According to an account later written by Fr Giuseppe of Roveto describing the last days of the Capuchin Mission, his fellow priest, Fr Michelangelo, healed the king's son, an act that served them well later when that same son showed his good will and concern for their plight.[14]

Prithvi Narayan, distrusting the missionaries, sent spies to keep a close watch over their activities. His suspicions were raised in 1767 when the Malla Raja of Kathmandu, desperate for help to fend off the encircling forces, sent a secret request to the British East India Company for help. In response, the British dispatched an expeditionary force to Sindhuli in the lowlands, followed by the ill-fated Kinloch military expedition, which penetrated slightly farther into Nepal. Kinloch's troops were readily beaten back by the indomitable Gorkhalis.[15]

Prithvi Narayan assumed (incorrectly) that the Italian Capuchins had some part in calling the British. He believed them to have a close association with the besieged Raja of Kathmandu, as well as with the British authorities in India. The Capuchins denied it.[16] Immediately after Kinloch's defeat, Prithvi Narayan decreed that henceforth the missionaries must cease all communications out of Nepal except in the Hindustani language (which he could check). Under these conditions, and without access to funds and supplies from Rome, the Capuchins found it difficult to continue.

As the situation worsened, the Raja of Kathmandu warned the Capuchins to flee for their lives. He had heard that Prithvi Narayan was certain to put them to death. As the three valley kingdoms fell one after the other to the Gorkha troops, the priests lived in great fear and moved about frequently to avoid the sieges and battles. A major concern among them was the fate of several dozen Nepalese Christian converts.[17]

By 1769, the siege was over and the Gorkhas were under full control of the valley. Prithvi Narayan's dynasty was firmly established. (It lasted over two centuries, until 2008.)[18] The victorious king's immediate reward was a valley rich in agricultural resources and a critical link in the coveted trade between India and Tibet.[19]

Under the new Shah king, and particularly under the suzerainty of the Governor of Kathmandu, life for the Christians became unbearable. By one exaggerated account, "the new regime of the Gorkhalis took away the leased lands of the Christians so that they had no way of making a living. The Fathers were under heavy suspicion and disgrace and were unable to do their usual work. They were cut off from communication and support from their colleagues in India. One Father reported that the new Gorkha governor in Kathmandu maltreated the missionaries and tortured Christian converts. For a while King Prithvinarayan held the Fathers as hostages against a further possible attack by the British."[20]

The various difficulties suffered by the priests and their Christian converts sealed the fate of the Capuchin mission and forced them into exile in India. The final decision to leave Nepal, however, was not the raja's but was that of the Nepalese Christian converts themselves. Fulgentius Vannini, the Capuchin historian, quotes Fr Giuseppe of Roveto who described the final events leading to the Christians' departure. At Patan, he writes, "After having caused all the nobles who were in his power to be put to death, or rather their bodies to be mangled in a horrid manner, he (the new king) departed with a design for besieging *B'hatgan* (Bhatgaon), and we retained permission, through the interest of his son, to retire with all the Christians into the possessions of the English" (meaning, south into British India).[21]

On February 4, 1769, escorted by Fr Giuseppe of Roveto, the Nepalese Christian converts left Nepal. They numbered no more than sixty men, women and children, including five young catechumens (studying to be Christians). "With a sad and heavy heart they bade farewell to their homeland, to their relations and friends and walked out into the unknown, without means of support, sustained in their ordeal by an abiding faith."[22]

After two weeks the converts reached India and entered Bettiah District, a few miles across the border in the Kingdom of Bihar, and within a few weeks the remaining two Capuchins were also given permission to leave Kathmandu for India. There, in the tiny village of Chuhari, they settled on land obtained earlier by the Capuchin India Mission from the British East India Company. Their descendants, still devout Catholics, reside in Chuhari today, over two centuries and many generations later. Among them, however, the dramatic history of their origins has grown dim, and the Newari language, which their founding ancestors spoke, has been forgotten.[23]

The Last Capuchin in Nepal
The Capuchin retreat from Nepal back to India was not the last word from the determined Capuchins to keep a mission to Nepal.[24] On January 11, 1775, Prithvi Narayan Shah died and life in the valley of Nepal settled down in the newly consolidated kingdom under his son, the new Gorkhali Raja, Pratap Singh Shah. The new king promptly invited the priests to return, but at that time there was no one available to go. A few years later, after Pratap Singh and his *rani* (queen), Rajendra Laksmi, had died, Bahadur Shah (younger brother to Pratap Singh Shah) renewed the invitation under his authority as regent to the new infant king, his nephew. Bahadur Shah even offered money, an elephant and a personal escort to accompany the priests overland from India to Kathmandu.

Finally, in 1786, seventeen years after the capture of Kathmandu Valley by the Gorkhalis and the Capuchin departure with their congregation of Newar converts to settle in India, the Italian Fr Giuseppe of San Marcello was sent to Kathmandu. He stayed for three years, and was joined for one year by Fr Carlo Maria of Alatri. Shortage of priests in India, however, forced the Capuchin superiors to recall both priests back to India to fill other posts. Then, in 1794, Fr Giuseppe returned with another Capuchin, Fr Romualdo of Sanagallia. But Fr Romualdo soon left due to ill health. Henceforth, Fr Giuseppe of San Marcello remained alone in Kathmandu, until his death on November 9, 1810.

Unfortunately, the circumstances of Fr Giuseppe's personal life were his undoing as a priest—he failed to evangelize, he kept a concubine, and he was involved in some questionable financial dealing that led to a civil case against him in India. He was, therefore, declared disobedient and rebellious and was excommunicated by the church. Nonetheless, he stayed on in Nepal, maintaining himself thereafter doing business and living off the alms of local Christians. According to one account, after his death in Nepal the church authorities re-recognized Fr Giuseppe as a Capuchin, which implies that the excommunication order may have been rescinded.[25]

No other Capuchins were known to have gone to Nepal; although, once again, the record is unclear. There were further invitations from the royal palace in Kathmandu, but they were apparently not followed up, due in part to political circumstances within British India and, not least, to a growing weakness within the Capuchin Mission itself. History repeated itself—a scarcity of priests again undermined the Capuchin attempts to manage both the India and Nepal missions.

As a footnote to these difficulties, in 1782, Bahadur Shah, in a friendly gesture towards the missionaries, dedicated a large bell in the recently completed sanctuary of the Patna Cathedral. The inscription reads: *Bahadur Shah, Priti Naraen Regis Nepal Filius dono dedit Anno 1789* ('Given by Bahadur Shah, the Son of Priti Naraen Shah, the King of Nepal, in the Year 1789'; Priti Naraen being an alternate spelling of Prithvi Narayan, Bahadur Shah's father and the Gorkhali conqueror of Kathmandu valley).

By the early nineteenth century, the Capuchin Mission to Nepal was finished. As late as 1813, however, the government of Nepal again gave permission for a missionary to come. None was sent. Over time, social and political conditions within Nepal itself were deteriorating. By mid-century a bloody palace coup by a rebellious noble, Jang Bahadur Kunwar, propelled the kingdom into a century of repressive autocracy and despotism. During that time the Shah Kings were retained as puppets in the palace under a succession of powerful Rana prime ministers.[26]

Recent Findings

In his history of early Christian activity in Nepal, the mid-twentieth century Protestant missionary to Nepal, Jonathan Lindell, ends his chapter on the Capuchins with this summation: "The Capuchins considered their mission in Nepal largely a failure. With the passing of the years practically all the remains of their presence in the Valley disappeared: houses, gravestones, crosses and the like. It is reported that there are extant in Kathmandu manuscript copies of the Capuchins' books. From time to time people have looked for evidences of that early mission but with very little success; some day more may be found."[27]

The only physical evidence that remains today are three Capuchin manuscripts in the Newari script—two copper plates and one palm leaf document that served as deeds to the mission houses and lands. The deeds give the locations of Capuchin houses in Patan, Bhatgaon and Kathmandu. Fr John Locke, SJ, who (in the mid-twentieth century) conducted the most research on the Capuchin presence in Nepal, reported that "The places where they lived in the three cities are fairly clear, but the buildings no longer exist. Nepal has had two major earthquakes (1833 and 1934) since they left, and few buildings of any kind predate 1833... [T]he house in Patan was situated on the corner of the main road leading from Mangal Bazar towards Lagan Khel in the lane leading into the Ta Baha compound (location of the Machhendranath Temple). The site was a vacant lot until about 1986. The house in Bhatgaon was just off the southeast corner of the large open area around the Nyatpola temple. The house in Kathmandu was in Wotu Tole right along the old city wall..."[28]

Early in the twentieth century, Sylvain Levi saw and photographed the tombstone of Fr Horace of Pennabilli where it was set up in the Capuchin graveyard outside the north wall of Patan, near the Bagmati River (somewhere in or near the neighborhood of Sankamuhl). Its precise location today is unknown, although it has been searched for diligently on several occasions. The area is now built over with houses.

Fr Locke concluded that "The only real link that exists between that early Nepal mission and the present is the community in Chuhari near Bettiah, where the people from Patan settled when they left Nepal with the Capuchins. Many of their descendants are still there, and until about 50 years ago remained a separate community still speaking Newari."[29]

Not until the mid-20th century did Nepal reopen its border to outsiders, with the demise of the Rana regime in 1951 and return of the Shah kings to power. Under the popular King Tribhuvan Bir Bikram Shah, political and social conditions inside Nepal were greatly improved and new ideas were welcomed.

By this time, the Jesuits had replaced the Capuchins in the Patna Mission in neighboring Bihar, India. Since the 1920s, the Jesuits in Patna had become well known and respected by member of the Nepalese ruling class, who considered them to be excellent educators. Sons of the Kathmandu elite attended the Jesuit schools in Patna, and for several years around mid-century, some Nepalese leaders talked about the need for such schooling in Nepal, itself. Marshall Moran was one to whom they talked. The turbulent history of the Capuchins in Nepal, as well as both Jesuits and Capuchins in Tibet, was not lost on him. He was ready and well prepared for the task of leading the return of a Catholic mission to Nepal, one focused on education, with full attention to conditions necessary to keep the mission alive and well.

With this brief background about early Christian missions and explorations in Nepal and Tibet, including Fr Moran's predecessors in Nepal, we can return to the account of his own first few years on the subcontinent, in the 1930s, preparatory to his going to Nepal for the first time at mid-century.

Notes to Chapter 5: Early Christian Missions in Nepal

1. Nigg, *Warriors of God* (1959, p.235); see also R.P. Cuthbert, *The Capuchins* (1930).
2. Fulgentius Vannini, *Christian Settlements in Nepal* (1977, p.5).
3. Charles Bell, *The Religions of Tibet* (1931, p.144).
4. The Tarai (Terai) is the malarious jungle lowland of Nepal that travelers from Patna had to cross before ascending into the Himalayan foothills.
5. Vannini, *Christian Settlements* (1977, pp.8-9).
6. Sylvain Levi, *Le Nepal* (1905, v.1, n.p.), from an unpublished English translation by Mary Harris, edited by Deepak Shimkhada.
7. Bell, *Religions of Tibet* (pp.144-145).
8. *Ibid.*
9. Desideri, *An Account of Tibet* (1932, pp.312-318). The brackets and parentheses are in Wessel's edited version of Desideri's account, and the original (mis)spellings have been retained. Only the footnotes within the passage (nrs.10-11) are added.

    In the *Nepal Jesuit Chronology*, Fr Desideri is listed as the fourth and last Jesuit to set foot in Nepal until Fr Marshall Moran arrived over two centuries later. See John K. Locke, SJ, *Jesuits in Nepal* (1986). As one of Moran's principal inspirations, Desideri's description of Nepal fueled Marshall's imagination and resolve to live and teach among the Nepalese people. But in contradistinction to Desideri's short acquaintance with, and rather critical view of, the Nepalese people, Fr Moran, before ever going to Nepal, was well acquainted with them through long association with Nepalese boys whom he taught in the school at Patna. He knew them to be a far more generous and respectable people than Desideri narrowly made them out to be.
10. The goddess Bhavani is also known as Durga.
11. Metempsychosis is reincarnation.
12. Desideri, *An Account of Tibet* (1932, p.314).
13. *Ibid.* (p.318).
14. See Ludwig F. Stiller, SJ, 'A Letter of Fr Giuseppe da Roveto...' (1970).

15. For a history of the Gorkha Conquest of Kathmandu Valley and the unification of Nepal under Prithvi Narayan Shah, see Ludwig F. Stiller, SJ, *The Rise of the House of Gorkha* (1973). John Whelpton also gives a synopsis in *A History of Nepal* (2005).
16. Recent scholarship supports their denial. See Ludwig F. Stiller, SJ, 'A Letter of Fr Giuseppe da Roveto...' (1970, pp.6-20). Giuseppe writes (p.10): "The show of strength that the English made against Nepal really increased the difficulties that we had with the King of Gorkha, because the King of Gorkha erroneously supposed that the English had been called by us, because he thought, even though experience should have shown the contrary to him, that the Europeans were all of one mass (*una pasta*), and that the Fathers actually direct them in their military efforts because, as it seems to me, he thinks that we do for the English what the Brahmins do for him."
17. Fr Giuseppe's letter (*ibid.*, p.9) provides a very moving account of the terror to priests and valley dwellers, alike, during these times. One famous incident took place at the fall of Kirtipur, a fortified town about three miles southwest of Kathmandu. There "after the Gurkhas had taken the place... they cut off the noses and lips of all the men, except the male children who were in the arms of their mothers... To leave to posterity the memory of their vengeance the king gave the order that the said city would now be called Naskatapur, which means the City of the Cut-off Noses. This procedure of the Gurkhas so struck terror into everybody in the rest of Nepal (valley) that they did not want to suffer a like misfortune..."
18. On May 28, 2008, Nepal's Constituent Assembly (formed under a newly empowered Maoist-led government following a decade of insurgency), declared the establishment of a federal democratic republic, thus ending the monarchy that Prithvi Narayan Shah had founded 240 years earlier.
19. Prithvi Narayan and his successors were not content to stop with the Kathmandu Valley, however. His Gorkha Conquest continued east and west across the Himalayan hills for many more years, eventually knitting together a vast territory stretching, at one point, from Sikkim in the east nearly to Kashmir in the west, and from Tibet southward out on to the Ganges plain. Nepalese expansionism greatly alarmed the British in India, who mounted several campaigns against the Gorkhalis and finally stopped them in 1816. With the Treaty of Sagauli that year, the Kingdom of Nepal was cut back to nearly its modern size. (On the history of the Gorkha conquest see Kumar Pradhan, *The Gorkha Conquests*, 1991).
20. Jonathan Lindell, *Nepal and the Gospel of God* (1979, p.36).

    Fr John Locke (personal communication, 1989) notes, however, that while "It seems clear that the Gorkhalis confiscated the lands of the Christians..., this need not have had anything to do with them being Christians. The Gorkhalis confiscated a large percentage of Newar lands: all the land belonging to the old Malla aristocracy, land belonging to Newar institutions..., etc.... The hostage business is (also) a bit misleading. When the Christians left, the king granted permission for one Capuchin to leave with (them), the other two were to stay. The *Capuchins* surmised that these were asked to stay behind so that they could be used as hostages if the British ever attacked again. They certainly were not arrested and held as hostages. In fact they too got permission to leave shortly after. It is important to note that this harassment and persecution of the (Nepalese) Christians was carried out by the governor of Kathmandu while Prithvinarayan was in Nuwakot. He later rescinded the orders of the governor at the request of his sons" (presumably by Pratap Singh Shah, who had been healed by Fr Michelangelo).

The reader should also bear in mind that Nepalese royal authorities repeatedly, over a period of many years, invited the missionaries to return to Kathmandu and, at one point, to two districts in the central midhills west of Kathmandu.

21. Fr Giuseppe, 'Account of the Kingdom of Nepal' (1801, vol.2, n.p.); original italics, but bracketed explanations added.
22. Vannini, *Christian Settlements* (1977, p.97).
23. See Theodore Riccardi, 'The Nevars of Chuhari' (1990).
24. Lindell, in *Nepal and the Gospel of God*, writes incorrectly that no Capuchins were ever formally appointed to serve in Nepal after 1769. More recent scholarship shows quite conclusively that the Capuchins did return, although the mission was weakly maintained under rather trying personal and financial circumstances.
25. John Locke, SJ, personal communication (1989). Much of this account of the last Capuchins to reside in Nepal is described by Dipak Raj Pant in Vannini, *Christian Settlements* (1977, pp.35-36), based on the scholarship of Luciano Petech, *I Missionari Italiani nel Tibet e nel Nepal* (1952-56).
26. After ascending to power in a bloody coup called the "Kot Massacre," Jang Bahadur Kunwar (who changed his name from Kunwar to Rana) ushered in the century-long Rana autocracy until it collapsed in 1951. For an appreciation of the turbulent histories of the Shah dynasty in Nepal and the rise and fall of the Ranas, see Ludwig Stiller, SJ, *The Rise of the House of Gorkha* (1973), *The Silent Cry* (1976) and *The Kot Massacre* (1981).
27. Lindell, *Nepal and the Gospel of God* (1979, p.37).
28. Locke, personal communication (1989). Fr Locke, SJ (1933-2009) was a well known scholar of Newar Buddhism, and for many years maintained the *Nepal Jesuit Chronology*.
29. *Ibid.* More recent evidence is that Newari is no longer spoken by anyone in the Chuhari community.

MORAN IN NORTH INDIA

6

Two Years in Bettiah

...in one respect Bettiah really bulks plenty big on the horizon, for it can boast that it has the oldest and largest Catholic community in the whole of Patna Diocese. The little town will always rate a warm spot in my heart...
  Richard Welfle, SJ, *Pieces of India* (1963)

We never felt anything but happy. Hear no complaints, made none myself.
  Fr Moran, SJ, on his life in Bettiah

In the early winter of 1929, Marshall Moran arrived in Patna, in the Province of Bihar, after his train ride across India from Bombay. Patna city was steeped in the history of Christian Mission work but was otherwise little known to outsiders. One wonders what Marshall first thought of this dusty, dirty Indian town, so far from the familiar clean streets of Chicago or St Louis. He never uttered a disparaging word about the place, however; but said only that despite its inconsequence to most of the rest of the world, it was to him a striking and important place. That was his way of handling difficulties—he looked to the bright side, while knowing there would be difficulties in adapting.

Patna was an old city, with narrow, rutted lanes and once whitewashed buildings now dark with the stains of neglect. And, while he arrived during the cool of the winter, Marshall knew it would be beastly hot in summer. The city was not totally unfamiliar to Marshall. He had read all he could find about it and knew something of its long history and religious significance to both Hindus and Christians. For Catholics, it had started as a Capuchin Mission center. The Capuchins had built and left its central Christian edifice, the Patna Cathedral. Now, the cathedral, the city and its environs were the focal points of Jesuit enterprise; and for all Marshall knew, they would be his focal points for the rest of his life. He quickly oriented himself to the city and the wider region of Bihar and began to delve into its various stories and mysteries, closely observing its culture and geography.

Situated on the south bank of the Ganges river, "Mother Ganga" to the locals, Patna dominates that broad and sacred waterway that for countless centuries has focused and guided Hindu religious devotion as well as traffic and commerce across much of the northern subcontinent. It has been said that Patna is not a "city" in any real sense, but "an overgrown village three blocks wide and twelve miles long."[1] It is a place of rich and archaic significance, with crumbling ruins nearby that attest to its former stature and importance. Modern Patna was founded in 1541 near the site of Pataliputra, once a capital for two Indian empires, the Mauryan from the fourth to second centuries BC when much of the subcontinent was first unified, and the Gupta from the fourth to sixth centuries AD when Hinduism flowered.

On arriving in November 1929, Marshall and his companions stayed at the Bishop's House. Reverend Bernard Sullivan, SJ, was the second Jesuit bishop to be appointed to this ten-year-old Jesuit diocese, and the first from America. His consecration as Bishop had taken place only a few months earlier. He remained there as Bishop

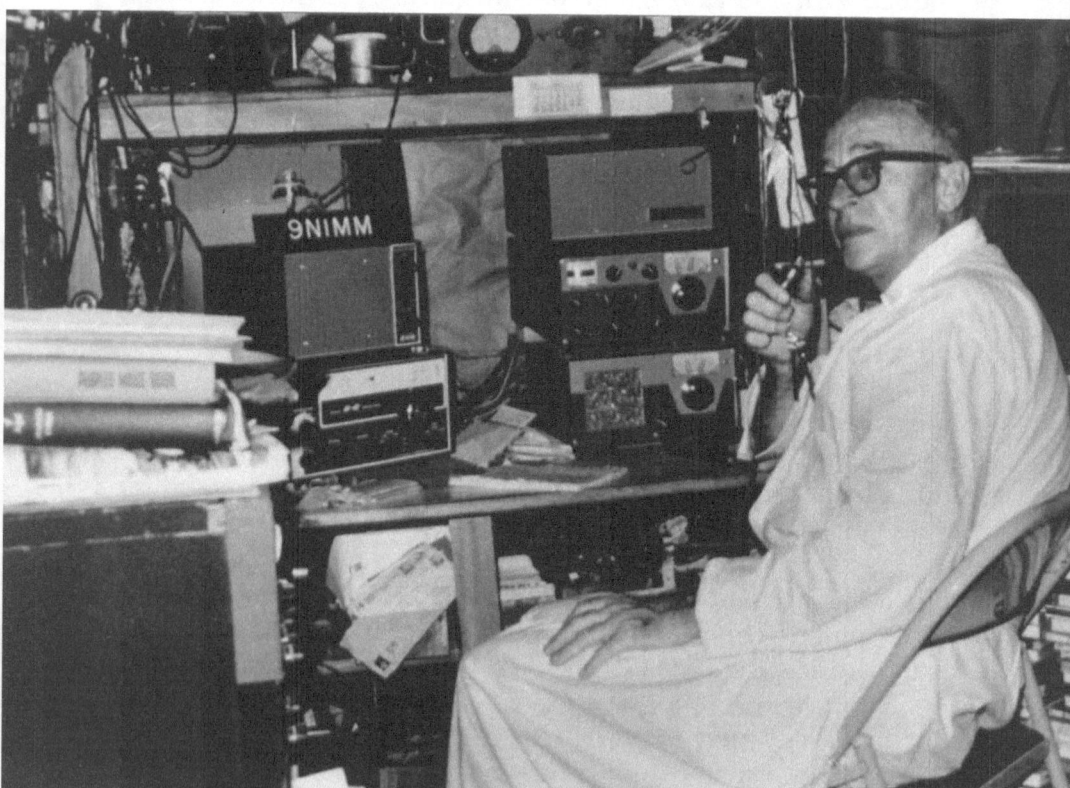

6. Fr Moran at his ham rig.

through virtually all of Marshall's India experience, retiring only in 1947, after a long, successful and respected career.

First Impressions
Within a few days of arriving in Patna, Marshall was informed by the superior of the mission, Fr Eline, that he was being assigned to teach in the parish school of Bettiah, ninety miles north. Bettiah, which in 1929 had a population of twenty-five thousand people, is situated on the flat Gangetic plain north of the river and south of the fearful Tarai, a low, malarial jungle belt that separates north India's vast flatlands from the rugged foothills of the Nepal Himalayas.

Before starting his work in Bettiah, however, Marshall still had a year of studies in the philosophate, for which he would attend a Jesuit college in the south of India. His schooling there would commence in January, he was told. In the intervening weeks he determined to become acquainted with Patna and Bettiah and other nearby parts of the diocese. Standing still was not his manner.

So Marshall eagerly joined a group of several other young scholastics and a few older priests for a short tour. First they visited the mission's churches and chapels in nearby Kurji and Dinapur and were impressed that the entire Patna area clerical services and sacramentals had been served to date by only four priests. A great deal of work was expected of them as the new batch from America, they were told.[2] One highlight of their introduction was a tour of the eighteenth century Patna Cathedral. It was situated four miles away from the city center in an older part of town known, today, as "Old Patna City." Marshall never forgot his first impressions.

Looking Back
The Patna Cathedral
Fr Moran

The foundation stone for the Patna Cathedral was laid by the Capuchins in 1772. This graceful, solid, lofty structure was opened for divine service in 1779. It has four impressive Ionic pillars along the front of the porch, perhaps thirty feet high. The inside is in the Corinthian style.

At the time of my first visit in November 1929, there was no real parish activity. That part of Patna had lost its luster and the heart of the city had moved four miles west to Bankipur where the British had built large structures and beautiful residences for the civil servants in an extensive park-like area with beautiful driveways. That's where they built the colonial secretariat, the high court and numerous administrative and departmental office buildings. The picturesque old cathedral was left behind, stranded in Patna's old bazaar district surrounded by run-down buildings and neglected shops and warehouses.

Still, the old cathedral impressed me with its austere beauty and its long history. The fact that the saintly Bishop Hartmann had lived there made me very respectful and devout, as one would feel toward a holy shrine.

When the roof was damaged in the 1934 earthquake, the Bihar government generously paid for repairs, due to the Patna Cathedral's historical importance.

Later, during the 1940s, when I was chaplain to the Medical Missionary Sisters in Patna, I rode my motorcycle each morning to the cathedral to say mass. More recently, Mother Teresa has established her Missionaries of Charity at the cathedral to do their wonderful works of charity among the poor of the city.

That glorious old cathedral has been witness to a great deal of Patna's church history through the centuries.

Then Marshall set off for a month's stay in Bettiah, to visit the school and parish where he would be posted after his year of further studies. The trip north coincided with the annual Sonepur *mela,* a huge fair. Sonepur is a sacred Hindu pilgrimage site on the north bank of the Ganges, across from Patna. Fairs are commonplace in India during the dry winter months following the rice harvest and, as this one was on their way to Bettiah, Marshall and his companions decided to stop and see it.

Since the trip took most of the day, the company of young Jesuits booked seats on an early morning train along the north bank of the Ganges. To get to the train they first had to ride across Patna in a two-horse carriage, from the mission headquarters to the *ghat,* or levee, where the river boats departed. There they caught a side-wheel ferry boat to cross the Ganges. Marshall recalled Mark Twain's description of side-wheelers and imagined what it must have been like on the Mississipi. One of the most striking differences was that passengers here were quite likely to see half-burned human corpses floating down river, eastward toward the Bay of Bengal. And gigantic trees, uprooted during the previous summer's monsoon flood lay stranded on the river banks, some of them thirty or forty feet above the winter water level. To devout Hindus, the great Mother Ganga is known far and wide for both its natural and supernatural powers.

The Sonepur mela reminded Marshall of his first days in India, at Bombay. It was just as crowded, or more so, with a veritable crush of humanity. The hawkers were loudly selling all imaginable goods and services amidst indescribable smells and the ever-present flies, attracted to the sweets and the refuse that accumulates when so many people gather for festivities. He saw poor peasants from the plains and, for his first time, some of the rough hewn traders from the mountains; people wearing all manner of coarse dress, peddling their wares, buying supplies and wandering about in awe of the spectacular cattle fair, a main attraction of this mela. Everyone was enjoying a grand winter holiday.

There were Hindu holy men, the ubiquitous *sadhus, fakirs* and *jogis* of India in all stages of dress and undress, practicing exotic masochistic and contortionist arts on their bodies. Snake charmers and snake-oil peddlers hawked miraculous cures (to hear them tell it), "fully guaranteed" medicines for all and sundry ailments, from warts to ulcers to infertility. There were dozens of stalls where people could sip warm tea, eat roasted peanuts and smoke pungent little Indian cigars. All about they heard the cries of *"chai garam!"* (warm tea), *"badam-badam!"* (peanuts) and *"bidi-bidi!"* (a kind of small cigarette hand rolled from a single leaf).

A major purpose of the fair was the livestock exchange. The animal merchants bought and sold cattle and water buffaloes, goats and sheep, horses and even elephants. And there were blacksmiths selling hand-forged tools and cooking utensils. All manner of merchandise manufactured in village lanes and in city factories was available— "nearly anything under the sun," as Marshall put it. This gathering of industrious but simple village people impressed him greatly, etched indelibly in the earliest memories of his new life abroad.

After the Sonepur fair the priests boarded the coal-fired narrow-gauge train of the Bengal Northwestern, a branch line of the greater Indian railway system. It took them first to Muzaffarpur, where they ate a meal of rice, then on through Motihari to Bettiah, where they arrived, exhausted, in the evening.

There Marshall settled in to the parish house for a month's stay. He used his time to get to know other scholastics, priests and staff and to meet some of the Indian parishioners, townspeople and peasants among whom he would soon return to live and work.

He was back in Patna in time for Christmas, which he spent in the cheerful company of fellow Jesuit missionaries, enjoying the pleasures of the Bishop's fine but simple hospitality. The Bishop's House was the center of the action, so it seemed, near to the Ganges on a busy main street with noise and chatter and the loud patter of horses passing by night and day. "It took me at least a year to get used to the voices and traffic noises, the railway train whistles and the blaring bulbous horns of the horse cart and carriage drivers," he recalled. "But that's India—a long way from Chicago and St Louis!"

The local conveyances were a special challenge. "Once when Father Peter Sontag, our superior, was rushing to the railway station in Patna, riding on a bouncy two-wheel *ekka*, the horse stumbled and fell on his knees and the cart tipped sharply forward. Fr Sontag and the driver tumbled head first into the dust, handbags and bed roll flying after them. Such were the perils of travel in those days. But today, of course, one takes as much or more of a risk riding with the wild taxi drivers through the crowded city streets."

Studies at Shambaganur, in South India

Shortly after Christmas Marshall set off for his required year of study of philosophy at the College of the Sacred Heart, located in the picturesque hill station of Shambaganur in the Madura Mission of South India. Shambaganur was a fully approved house for novices, juniors and philosophers of the Society. There he completed studies for his Masters in Philosophy degree.

Looking Back
Shambaganur
Fr Moran

I traveled by rail east from Patna to Calcutta, where I changed to a train going south to Madras, or Trichinopoly as we used to call it.

Calcutta was interesting. The Houghly river divided the city into two parts and as there was no proper bridge between them, the people crossed on a floating pontoon structure. The city had hardly any buildings more than four or five stories high and the streets were very narrow and crowded. Later, of course, it was transformed into a metropolis with huge bridges, broad boulevards and even the beginnings of a subway. In January 1930, however, it seemed a rather sleepy place.

I traveled for two full days and noticed as I passed through central India into the southern parts that the people became much more subdued, quiet, polite, gentle and quite friendly. The stations were cleaner than in the north and the station restaurants were better maintained. And, in the preparation of coffee, the south Indians are experts. The coffee was superb. I always liked coffee and the best I've ever had was in south India.

From Madras city my destination was an overnight journey up into the Palni hills to about five thousand feet. Shambaganur sits in a beautiful eucalyptus forest and is only a few miles from Kodi Kanal, a popular hill station. At night in my room at the college, I could smell the eucalyptus trees and could hear the ox cart drivers singing along with the shrill, loud squeaking of the cart wheels.

It was winter when I arrived, but there was no real winter there.

The temperature was always mild, usually seventy to seventy-five degrees Fahrenheit, never rising above eighty by day, cooling down to sixty-five in the evening. That's what they called "winter"!

After the harsh winters of the American Midwest, this mild, pleasant place was like heaven.

There were several dozen students in my class, of many nationalities—Walloon and Flemish Belgian, English and Irish, German, Spanish, French and Italian, a few Americans and many Indians from all corners of the subcontinent.

Being with such an international group was a new experience, something surprising, always interesting.

My new companions gave me many ideas and I was constantly stimulated by their keen sense of philosophy and of life. There were many excellent students among them; but more value than all the Europeans, I thought, were the Indians. The reason I had come to India was to be with the Indians and there were many in the school to get to know. As students they were just as good as the Europeans and a few were much better. I can think of only one English student who excelled beyond the best Indian students in my class.

I especially remember Fr Kevin Angelo, an Indian, and Fr Kevin Cleary of Irish ancestry but born in India. Fr Cleary later joined the Patna Mission where he helped me very much in starting St Xavier High School. There was also Fr John Brennan and Fr David Pinto. Pinto was one of my earliest and best friends at Shambaganur. Both Brennan and Pinto were expecting to go to Bettiah, as I was. Fr David Pinto had a wonderful grasp of philosophy, our main subject, and he often helped me prepare for exams. I appreciated his keen sense of history and his ability to explain the opinions of Aristotle and Plato and Saints Augustine and Thomas Aquinas.

We had some remarkable professors. Fr Ravel, a shy French priest, taught theodicy or natural theology, using Thomas Aquinas's *Summa Theologica* as his text. Despite his shyness we all appreciated his well-ordered lectures and his guidance and suggestions for our readings, such as the sermons and commentaries of St Augustine on the Gospel of St John and various interpretations of St Thomas like Etienne Gilson and other neo-Thomists (and, a few years later, Jacques Maritain). I often turned to them later for continuing inspiration.[3]

Our ethics teacher was Fr Klein, a Luxembourger, much different from the other Frenchmen, quite outspoken and blunt. He was an interesting teacher, with many examples and stories to explain some very abstract points of ethics.

Several times I had to engage in debate, all in Latin, on some of the subjects. I remember one debate with the Spanish student, Fr Joseph More—spelled M-O-R-E, but pronounced "mo-ray." I had to defend a particular thesis and he worked hard to knock down my arguments. We became very good friends.

> The days and evenings of my stay in Shambaganur were full of study. I had little chance to enjoy any music and I missed choir and singing, phonograph records and radio. Instead, I did a great deal of reading. During holidays I concentrated on history and on the biographies of important historical characters such as the saints or the "Fathers of the Church," as we called them—Basil, Gregory of Nyssa, Athanasius of the Greek church, and other such great philosophers and theologians.
>
> In November 1930, at the end of my first year in India, I took my final exams and was graduated with a degree in philosophy. Then I bid my new-found friends goodbye and left Shambaganur to return to Patna Diocese and the Bettiah parish, where I would begin my life's work as a teacher.

While living in Shambaganur, Marshall realized again that he had serious trouble with the traditional and normally spicy Indian food. The strong peppers and other seasonings simply did not agree with him and he had to learn to take much milder fare. "It was only a minor complaint," he said, playing down a problem that caused him a great deal of discomfort over the years.

One strong flavor that he did enjoy, however, was the bold south Indian coffee. He has often commented with pleasure on the strong aroma and flavors of the drink that he so enjoyed at Shambaganur. He was never known to refuse a cup of fresh-ground brew.

Return to the North

On a cool November morning in 1930, a year after his arrival on the subcontinent, and with his year's study complete, Marshall left Shambaganur to return by a rather winding route back north to Patna. He traveled first to Mangalore on India's west coast, where he spent a day in what he described as "a very old, intelligent and industrious Catholic community, among people who spoke Konkani. I saw their flourishing college and delightful parishes and excellent schools."

He was joined there by two new companions, Frs Raymond Mullen and John Sloan. In Mangalore they boarded a coastal steamer bound for Goa and Bombay. Every few hours the steamer put in to port to load coconut and cashew nuts, all being readied for shipment to the United States.

Goa was the Portuguese colonial headquarters and main European settlement of India during the sixteenth century and it was there that St Francis Xavier had first landed in India, on May 6, 1542. "I knew all that, but was no less astounded there to see the huge churches, many special shrines and the remarkable devotion of the people visiting them. It seemed more like a corner of France or Spain, or Portugal or Germany—Bavarian Germany, that is, the Catholic part—for the devotion of the people and number of priests and nuns and Catholic institutions, schools and hospitals. This was a great surprise to me."

Settling in at Bettiah

By December, Marshall had returned to the Bishop's House in Patna. After a brief stay, he set out in January to take up his new assignment at Bettiah, in northern Bihar. Marshall had begun to speak the Hindi language by now and it pleased him that at the frequent stops along the way he was able to understand what was going on around him. "My Hindi was improving and I began to distinguish Hindu from Urdu, as well as the Hindus from the Muslims who spoke these two principal languages. And I could recognize the different types of merchants and caste people by their clothes and often by their accented language."

He noted that many of the railway personnel, such as the station masters and ticket collectors, were from other parts of India, like the Punjab and Bengal. "There were Sikhs and Bengalis and many Anglo-Indians of mixed heritage, all with unique features and of different bearing from the local Biharis. The Bengalis, especially, expressed a certain superiority in their manner of speaking and attitude."

Marshall's traveling companions from Patna to Bettiah were three other scholastics, each of whom had been with him in South India and were now setting out to do their first teaching together. "We made an interesting study in international relations. There was David Pinto, one of the first Indians to join the Patna Jesuits. He was of an old Goan family whose Christian roots dated back two or three hundred years. Fr John Sloan was also with us, a man from southern England, but very Irish. I remember that although he was nervous and did poorly at speaking Hindi, he was nonetheless a dynamic character. He turned out to be a great preacher in English. My other companion was Fr John Brennan, an American Irish from Cleveland. He had flaming red hair and was a good linguist, very conversant in colloquial Hindi. Brennan was very animated and whenever he spoke, even about ordinary things, he'd use his hands and flash his eyes in punctuation."

At Bettiah, his friends Pinto, Sloan and Brennan were assigned to the new Khrist Raja (Christ the King) high school. The school was two miles away from the city, amidst pleasant and refreshingly cool mango groves that bordered on expansive rice fields. It was so new that the classrooms and living quarters were still without window glass or finished floors. They had to live and work for several months under rather austere conditions, but they were cheerful about it, knowing that they were pioneers of a sort. Their school represented the first development in higher education (above middle school level) for the mission in over two hundred years of Catholic settlement there. Over the years the Khrist Raja School became known, as one observer put it, as "The pride of Bihar."[4]

Marshall was assigned to a grammar school in the heart of Bettiah proper. It had grades one through seven for boys from about the age of five to twelve or thirteen. Although a school in the center of the small city was not as attractive to some as the high school was out in the country, teaching in the middle school was his wish. "It was what I expected and had volunteered for. I wanted to be with small boys and live and work in an environment where I was obliged to speak Hindi and where I could attend classes where Hindi was spoken. I found that boys eight or ten years old were better teachers of Hindi for me than were high school boys who, although they knew much more of their native language, were shy in speaking it with me and more keen on practicing their English. I wanted practice in the simple language of the younger people. And I knew that most parents there did not speak English, so I would be forced to carry on all conversation and business in Hindi with them, as well."

Hindi did not come easily to Marshall. He worked on it with a boy named Lazarus Pascal, whom the other children called *"pundit-ji"* (respected teacher), because of his seriousness as a tutor, of sorts, to the school master. Marshall and Lazarus met daily to read Hindi, using the New Testament in translation as their text. "We went completely through the four gospels at least three or four times, very slowly. I thought that because the Gospels were in short sentences and simple words that I would do better. That way I could use what I learned, the parables especially, more quickly. Within a year I was quoting whole passages in Hindi, verbatim."

It took two years before Marshall was at ease speaking colloquial Hindi. He was proud of his ability to read the newspapers with facility and to understand radio broadcasts when he heard them, which was seldom. "I greatly enjoyed using Hindi. It was a real accomplishment for me." In the meantime, however, he had his difficulties and setbacks. On one occasion, soon after he began teaching, he met one of the school boys and his mother on the street. He tried to tell her in Hindi what a good boy her son was in school. She listened patiently, then turned to the boy and said in the local dialect, "Tell Father that I do not speak English." She was probably most comfortable in Bhojpuri, the colloquial dialect of the district. Marshall never tried to learn Bhojpuri, for "Hindi was difficult enough to master," he said.

Urdu was another language often heard in the region, especially among the Muslim villagers. It dated to the time of Akbar the Great (late sixteenth century), when the Muslims ruled north India. Some of the early church hymns, Marshall found, were still sung in Urdu. Although closely related to spoken Hindi, Urdu utilizes an Arabic script in place of the Devanagri script of written Hindi. It is also the language of popular poetry.[5]

The Bettiah Grammar School had about six hundred boys in seven classes, some as large as forty-five or fifth students. There were twenty teachers, mostly Indians recruited from the local Christian community. The attached kindergarten was handled by four Indian nuns and met daily on the verandah of the local church.

Marshall's main subject was English and, within a few months of starting out, the boys of his fourth and fifth standard classes were able to use a vocabulary of about a thousand words "in proper sentences," as he put it. The energetic young Fr Moran stimulated the boys' interest in spoken English by using dialogue and staging dramatic performances in the classroom—poetry, theater and English songs. Every four or five months "my boys," as he called them, staged plays for their parents, that hundreds of townspeople and students from others schools came to see. The sisters of the Swiss Order of the Holy Cross, who ran a nearby girls' convent school and orphanage, often praised Marshall for the progress his boys made in spoken English.

"Two and three decades later, when I'd meet former students from Bettiah, they talked about the little plays that we put on—'Hansel and Gretel,' 'Ali Baba and the Forth Thieves,' and others. And whenever we had a story in the English reader, they'd memorize and dramatize it, pretending it was a radio program with an announcer and assigned parts. Those with good memories got on quite well. I'd give them a lot of dictation, spelling contests and a memory lesson every day, for our five lines from the reader so that they also got facility in writing English."

Of all his work, classroom teaching was Marshall's first love. "My teaching and life in Bettiah was very rewarding, and very busy. I especially enjoyed watching those boys mature and become responsible citizens and family men. Many of the boys from that small town, in that backward community, later went on to the university and took degrees and found jobs in commerce, the civil service and professions as doctors and lawyers. One even became a very popular parish priest."

His concern for the boys' welfare went deep. "I remember one boy who was ill with typhoid fever in the hospital. When he had a relapse his family gave up on him and brought him home to die. I went to his home by carriage and put him back in bed at the hospital. It took forty days, but he recovered. After that I followed his career with special interest. He married and had several sons who were very bright, especially in mathematics. One went to work as an engineer in a motor scooter factory in the Punjab. For as long as I lived in India, we kept in touch."

Marshall made many friends among the Indian families in Bettiah. Many of the school boys were Christian, but there were also Hindus and Mohammedans (Muslims) among them, whose parents became good friends and treated him with kindness. Some of his first students and their parents travelled to Patna to visit him for many years after.

"I was very fortunate to have good relations with the parents and children of Bettiah. We seemed to have their confidence and trust. There were only one or two cases of student insubordination or of individuals who didn't want to study, or who wouldn't let others study. Bullies were rare; there was very little of that. I always felt good that we accomplished so much with those students and had such good discipline without corporal punishment."

The two years in Bettiah had an important effect on Fr Moran and in his maturation as a person, a priest and a mission educator. In later years, he often reflected back on this period in his career. Among the memories were his first glimpses of Nepal and of the mountain people, including the Bhotia (Tibetans), who sometimes visited the parish while on pilgrimage to their own Buddhist religious shrine at Bodh Gaya.

People from the Himalayas

Sometimes Marshall rewarded his students (and himself) by taking weekend trips to visit outlying mission stations. More than once these special trips took them to the Nepal border, at Raxaul. It was only a short train ride. He would do it for the fun of saying that he and the boys had stood at the entrance to the Himalayan kingdom. They could not enter Nepal in those days—it was firmly closed to outsiders—but they could stand and look across the border and meet the interesting Himalayan people who crossed into India.

Looking Back
Glimpses of Nepal and the Tibetans
Fr Moran

From my very first days in Bettiah, and on those holidays spent in Raxaul, I loved to look up to the snow peaks rising over Nepal and

Tibet. Hindus call those mountains the "Abode of the Gods." I could see why—they inspire awe and reverence. On clear days I could make out some of the more famous peaks, like Annapurna and Dhaulagiri, and many others whose names I did not know until years later.

From the Nepalese town of Birganj, just across the Indian border from Raxaul, the Nepalese ran a little narrow-gauge railroad inland across the Tarai to Amlekhganj. One time at Raxaul I telephoned to Birganj, to the Nepal railroad director, and asked him to come across to see me if he was interested in having his tickets and forms for his office, the account books, letter heads and envelopes or any other printing done by the mission press. In that way I got new orders for Brother Pias and his printing press back at Bettiah parish.

In winter, hundreds of Nepalese hill people came down to India to towns like Bettiah, looking for seasonal work. Others came on holiday to escape the mountain cold. Some among them were from the highest mountains along the Nepal-Tibet border. Their religion and culture were Tibetan, but Hindus called them "Bhoté." These Bhotia people would walk for weeks down to the edge of the plains, then another four or five days to Bettiah. They were all Lamaists, Tibetan Buddhists, but for some reason they were attracted to our Christian parish church. They would enter quietly, prostrate themselves in the sanctuary, flat out, and go through various Tibetan rites and prayers. It was an important pilgrimage for them and their devotion was remarkable. We never turned them away.

The Bhotias then took the train ten hours down to the Ganges and took the ferry across to Patna, from where they continued the rest of the way four hours farther south to their destination at Bodh Gaya. Gaya is especially sacred for Buddhists. In the sixth century BC Gautama Buddha, or Siddhartha as he is sometimes called, meditated there under the famous Bo tree seeking enlightenment concerning salvation, human suffering and Nirvana, "eternal bliss." Siddhartha spent the rest of his life teaching and preaching and established the foundations of Buddhism.

Opening a Country School

Marshall's teaching responsibilities in the middle school at Bettiah kept him busy. But it was apparently not enough to satisfy his high energy level and determination to excel. So, in addition, he sought out a nearby place to experiment in starting a new grammar school. He chose the tiny community of Majowlia, a village of about a hundred houses six miles east of the city. To start out he hired an unemployed "old boy" Jesuit school graduate. The teacher, a high caste Brahmin, acted as a school master and responded quickly to the responsibilities and routine of teaching.

Once or twice a week Marshall bicycled out to Majowlia to mark the school's and the boy's progress. In winter the cart track was rutted and dusty. During the monsoon it was a quagmire. In summer he rode in thin white cotton trousers to keep cool. He inevitably came home spattered with mud. In winter he dressed more warmly, only to arrive at the school house covered in dust and grime. "I must have ridden hundreds of miles on my bicycle. Enough exercise, I used to think, for the next ten years!"

He was encouraged by the initial show of support for the school by the fathers of the village boys. "To get started, I asked them to supply the land and put up a grass hut with plenty of ventilation. The children needed to be protected from the hot sun and from the rains. Then, I thought, after this first experiment, if we could get another teacher trained to be a real headmaster, the Majowlia School might become more permanent, with a *pakka* (first class) building."

Marshall was also encouraged by fellow priests, many of whom accompanied him at one time or another on the bicycle ride to the village, or came out from Bettiah or up from Patna to observe. "Some would visit out of curiosity or for an outing. Others did it as a sort of devotion. Some of the older men would come and give me advice on teaching and sometimes help me improve my language and manners with the local people." He remembers the help of Frs Miller, Pettit and Sontag of the Bettiah Mission and especially of Fr Gus Wildermuth, who later succeeded Reverend Sullivan as Bishop of Patna.

The visit of a bishop to the rural schools was always a big event. We are fortunate to have a graphic description of a visit to villages near Bettiah by Bishop Louis Van Hoeck, SJ, a few years before Marshall arrived. Although it predates Fr Moran's work in the villages, it gives us an insightful view of the big event and a glimpse into the life of the rural mission communities and schools.[6]

Looking Back
Visiting the Village Schools
Joseph A. Gschwend, SJ

(*The Bishop's party started out into the countryside on local transport—*) We took our seats in the tonga (bullock-cart with springs) and began our journey of about six miles over a good but dusty road. On both sides of the road the fields extend as far as you can see... When we reached the Mission it was about ten o'clock; the bells were ringing, announcing the arrival of *Lat Padri*. The Hindus and the Christians were busy in their fields cutting the cold weather crops. They now came hurrying up to the milras (arch) erected in front of the church; the Christians were anxious to kiss the Bishop's ring, the Hindus to salaam the *Lat Padri*. The Bishop vests in surplice and cappa, the canopy is brought forward, the Te Deum is intoned, the procession forms and proceeds to the church...

In the afternoon the Hindu assamis (tenants) came to pay their respects to the Bishop, their landlord. A number of castes are gathered together in the Hindu tolah (or hamlet): Brahmins, Manias (tradesmen), Kayasthas (writer-caste), Munias (salt workers) Chamars (leather workers), Turahas (fishermen), Ahirs (cowherds), Gonrs, Lohars (blacksmiths). There are also a number of Mohammedans. The assamis had come in true oriental fashion with their dalis (baskets with offerings). A few began by placing a rupee at the feet, or rather on the feet of the Bishop; then the others came forward with their baskets of vegetables and fruit. In one basket there were some baigans (egg-plant), some alu (potatoes), some salt, some achar (pickle), in another, kobees (cabbages), rice, dal, marcha (chilis), and again in another, guavas, plantains, etc. The Bishop touched each basket in token of acceptance, and the contents were taken away by the servants of the bungalow...

(At another village, the scene was even more spectacular, rich in pomp and circumstance and acts of deference and respect, in honor of Bishop Van Hoeck—)
At 11 a.m., we all went out, camels, elephants, etc., one mile to meet His Lordship. To the beating of drums and amidst great cries of jubilation he was received at the Mission. At three o'clock in the afternoon the space round the Mission was packed with huge crowds, and the procession with the Blessed Sacrament commenced. The cross with a bodyguard of two immense elephants headed the procession. Then came a lot of children in white, followed by two large camels. Then more children in white and with flowers, followed by His Lordship with the Blessed Sacrament. Then came a huge number of people followed by fourteen more elephants. The procession wound around through the country roads for nearly a mile and finally returned to the 'Square' in front of the Mission...

Then the sixteen elephants all lined up, and, raising their trunks saluted the Eucharistic King, whilst thousands of people, Christian, Pagan and Mohammedan, knelt around in reverence as His Lordship gave a stirring address suited to the audience. Apparently, as far as we could judge, the address made a deep impression.

(In the same account we also find a description of the rural schools. Then, and later in Moran's time, the village schools were simple affairs—)
...a few bamboo poles stuck into the ground, supporting a thatched roof. The ground is the blackboard. The luxury of desks is not known and the children, very scantily clad, squat on the ground. They are taught writing, arithmetic and reading...

> We spent the greater part of the next morning inspecting the boys' school. Not that we had to waste any time going from class-room to class-room. Oh, no. Picture to yourself a plot of ground 12 feet long by 5 feet broad, four wooden posts, one at each corner, supporting a roof thatched with khair...[7]
>
> The school furniture was in keeping with the building: that is to say, there was none." In place of books and paper, each student had on "a small remnant of a slate, an irregular piece, almost as large as the hand, and slate pencils on the same scale, that is, about one inch long. Others had a small plank on which they traced with a piece of chalk... hard to read.

Such were the conditions at the school in Chaknee, but it could have been Marshall's little school in Majowlia or any one of the others throughout the large diocese. Marshall pursued his experiment at Majowlia for two years, then turned it over to another priest to continue. It was not an easy assignment and within a few years, to his disappointment, it was abandoned.

Daily life in Bettiah and out in the countryside was rugged but not unpleasant for the young priest. There were moments of joy and moments of discomfort. Marshall and his companions had rooms in the school staff house at Bettiah and shared their board at a common kitchen. Here on the northern Gangetic plain it could get very hot, with temperatures soaring to well over 100 degrees Fahrenheit (over 38° Celsius) during the days and hardly less than the nineties at night. At night, to escape the heat, Marshall joined the others to sleep on the roof, seeking even the tiniest night breeze. When a rain storm hit them (sudden, violent downpours were common), they scrambled to get their beds and bedding back into the rooms. Nonetheless, he recalled, "We never felt anything but happy. Heard no complaints, made none myself."

A Day in the Life...

A typical day for Marshall in Bettiah began at five o'clock a.m. He attended mass at 5:30. It was his responsibility to unlock the doors to let in the church warden and the sexton for preparations. They could expect up to two hundred parishioners to show up regularly for early mass, from a congregation of two thousand, town and city dwellers and farmers alike.

After mass he practiced an hour of private meditation, followed by breakfast at seven o'clock. By eight o'clock, when the first period of school began, Marshall was in his office preparing for class. In his second year at Bettiah he was recognized and rewarded for his teaching and administrative skills by being appointed headmaster of the grammar school. This was his first administrative post in what became a lifetime of school management and institution building. After that he devoted his first hour at the school each morning to business and always opened his office for visits by teachers and staff, students and parents.

During second and third periods he taught English and "moral science" (citizenship and ethics), and sometimes the catechism. Then, in the hour before noon, he would visit other classrooms, test the children, encourage the teachers, and try to keep up good relations and some dynamic movement to energize both the teaching and the learning.

Lunch was served promptly at twelve o'clock, with more classes following from one o'clock. Afternoon tea was served at 3:30. From four to five o'clock he faithfully practiced his Hindi lessons with the student, Lazarus Pascal, six days a week.

Over a relaxed evening meal, Marshall often discussed the day's highlights. Then followed a few hours of reading and reflection in the parish library before returning to the chapel for evening prayer.

That evening hour or so in the library is a cherished part of every priest's day in the missions. It allows for some relaxation and privacy after a busy day, away from the school boys and others with whom they deal all day long. The shelves are typically lined with books on church history, philosophy, literature, travel and religious reflection.

In Bettiah back in the early 1930s, however, evening reading was not easy, since without electricity the priests depended on oil wick lamps. Sometimes Marshall and his fellow priests and brothers liked nothing better than to play a board game, while sipping hot coffee or tea and enjoying a cookie or two over idle chatter. In these ways they could rest and refresh themselves and reinforce the group's communal bonds.

One day each week, Thursdays, Marshall made a special trip out to Khrist Raja School to join the little community of eight Jesuit teachers there over supper. With a wry smile he once admitted that "The big feature on Thursdays was ice cream. I was accused of being addicted. Guilty!"

An equally serious reason for visiting Khrist Raja was to use the high school library. Marshall always found a few hours of repose among a set of excellent books, including the translations of Saint Augustine and Saint Thomas Aquinas. "I was very serious about preparing myself with the Holy Scriptures, and I would get books from the high school library or from the Bishop's House in Patna. I'd use them to improve my prayer and spiritual life as well as prepare myself for my further technical theology studies."

The Bettiah Catholic community was led by Fr Heraclitis Alban, the parish priest. Parishioners had difficulty with his name, and he became more popularly known as "Father Rakilo," instead. Fr Rakilo was a short, stocky man with a pleasant face framed by a short beard. A local Bihari by birth, he had studied theology in Kandy, in the hills of Ceylon (Sri Lanka). His assistant was Fr Walter E. Marquard from Cleveland, Ohio, a tall, thin, sharp-featured man "with a face like Woodrow Wilson," Marshall thought. "He had a very serious professional deportment and style of speaking, and was deeply spiritual, a mystic I believe. We differed somewhat in our respective approaches to theology, however; but that only added interest to our discussions. He taught me a great deal about the scriptures. We were good friends."

Another member of the Bettiah parish staff was Brother John Pias, an Indian from Mangalore. Br Pias ran an old fashioned letter press, printing in both English and Hindi. He had about twenty-five workers and favored hiring handicapped men and unemployed Indian Christians. Marshall saw in him a very quiet, serious, spiritual man who held strong ideas about justice and fairness. Marshall thought that in some ways Br Pias' feelings got the better of him. He reacted strongly to any lack of loyalty or any dishonesty on the part of his workers. Being very idealistic, Br Pias could not understand weakness of will nor the limited knowledge and low moral convictions of some of his workers. Marshall saw that this depressed him very much. "Br Pias had difficulty making allowances for any failings or weakness among his fellow Indians."

Marshall remembered Bettiah in general as "a backward, underdeveloped city. The streets were unpaved—dusty in winter, muddy in the monsoons. There were only one or two proper drug stores or, as the British would say, "chemist shops." And no electricity, so of course, no radio. The only newspapers available to us came up on the train from Patna and Calcutta. They usually arrived two or three days late, if at all. Without electric lights and reading by oil lamp at night, it wasn't long until my eyes began to trouble me. Since Bettiah had no proper optician, I had to travel all the way back to Patna by train, ferry and horse cart, to have glasses fitted at the medical college. After two years in Bettiah the bright lights of even a small town with electricity were a welcome sight to my poor eyes."

Fr Richard Welfle, who had accompanied Marshall out to India in 1929, was one of Marshall's Bettiah companions. Fr Welfle once described the "little town of Bettiah" as an "overgrown village with narrow, twisting lanes threading their way through a sprawling cluster of mud-walled, whitewashed houses. Years ago the town was much more impressive, for it then had something of the glamour of the East. It had a wealthy raja who maintained a splendid palace. He had elephants, camels, thoroughbred horses and the other trappings that usually go with Oriental royalty. But all that has gone with the wind." The place was "so insignificant that sometimes cartographers do not even bother to mark it on their maps. Yet the fact remains, that in one respect Bettiah really bulks plenty big on the horizon, for it can boast that it has the oldest and largest Catholic community in the whole of Patna Diocese. The little town will always rate a warm spot in my heart..."[8]

Fr Welfle lived in Bettiah for ten years. Fr Moran stayed for only two, but it left a lasting impression. Here is how Marshall described Bettiah, looking back after a lifetime of mission work elsewhere.

Looking Back
Life in Bettiah
Fr Moran

When I first came to Bettiah I was bothered by the noises at night, especially a high-pitched "whoop, whoop," the wailing bark of jackals, and the odors, some of them quite fetid. The sweet aromas of honeysuckle and other flowers in the garden were a pleasant counterpoint, especially during the winter months. The poverty, the dirt and the lack of sanitation in the city were rather shocking to me at first. I was surprised how fast I got used to all this. I sometimes thought about the danger of accepting it and coming to think that nothing needed to be done. I used to warn myself, and I told others, that "must not think that we can't make any improvements."

Nowadays, I'd roughly estimate that perhaps sixty to seventy percent of the noise, bad manners and lack of sanitation have disappeared. Now there are no more open sewers, and there is a better water supply so people can bathe more frequently. Education has taught them better manners; and they have more prosperity; their clothes are much better. Back in the 1930s, few children came to school with shoes on. Now no child would think of coming without shoes.

Among the inconveniences for us was the lack of electricity. That meant that every evening I had to prepare my oil lamp. I found that distasteful, not only because of the odor of the kerosene and the smoke, but the poor light it produced, even with it right at my elbow. And the heat from the lamp, it had to be so close. It attracted mosquitoes. Bettiah was plagued with mosquitoes. It is no exaggeration to say that there were twenty, thirty, or forty mosquitoes in my room every night, particularly during the hot season. I had to go to bed very carefully, sure to tuck the mosquito net very tightly. Just a few inches exposed or unfastened at the corner inevitably let in mosquitoes.

Aside from the annoyance of the biting and scratching, it is a scientific fact that these mosquitoes carried three or four virulent diseases that kept the Bettiah hospitals filled with patients. Malaria was only one and, by the grace of God, I never contracted it. An even more insidious disease was filariasis, which is sometimes called elephantiasis. The tiny parasitic filarial worm (*Wucheria bancrofti*) causes the legs and feet of many persons to swell. If untreated they never return to normal, but become more and more painful and disabling. In those early years there was no medicine to cure the disease. Only later, in the 1940s, was a medicine (*Diethylcorbamazine*) available that would arrest the disease, but would never restore the damage done to the body tissues.

There was also the dreaded leishmaniasis, or black fever, that Hindi speakers called "kala-azar." This disease is passed by sand flies (of the genus *Phlebotomus*). It attacks the spleen, liver and lymph nodes and is very debilitating. Another was breakbone fever (dengue fever) so-called, which rather cured itself after three or four painful days. And leprosy. There were many lepers in the market, on the roadsides, everywhere, showing their festering stumps of hands and feet, and begging.

I did not worry much about contracting diseases until my second year, when I began to suffer from repeated attacks of amoebic dysentery. The medicines used for dysentery in those days were not very good, especially the injections of emetine. They were painful and debilitating.

My health deteriorated when I had an attack of jaundice (contagious hepatitis) and I fell more seriously ill. At first I was sent to convalesce at the Dinapur cantonment near Patna in the company of one of the senior members of the mission. Then the superior and the Bishop formally recalled me from Bettiah and sent me to the hills to recover. I went to Kurseong, near Darjeeling in northern Bengal.

My illness proved to be a great blessing, of a sort. At Saint Mary's Seminary in Kurseong the climate was milder. And it was there that I completed my theological studies for the priesthood.

Notes to Chapter 6: Two Years in Bettiah
1. John K. Locke, SJ (personal communication, 1989).
2. Nowadays, more than forty priests carry on the various parish, school and social work of the church in Patna and vicinity.
3. On neo-Thomist thinking, see Jacques Maritain, *St Thomas Aquinas* (1933, and 1958) and Etienne Gilson, *The Philosophy of St Thomas Aquinas* (1924).
4. Henry Pascual Oiz, SJ, *Blessed of the Lord* (1991, p.128).

5. Urdu is still spoken in Bihar, but not as commonly as before 1947. With the partition of British India into separate Muslim and Hindu nation states, millions of Urdu speakers migrated to Pakistan. Urdu is now the national language of predominantly Muslim Pakistan.
6. All descriptions of the village schools on these pages are from Joseph A. Gschwend, SJ., *The Patna Mission, India* (1925, pp.14-19). While reading this account of these visits today, recall that they occurred in another time, the 1920s.
7. *Khair* (or *khar*) is a species of wild thatch grass commonly used as a roofing material in the villages.
8. Richard A. Wefle, SJ, *Pieces of India* (1963, p.67). Fr Welfle was one of the cohort of six young priests with whom Moran came out to India in 1929 (see Ch.3). Welfle lived and worked his entire career in the service of the Patna diocese. He died in India on May 15, 1987.

7

Ordination Studies at Kurseong

Selected for their spirit and learning, thoroughly and lengthily tested, and known with edification and satisfaction to all after various proofs of virtue and abnegation of themselves...
  St Ignatius of Loyola's ideal for professed priests

Marshall Moran left Bettiah in December 1932 for medical treatment, rest and recuperation at the parish house in Dinapur (or Danapur), a quiet suburb of Patna. He was twenty-six years old, still young but thin and weak from many months of recurring and debilitating bouts of amoebic dysentery combined with the jaundice of contagious hepatitis, two of the most common afflictions of India. He was told it would take at least six weeks of forced rest to regain his strength and some time beyond that before he would feel fully recovered.

11. Fr Moran in front of Xavier Hall, Godavari School, with his Ham radio antennas on the roof.

At Dinapur, Marshall was put in the care of the elderly, shy but busy Fr William I. Eline. Fr Eline was the pioneering first Jesuit superior of the Patna Mission, pastor of the Dinapur church, and chaplain for soldiers posted to the British Army's Dinapur cantonment. Eline also ran the mission's apostolic school; its library attracted Marshall like a magnet. Marshall spent as much time as he could in the library, reading philosophy and religion. He paid special attention to the nature of the holy scripture, revelation and inspiration. The books kept his mind off his illness and focused on his forthcoming theological studies.

The parish house, as he remembered it later, "had a beautiful garden, larger than a football field, with rose bushes and a very quiet environment. There I could get on with a lot of study and could read scripture knowing that the first source for theology is the revelation of God as we find it in the Old and New Testaments."

In this idyllic setting he actually enjoyed his recovery. The time passed quickly, and he steadily gained back some of his strength and health. The setting was comfortable, as the December weather on the Gangetic plain is mild, neither too cold nor too hot. "All I needed was a sweater in the evenings and a light blanket on the bed." At Christmas, he celebrated mass and a modest feast with several priests and fellow scholastics assigned to Patna and vicinity.

His sojourn at Dinapur marked a transition in Marshall's life and career, the beginning of a change from his role as a scholastic to being a "professor" in the Jesuit sense of the term. His superiors decided that it was time for him to resume formal theological studies towards his eventual completion, or "profession," of the four vows that bind Jesuits to their Society and to the work of the church. He was sent east into the West Bengal hills, to Saint Mary's Seminary at Kurseong, near Darjeeling. There, under the rigorous tutelage of priests from Belgium and Luxembourg, he began the last phase of the theological and philosophical studies in preparation for ordination, and the rest of his life as a fully professed Jesuit priest.

The Cold of Kurseong
Marshall started out from Patna by train on a morning in mid-January 1933, traveling down the broad Ganges valley first to Calcutta, then north to the town of Siliguri near the place where the Teesta River spills out of the Kanchenjunga foothills on to the plains. At Siliguri he boarded a coal-powered, smoke-belching narrow gauge railway for the ponderously slow, zig-zag ascent to his destination on a mountainside at five thousand feet elevation.

Its invigorating environment gave Kurseong a reputation as a health resort in addition to its fame as a scholarly religious center and retreat. After the insufferable heat of the plains, the cool, clean environment of the Himalayan foothills was refreshing to Marshall, even if not very warm.

The seminary's main building was a three-storey, thick-walled stone and stucco structure; and temperatures both inside and out were never quite comfortable. Its massive style was more appropriate to the hot plains than to the cool hills. The rooms were unheated, and the temperature sometimes fell below forty degrees Fahrenheit (four degrees Celsius.) at night. It took Marshall some time to get used to the cold nights and mornings, and while mornings tended to start out clear, by mid-day a thick cloud often enveloped the hillside, creating a damp and uncomfortable chill

"The climate was a shock," Marshall recalled later, "especially after two years on the hot plains of Bihar. When I arrived I had few warm clothes and had to borrow a sweater and woolen trousers from fellow students. Even summer was never very warm at St Mary's. It was always chilly. And although I can't say that I really suffered, I was never very comfortable. The cold was good for at least one thing—it kept me awake at my books!"

The only heated room was the library, where Marshall often studied and where he and other seminarians and the professors assembled informally each evening after their meal to talk, play board games or read for recreation.

St Mary's Belgian Priests

The rector of the Kurseong theologate was Fr Joseph Genicot, a genial, friendly, cheerful man who believed in a minimum of rules and regulations. Fr Genicot's non-interfering, non-threatening demeanor was respected and well liked by the staff and the young theologians alike.

The dean was Fr Joseph Pütz, one of Marshall's favorite teachers, a scholarly, studious and productive man. Fr Pütz had studied at one of the Jesuits' oldest universities, the Louvain in Belgium, as well as in Naples, Italy, and at Innsbruck in the Society's Austrian Province. Marshall remembered him as a man very much abreast of the times, frequently praised for his understanding and support of the growth of a dynamic religious scholarship. For over forty years Fr Pütz published a monthly theological magazine, *The Clergy Monthly* (now the *Vidyajyoti*), through which other priests in India were kept up to date on Catholic thinking. His work brought him great respect as one who understood scripture and church dogma, as he was widely acknowledged for his sound theological opinions and teachings. Years later he served as a special advisor to the Bishops of India at the 1962-63 Vatican II meeting in Rome.

During his four years at St Mary's, Marshall came to know Fr Pütz well. As Marshall described it, "Fr Pütz would come to me each morning with the day's lecture outline, neatly typed, which it was my job to duplicate for class. Sometimes we'd take walks in the seminary garden or along the Cart Road." The main road past St Mary's was called Cart Road because, in the old days before railroad or motor cars, travel to Darjeeling, fifteen miles away, was by ox-cart. Later it became a motorable road. Marshal and Fr Pütz usually walked the road by evening when traffic was light. It was a comfortable and scenic hike, one which "gave us a bit of refreshment, especially after a hard day of study." On these occasions they talked very frankly and honestly about mission policies and history, and sometimes compared North American and European methods and techniques with those of the Fathers in the nearby Indian missions at Patna, Ranchi, and Calcutta

Looking Back
Life at St Mary's Seminary
Fr Moran

St Mary's College was located at 5.454 feet in elevation on the side of a steep hill that drops off to the Cart Road and the railroad tracks, three hundred feet below. We sometimes heard the trains go by, but motor cars never. My room was on the ground floor, on the northwest corner of the big main building. From there I looked out westward over a drop of several thousand feet down into the Balasan River Valley. On a clear day, looking out of my window, I could see out over the Himalayan foothills and near mountains— although Mount Everest was hidden from view, except from the viewpoint atop Tiger Hill in Darjeeling. From my north window, however, I saw a magnificent panorama including Kanchenjunga, the world's third highest peak. It was especially inspiring, truly spectacular, by moonlight.

A main drawback to the location of the college was that it attracted frequent clouds and mist. As a result, winter mornings were foggy and damp. The place was rather infamously known among some students for its lack of sunlight and especially for its misty days. But I never felt it was oppressive. Just cold. It was an atmosphere good for study and reflection, and had a certain mystical dimension that made us give more attention to the inner life and to prayer. Many of my fellow Indian confreres, however, being from the plains, complained about the cold winters and wet summers both. Some suffered chilblains.

My days at St Mary's began at 5 o'clock in the morning. The bell would ring at five, but I would wake up at four to do simple ablutions (bathing) followed by my meditations, usually reflecting on a scriptural theme I had prepared the evening before. At six o'clock I went to the chapel for mass, followed by breakfast at 7:15. Breakfast was always very simple, typically cereal, a boiled egg, toast and some well-made coffee with creamy milk from the seminary's own dairy cows.

After breakfast I read the Greek New Testament for about ten minutes, just to keep up my Greek language. Then I would repeat the same passage from a Hindi Bible. I worked very hard on Hindi and often practiced it with fellow Indian seminarians. One of these was Martin Topno, who later became an outstanding priest in the mission at Ranchi, south of Patna. We frequently sat together on holidays making notes in Hindi for retreats and translating the *Spiritual Exercises*. Our goal was to prepare a retreat vocabulary in very simple Hindi within the grasp of high school students who participated or were interested.

From eight to nine o'clock each morning I prepared for the day's classes, and thereafter our day followed a very strict schedule. First lecture was at nine o'clock; the second was at ten. Eleven to twelve noon was a free time when we put our notes together and reflected on the morning lessons. Lunch was served promptly at twelve.

It may surprise some, but in those days we kept perfect silence around the house. There was no conversation, no talking, no socializing until after lunch.

Then we took a break from 12:15 until afternoon classes began at two o'clock. This was a time when we were free to walk outside in the sunshine (if there was any) to get a little exercise.

Afternoon classes were held at two and three o'clock. Tea was served, in the British style, at four, followed by an hour of outdoor games, if we felt up to it. Normally from about five to seven o'clock we studied quietly in our rooms or in the library.

Supper was always a very modest affair, rather austere, simple, but satisfying and sufficient. After the meal we'd customarily retire to the library for chatting and visiting with one another. Or sometimes we'd take a short walk around the garden, two or three or four of us together, discussing any topic imaginable. About half the time, as I recall, we talked about our classes, which were uppermost on our minds. The professors were also a frequent subject of conversation, or sometimes a companion, or plans for the Thursday holiday, or an upcoming picnic.

These late evening hours before retiring were very important, very meaningful to me. Often I would use the time to practice my Hindi or listen to the personal history of one of my companions, an Italian, a Spaniard or a Belgian, of their college days, or their memories of the Great War in 1914 to 1918, when they, like myself, were only ten or twelve years old. A time when memories go deep.

Fellow Seminarians

The company of students at St Mary's during Marshall's stay numbered about a hundred, almost half of whom were Indian. Marshall's class had twenty-six students, from six European countries, the USA, and India.[1]

Having so many nationalities and languages represented at the seminary was an advantage to the students. "Theological publications in English were limited, so we relied on many sources in French, German and Spanish. We needed students of these other languages to help us come to a better understanding of divine scripture, ethics, history, the New Testament, and the teachings of European church scholars."

One of his frequent companions was a young Indian scholastic named Kevin Angelo. Kevin was from Goa, the Portuguese colony on India's west coast. "Kevin and Richard Welfle were both ahead of me in the seminary, and they'd loan me their last year's notes to classes I was not taking. The notes, of course, were all in Latin, because our lectures were in Latin. Kevin's grasp of Latin was excellent, and his notes were remarkably clear and simple. By reading them ahead I could anticipate and prepare my mind, which made it easier to remember the lectures when I heard them." For nearly thirty years after his ordination, Fr Kevin Angelo served as a mission pastor in the Bettiah parish, where Marshall occasionally visited him.

The professors usually read their notes verbatim to class, all except Fr Pütz, who handed his notes out in printed form and used the class periods to elucidate the main points through discussion. Marshall never told his professors about the practice of passing on last year's notes. Looking back on it, however, he was sure that they knew.

Another of Marshall's friends at Kurseong was Joseph More, the Spaniard he had roomed with earlier while studying at Shambaganur. He was a very strong character, "a bit more Germanic than Spanish," Marshall thought, "rather serious, but rugged and blunt." At the time they could only speak to each other in Latin, as Marshall did not speak Spanish and the scholastics were not allowed to converse in their native languages. It was one of the many rules of the seminary.

And, as at Shambaganur, in Kurseong, Joseph and Marshall continued their habit of holding long and wide-ranging philosophical discussions on such topics as the mystery of free will and of evil and suffering in the world. They also practiced a sort of linguistic crossword puzzle, translating the Psalms in columns across a page from Septuagint Greek and Vulgate Latin into English, Sanskrit, Gujarati (the language Fr More was expecting to use for the rest of his life in western India) and Hindi (the language Fr Moran used in north India).

They also discussed a great deal of theology, Joseph More from the perspective of the Spanish metaphysicist Francis Suarez and Marshall from the view of a neo-Thomist. Joseph, however, was unimpressed with Thomist thought at first, but by 1936 when he left the seminary he was won over to this form of metaphysics.

Another near neighbor in the seminary quarters was an Italian scholastic named Cyrus Starace, "Ciro" for short. Ciro was from Naples and the nephew of one of the men of the Quadrum Virs, the four companions of Benito Mussolini in 1922 when he marched on Rome in his rise to power as the fascist leader of Italy. In contrast to that part of his family heritage, Marshall remembered Ciro as "a mild-mannered person, gentle, thoughtful, very considerate of others, and not easily ruffled. He often spoke vividly of his youth in Italy, of starvation during World War I and of the sufferings of his own family members who, although they were supposed to be of the nobility and presumably affluent, nonetheless had a very difficult time surviving. Perhaps that experience is what influenced his uncle toward the radical fascist politics of Mussolini. But it also influenced Ciro's mild approach as a priest. It is interesting how a single event can trigger such different reactions in people who experience it."

When Marshall first met Ciro, he thought him cold and unemotional; yet he soon saw in his friend an openness to new ideas, and they easily became the best of companions. Ciro was later posted to South India. "We did not keep up a very strong correspondence. I never saw Ciro again after 1936, and soon lost contact with him. Perhaps it was my fault. I am not a very good letter writer, being easily distracted by daily duties. It is hard for me to find the time."

Moral Philosophy and Liberalism

One of Marshall's regular mental exercises in the seminary was the study of morals from *The Book of Cases*. He and Fr Gus Wildermuth would often discuss various ethical and moral principles from the book for a few minutes just before dinner each evening. The case book helped students prepare for a variety of problems and dilemmas they might encounter in life, or that they might hear described by parishioners in the confessional. "The purpose of this study was not to wax metaphysical or abstract, but to be able to give short, clear, decisive explanations and advice based on the traditional rules and teaching of the church, especially those of the Ten Commandments."

Marshall's training in moral philosophy followed what the Jesuits call "probabilism". When a Jesuit is in doubt as to the meaning of the law he constructs a probable opinion; that is, an opinion that is reasonable, based on teachings or opinions of good teachers, well-known theologians and moralists and, especially, of the saints. Jesuits do not independently construct an opinion, but seek one in the authority of well known moral theologians. Where the authorities appear to disagree, the rule of thumb is to side with the majority; that is, with the probable opinion of the larger number of authorities. "We Jesuits tend to follow the more liberal and easier opinions," Marshall once explained, "which means that after three hundred years of the teaching of morals, there is a strong spirit of liberalism among Jesuits. This is quite the opposite of the puritanical obligation to uphold a stricter or harder opinion. To prepare ourselves as Jesuits we are required, particularly, to study carefully the teachings of St Alphonsus Ligouri, a strong defender of liberalism."

Jesuits are sometimes criticized by more conservative elements in the church for their liberal approach. Yet, that very liberalism is considered by many others as one of the Society's major strengths in the face of many conflicting situations in the modern world. As Marshall well knew, liberalism can be a double-edged sword, and over time (well beyond his stay at Kurseong) some expressions of it in society, and especially within the church, disturbed him. He also had misgivings about what could be heard or seen being done on the Indian scene by some of the followers of Mahatma Gandhi.

Gandhi avowed "passive resistance," the non-violent liberal philosophy and social movement with which he confronted the troubling political and social inequities of his time. What bothered Marshall, however, was the extremes to which such liberal thinking could be taken—were being taken—by people whose purposes were ostensibly noble, no doubt, based on high social or political ideals. But he interpreted many of those defiant and confrontational acts as lacking true brotherhood and love.

The basis of Gandhi's passive resistance was belief in "the approach, the underlying philosophy, and the technique... of a new kind of resistance," based on the concept of *satyagraha*, a Sanskrit term that he interpreted to mean "truth-force" or the power of truth, force born of truth and love or nonviolence."[2] In his thinking, Marshall was sympathetic to the opinions of R.R. Diwaker who wrote about Gandian philosophy and *satyagraha* at some length. Diwaker felt that Gandhi had slanted the Sanskrit term to his purposes, distorting its original meaning from "truth-force" to something ultimately more powerful and potentially more harmful.[3] Diwaker wrote that "Passive resistance, as commonly understood in the West in its historical setting and as understood by us now, is a weapon of the weak, of the unarmed and helpless. It does not eschew violence as a matter of principle but only because of lack of means of violence, or out of sheer expediency. It would use arms if and when they are available or when on account of their use there is reasonable chance of success. Passive resistance may even be preparatory to or go hand in hand with armed resistance. The underlying object is to harness the opponent and thus force him into the desired course of action. *Love has no place in it. ...It cannot become a philosophy of life."*[4]

At one level, working from his own experiences watching satyagraha in action, in the India of the 1930s and 1940s (and to a much smaller extent later in Nepal, during the revolution of 1990), Marshall equated it loosely, during the 1970s and 1980s, with Liberation Theology, which some activist priests in the church have practiced in the face of serious social and political injustice, especially in Latin America. What Marshall knew of Liberation Theology he had read (he had no direct experience). He was distressed by the moral implications of both *satyagraha* and Liberation Theology, but particularly the latter because it involved many Catholic priests. To him, it implied both spiritual and temporal weakness, something he clearly eschewed. He was concerned about "the political slant, or bias, that Liberation Theology gives to Christian activity, to the Bible itself. It skirts dangerously on politics," he said, "and priests involved in politics is something of which our present Pope and his predecessors did not approve. They want to see fundamental human rights guaranteed, of course, but they do not think that priests are the ones to lead directly in resistance, in defiance, in *satyagraha*. If it is political, that means there are factions—extreme right, extreme left, and so-called conservatives and radicals. And this leads to disunity, right into the church itself, which should never be permitted."

Within the church, Liberation Theology raises three contentious issues—priests involved in party politics (running for office), class warfare (after Marxism), and the use of violence as a means of action. Marshall, like many priests, fully realized the need for social justice, progress, change, improvement—but not by violence.

All of this weighed on him in his thoughts and meditations over the years; and it profoundly influenced his thinking as a priestly counselor and confessor; and as a kind of activist, himself, albeit at the more conservative end of the spectrum.

Spiritual counseling, especially from within the confessional, is an important aspect of every Jesuit's life. Their role as confessors to the faithful is something for which the Society is well known and proud. As a student, Marshall prepared himself for this part of the priestly role through seminary course work in moral philosophy, theology and logic, pursuing probabilism as well as other forms of casuist reasoning, in order to deal with everyday questions of right and wrong, truth and untruth, good and evil, love and hate. Historically, priests of the Society of Jesus have become quite well known for their skill as confessors and counselors to all manner of Catholic men and women—from the rich and powerful in seventeenth and eighteenth century Europe, to the poor and powerless on the front lines of today's widely scattered world missions.

Some historians describe the Jesuit confessional as attractively flexible, even lenient, and spiritually comforting to the repentant believer. Their generally relaxed and rational style of hearing and responding to all manner of human faults has led one historian to praise the Jesuits for their legacy of success in reforming the system, in changing the role of the priest-confessor away from the image of stern magistrate to that of a wise and warm-spirited adviser and, in short, for turning the once "gloomy rite of penitence and absolution into a kind of spiritual counseling service."[5] Every Jesuit is admonished by Ignatius, himself, "not to allow anyone to leave the confessional entirely without comfort."[6]

At St Mary's, Marshall's attentions were very scriptural; he paid special attention to the life of Christ and to the New Testament letters of Saint Paul. He concentrated on the great apostle's theology about the mystical body of Christ. "I selected this topic as my main theme for the year of 1933, because it epitomizes the inner essence of the Catholic Church. Of course, the church is also visible through its bishops, the Pope and the priestly hierarchy. But I had long before reached the conclusion that this visible aspect, the human side, was the weaker side of the church"—and it was this weaker dimension that especially bothered him. "I wanted to get down to its spiritual essence, to the grace of God given to Christians through baptism. It is this spiritual aspect that links us with Christ and with one another. Through Christ we are all joined together in what we call the 'mystical body' of the church."

He remembered Fr Pütz and others of his mentors recommending many excellent treatises and special studies—"textbooks and more textbooks!" as Marshall put it—on these topics, particularly on the essential, invisible, spiritual church. The seminary had an excellent library of Catholic theology in modern languages, as well as medieval and early church publications in Latin and Greek. There, Marshall was able to study the writings of some of the first great theologians of the church, early saints like Basil the Great, Origen, Chrysostom and Augustine. He found a great deal of wisdom in them, wisdom with which to deal with daily life and face a troubled world.

Keeping Up with World Events

Each Thursday was a holiday at the seminary. The students called it "ville day," and if the weather was warm they would go on hikes, sometimes all the way down the ridge to the riverside, two thousand feet below. Marshall remembered those hikes with pleasure. "Although it was only seventy or seventy-five degrees Fahrenheit down there by the river—I say 'only' because I was used to the greater heat of the plains compared with the cool of Kurseong—it was heavenly. It was warm enough for us to bathe in the river. I couldn't go on these hikes during my first year at the seminary, however, because I was still recuperating from my illness, still taking medicines, and still weak. I found walking difficult and painful until my second year. It was only then, with a little therapy and gentle exercise, that the discomfort passed away and I got back to normal. Once I could hike again in the fresh mountain air I felt much better." When he wasn't out on a hike he began each Thursday with special studies in the library, and in the afternoon he practiced his Hindi.

Part of Sunday, too, was a holiday of sorts. Sunday mornings featured high mass in the chapel. This was a formal event with deacons and sub-deacons. On feast days (set aside to honor the Lord, the Virgin Mary, or a saint) the mass was especially colorful and pompous. Sunday afternoons were very special but for a different reason; it was the one day each week when Marshall caught up on world events and indulged in his passion for the news, although he never looked at a daily newspaper nor heard the radio during his four years in Kurseong. Rather, he read and heard about the news second hand, in periodicals at the library and, occasionally, when the staff (who had the only radio) reported what they considered important for the students to know.

In this roundabout way he learned of the dramatic events in Europe that led to the rise of Nazism and the second world war. In 1933 and 1934 he learned, with keen interest and concern, news of the burning of the Reichstag, Germany's Imperial Diet, and of Hitler's rapid ascent to dominance in German politics. Years later he would recount to the boys in his school classes in Patna, and in Kathmandu, how the Nazis rose to power and changed the face of Europe and the history of the world. Many of Hitler's tyrannical acts were designed to quash political freedom and human rights, he would tell them.

Stalin's repressive acts in the Soviet Union were also happening about this time. The notion of forced collectivization disturbed Marshall with its dislocation and waste of human life, and the widespread starvation that followed it.

Spain, too, was the focus of great troubles and worry to humanity. While living at Bettiah in 1931 and 1932, Marshall remembers reading about the riots and disturbances caused by the Leftists and the labor unions, especially in Catalonia, northern Spain. They soon erupted into the Spanish Civil War of 1936-39.

All of this troubling news meant a great deal to him now as he listened to his European classmates at the seminary retell events of the previous few years and describe their worries about the families and friends left behind at home. "There I was in Kurseong, in my theology, with many Spanish fellow seminarians. I listened to their version of the events of 1932 and their explanations of the cause of all the chaos in their home country, about which I was reading: the labor unions with loyalties to communism, which meant loyalty to Stalin's cause and Soviet machinations, and so many subversive activities, bombings and murders and assassinations, and the burning of Catholic convents and churches. Sad reading it was."

He was quite surprised at the amount of suffering in Europe— the food and fuel shortages, the repression of human rights and the human spirit, the preparations for war, all "lessons from history" as he called them when he taught his students in later years. "Much of it was virtually ignored or avoided by Americans at the time," he thought. "Few people realized the great poverty of Europe after the Great War, during the 1920s and 1930s. Americans in those days rather avoided the negative and depressing points of the news, while nowadays, I think, they exaggerate it."

"The future of the world, not only of Europe and the United States, worried me. Franklin Roosevelt was just elected president, and I put a lot of trust in his abilities. But I noticed in the English weeklies and from reaction in magazines from America strong feelings both for and against Mr Roosevelt. Some people thought him as a 'savior,' but critics called him a 'dictator.' Extreme opinions."

Marshall recalled with a touch of bitterness that "one leader in the group against President Roosevelt was my own city's daily newspaper, the Chicago *Tribune*. It haughtily gave itself the title of 'The World's Greatest Newspaper,' run by its erratic proprietor, Colonel Robert McCormick, who found fault with everything Roosevelt did."

"Another voice against the president was a Catholic priest from Detroit named Charles Edward Coughlin. In the 1930s he was known as 'the radio priest,' broadcasting extreme anti-Roosevelt opinions to an estimated 10 million listeners in North America. His style was dramatic, very rhetorical and rabble-rousing. Fr Coughlin went on to oppose Roosevelt in 1936 by forming the Union Party. By the early

1940s his preachings became very pro-Nazi and anti-Semitic until, only in 1942, he was finally silenced by his superiors."

"So it was," in Marshall's summation, "that during my Sunday afternoons at Kurseong I dipped into the secular world, the world beyond our isolation in the Himalayan foothills, the world of economics and politics. I thought it an important thing for me to do, to know what was going on in the world at large to prepare myself for teaching. But it was disturbing and quite depressing." It all raised in his mind and, he noted, in the thinking and writing of many others of that time, some basic and serious moral and theological questions about the nature of Western civilization.

He also studied Indian affairs. Every two weeks the students and staff held a seminar on Indian history and philosophy. To understand Hindu teachings they read deeply of Hindu theology and mysticism, especially the Vedas and the Bhagavad Gita. They also studied Islamic and Buddhist thought and theology. The India seminar was conducted by Fr Turmes, a Belgian priest who was himself a respected philosopher, theologian, and historian. The seminar was entirely voluntary, but Marshall never missed a meeting in all four years. In his last year he was elected president of the group.

Magazines for India

Not all his activities were academic, In Marshall's first year, for one or two hours a week right after lunch, a group of American and several Belgian seminarians voluntarily collected and remailed American and European Catholic magazines from Kurseong to several hundred addresses across India. The magazines included the Jesuit weekly *America* from New York City, the popular *Sign* magazine from the Passionate Fathers of New Jersey, as well as *Commonweal*, *Catholic World* and several others. The mailing list included university professors, libraries in Calcutta, Benares, Delhi, Bombay and Madras, and selected politicians and social leaders. Besides their theological themes, these magazines and papers printed essays on the economic, social and political affairs of the time.

Marshall took full charge of this extracurricular activity in his second year at Kurseong, recruiting other students to help. The mailing list included the young Jawaharlal Nehru, then an up-and-coming Indian politician. "Nehru was quite interested in writing on social issues in particular. Even when he was imprisoned for his nationalistic activities in opposition to British rule, our mailings continued to reach him through his wife and friends at Allahabad, his home city." Later, when Marshall read Nehru's autobiography, he recognized various thoughts, themes and commentaries on social theory and human welfare from the magazines he and his colleagues had sent from their hill top seminary in West Bengal.

Living so far from home, the seminarians and priests all depended on the erratic local postal system to keep in touch with friends and family in America and Europe, and remote parts of the Indian subcontinent. And the seminary leaders depended on the Indian post to keep in touch with church offices in Calcutta and those in other far distant parts of India. Marshall was especially conscious of the postal system and its foibles because of his responsibility for mailing out all the periodicals and in his frequent correspondence with his mother back in Chicago. Occasionally there was trouble.

Looking Back
Corrupt Officials
Fr Moran

In 1934 we began to notice that some mail from the college was not getting through to its destination. Somebody, somewhere, was stealing our letters, probably not for reading but for their uncancelled stamps. Sometimes our mailings numbered hundreds of items. The value of stamps on just one piece of mail might equal a half day's wage of one of the lowly postal clerks. Considering that a clerk could collect in one day well over a month's wage from the resale of stamps from our heavily stamped mailings, it must have been very tempting. Suspicion fell immediately on employees of the Kurseong Post Office.

We filed a complaint with higher authorities in Calcutta, and a few days later a postal detective arrived. First, he counted the stamped letters leaving the seminary, then he watched as they were put into a locked bag for delivery to the post office. There the detective watched unobtrusively as the mail was put into the hands of the postal clerks. When the mail was finally carried out to the train, he stopped the process for inspection. As suspected, our letters were missing. Unscrupulous clerks had set them aside to remove the uncancelled stamps, then destroy the evidence. They were sacked immediately.

Only a year before, when I was still living in Bettiah, another incident occurred with the mail. My mother, who wrote frequently, got an envelope back marked "Undeliverable—Addressee Unknown—No Forwarding Address". Mother was upset. She knew I was in Bettiah. We had been exchanging letters for a year and a half already. So she took action, and before I knew it she had written to the U.S. Senator from Illinois. He, in turn, contacted the Postmaster General of India directly.

It is unbelievable the action taken by the Indian authorities. The Postmaster General sent a special investigator all the way up to Bettiah from Bombay. In those days Bombay was the official port of entry for all foreign mail arriving in India.

One day this stranger arrived at my door and said, "Your students tell me you are Marshall Moran. And you've lived here long? You haven't been away?"

I told him I had gone briefly into Patna a few times. "But I am well known in this town," I said, "and the parish priest takes care of my mail when I'm gone."

"Well," he said, "there has been a complaint from the United States that this post office has not been delivering your mail. So we are dismissing the Bettiah Postmaster."

And it was done. Just like that. One example of the unfair way of life among many of the lower government officials.

Counterfeit money also gave us trouble. One day I gave a boy two silver rupees to buy a ticket home on the train for holiday. In a few minutes he was back. He couldn't buy the ticket, he said, because the rupees were "bad." I knew that I had given him silver rupees, because I always tested them. We would drop them on the floor to listen for the clear metallic ring of the silver; counterfeits had a dull sound to them. All coins in our money box were good. The boy didn't know that, however, and had somehow been tricked. The ones he now handed back to me were counterfeits.

"Come with me," I said. "We're going to the station. *Jaldi!* Quickly! Before the ticket agent goes off duty."

I went first to my friend the station master and said, "I'd like you to come with me. I have a complaint against the man at window number two. He's switching counterfeit money for good silver, then telling people their coins are 'bad' and cheating them."

Sure enough, behind the window we found a box of counterfeit rupees. Of course the agent didn't dare trick everyone, only the poor ignorant, those who wouldn't catch on or, if they did, were too afraid to approach the station master's office to complain. To get into his office they'd have to pay a bribe and they weren't going to pay a rupee just to save a rupee.

These sorts of problems taught me rather quickly about the dark side of local culture and of the unfair dealings and injustices that the poor and illiterate in particular had to endure. India, of course, has no monopoly on corruption, and Indian ways are not all bad. I have many more memories of the bright side, the good people and the wonderful things of life there.

Master of Ceremonies for the Mass
In his second and third years at St Mary's, Marshall served as Master of Ceremonies for the mass. It was his job to select the priests and

arrange during the year for volunteers to handle various ritual duties. He took care of the ceremonial parts, the movement of the lectors (readers) and the priests. His most elaborate preparations were on the occasion of Holy Week each spring. "Palm Sunday mass began with a special choir singing the *Lamentations of Jeremiah* and selections from Palestrina. The Good Friday and Easter Sunday services were especially rich and colorful. They have been simplified in recent years."

He considered it a great privilege. "And although it consumed a lot of time in preparations, it certainly kept me busy and interested." He also served as a sort of guest master, guiding visiting clerics around the seminary. "I met many visiting priests and bishops and became especially friendly with the Archbishop of Calcutta, Monsignor Perier."

Monsignor Perier came up to St Mary's several times during the year. Each November he conducted the year's ordination ceremonies. Sometimes when he went on up to Darjeeling, he invited Marshall along to serve as his personal master of ceremonies. "I helped him put on his mitre and arrange his crozier, a special staff, and his *cappa magna*, a long cape which I called his 'tail'. Archbishop Perier always wore a ring, and a small red skull cap, both of which he'd take off at certain points during the mass."

One time during Pentacost, when Marshall was staying at the Archbishop's house in Darjeeling, he overheard some classical music being played on the library piano. He entered quietly at the back and sat listening. "The Monsignor never played in public, and his fellow Jesuits never really knew how accomplished a pianist he was. When he looked up and saw me sitting there, enjoying the music, he challenged me. 'Can you name that piece?' he asked. 'A Chopin mazurka,' I answered. That pleased him, and he played some etudes as an encore. The following November, in the evening after my own ordination, when various priests gave little speeches and we sat around listening to music in the library, I asked the Monsignor if he would play some Chopin for me. 'Of course,' he said, 'but I have no music'—at which I produced sheet music of several selections I'd heard him practice earlier."

"Afterward, some of the old Belgian Fathers who had lived with the Archbishop for so long, one of them for at least forty years, congratulated me on so successfully persuading him to play. They had tried many times without result, they said. It just showed how considerate Msgr Perier was and how friendly and yielding, provided you could anticipate his excuses."

Final Preparations for Ordination

By January 1935 Marshall was planning ahead for his anticipated ordination. He more carefully focused his time on the practice of the spiritual life and on sacred readings, "to be more prayerful, more recollected, to understand more about the life of grace and union with God and with the saints. To be fully prepared," as he put it.

He especially concentrated on the sacraments, which were the topic of study that year by his professors. He mastered St Augustine's commentary on the Gospel of St John, paying special attention to the promises of the Holy Eucharist, or Holy Communion. He also pursued special studies on various medieval writers of the mass and delved into the history of the Reformation and Counter Reformation in regards to the mass and the sacraments.

The Counter Reformation ran from the mid-sixteenth to the mid-seventeenth centuries, during which time heresies were eradicated and reforms accomplished within the Roman church. A main event was the Council of Trent (1545-63), called by Pope Paul III to counter the challenges of Protestantism, to clarify doctrine and to strengthen church authority. One outcome of the Counter Reformation was the creation of the Society of Jesus by Ignatius Loyola. The Jesuits were established to be the "Pope's men," to serve as the church's "fighting unit" as educators and as missionaries to the far corners of the globe.

Later, reflecting on this phase of his studies, on the subject of the sacraments, the Protestant Reformation and the effects of the church's Counter Reformation, Marshall offered what he called "a bit of theology" in this observation: "Our Anglican and Lutheran fellow Christians have now come back, so to say, more closely reconciling to the traditional Catholic belief in the real presence of Christ in the Eucharist, and in the continuation of the sacrifices. It is not a question of repeating the sacrifice, for it continues as something eternal. Christ does not change His mind, but in eternity He remains our savior and redeemer. We can make the offering, but the sacrifice is forever."

Marshall also gave special attention to the theology of St Paul. "The only treatise available on St Paul to me at Kurseong was an English translation of the work of a French priest named Prat. Today there are abundant translations from writers in German, Spanish, French and other languages, and other treatises to refer to in English. For some of my theological studies, I read the *Verbum Dei*, a publication from the Gregorian University in Rome, as well as the *Theological Quarterly* from Fordham University in the United States. I also remember reading the American *Theology Digest*, edited by one of my fellow novices from St Louis University days."

On November 12, 1935, after three years of study at St Mary's, Marshall and thirty-nine other young men were ordained into the priesthood. "We were a great mixture of nationalities—American, British, Indian, French, Italian, German, Spanish, and others." This group included the twenty-six in his class and fourteen others from earlier classes who had only just finished their studies.

The ordination service was conducted by Archbishop Perier. Marshall was "well prepared for all the pomp and ritual of the occasion, having assisted the Archbishop the previous years as his master of ceremonies. But it was still the most exhilarating experience of my life. For three weeks we practiced the sequence of the liturgy in all its parts, learning when to stand, when to kneel, when to prostrate ourselves face down on the ground at the beginning of the mass, when to recite the confession of sins, and so forth. The great moment came when my hands were bound, as is the custom, and I was anointed with oil. Then I pledged my vows and proclaimed the Profession of Faith."

In the moment of ordination, Marshall Denis Moran became the priest he had sought to become since his youth, having successfully passed the series of rigorous scholastic examinations and proven his theological abilities and religious qualities as a man. During ordination, he took on the full responsibilities of the Catholic priesthood. A few years later, after the requisite tertianship (a long retreat of serious recollection and prayer) he proclaimed his final solemn vow and entered the ranks of the fully professed Jesuit priests. That fourth vow is a special Jesuit vow imposed by St Ignatius, swearing special obedience to the Pope. It is this fourth vow that distinguishes Jesuits from other priests of the church, and fully professed Jesuits from others within the order.

He had not become the doctor his mother had once so fervently wished him to be, but he was now the priest that she had ultimately agreed he should be. She had already taken up responsibility for raising money to help the Jesuit Indian Mission. And although he missed her presence at his ordination (no family members were there to witness the event), he now moved forward in his calling with her special blessing and support.

Leaving St Mary's

Following ordination, Marshall stayed on at Kurseong for one more year to complete his studies of theology. For that he finished several treatises on theology and put the final touches on special retreat studies that he anticipated leading once he had left the seminary and returned to the Patna Diocese.

"It was a wonderful day. On the eleventh of November 1936, at the eleventh hour in the morning, I finished up my last oral examination. It had gone on for two hours that morning, all in Latin. I felt confident in completing my studies. Now I could say they were over. I was just thirty years old."

Marshall departed Kurseong at the end of November 1936. He took the narrow-gauge train from Kurseong down to Siliguri, then boarded a standard gauge train for the overnight ride back to Patna. His traveling companion was his good friend Fr Joseph More. After getting settled in their sleeper coach, an Indian man came in and sat in the berth opposite. It was early evening but not yet time to sleep, so the two priests sat on their lower berth talking quietly in the gathering darkness. Marshall was relaxed and happy, and he once admitted as he recounted the story to friends, that he felt a bit mischievous that evening. He glanced across the aisle and thought he recognized the stranger.

Looking Back
The Man on the Train
Marshall Moran

"I think I know that man," I whispered to Fr More.

"How could you" More asked. "You've been up in the hills for four years at your studies. You haven't been down here, and you've never lived in this area. How could you possibly know him?"

"He's a singer," I said.

"You're just guessing."

"No. I'm positive. He's a singer. He works for the railway, and he's a Bengali. He doesn't speak much Hindi."

Fr More was taken aback. "The man has no uniform. How can you say that he works for the railway?"

I was having a bit of fun with Fr More. And how did I know all about the stranger in the same compartment? Because I had met him on the train a year earlier, during my only trip away from Kurseong during those four years of study. I'd gone to Patna the previous winter to be fitted for new glasses. My eyes had become weaker—all that reading, I guess. I stayed in Patna only for three days, though; they were very strict with scholastics in those days, and I didn't want to appear to abuse the privilege. I wanted to show my seriousness, my obedience, as it was called, so I returned back immediately.

It was on the return journey that I met the man. I was riding in an empty coach when the ticket collector came aboard. He didn't ask for my ticket, but began, instead, to ask me questions, like "Where are you going?" and "What are you doing?". He was practicing his English on me.

So I went along with him and talked in English. After awhile I told him, "You have a very nice voice. Are you also a singer?"

"Yes," he said, somewhat surprised; he was a singer.

And I said, "You don't know Hindi, but you speak Bengali." To which he responded, "Yes. How do you know that?"

"By the way you pronounce your vowels."

Bengali speakers can be recognized in English by the way they handle "a" and "o" sounds, for example. Where a Hindi speaker says "Ganga" for the River Ganges, a Bengali says something like "Gongo." Or compare the Hindi word *"jal,"* for water, with the Bengali *"jol."* And so forth. I teased him about it, and told him how often I amused myself by trying to place a person's place of birth or where he had studied by his accent, even in English.

Then I asked the man if he would sing a Bengali song for me. He hesitated, as he was a bit shy. So I urged him by striking a bargain.

"It you sing a Bengali song," I said, "I will sing one in Hindi."

"You can sing a Hindi song?" he asked incredulously.

"Yes," I said, "but not until I hear your Bengali song."

So there we were in this otherwise empty train car, singing in Bengali and Hindi to each other! And, now, a year later we were sitting across from each other in the same train. I turned to him and said, "Weren't you on this train a year ago? Aren't you a ticket collector?"

"Yes, I am," he said. Fr More was impressed.

"And you are a Bengali?" I asked.

"Yes."

"And you sing?" I said.

He looked puzzled. He didn't recognize me. It was dark in the coach, and he couldn't see my face. "Yes," he said. "How do you know?"

I reminded him of our travels together the year before.

"Yes, yes," he said. "Now I remember you. Yes, and you sang a Hindi song."

The three of us had a great laugh at the coincidence.

In the morning the train arrived at Patna, and the traveling companions parted company. Frs Moran and More took a horse cart to the Bishop's House. Their Bengali friend continued on his journey.

Several years had passed since Marshall first arrived in Patna as a young, inexperienced scholastic from America. Now he had come full circle, returning as a mature, professed priest of the Order. Well over a half century of work lay ahead of him, during which he would serve the Society as a priest, educator, and mission builder. Over the years since then, he often thought back with nostalgia on his school days at St Mary's, Kurseong. It was a high point in his preparations for the priesthood. "They were wonderful days, studying theology with such experienced professors, and having access to the seminary's good library. It meant a lot to me. And I often think of the companionship I had enjoyed with so many fine young scholastics from India, America, and Europe. I couldn't have gotten any better training in America, I knew, having already studied there. At Kurseong I learned so much about India, its history, its politics, its religions and its people, all of which stood me in good stead and prepared me well for the work ahead."

Notes to Chapter 7: Ordination Studies at Kurseong

1. By comparison, Marshall's class at Shambaganur a few years earlier consisted of the nine seminarians from India, five from Belgium, four from the United States, three from Italy, two from Spain and one each from Britain, Malta and Yugoslavia.
2. R.R. Diwaker, *Saga of Satyagraha* (1969, pp.1-2).
3. One could argue, of course, that Gandhi's concept of Satyagraha was entirely virtuous, but that some who called themselves "Ghandians" distorted its meaning or essence in carrying it out.
4. Diwaker, *Saga of Satyagraha* (1969, p.2). Diwaker lists the vows, rules, pledges and constructive program of satyagraha in Appendices 5-8, (pp.225-234).
5. Manfred Barthel, *Jesuits: History and Legend of the Society of Jesus* (1931, p.87). More conservative writers, however, claim that this sort of liberalism is the Jesuits' failing. In one particularly vitriolic account, Jesuit liberalism is said to account for a "betrayal" of the tenets of the church (Malachi Martin, *The Jesuits*, 1987).
6. Ignatius Loyola, quoted by Manfred Barthel in *Jesuits: History and Legend of the Society of Jesus* (1931, p.86).
7. Giovanni Pierluigi da Palestrina (1515?-1594) has been called "The greatest composer of liturgical music of all time" according to the *Catholic Encyclopedia* (www.newadvent.org). During his lifetime Palestrina had many assignments with the church in Rome, including choirmaster at Saint Peter's Basilica and composer to the papal chapel in the Vatican. Many of the liturgical compositions that this Prince of Music composed, including madrigals, motets, psalms, hymns and masses, are still sung. He was especially noted for his version of the ever popular Gregorian chant. Altogether, his complete works fill thirty-three volumes. Palestrina's offertories for the ecclesiastical year may have been what Fr Moran meant when he described the elaborate preparations, including the music, that he oversaw during the seminary's Holy Week observances.

8

The Patna Years

Fix your mind on me;
Be devoted to me;
Sacrifice to me;
Prostrate yourself before me (your God).
I promise truly,
For you are dear to me.
    Bhagavad Gita (XVIII-65)[1]

Arriving in Patna, the newly ordained Reverend Marshall Denis Moran, SJ, anticipated his formal assignment somewhere in the Patna Diocese. But first, before his superiors could address his long term future, there was a more immediate job to be done. Marshall was placed in charge, for a week, of mission headquarters while the bishop and all the other priests were away at meetings. His responsibility included the Kurji School, Dinapur cantonment and the Patna cathedral. He was accompanied only by a newly arrived priest, his old friend and fellow novice from seminary days at Florissant, Fr Francis Welzmiller. "It shows you," he said later, "how in those days there were so few Christians and so few institutions in the diocese that two of us could look after the whole bit. Today, of course, they need thirty or forty priests to do it. And there is so much to keep up with now—various social works, the church press, a novitiate, a house of studies, several boys' schools and a hospital. And there we were, we two "greenhorns," so to say, just out of studies, running the whole works by ourselves."

Jesuit Organization
While Marshall had little real authority that week beyond minor caretaker functions, the general administration and management of a mission like the Patna Diocese and its outlying stations were not uncomplicated. Jesuit operations worldwide are large and many-faceted. Patna was no exception. The Society's streamlined organization and efficiency are often commented upon and mimicked by admirers and detractors alike. Several other Catholic men's orders

and sisterhoods are modeled on the system of governance so carefully designed so long ago by Ignatius of Loyola.[2]

By the mid-1930s, the staff of Patna Diocese looked after the usual range of Jesuit mission work, including the management of the priests' activities, preaching the gospel, teaching, ministering to local Christians and writing. In Patna there was the Bishop's House to look after as well as pastors living at Dinapur and the running of the Christian Brothers' School and St Michael's High School. In addition, there were pastors in outlying schools at Khagaul, Gaya, Bhagalpur, Bettiah, Chuhari, Chakni, Samastipur, Latonah, Rampur and Marpa. The main retreat house for the diocese was at Ranchi, a hundred miles from Patna.

Each functional house in the Jesuit plan has a father superior, who reports upwards to the father provincial. One of several consultors helps the superior of the house with administrative chores and activities. They are drawn from the members of the house. A minor superior, for example, may be assigned to manage house finances. A spiritual father serves house members and the wider community with spiritual advice and direction. And, as necessary, there may be a lesser superior in charge of a library, the health of the house, a farm operation, a printing press, or whatever is important to the upkeep of the house and its residents. Ultimately, everybody assigned to a mission performs an important function and the roles are rotated to make the best use of available talent and technical or administrative skills.

Life throughout a diocese in its various houses is communal and austere, functioning under the universal vow of poverty of its members. It is closely regulated in part through the vow of obedience. House life is conducted without undo harshness or discomfort to the members, however, and corporate unity and a consensus oriented around the fundamental principles of the Society is sought in all matters.

The life and operations of diocese, parish, house and schools are not without their problems, often personal and idiosyncratic; but the lines of communication are ostensibly always open at all levels. Communications help alleviate or anticipate problems. Even then, priests and others assigned to a house, for example, may find it difficult or not to their liking, and personal animosities between individuals may make daily life uncomfortable. In difficult cases, some individuals may be transferred or may leave the Society altogether, abandoning their vows and returning to lay life, either of their own volition or at the suggestion or on orders from above. The Jesuits try to select their members carefully, to be sure of a good

8. Xavier Hall, Godavari School, with Fr Moran's Ham radio antenna on the roof.

fit between individual personalities and the needs and expectations of the whole Society. The goal is to create and maintain communal harmony, and the challenge for all is to conform and prosper in their calling to the Church.

Group strength is facilitated by a special union of mind, spirit and action, locally and throughout the Society. Periodic changes of assignment within the local community help, as does the leveling effect of pious confession, periodic retreats and the practice of tolerance, patience and counseling.

Group understanding and cohesion are also maintained through regular correspondence and report writing. Reports sent from the outlying missions, to the diocesan office, to the province office and to the center in Rome, usually concern the spiritual condition of the members and their responsibilities, merits, demerits and special skills. Correspondence is also used to report on the conduct and financial well being of various mission works and activities. From the beginning, Ignatius encouraged correspondence among and between individual members of the Society. This aids in creating a mutual bond of interests and of wills, in a kind of communal camaraderie. And always uniting the Society in all places, in all things, are the mutually reinforcing bonds of authority and obedience.

Tertianship Retreat at Ranchi
To complete his preparations as a freshly minted priest, Marshall had one last, long obligation to fulfill, the tertianship retreat, before taking up his new assignment in Patna. In January 1937, barely two months after returning from Kurseong, he retired to the Jesuit retreat house at Ranchi. The Jesuit tertianship is normally a year-long, formal period of meditation, self examination and intense spiritual study and preparation.

Marshall's tertianship lasted ten months, "beginning with an entire month of retreat, followed by study of the principles of the spiritual life of prayer, recollection and devotion to the apostolate, the duty assigned to a priest." The idea of the tertianship began under St Ignatius, who determined that after so many years of academic study, before a young priest is put out to pastoral work or teaching or any other types of priestly duty, he should rather formally examine and renew his spiritual life. "Ranchi provided me a quiet and supportive environment where I carefully examined for myself the virtues needed to deal with people sincerely and honestly, yet tactfully and prudently, respecting their conscience." In recent years, he said while reflecting on the retreat experience, "a wonderful spirit of ecumenism, of understanding and respect for other religions, had entered the Society and the church. These things made my tertianship all the more important, preparing me for an apostolate among people of several other religions."

While there is only one formal tertianship in the life of a priest, each is expected to engage in an annual eight day retreat. And, as he gains seniority, a priest conducts retreats for others. The term "retreat" derives from the Latin *retrahere*, meaning "to withdraw" from the usual surroundings and distractions of daily life. It is not unlike the notion of pilgrimage among many religions. A pilgrimage is, in fact, a kind of retreat.

The retreat is both a place and a time set aside in solitude for strictly religious attention and, if desired, for personal guidance, redirection or renewal. Retreats are designed to help the retreatant to grasp the simple but fundamental beliefs of the church about god and the people's relationship to god, about sin and its penalties, about discipleship to Christ, and about the rules of Christian living. The ultimate goal is for the devout individual to rise above doing evil and to aim at a higher standard of life according to what the church professes to be the will of god as taught by Christ.[3]

Marshall was only 30 years old at the time of his tertianship, the youngest in his ordination class. Joining him in Ranchi were his American friends Augustine Wildermuth, Marion Batson, Felix Farrell, John Brennan and Francis Welzmiller, all assigned to Patna by the American Jesuits of the Missouri and Chicago provinces. There were also several Belgian, Spanish, French and Indian priests.

Looking Back
Studies on Retreat, of Ignatius, Nehru and Gandhi
Fr Moran

We made a good company of priests, sitting in seminars and study groups, attending to recent research in scripture and learning sermon techniques and liturgical customs. I was put in charge of the liturgy and the sacramental rites, with which we renewed our understanding and appreciation for the dogma and teachings of the church, including the formalities of baptism, weddings and other sacramental functions.

During the day we kept up a continuing discussion on the writings of St Ignatius, the *Constitutions* of the Society, current affairs and the need of social developments and proper social doctrine. And almost every evening, for exercise and some fresh air, some of us would go cycling for an hour with Fr Wildermuth, who later became our bishop. In current affairs, we kept up with the activities of certain Indian politicians who, in those days, were warming up in opposition to British colonial rule. Among them were the two great leaders, Gandhi and Nehru, who had two complementary but unique personalities and very different agendas.

It was about this time that I read the newly published autobiography of Jawaharlal Nehru. His book had a great influence on my thinking. It provided me a glimpse of his ability to express his thoughts in excellent English and of his grasp of India's history and politics. In it he also expressed a remarkably balanced approach and fair treatment towards the British in India. By reading Nehru I also found a key to understanding Gandhi, seeing how the two of them disagreed many times on points of general policy. I saw in Nehru's writings, and later when I met him, a world character of high caliber and morality, a very striking contrast to Stalin, Hitler and Mussolini, who were also very much in the news at this time.[4]

Mohandas Gandhi was a cautious man, even suspicious of things like machines and industrialism. He had a distaste for life in cities and for modernization. He was very religious and wanted people to retain the simple life. He especially sought the maintenance and strengthening of small cottage industries.

Nehru on the other hand was agnostic, had little to say about religion and was frequently caustic and outspoken about all the fakirs and beggars and religious charlatans roaming the cities and countryside. He was, however, very warm towards the minorities, whether they be Muslim or Christian or Sikh. He went out of his way to bring them into his Congress Party and gave them responsible positions. And both Gandhi and Nehru promoted the cause of the liberation of women, under the leadership of Mrs Amrit Kaur and the poet Sarojini Naidu. Sometimes Nehru's sister, Vijaya Lakshmi Pandit, and his mother, as well as Gandhi's wife, Kasturba, would appear in public with them, on the same platform where Nehru spoke or in the village lanes where Gandhi met the common folk. The presence of these women was a shock to the rather orthodox and reactionary aristocrats of India and to the village folk. Remember that in those days, girls in India rarely went to school and women's colleges were almost unheard of.

The simple teachings and innate spiritualism of Mohandas (Mahatma) Gandhi had always intrigued Marshall. They were discussed among his colleagues during tertianship, and they became an important part of Marshall's makings as an ecumenical priest. Over the years he often read Gandhi's writings, juxtapositioned with his own priestly studies and reflections on the Bible. He kept up with Gandhi's words and works in the spirit of religious tolerance and ecumenism while living in Patna and later in Nepal. They were a major force in Marshall's own thoughts and actions.

On Gandhi and the Gita

Marshall was intrigued by Gandhi's interest in the Sermon on the Mount, and his comparisons of the Bhagavad Gita to the Bible, particularly the New Testament. And quite understandably, Marshall's own interpretations of scripture and his broad-mindedness as a missionary in India and Nepal were greatly influenced by Gandhi the philosopher, as well as by Gandhi the man and social healer. Gandhi was impressed by parts of the New Testament, but he cared little for the Old Testament, which he found extremely difficult to read. He read it, he says, because of a promise to "a good Christian from Manchester" who gave him his first Bible. "I accepted his advice, and he got me a copy... [but] I could not possibly read through the Old Testament. I read the book of Genesis, and the chapters that followed invariably sent me to sleep..."[5] The Book of Numbers posed, for him, the greatest test of will and forbearance, he once wrote.

In contrast, reading the New Testament "produced a different impression, especially the Sermon on the Mount which went straight to my heart," Gandhi wrote. "I compared it with the Gita. The verses, 'But I say unto you, that ye resist not evil; but whosoever shall smite thee on thy right cheek, turn to him the other also. And if any man take away thy coat let him have thy cloak too,' delighted me beyond measure and put me in mind of Shamel Bhatt's 'For a bowl of water, give a goodly meal,' etc. My young mind tried to unify the teachings of the *Gita, The Light of Asia* and the Sermon on the Mount. That renunciation as the highest form of religion appealed to me greatly."[6]

In his book, *The Teaching of the Gita*, Gandhi has described Jesus's Sermon on the Mount as a graphic account of the Law of Love—what he preferred to call the "Law of Abandon." While the Gita reduced it "to a scientific formula... The Sermon on the Mount gives the same law a wonderful language... Today, supposing I was deprived of the Gita, and forgot all its contents but had a copy of the Sermon, I should derive the same joy from it as I do from the Gita."[7] Elsewhere he noted that "The spirit of the Sermon on the Mount competes almost on equal terms with the Bhagavad Gita for the domination of my heart."[8]

Gandhi once remarked about his uncritical approach to Hindu, Christian and Islamic scriptures. "I derive the greatest consolation from my reading of Tulsidas's *Ramayana*. I have also derived solace from the New Testament and the Quran... They are to me as important as the Bhagavad Gita, though everything in the former may not appeal to me—everything in the Epistles of Paul, for instance,—not everything in Tulsidas. The Gita is a pure religious discourse, given without any embellishment. It simply describes the progress of the pilgrim soul towards the Supreme Goal..."[9]

Marshall often turned to the saintly Gandhi's inspiration, based on an understanding of the variety of the world's religious scripture. Marshall's maturity and theological growth as a missionary in India, especially his life-long support of ecumenism, his acceptance of the wide variety of religious belief and expression in South Asia, owes a considerable debt to the Mahatma, "The Great One."

After his discover of Gandhi's writings in the 1930s, and in the intervening years, Marshall wove Gandhi's philosophy and tolerant spirit into his own pilgrim-like progress through a world populated by Hindus, Muslims, Sikhs, Buddhists, Christians and people of other beliefs and spiritual expressions, many of whom he worked with or studied and for whom he dedicated his apostolate and daily enterprise. His own life work and teachings as a priest and confessor, as an educator and a friend to many, reflected a tolerant and profound understanding of the variety of religious expressions he encountered in the scriptural writings and lives of millions of Asian people around him.

Gandhi once talked about the influence of the Gita on "a Christian friend telling me that the Gita shows him how to live the New Testament, and that many passages in the latter which used to be dark were intelligible to him through a study of the Gita."[10] Marshall's experience echoed the same sort of scriptural insight and revelation.

Looking Back
More Reflections on Gandhi and the *Gita*
Fr Moran

Ever since I came to India in 1929, I have been reading commentaries and explanations of the Bhagavad Gita.[11] Mahatma Gandhi said years ago that the Gita epitomizes the essentials of the whole Vedic teaching and that a knowledge of those teachings leads to a realization of all human aspirations. He was greatly attracted to Christianity at one time in his life and was well acquainted with the Bible. TheSermon on the Mount was especially meaningful to him, as he has said, but the Gita stands out as having a profound influence on his life and his thinking. Gandhi once wrote "...that Hinduism as I know it, entirely satisfies my soul, fills my whole being and... when doubts haunt me, when disappointments stare me in the face, and when I see not one ray of light on the horizon, I turn to the Bhagavad Gita, and find a verse to comfort me; and I immediately begin to smile in the midst of overwhelming sorrow..."[12]

Gandhi's life was certainly full of tragedies and sorrow; and as he has said somewhere, he owes it to the Bhagavad Gita that they left no visible scars.

Since the Gita has so much authority and gets so much attention from serious Hindus, I sought early on to study it and Gandhi's views of it. This, I felt, would help me to enter into the attitudes, convictions, religious feelings and the devotions of the dear people of India and Nepal. It can explain very much of their culture and daily life. I chose the Gita because from my earliest days in India I spent much of my time trying to understand what the Hindus really understand. It is their Bible.

The ninth century Hindu scholar, Sankaracharya, once wrote, "The ultimate aim of the Gita is, in a word, the attainment of the Highest Good."[13] I sought an understanding of that "highest good" by reading the Gita and by studying the reflections of Gandhi, as well as the more recent academic commentaries of Aldous Huxley.

Huxley was greatly impressed by the Gita, calling it "one of the clearest and most comprehensive summaries of the Perennial Philosophy ever to have been made. Hence, its enduring value, not only for Indians, but for all mankind. . . . The Bhagavad Gita is perhaps the most systematic scriptural statement of the Perennial Philosophy."[14]

I feel obligated, however, to criticize the last statement of Huxley, since I took a degree in philosophy and continue to take a great interest in philosophy as well as theology. I would say that he exaggerates the metaphysical aspects of the Gita. Rather, it is more of a poem with broad general statements aimed not at the metaphysical, but at purely religious, ritual devotion, which is called *bhakti* in Sanskrit. I think Gandhi would agree with me. It is trying to join the way of bhakti to that of abstract philosophy, a searching for the truth and finding of the divine self which is, of course, pantheistic, or monistic philosophy. That is my observation.

Challenging New Assignments

In November 1937, after completing his nearly year-long tertianship retreat at Ranchi, Marshall returned directly to Patna where he was assigned as the assistant to the Superior of Patna, Fr Frank Loesch. Fr Loesch had been in Kurseong in 1933 and Marshall knew him well. He was a young and dynamic leader, a pleasure to work with. Their first task was to find larger space for the expanding mission headquarters. For a modest fee they rented a two-storey house on Exhibition road from a prominent Anglo-Indian family named Connelly. The house had nine rooms on each of two floors. It was quiet and very comfortable, quite ideal for a new mission office.

Marshall served, as he called it, "as house keeper, so to say, or minister and administrative assistant to the Superior, organizing files and helping with letters and correspondence." Among his many duties was one that made use of his interest and limited early training in medicine. He was assigned to help missionaries, seminarians and students who took ill, to get admission to hospitals, meet the doctors and arrange for diagnosis and treatment. In this position he was able to meet many of the leading medical doctors in Patna as well as professors at the Patna University medical college.

St Xavier's High School for Boys

It was about this time that plans for opening a Jesuit high school for boys began to take shape.

Looking Back
Building Patna's St Xavier's School
Fr Moran

I remember being invited by the bishop of Patna, Reverend Monsignor Bernard J. Sullivan, to a function organized by the governor of Bihar. All the judges of the high court and ministers of the Bihar provincial government, legislators and department heads were assembled to hear the abdication of Edward as King of England and the accession of George V. On these sorts of occasions I met many of the leading personalities of the Patna community. We discussed plans for a Jesuit high school and invited a number of them to form a school advisory committee. They were a mixed professional and ecumenical group: three doctors, three lawyers, a judge from the high court, including representatives from both the Muslim and Hindu communities. The local Bengali community was also represented among them. In those days Bihar was rather backward and underdeveloped, and many Bengali professionals, mainly from Calcutta, were attracted there to fill the void.

The idea of a quality high school in Patna was attractive to them, and as our advisers they were a great help and became good friends. They were proud to lend their strong support and their names to the founding of St Xavier's High School, relying on the good reputation that the Jesuit schools had earned in other Indian cities as far away as Bombay. That made our beginnings much easier. And the support we received from both the Hindu and Muslim leaders made the parents of prospective school boys confident that the mission school would be fair and impartial from a both religious and social points of view.

With divine providence we procured a choice piece of land right opposite the central *maidan*, the city park, as the future site for our school. We bought it from the Imperial Bank. I believe God was helping us, for it was ideal, with plenty of room for high school buildings and the adjacent park available for football (soccer) games and cricket pitches. The *maidan* was public land, a large open space surrounded by trees and large drives. We couldn't have gotten a better site, a better location.

Fr Loesch was a good organizer and a good engineer. He soon had a group of workers preparing for construction. The plans were drawn up by one of the mission's Belgian priests, a talented architect. At that time, in 1938 and 1939, due to the Depression and unemployment, prices and wages were low and cement was quite cheap. We made our own bricks at a price of five rupees per thousand. The building went up quickly and by 1939 it was completed.

In 1934, Bihar had suffered a severe earthquake. Many two- and three-storied buildings had collapsed, buildings constructed only of mud mortar or ordinary clay without lime. They simply crumbled and fell into the city streets. The death toll was not so great because it happened in the early afternoon when people were alert and able to escape outside. Now, five years later, the face of the city was changing. In the midst of which was our magnificent new building, the most modern and up to date in Patna, with proper fixtures and fittings—a building such as Patna had not seen before. Even the government buildings had not used reinforced concrete and did not have the sanitary fittings that we used in the school.

St Xavier's High School formally opened its doors on January 15, 1940. The governor of Bihar cut the ribbon and Bishop Sullivan gave the blessing. School began with a few boys in three classes, but increased each year until, in five years, it boasted an enrollment of six hundred boys.

Fifty years later, at its golden jubilee, one of its early students wrote this about the school's long term success: "In its 50 years of eventful existence the service rendered by St Xavier's in building up young men and establishing healthy traditions is something it can justifiably be proud of... It takes many years to build up traditions. The selfless devotion of some men of vision, dedication and character built up St Xavier's. The achievements of some of its alumni place it among the very best of educational institutions in the country. ...A school is not its handful of brilliant boys, but the larger majority who carry the stamp of a particular code of conduct... the capacity to do the right and the just thing without fear of the consequences."[15]

St Xavier followed the Cambridge system of education, concluding with what was popularly called the O-level examinations or, more properly, the Joint Examination for the School Certificate and General Certificate of Education (G.C.E.) International Examinations. Cambridge University in England provided the syllabi and the textbooks. The school in Patna had excellent results with this system and the Bihar students proved that they were able, with a good foundation in grammar school, to compete successfully for good marks and a chance at a college career after graduation.

Marshall proudly recounted that "as St Xavier's High School grew, its success attracted attention and emulation. In 1943, the school was visited by Sir Mirza Ismail, the *diwan* or prime minister of Travancore, a large princely state in South India. When he came to Patna he was serving a similar function at Jaipur, a princely state in Rajasthan. It was only our third year of operation and he was so impressed with the general knowledge of the boys and their good command of English that he asked if I would open a similar school in Jaipur. He volunteered seventy-five percent of the construction costs and provided the land free of charge. I introduced him to our superior, Fr Loesch, and to the Bishop. They took it from there and today there is a big school in Jaipur, with an enrollment of about two thousand boys. That was the first offshoot of the Patna School.

Another opened in Delhi, in a converted hotel building. It began late in the 1950s and soon had nearly two thousand students."[16]

Looking Back
A Tribute to the Founding Fathers
Amar Mishra[17]

I recall that the 18th of January, 1940, was an unusually cold day. Perhaps it is only "first day nerves"... It was on this cold day that along with a handful of other nervous children, I was entrusted to the benign care of the (Jesuit Fathers)...

The "Fathers" who one encountered in those early days were indeed great visionaries, totally dedicated to building institutions and hopefully crafting a few "good" men. Father (Francis) Loesch, the tireless builder; Father Moran, the dynamic "Sultradhar"; Father (Edward) Niesen, the assiduous administrator; Father (Joseph) Wroblewski, the quintessential Guru; Father (Kevin) Cleary, forever spinning out worldly and not so worldly wisdom, were all part of an outstanding team who set about making St Xavier's a seat of excellence. There were also many others whose association may have been briefer but not less vital... What I recall most about this distinguished group of founders is the rare sense of humor with which they were all individually and collectively endowed. Life was to be lived vigorously and with good cheer.

It was in 1943, when the Second World War was at its horrific peak, that the first batch took their Senior Cambridge examination and the school's high academic credentials were immediately confirmed... They were rather eventful years and certainly nothing was going to be the same again. The Second World War and the Mahatma (Gandhi) saw to that...

It must be said to the everlasting credit of Father Moran that he kept us adequately, if judiciously, exposed to the political cross currents that were sweeping the country. There were numerous occasions when eminent political leaders were invited to speak to us. One such memorable occasion was the visit of Mrs (Vijaya Lakshmi) Pandit. She was a great hit with us because she spoke English with an "Oxbridge" accent and as always she was impeccably coiffured and dressed, very much the glamorous lady she then was. She had got out of jail after the Quit India Movement, although her illustrious brother (Jawaharlal Nehru) was still confined... The Quit India Movement led to much disruption and we, who were in the hostel, were "confined to barracks" for some weeks, but I remember that we were encouraged to wear "Indian clothes" during this period. Those of us who had the odd *dhoti* or *pajama* were greatly tickled by this opportunity to exhibit our patriotism!...

One afternoon, quite out of the blue, Father Moran spotted Ranjit Roy Choudhury and me strolling in the compound and asked us if we would like to go for a drive in his new car—the first post war model of the Ford V-8. Ranjit and I, of course, accepted his invitation with alacrity and soon we made off in the direction of what was then known as "New Capital." While we were driving along, Father Moran broke the news that we were in fact going to call on Pandit Nehru at the Circuit House. We could hardly believe this, but soon we were indeed turning into the gates of the Circuit House. On the verandah, we could spot eminent personalities like Khwaja Sir Nazimuddin, later Pakistan's Prime Minister and Governor General, Abdur Rab Nishtar, Nehru's Cabinet colleague, Sri Krishna Sinha, the Bihar Chief Minister and a host of others discussing the latest situation of the riots. In the adjoining room we were told that Pandit Nehru was conferring with officials.

Father Moran asked Ranjit and me to wait outside the room while he himself went in unannounced. The gentry, waiting in the verandah to meet Nehru, were all in an appropriate state of shock to see a foreign priest barge into the great man's private room. Later, Ranjit and I were summoned inside and introduced and pleasantries were duly exchanged. Both of us whispered rather hoarsely whether we could be favored with autographs. Of course we would. "Just leave your books with Upadhya," I still remember him saying. We did not have our books with us but these were duly sent to Mr Upadhya, Nehru's accompanying secretary, and promptly they were sent back to us suitably autographed.

The next few days, much to everyone's surprise, Nehru toured Bihar in Father Moran's new car with the latter personally driving him. This sort of thing would be unthinkable today, but there is perhaps a lesson in it somewhere for prime ministers.

Later, we heard from Father Moran that he and Pandit-ji (Nehru) had traveled together quite fortuitously, to Assam on a very slow train some months earlier and struck a close friendship.[18]

Nostalgia, they say, can be very destructive in that it makes one live in the past, but when one is in the autumn of one's life it is ever so delectable to go back occasionally to one's memorable archives.

Patna Women's College

During the 1940s, the Patna Diocese steadily expanded its number of priests, Christian members, and construction projects, in support of its growth in social, educational and medical works. But, while the Jesuits focused principally on boys' education, Indian girls were neither neglected nor forgotten. In the late 1930s, to start an advanced educational program for girls, the Jesuits invited the Apostolic Carmelite Sisters of Mangalore, who had proven themselves in South India, to come and build a women's college. Patna Women's College opened in 1940 in temporary quarters. Negotiations began soon after they arrived for the purchase of government land opposite the high court building on the main road called High Court Road in Patna's residential section. As with negotiations for the boys' high school, Marshall was closely involved. But unlike the ease with which land for the boys' school was purchased and built, preparations for the Patna Women's College were far more problematic and challenging.

For nearly four years, classes for women were held in the Bishop's House. The bishop had moved to temporary quarters in the high school, where Marshall now served as both the principal and the superior. As negotiations for the land for the Women's College were made public, complaints began appearing in the newspapers objecting to the project as Christian, foreign and Western. (The ultra-conservative opposition was careful not to state too openly a main underlying reason for their objections—the outrageously liberal notion of educating women!)

To silence the opposition, Marshall lobbied his acquaintances among the government, political and civic leaders of Patna and Bihar. "I met the British governor of Bihar; I told him I would try to turn opposition into support by enlisting their advice, involvement and consent. Then I went to Dr Rajendra Prasad, a leader in the Bihar Freedom Movement, president of the Bihar Congress Party and former president of the National Congress Party of India. He was one of the top four or five national leaders in the independence movement, alongside Nehru and Gandhi. Dr Prasad was well known in Bihar, especially for his handling of emergency relief activities following the devastating 1934 earthquake. Not only were cities and towns devastated by the quake, but two hundred miles of the railway system on the north side of the Ganges were knocked out. Dr Prasad oversaw relief efforts and the railway's complete reconstruction.

"As Dr Prasad was already a supporter of the mission's medical and educational works, I described to him our new plans for the women's college and asked him to participate in the inauguration ceremonies. I knew that if we got his involvement it would be seen as a recommendation for the rest of the public to agree, and we could avoid further acrimony and argument."

Fr Moran and Dr Prasad then called a press conference on the proposed location for the college, to talk with journalists and others of their plans. A number of prominent local leaders and educators, members of the high school committee and various other college and university officials and friends of the Jesuits were invited to participate in the inaugural opening.

"All of this was arranged. Fr Loesch engineered its construction, several four-storied buildings for classrooms and dormitories. It quickly became one of the sights of the city, for in those days there were few buildings over three stories high. In 1948, shortly after Indian Independence, the Patna Women's College was formally opened. It was the first degree college for women in north India between Benares and Calcutta, which are more than eight hundred miles apart. It included a high school department and in a short time they had over three thousand school girls and college women enrolled. We accomplished all this in the end with the full cooperation of Hindus, Muslims, Sikhs and Christians working together."

Holy Family Hospital
After Indian Independence in 1947, the Patna Diocese leaders found in the new civil service and government officials a continued sympathetic and cooperative attitude toward Jesuit educational projects. They were also willing to promote much-needed hospital development and a nurses' training facility. That goal was pursued by a group of nuns known as the Medical Missionary Sisters, with considerable Jesuit help. Their goal was to build both a hospital in Patna and a nurses' training facility to support it at Mokama, forty miles east.

The Medical Missionary Sisters are an order of Dutch origin that attract mostly Dutch and American women. Prior to coming to Patna they had built a hospital at Rawalpindi in the western Punjab (now Pakistan) and in East Bengal (now Bangladesh). They are also known for their pioneering work in public health and disease prevention in rural villages. Their first facility in Patna was opened in the old Patna cathedral. In 1943, temporary buildings were erected on newly acquired property near the Ganges, and in 1950 the Holy Family Hospital formally opened in permanent quarters there.

Marshall was instrumental in helping the Sisters cut through the formidable red tape to secure building materials, which were in short supply following the war. "The kindness of the Congress Party of India and some of its ministers was very generous, and with their help we obtained a special freight car full of cement for construction. They raised not the least opposition or criticism of our plans. That hospital still thrives, a favorite institution for the people of the city and well known across north India. Our workers in mission stations throughout Bihar send their most difficult medical cases to Holy Family Hospital."

Moran and India's Independence Leaders
Those three capital developments in Patna—the high school, the women's college, and the hospital—were all proud achievements for the mission and for Marshall, personally, in his various roles of helping in their creation and ensuring their success. But above all, he

was most pleased and proud to serve as the principal and superior of St Xavier's High School. He liked being in charge of things and was never shy of the recognition it brought him from the wider community. In his position as principal, he was able to associate with many other educators and civic leaders of Patna and greater Bihar. Dr Rajendra Prasad was one of those he met in this capacity, and it was Dr Prasad who introduced him to others, including Mahatma Gandhi.

One evening in May 1939, Marshall was attending an open air discussion about Gandhiji's controversial "Wardha Scheme" for Indian education. Gandhi, himself, was present. The lecture began at seven o'clock. It was dark and, as Marshall was listening at the edge of the crowd, a stranger asked, "Father, are you able to understand the Mahatma's Hindi?"

"Yes," Marshall replied in Hindi. "I find it quite easy. He speaks so slowly."

Then he recognized the stranger as Rajendra Prasad and introduced himself. It was the first time they had met. They talked briefly about their mutual interest in good education. Then Dr Prasad said, "Would you like to meet Gandhi? I can arrange an interview."

Of course he would! Gandhi's Wardha Scheme interested Marshall; it was a reform movement advocating practical education based on simple handicrafts, as opposed to the college preparatory type training that so many aspiring Indian leaders wanted to provide for the new nation's children. Marshall certainly wanted to hear more about it and took Dr Prasad up on the offer.

Looking Back
Meeting Gandhi-ji
Fr Moran

The meeting with Gandhi was set for the following afternoon. It was hot, very hot! We met in an open straw hut about fifty feet square, specially made for the occasion. With me was Fr Wildermuth, Rector of the Khrist Raja High School, who had come down from Bettiah. Another Father, Cecil Chamberlain, was also there. We sat on a carpet with "Gandhiji" (the suffix *-ji* denotes a highly respectable person in India). He offered us chairs, but we declined. "When in Rome...," and all that.

Outside the hut, five to eight thousand people were standing in line, three or four abreast. Just to walk past and take *darshan*. Darshan is a tradition in India. It has an elusive meaning, a subtle belief, highly emotional, a kind of psychological blessing one gets just from seeing such a great person as the Mahatma.

There were many prominent men around Gandhi, local personalities like Badri Varma—"Badri Babu" we called him—the minister of education for Bihar, and Bulabhai Patel, one of Nehru's deputy prime ministers, and Dr Prasad, of course, who had arranged the meeting.

Gandhi struck me as being frail but not at all timid. Bold, pleasantly bold. Outspoken, but not the type to give lectures. Full of questions.

He was constantly putting questions to us and discussion points in a friendly, open and intelligent manner. We talked mainly about education. I mentioned that I had, myself, experimented with village schools in Bettiah. Then he asked my opinion of the Wardha Scheme. I said, rather freely, that I thought there should be more attention given to agriculture, horticulture, cash crops and irrigation. I also said that there was too much of spinning in the Wardha Scheme. Spinning was one of Gandhi's favorite themes. It would be better to have weaving, I suggested, where the children could take home a shirt or some other clothing or a piece of cloth that they had made themselves. Whereas spinning yarn, I said, was very boring and machines could do it so much faster. That, of course, was also Pandit Nehru's criticism of the Wardha Scheme, and I agreed.

Gandhi suddenly said to me, "You sound like Sam Higgenbotham." When I said I didn't know who that was, he said, "You should meet him." (I later learned that Sam Higgenbotham was a progressive Presbyterian missionary at India's first modern agricultural college in Naini, near Allahabad, in the plains west of Patna. Later, in 1960, I met his daughter, the wife of Lyndon Clough, a British official in Kathmandu.)

Before the meeting was over, Gandhi asked me to serve on the Wardha executive committee for Bihar. I agreed and served for twelve years, until I left India for Nepal in 1951. During those years the government adopted several Wardha themes, but not universally. A few years after Gandhi's assassination it was given up and the government turned back to the previous scheme. They had trouble getting the necessary handicraft teachers, and the people did not have much faith in a system that promoted simple technical training over a more academic and college preparatory education. Everyone wanted to go to college. That's why India today has such a glut of unemployed engineers and doctors, for example, who do not want to go to the rural areas. Even the trained educators want to work in the big cities to the neglect of the rural areas, while it is in the countryside that more teachers and more schools are needed.

I met with Gandhi on several later occasions. Whenever he came to Patna, he would phone me through his secretary and ask permission to use the school playground for his prayer meetings. We were on excellent terms and later, in 1946 and 1947 during the

Hindu-Muslim riots in Bihar, I took him around in my jeep to help restore peace and harmony.

Riots and Indian Independence

About Easter, 1942, a delegation of British parliamentarians and ministers led by Sir Stafford Cripps visited India to try to reach a compromise on the political future of the country, one that would be agreeable to the Indian Congress Party. There were several difficult issues, including the status of the minority Muslims and the future of the Indian army. From all appearances, Prime Minister Churchill did not give the Cripps mission much power, and in the end no real agreement was reached. Over the summer, the patience of the Indians was stretched thin and although they valiantly supported the British and the Allies in the war effort in Asia, sentiment against continued British rule of the subcontinent was rising sharply. The Indians wanted dominion status, but the British would not budge.

It was at this time that Gandhi's "Quit India" movement caught on and became a rallying cry for many frustrated Indians. It was punctuated by a series of non-violent, passive acts of civil disobedience under his leadership. But despite Gandhi's appeals for passive resistance, political and social disorder raged openly, much of the worst of it in Bihar. Railway tracks were torn up and stations burned, police offices were attacked, electric wires and power lines were cut and telephone services were disrupted. The violence encouraged public acts of lawlessness by the criminal elements, and seeing the embarrassment of the police, looting and murder increased, all in the name of politics, but often far removed from political motive. It finally took a contingent of the British army in training for war duty in Burma to restore local order. But it was many weeks before communications were repaired and the trains ran again.

In the midst of the strife, on August 10, 1942, the mission office got a call from police and railway authorities asking for help. Thirty Salesian priests and Italian and German seminarians, all considered to be wartime enemies of the Allies (because of their nationalities as citizens of the Axis) were passing through Bihar under guard, heading for an internment camp at Dehra Dun. Because of local anti-British rioting, their train was stopped and the railway officials and police requested the American Jesuits to take them in. Marshall was contacted for help. He offered temporary accommodations for them in the high school where they stayed in safety for a week before moving on to a government internment camp for the duration of the war.

During the war, divisiveness between the Hindu and Muslim communities increased at all levels, affecting people all the way from the ranks of the Indian leadership to the poorest, most remote villagers. Mohammed Ali Jinnah was the leader of the Muslim League and a former member of the Indian National Congress from which he had resigned in opposition to Mahatma Gandhi. While at one time he favored Hindu-Muslim unity, as the war neared its end and independence seemed near, he held out for an autonomous Muslim state of Pakistan (including East Bengal or East Pakistan, now Bangladesh). Marshall always held the opinion that "Jinnah did more harm than good to the cause of Indian nationalism and social unity. I was especially concerned," he said, "when, in 1946 and 1947 in Bihar, bloody Hindu-Muslim riots were turning the countryside into a battlefield, and Jinnah did virtually nothing about it."

The rioting in the spring of 1947 attracted both Gandhi, the passivist, and Nehru, then the acting prime minister, to Bihar to talk with the people and try to calm their fears. When Marshall recounted the events of those hectic days, it reflected his strong admiration for these two great leaders and statesmen of India. "I met them both and went around with them to the villages in their efforts to restore peace and confidence. Wherever they went they were successful, but there were always new outbreaks of violence somewhere else."

In neighboring Bengal the disturbances went on for many months. "The daily news was tragic. The streets of Calcutta were littered with corpses and there was arson and other outrageous acts pitting one community against the other, Hindu against Muslim, Muslim against Hindu." It was in the midst of the worst rioting in Calcutta that Gandhi staged one of his famous fasts for civil peace, nearly dying before Hindu and Muslim leaders begged him to eat and live, in exchange for their own promises to avoid inciting further violence.

Once, when Jawaharlal Nehru was in Patna, Marshall offered his jeep—it was probably the only available jeep in all of Bihar at the time—for trips out into the riot torn villages.

Looking Back
With Nehru in Bihar, 1947
Fr Moran

I drove my jeep from Patna out into the countryside to the scene of some of the worst rioting. Nehru sat with me in front, in the passenger seat. When we came to one town we were stopped by security police. Just then the local chief magistrate, the top police officer of the district, drove up, jumped out of his car and rushed over to us. He was in a great panic over the rioting and started shouting, "Go back to Patna. Tell the government what's happening. Tell the prime minister. Please, go at once!"

I said to the man, pointing at Nehru. "Look who's here."

"He looks like Mr Nehru," the magistrate said. "Who is he?"

Nehru was amused by the incident, although the situation in the town was not funny. Nehru had come rather suddenly to Patna and his travels into the districts were not planned ahead. "Well, Father," he said, "I expect they might know you here, but they don't expect me. This trip wasn't announced."

For three days I drove him through the villages, where he talked to rural leaders and tried to calm the people. He wanted me to be with him, I think, because as a Christian I was seen as a neutral. He also valued my testimony as an American; that is, as someone who could tell others about his efforts to try to save the Mohammedans. In comparison, the national Muslim leader, Mohammed Ali Jinnah, never seemed to try in the same public way to save the Hindus. At least that was the impression. Many Hindus saw him as a villain.

Both Gandhi and Nehru were determined that there should be no violence and that Muslims should not suffer from the sins of people in the new Pakistan who were killing Hindus. Jinnah once said to Lord Mountbatten, the last British viceroy of India,[19] something like he "would rather have a month-eaten Pakistan than no Pakistan."[20] He meant that at any price, no matter how many people died, he was going to have his Pakistan. And it was in this political atmosphere that the Hindus and Muslims engaged in bloody religious riots in the villages and cities.

Travels Abroad

In early December 1947, Marshall was invited to Bahrain, a small oil-rich country on the Persian Gulf, and to Saudi Arabia, as a guest of BAPCO—the British Arab Petroleum Company, and ARAMCO—the Arabian American Oil Company. It was common for these companies to invite clerics to conduct special religious services and lectures to their European and American employees. Thus, for several weeks, Fr Moran was their chaplain and served Christmas mass to the Catholics among them.

On his return to India, a companion, Fr John G. Sloan, urged him to stop by Bombay for a visit. Marshall declined the invitation on the excuse that he had been gone too long from Patna and as principal he was needed there to oversee the opening of school for the new year. "There is so much work to be caught up," I told him. So when our Indian Airlines plane made its scheduled stop in Karachi, we separated. I caught the next flight for Calcutta and he for Bombay. When his plane took off, it crashed on the beach, and all passengers were killed. Sabotage seemed certain. When my family in Chicago read in the newspapers of the crash, they recognized Fr Sloan's name and knew from my letters that we had been together on the trip. They were frantic about my safety. When I arrived in Patna, I cabled them that Sloan had been lost but that I was safe in Patna."

Going Home
The following year, Marshall few home to America, his first trip in the nineteen years since he had come out to India. Before the advent of modern air travel, missionary priests did not expect to every go back, since the sea voyage took so long. But with the trip reduced to a few days by air, it was now possible. He was excited to go back to Chicago, to see his mother again and his brothers and some of his old school chums. It was a momentous occasion when he arrived and for several weeks he was feted and fed like a king. He was quizzed about conditions in India as an exotic guest, of sorts, in the homes of his various relatives and old friends.

The America he saw in 1948 surprised him. The rationing scheme left over from the war was still in effect, on meat for example, while back in Patna, he told his family, the only thing he had trouble with any more was an occasional shortage of petrol (gasoline) for cars. He described how in India he used to mix his petrol with cheap commercial alcohol to stretch the supply. The alcohol came from the sugar mills of Bihar, sugar cane being a popular cash crop among the farmers on the Gangetic Plain. The surplus molasses was sold to distilleries for making commercial alcohol for industrial and medicinal use, and for potable alcohol.

He found his home town of Chicago greatly changed, and somewhat depressing. "It needed wider streets and throughways, I thought. While there, I gave many talks to friends, relatives, mission benefactors, schools and other institutions. When I lectured to the rotary and Lions Clubs, the most popular question I heard was 'What is the future of India?' India was then under the prime ministership of Jawaharlal Nehru, I told them. Give him fifteen or twenty years for India to settle down and develop, I said."

Marshall felt, however, that Nehru exaggerated India's need for development of heavy industry, to the neglect of agriculture. His greatest fears about this came true a few years later when India began to experience devastating droughts and famines, which heavy industry could not help.

The decade after independence was a sort of honeymoon period, he thought, particularly in relations between India and the United States. "But there was an eventual turnabout in relations. When the U.S. government started giving planes and sophisticated weapons to Pakistan, the Americans became rather unpopular in India. At the same time, the Russians, coming out from under Stalinism, were mending their fences with India. Three times there was war between India and Pakistan, and I regret to say that the U.S. seemed to be, each time, on the wrong side. I say 'seemed to be' because they were always willing to help and negotiate, but there is a limit to what they could do to interfere with the 'local insanity,' as it was called, because both sides were so easily stirred to retaliate with vengeance, to take an eye for an eye and a tooth for a tooth. In some areas there weren't many eyes and teeth left. I mean that literally, for when riots erupt on the subcontinent, it can be very savage."

His departure back to India after his trip home in 1948 was nothing like his first, in 1929. Somehow, flying away from an airport has none of the drama of leaving on a ship. Marshall was sad at this departure, wondering if he would ever see his mother or his brothers again. He did not anticipate being able to come home ever again and the likelihood of their visiting him was very small.

Marshall returned to an India unchanged during his sojourn abroad. Nor were his responsibilities in the mission much different after his brief absence. He returned to a heavy mission work load, more than enough to keep this energetic man busy, both in religious and civic activities.

Civic Involvement

Through Marshall's work as superior and as principal of St Xavier's High School, he became involved in other educational enterprises and responsibilities. For many years, he was a member of the textbook committee, as a member of the Board of Secondary Education for high schools all across Bihar. The BSE oversaw about three hundred and fifty high schools; its members held periodic inspection tours and oversaw capital and academic improvements. While serving on the board, Marshall traveled to all parts of the state, hundreds of miles at a time, to carry out his responsibilities.

One year he was elected president of the high school teachers' union and immediately found himself placed in a difficult position when the teachers raised a strike vote against the government. Marshall vetoed the move, insisting that the union negotiate. "We must parlay before issuing ultimatums," he told the teachers. "We must negotiate. If negotiations fail, then you can have your strike, but I cannot be a strike leader. As a foreign resident in India, I am at the mercy of the government, and I don't think they will countenance any agitation from me." The negotiations he advocated were opened with the Bihar state minister of finance, Anuragh N. Sinha, and the strike was avoided. A satisfactory agreement was reached within two days.

The Patna Museum officers also put him on their governing committee. While the Patna Museum never came up to the standard of larger ones in Calcutta or Bombay, it did boast some rare objects and artifacts of considerable antiquity, value and local pride. They included relics and art pieces, bronze and stone images dating from the Mauryan Empire (*c.*320-195 BC), which had unified much of India from its base in Bihar at Pataliputra (now Patna). One of the museum's most interesting collections was a set of gold and silver Greek coins, dating to the invasion of the subcontinent by Alexander the Great in 327-325 BC. "One afternoon," Marshall recalled with a touch of bitterness, "a thief hid in the museum and that night he made off with most of the coin collection. They were later found to have been sold to a government museum in Allahabad. So 'Peter robbed Paul,'" he said, "one government institution secured the collection at the expense of another."

Among his other civic responsibilities, and they were many, was his appointment as treasurer for the boy scouts of the state of Bihar. During and after World War II, he helped promote and spread scouting throughout the state. He was also on the state's Red Cross Committee and once attended a national convention of the Red Cross in Delhi as the delegate from Bihar. He met the president of India there and got from him a guarantee of concessions to mission hospitals to import drugs and medicines on the condition that they be distributed to the poor irrespective of race, caste, or creed.

During this period after the war, Marshall also rekindled his interest in radio. After meeting amateur radio hobbyists in Patna, he filed for a license for the high school and set up a low-wattage school station for experimentation and broadcast. This brought him well into the ham (amateur) radio fraternity of India, among whom he made many lifelong friends. One thing led to another and before he left India for Nepal, he was even appointed to the board of the Bihar section of the Indian broadcasting services of All India Radio (AIR).[21]

At about the time of India's independence, Marshall was approached by a friendly English Baptist educator, a Reverend Bridges, who was teaching at Patna University. Bridges encouraged Moran to help compose course syllabi and exams in Latin and Greek, and later in philosophy. Bridges was impressed with Marshall's abilities and recommended his name to the governor of Bihar for an appointment to the Patna University senate.

The university senate was comprised of over a hundred educators, lawyers from the law college and doctors from the medical school, along with the deans of the colleges as ex-officio members. He responded positively to their invitation to join this august group of advisers. "From that group of distinguished scholars, I was able to meet many prominent professional people such as judges from the high court, retired educators and young professors. The Senate met twice annually to draw up legislation and statues, laws and by-laws for the university. I was also on the Philosophy Board of Studies, where I helped prepare examination questions for the degree courses. I found my association with the university very rewarding and satisfying, and it helped me keep contact with the thinkers and leaders of Patna and greater Bihar society. This, in turn, was useful to me in the development of St Xavier's High School, to get assistance and advice from these good people."

Marshall's association with Patna University had other rewards, as well. For it was in his combined role as a member of the university senate, teacher and sometime examination proctor that he embarked in 1949 on a month long sojourn into Nepal to administer degree exams at Kathmandu's Trichandra College, an affiliate of Patna University. His first brief encounter with Nepal was destined to change Marshall's life, the course of Jesuit involvement in South Asia and, not least, the history of education in Nepal. It marked a return of the Catholic Church to Nepal after a hiatus of nearly two centuries. It opened up a richly rewarding new life for Marshall Moran. And by his vision, leadership and drive for educational development, it brought new prospects for many of the people of that tiny landlocked Himalayan kingdom.

Notes to Chapter 8: The Patna Years

1. This was one of Fr Moran's favorite verses from Hindu scripture.
2. Even Adolph Hitler's infamous collaborator, Heinrich Himmler, is said to have expressed such an attraction to the model of Jesuitical efficiency and effectiveness that he contemplated developing his select Waffen SS storm troops after them—without the Society's religious and social agenda, which he undoubtedly did not share.
3. *New Catholic Dictionary* (1929).
4. See Jawaharlal Nehru, *An Autobiography* (1936).
5. Mohandas K. Gandhi, *An Autobiography: The Story of My Experiments with Truth* (1927, p.51).
6. *Ibid.*
7. Gandhi, *The Teaching of the Gita* (1962, pp.36-37). The Gita, or Bhagavad Gita (in Sanskrit: Song of the Lord) is a Hindu poem composed in approximately 300 BC. It is the sixth book of the Mahabharata, the great eighteen-part Indian epic. The Gita blends and reconciles a number of Hindu philosophies and, in its way, it presents a cultural prescription for the virtuous life. It tells of the deeds of the great warrior-hero, Arjuna, whose charioteer, Krishna, persuades him of the value of

selfless attention to the duties of caste and of the ways by which one gains liberation from earthly matters—by virtuous actions, devotion to god (*bhakti*), philosophical speculation, asceticism and meditation. For more of Gandhi's viewpoint on the Gita, besides *The Teaching of the Gita*, see also his autobiographical periodical *Young India* (1919-31), and Louis Fisher, *The Essential Gandhi: An Anthology* (1963).

8. Gandhi, *Speeches and Writings* (1932, p.338), as quoted in *The Teaching of the Gita* (p.37n.).
9. Gandhi, as quoted from the periodical *Harijan* (Amedabad, India; December 5, 1936) in *The Teaching of the Gita* (p.37).
10. *Ibid.* (May 25, 1935, p.38).
11. Gandhi, *Young India* (1919-31).
12. Gandhi, 'An address to missionaries,' *Young India* (August 6, 1925, v.7, n.32, p.274).
13. From Sankaracharya's introduction to what is the earliest known existing commentary on the Gita, reprinted in Swami Nikhilananda's translation of *The Bhagavad Gita* (1944, p.53).
14. As quoted in S. Radhakrishnan, *Bhagavadgita* (1953, p.12n), from an introduction to *Bhagavadgītā*, by Swāmi Prabhavānanda and Christopher Isherwood (1945, p.6-7, 9). Aldous Huxley's famous book, *The Perennial Philosophy* (1944), was greatly influenced by the Bhagavad Gita.
15. Samuel Birendra, in SXAA, *St Xavier's High School Patna* (1990).
16. In Moran's own short speech on the occasion he recalled "the good old days, the building of the school, a few of the problems and some of the fortunate aspects of the timing of the school. Though the war (World War II) had begun the previous August in Europe, there was still no shortage of building materials and cement and because of the Great Depression of the 1930s, prices and the cost of labor were very low by today's standards." Then Moran presented the first Marshall Moran Award to Sonal Ranjan, the graduating senior with the highest marks. This award was created in Moran's honor and memory some years before by a group of Patna old boy alumni.
17. Amar Mishra (St Xavier's, Patna, Class of '46), 'A tribute to the founding fathers,' in SXAA, *St Xavier's High School Patna* (1990, pp.42-44).
18. Sometime earlier, when Marshall was traveling on mission business in eastern India, he found that the preferred train, an express, was behind schedule. Rather than wait for it, he took the next available train only to discover that it was carrying Jawaharlal Nehru on a whistle stop political speech-making tour of the stations along the way. At one stop Marshall joined the platform crowd to listen. When Nehru's aides had trouble with the loud speaker system, Marshall offered to help. In a minute he found the problem, a disconnected wire, and fixed it, then stood at the back while Nehru spoke. Before the train moved on, Nehru invited Marshall into his special car to thank him, and to find out more about the priest and his travels. This was the first time they met.

19. First Earl Lord Mountbatten of Burma served as viceroy of India in 1947, presiding over the partition of British India into Pakistan and India. He then served as governor general of India until 1948.
20. Jinnah's exact words were "Even if it is a moth-eaten truncated Pakistan, we'll take it," spoken on the eve of the founding of Pakistan in 1947. It is interesting to note that despite his goal of saving Islam in South Asia by creating a Muslim state, Jinnah was personally not a strong Muslim and could not speak Urdu. One political analyst recently pointed out that "those who continue to rave about this speech also need to be reminded that Jinnah was never a practising Muslim. He loved his Scotch and soda and preferred ham to chicken in his sandwiches. Namaz (obligatory prayer to Allah) was alien to him. The slogan 'Islam in Danger' and the two-nation theory came in handy to him to achieve his objective of getting a sovereign country—'truncated and moth-eaten,' in his own words—that he could rule."
21. The full story is told in Chapter 13: First Radio.

MORAN IN NEPAL

9

Into Nepal

Most people who become missionaries have an adventuresome streak in them, a fascination with the unknown, a readiness to undertake things they were not prepared to do. It's good that they have, because very few missionaries know beforehand what they are actually getting into.
  Thomas Hale, an American missionary to Nepal[1]

The readiness is all. Hamlet V, ii, 232.

Marshall's life in Patna during the 1940s was closely tied to the founding and growth of St Xavier's High School. He served for over ten years as its principal, giving up the post only on the eve of his permanent move to Nepal in 1951. And from 1940 to 1948, he also served as rector of the Jesuit Mission House in Patna.

Many other activities had also kept him busy. He helped found the Patna Women's College and Patna's Holy Family Hospital, and assisted with many other mission building projects around Bihar. During the war years and afterward, Marshall matured greatly as a priest. He became a respected administrator. He was particularly astute at garnering support for educational projects. He was skilled at negotiating land purchases and contracts. And in other ways, he was very adept at threading his way skillfully through the political and social mazes of pre- and post-independence Indian society.

Among his many activities, Marshall served as a senior advisor to the Indian administrators of Patna University. He sat on the boards of studies for Education, Philosophy, Latin and Greek, and was honored with a governor's appointment to the University Senate. The latter gave him considerable influence over the educational directions and standards of the university, in decisions about course offerings and selection of textbooks. At the time, Patna University was the only university in all of Bihar.[2] It was a busy academic center with a linkage to Nepal that eventually took Marshall on his first visit to Kathmandu.

9. Young priests on board the ship to India, 1920. L-R: Frs. George Dertinger, Charles Bonnot, Marshall Moran, Richard Welfle, Dick Mehren, John Morrison.

Since 1919, the Rana government of Nepal had supported one small institution of higher learning, Trichandra College, located at the clock tower in the heart of Kathmandu. The college, however, served only the sons of the Nepalese elite and a few others who enjoyed their favor. Its association with Patna University assured that its few annual graduates qualified for further study at universities in India. Over the years, various Nepalese educators had visited the Patna campus where they met Fr Moran. He considered some of them as his friends. He was also well acquainted with certain members of the outlawed Nepalese political opposition living in exile in north India. During those years, the opposition had as their avowed aim the overthrow of the Rana rulers, whose isolationist policies and repressive government they despised.

The Ranas had usurped power from the Shah Kings of Nepal a century earlier, when a young, relatively minor but ambitious courtier named Jang Bahadur Kunwar staged a dramatic and bloody coup known as the Kot Massacre on the night of September 14-15, 1846. After killing off most of the palace courtiers and monarchist retainers, Jang Bahadur changed his family name to "Rana" (it had a more prestigious ring to it) and established his family as the ultimate power and authority in the land, in perpetuity, through hereditary succession. The Rana government survived for over a century, passing power along through Jang Bahadur's brothers and their sons. Ultimately, it crumbled from within and was overthrown in 1951.

All this time, the Shah royal family was maintained in strict isolation, virtually imprisoned in the palace, available to public view only on ceremonial occasions. Among the peasantry, the royalty was considered sacred—the King was believed to be a reincarnation of Lord Vishnu, so the Ranas dared not destroy the monarchy entirely.

Under the Rana regime, only the sons of the Ranas and a few other elite families, such as Pandey, Upadhyaya and Koirala, were allowed to study at Kathmandu's Durbar High School and Trichandra College, and in a few foreign universities, mostly in India. There was a custom among a few well-to-do Nepalese families to send their young sons to elementary school and high school in India. Marshall had taught a number of them at St Xavier's in Patna and was impressed as much by the Nepalese national character as by their scholastic abilities. Nepalese respect for Jesuit education had grown strong under the positive effects of academic discipline, diligence and success. Some of the boys whom Marshall and other Jesuits taught at Patna returned to Nepal to take up positions of authority within the government. And some joined the Nepalese political opposition.

As Marshall became acquainted with the fathers and uncles of his Nepalese students, of both pro- and anti-Rana persuasions, he occasionally spoke with them about education in Nepal. He detected a strong desire and conviction among the Nepalese for new and better schools (in confidential conversations, for they dared not speak openly of such radical notions). Marshall quietly encouraged them, and as time passed he felt a special calling to help Nepal improve its educational foundations. Perhaps, he thought, he could assist by introducing a modern Jesuit boys' school on the order of those in India.

In 1949, the Nepalese prime minister was General Mohan Shamsher Jang Bahadur Rana, a grand nephew of the original Jang Bahadur. Mohan's own nephew, General Mrigendra Rana, served as Director-General of Education. In Patna, Marshall occasionally met General Mrigendra, a man in whom he heard a voice of reason and quiet dedication to modernization.

But while Mrigendra and others like him sought reform, the time was not yet right for sweeping educational change in Kathmandu. The Rana Prime Minister had recently condescended to allow some minor reforms in the social system, but neither the Rana supporters nor the opposition were yet prepared or able to force the establishment of a more open society. Leaders on both sides often spoke of much needed social and educational improvement, but Marshall kept his distance from any moves for radical change. Instead, he bided his time, ready and waiting to help when needed. Eventually, his readiness paid off.

Trichandra College Exams

Meanwhile, Nepal had come to rely on Patna University for help in two ways. One was through the university's oversight of a system of high school examinations leading to the SLC, the coveted School Leaving Certificate. A high pass in the SLC exams at Kathmandu's Durbar High School assured graduates of entry into nearby Trichandra College as well as to Patna University. The university also guided the educational system at Trichandra College, which relied on Indian university textbooks, matriculation procedures and systems of annual entrance and degree examinations.

Each year at examination time, a representative of the university was sent to Kathmandu to serve as the supervisor of examinations, to proctor both the Intermediate and the Bachelor of Arts and Sciences degree exams at the college. Usually, the rector of Patna University sent one of his Indian professors up for the month-long duty. After the exams were given, the test sheets were sealed and hand-carried back to Patna for scoring. In going to Kathmandu, these representatives left the comforts of urban India behind, to suffer what they considered to be both an arduous overland trek and primitive accommodations on arrival. The Indian examiners typically endured the hardships of this duty only once, unlikely to do it again.

Despite the reports of appalling conditions, Marshall was personally very keen on proctoring the Nepal exams; he had long been envious of his Indian colleagues who had gone, despite their complaints. Regardless of the conditions, he hoped one day to have the same opportunity. As a member of the University Senate, he was certainly qualified. But as a foreigner and a non-Indian, his welcome by the Rana authorities in Kathmandu was not likely; particularly, he thought, if they knew he was an American. The Nepalese rarely welcomed any outside visitors, although they tolerated with severe restrictions the presence of an official British government diplomat, or Resident. Under such xenophobic circumstances, the best Marshall could do was wait and see. His patience was immense; he had already waited nearly twenty years since first catching the Nepal fever after glimpsing the distant snowcapped Himalayas from the school in Bettiah.

Looking Back
"Then you go," said the Vice Chancellor
Fr Moran

In the summer of 1949, my friend Sarangdhar Sinha, Vice Chancellor of Patna University, called me into his office. After the usual pleasantries, he told me he had been invited to attend the Commonwealth Vice Chancellors' Conference in London late in the fall. But he was reluctant to go. He didn't think his English was good enough and he felt that he might not be welcome there so soon after Independence. He asked if I would kindly go in his place.

The London meeting was very prestigious and I was honored at the suggestion, but I declined. I spoke quite frankly to him, convincing him without much effort that he really ought to go. India was free of the British now and the sooner they got used to an independent India, the better. And they certainly didn't want to see an American face, I told him.

Then I said, "You go to London. Let *me* go to Nepal." It came out of my heart, just like that.

Jamuna Prasad, the Registrar, responded immediately and said, "Oh, that's nothing. I can arrange for that. But do you *really* want to go there? They haven't got a hotel, there's not a single paved street. It's dirty, you know. There is no sanitation. All of our men who've gone there as examiners in the past say they never want to go back again." He obviously didn't think I would like it any better.

"Yes," I said, "I want to go."

I had thought long and hard about Nepal for years and felt I had to get into the country somehow. I'd tried unsuccessfully to persuade British diplomats to invite me up for Christmas. They always said it was impossible. And, for them, it *was* impossible. Nor did I want to be seen tagging along with any American diplomats. That wouldn't seem quite proper or neutral. I could almost hear the cries from some quarters if I'd done that: "What's Uncle Sam's neutrality all about, non-religious and all that?" someone might say.

"I still want to go," I told the vice chancellor, despite all the negative description of conditions in Kathmandu.

It worked. "Then you go," said the Vice Chancellor.

So Sinha flew to England and I walked to Nepal, assigned to "invigilate" the exams, as the Indians say it in their British-Indian English style of speech.

The Trail to Kathmandu

Fr Moran had to wait for the monsoon to end before he could start out on his first journey into Nepal. The exams were scheduled for most of the month of October, when the days are typically clear and warm in Nepal and the mountain views are inspiring. But to Marshall, it seemed as if the snowcapped peaks had come out in their crystal clearness just for him. After years of gazing north, he was now, at last, actually going north into the mountains to the Valley of Kathmandu.

He departed Patna on October 1, 1949, starting out on a route that for the first part was already quite familiar to him. This time he was driven by car to the levee, where he crossed the Ganges on a side-wheel ferry to Sonepur on the north bank. From there he boarded a night train for the trip northward toward the border. The train passed through the Bihari towns of Muzaffarpur and Motihari, which he had come to know during his early years in Bettiah. At Sagauli he changed to a train headed for Raxaul on the India-Nepal border. Sagauli was only a small village, made briefly famous as the place where the British and the Nepalese Gorkhalis had made peace under the Treaty of Sagauli, which ended their little war of 1814-16.

In the morning at Raxaul, Marshall crossed to Nepal by horse-cart and rode into the dirty little town of Birganj. There, for the first time, he stood on Nepalese soil. He was met by Nepalese officials and taken to the government guesthouse for breakfast.

Marshall was not traveling alone. At the last moment he was joined, in Patna, by Pradyumna Rana, an eleven year old Nepalese boy, who was going home from school in Patna to celebrate the upcoming Hindu holidays with his family in Kathmandu. Young Pradyumna was the son of Major Mahendra Rana, an officer in the Rana Prime Minister's army. Major Rana, like many Nepalese from the elite class, had sent his son to be schooled in India. The boy was in the fourth standard class. For this trip home, Marshall was Pradyumna's chaperone. Pradyumna, however, thought of himself as Fr Moran's special guide.

The ride from Birganj on into Nepal in those days was by an ancient coal-fired narrow gauge railway. The train huffed and puffed across Nepal's Tarai lowlands past open fields where villagers were busy reaping the rice crop, then through the fearful *Chaar Koshi Jhari*, an eight-mile stretch of malaria-infested jungle that separated the plains from the foothills. This malarial forest had repulsed British troops during their first assault on Nepal in 1814. Every few miles the train stopped to take on water. Marshall thought he'd seen narrow gauge trains, but to him, this one was "*extra* narrow and *extra* slow. It took three hours to go twenty miles."

The road beside the train track was narrow and dusty. The common people walked this lane or, if they were lucky, rode on bullock carts drawn by high-humped zebu oxen. Now and then the train passed a one-horse *tonga* cart. "Or, should I say *they* passed *us*, the train was so slow," Marshall remarked.

At the end of the line was sleepy little Amlekhganj, a village at the base of the outlying Churia hills. The Churia is an extension of the north Indian Siwalik range, a long line of low and geologically degraded hills that mark the southernmost first step into the Himalayas.

At Amlekhganj, the priest and the schoolboy had to wait for a bus to take them on the next stage of their journey, to the start of the mountain trail above Bimphedi. While waiting, they sipped sweet, milky tea at one of the shops in the shade of a huge tree near the railway station. Finally, a decrepit old bus arrived and began to load. In no time it was packed with villagers and their baskets, bags, goats, chickens and crying babies. The bus bumped north alongside the Padewa (Pigeon) River into the hills. For awhile it wound along past the stony riverbed through a beautiful forest of *sal* hardwood trees and, higher up, through tall pines. Black-faced langur monkeys scampered across the way in front of them and bright tropical birds darted in and out of the green foliage.

Finally, after crossing a low pass, they descended down through the sal forest on the other side towards the slow flowing Rapti river. After crossing on a rickety bridge they entered the tiny trading town of Hetauda, then only a few shops and dingy tea stalls, but today a bustling truck stop and major center of commerce and education. A few miles farther along, they came to a halt on the edge of the gushing Bhaise (Water Buffalo) River. This marked the end of the road and the start of the walk.

As it was still early in the day, the two travelers, man and boy, set out uphill to reach the guesthouse at Chisopani Gardhi. They were now entering the Mahabharat *lekh*, literally "the great India hills," a huge forested mountain range, a major obstacle on the trail to Kathmandu rising abruptly from the Rapti Valley floor. Young Pradyumna Rana assured Marshall that they would reach Kathmandu by the following afternoon.

Looking Back
Into Nepal with Fr Moran
Pradyumna Rana, Godavari Class of '56

I accompanied Father Moran on his first visit to Nepal because I was going home on holiday. I used to like riding the ferry steamer across the Ganges and the trains up to Raxaul. Father—we boys always called Moran just "Father"—was treated on that trip as a very special guest of the Rana prime minister. The Prime Minister was a distant relative of mine.

We rode the NGR, the Nepal Government Railway, all the way from Birganj to Amlekhganj. We usually called it the "Never Going Railway." The NGR tracks were narrow gauge, very narrow. The distance wasn't very far, but to me, a boy, it seemed forever.

I traveled this way many times, going to and from school in Patna each year. The big forest always impressed me and I used to wonder at all the wild animals and birds. Every time my parents warmed me: "Never sleep there; you'll catch malaria." That was many years before the government's malaria eradication campaign, which led to the deforestation and opened the Tarai to farming. Now there's hardly a tree to be seen, only flat farmland for miles and miles.

On the bus to Bhimphedi we were lucky—no breakdowns. I wasn't usually so lucky and remember many times when it took a whole day with many delays.

At the guesthouse that first night, the officials checked our travel papers. Father had a visa but since I had decided to come rather suddenly, I had no proper permission. I had to call ahead to the Prime Minister's palace in Kathmandu. I was a Rana, so they allowed me, but the telephone line was terrible and I had to shout to be heard. But of course, I was given permission to come.

The next morning we started walking up the mountain trail. As a privileged Rana boy, I was expected to ride in a *tamdan* litter chair that was always provided. The tamdan was slung on a pole, carried by two men on their shoulders. Father was politely offered a horse and *syce* (attendant), but we both preferred to walk. Still, he teased me about riding in the litter. We had six porters for all our luggage, plus four for the tamdan. They traded off carrying it, two at a time.

Marshall Moran's own account of the trip continues from there.

Looking Back
Over the Mountains
Fr Moran

Already I was feeling the cooler weather of the mountains, and by the time we reached Chisopani Gardhi it was quite chilly. We made ourselves comfortable in a very primitive stone and brick guesthouse. After a simple rice supper we went to bed. We would start out again at six in the morning.

Ahead of us was the valley of Chitlang and the Chandragiri ridge, and beyond that Thankot, the formal check post at the entrance to Kathmandu valley. I knew the names of the villages along the way from a map I carried. I had prepared myself by reading Perceval Landon's *Nepal*, in which he described the kingdom as he'd seen it in the 1920s.

The following day was bright and beautiful, and the route was very picturesque. I remember walking through vast fields of ripening rice, now turning to gold. And it is no exaggeration to say I appreciated the clear, clean, cool mountain air, refreshingly so after the hot dusty plains of India. Big yellow-green *pomelos*, like American grapefruit, were ripening on the trees. And birds were singing as they passed through the mountains on their fall migration out of Tibet and Siberia towards India and South Africa. The people along the way were very jolly, in a holiday mood. It was festival time and the people were celebrating Dasain, the same as our Dassahra in India. Dasain honors Durga, a powerful demon slayer, the Nepalese version of the Hindu goddess Kali.

By three o'clock in the afternoon we were on the last uphill stretch, ascending Chandragiri. From the top, at an elevation of 7,400 feet (according to Landon), we got our first glimpse of the Kathmandu valley. It was a beautiful view, fifteen miles across to the eastern side. Thankot was at the western corner, below us. Out on the valley floor lay Patan on the south side of the Bagmati River and, of course, there was Kathmandu city itself. Rising above the rather medieval-looking red brick buildings and red-tiled pagoda roofs of the city's many temples, I recognized two prominent white landmarks—the minaret called Bhimsen's Tower and the "Bell House," or *Ghanti Ghar*, the clock tower of Trichandra College.

The Royal Guesthouse

That first glimpse of Kathmandu was an inspiring and unforgettable moment. While Marshall caught his breath from the steep climb and gazed out across the valley, he tried to visualize the scene over two hundred years earlier, when Fr Ippolito Desideri had passed here on his way home from Lhasa to Rome.[3] The scene cannot have changed much, he thought. For the Jesuits, the wait to return was a long one. But for Fr Moran, "Personally, being here the first time was answer to many prayers, dreams and aspirations," he said.

A maroon 1927 Chevrolet touring car with a canvas top was waiting for Marshall and young Pradyumna Rana at the Thankot checkpost. Pradyumna assumed that his father had sent it, but Marshall was sure it was sent there on orders from the Prime Minister himself. He knew that the few cars that existed in the nearly roadless valley had been carried in by teams of sweating porters over the same torturous mountain trail he had just walked. He had seen pictures of that feat in old *National Geographic* magazines, so he appreciated the ride. He and Pradyumna were driven the six miles into the city over a rough, unpaved road. While Marshall was shown to his quarters in No.2 Guesthouse in Tripureshwar, near the Bagmati river, young Pradyumna was driven home to his mother and father.[4]

After a quick wash up, Marshall was served a sumptuous tea. The table was set very generously for any taste, he recalls, with fresh fruit and imported crackers, cocoa and malted milk. His quarters were Spartan, but good enough, and he settled into them quickly for the month long stay.

The next morning, the Principal of Trichandra College, Rudra Raj Pandey, came to the guesthouse to greet him and to lay out the time table and schedule of events. He seemed surprised to see that Marshall was a Westerner, but nothing was said. An audience with Prime Minister General Mohan Shamsher Jang Bahadur Rana was set for the following day. After that, Marshall would proctor the exams at the college every weekday except Saturdays until the end of the month, from 9 o'clock to noon each morning and from 1 to 4 o'clock each afternoon. The principal offered to have him driven back to the guesthouse daily for lunch, but Marshall declined. Instead, he asked the guesthouse cook to prepare some sandwiches and a thermos of tea. "I decided to eat my snacks in the college library and save the horses, and my time, running back and forth through the city."

The horses Marshall referred to pulled the royal landau carriage that was put at his disposal. The Prime Minister had offered his carriage or his motor car. Marshall chose the carriage. "I knew that a motor car would only stir up the dust and I wouldn't see much of the shops and the people," he said. His choice also reflected a certain quiet flamboyance when it came to conveyances, reminiscent of his youth in Chicago when he drove his grandfather's stately old Kissel motor car to his summer job at the bank. And it preceded the time, a few years later, when he could be seen roaring through the streets and alleyways of Kathmandu on his motorcycle, wearing a beret and scarf and looking a bit out of character, like the Red Baron.

"As the carriage was a very regal affair, I would be recognized as an important person," he thought. "I rode with the top down. It was pulled by a team of excellent thoroughbreds, and two attendants sat behind me in a sort of rumble seat. They added to the pomp and dignity of it all. My hosts went to all this fuss as soon as they realized that I was not just another Indian professor from Patna, but someone whom they assumed must be a proper Englishman. I liked this merry open conveyance because I could look into the shops and into the peoples' eyes along the street side. I was a bit of a spectacle and the people wondered, you know, 'Who is this pale faced visitor?' At the time I thought it was good to 'fly the flag', so to say."

The next day, General Mrigendra S.J.B. Rana, Director-General of Education, came by the guesthouse to renew his acquaintance with Fr Moran. They had met before, in Patna. He had come to greet Moran and accompany him to meet the Prime Minister. Mrigendra was the son of General Babar S.J.B. Rana, who as commander-in-chief of the army and brother to the Prime Minister, was the second most powerful man in the country.

Audience with the Prime Minister
Marshall's audience with the Prime Minister was held at 5 o'clock in the afternoon. He arrived at Singha Durbar, the Prime Minister's palace (now the government's main secretariat building), in time to witness the daily public audience, or *durbar*. At this time each day the Prime Minister would stand out on the balcony of the palace, in front of the famous Crystal Room, to greet all the civil servants and give them his final "Namaste" greeting before they went home for the evening. After observing this ritual, Marshall and General Mrigendra were ushered into the Prime Minister's quarters for a private but very formal meeting.

Mohan Shamsher talked for a long time about the weather and the overland route up from India. He had many questions. "What part of Britain do you come from?" he asked. Marshall politely joked that he came from a place several thousand miles away on the other side of the Atlantic, a place called Chicago. "I'm an American," he said.

"Oh, you are?" the Prime Minister asked, a little surprised. Then he abruptly changed the subject to inquire if his quarters were comfortable.

"Yes," said Marshall, "although they are limited. But they are clean and satisfactory. If this is what is usual, then it is acceptable to me."

"Oh!—No, no!" the Prime Minister protested. "We'll have you shifted immediately." And before he got back to his quarters at Tripureshwar, Marshall's gear had been moved to the more commodious and luxurious No.1 Guesthouse, a special bungalow reserved for only the highest-ranking visitors.

"There I was given a special cook who took orders, and a bearer, and a cleaning boy," Marshall later described it. "Now I had three rooms all to myself, a sitting room right in the front, a bedroom and a small dining room. But the washroom was primitive, Bettiah style, I thought, with rather antiquated sanitation."

Proctoring the Exams
Every morning at quarter to nine, the carriage stood ready to carry him through the city to the college. There, wooden desks were

arranged for the exams in the spacious library room directly under the famous clock tower. Groups of ten to thirty students sat for the various examinations, fewer for chemistry and biology, more for the arts, economics and literature. And while the boys were writing, Marshall was pulling down books that interested him from the library shelves, for reading. First he read all the books on mountain climbing. He finished those the first week. During the second week he read from various histories of Nepal, then of Tibet, the published journals from early expeditions. He even found Fr Desideri's *Account of Tibet* which he had first encountered while studying at Kurseong. Tibetan and Nepalese Buddhism especially interested him. He pored over everything in the library that touched on that subject, which wasn't much.

"During the exams in economics, I asked the professors if they could give me papers that the boys had written about village visits, in which the economics of rural life might be described. I wanted to find out about the availability of milk, for example, and how many cows and buffalo there were per capita, the number of people and how much was available for babies and small children. I could guess that Nepalese children suffered from a poor diet. Years later, at Shanta Bhawan Hospital in Kathmandu, it was borne out that many children were not getting a child's diet. The villagers fed them highly spiced rice, exposing their children to digestive problems before they were old enough to eat an adult diet. It was mainly due to a lack of simple, more digestible foods."

Marshall was all alone there overseeing the students, but he had no trouble keeping busy during the exams. His curiosity about Nepal never flagged. His mind was racing. "All those books! My desk was perpetually loaded with books. I never had an idle minute. It made my sojourn at the college very enjoyable, as a welcome break from my work in India. New books, new ideas, new experiences, new kinds of people."

Despite the presence of Trichandra College, and Durbar High School a few blocks away, schooling under the Ranas was stifled by fear and suspicion. Few people came to talk with Fr Moran. What conversations he held were generally truncated and disappointing. "The professors at the college were very careful not to appear too interested in me or in any scholarly topics I might bring up. People were so cautious in those days lest they appear too friendly, too intimate, too curious. They feared even the slightest appearance of being eager to learn, of falling under some unsanctioned foreign influence."

Nonetheless, despite the reserve and strict protocol about meeting Moran, Pradyumna Rana's family decided to risk inviting him to dinner.

Looking Back
Moran Comes to Dinner
Pradyumna Rana, Godavari Class of '56

After leaving Father at the guesthouse, I was taken home to our house in Naxaul Gaucher, in the northeast part of the city.[5] My father wanted to invite Father Moran to dinner during his visit. To do that we had to get permission from the Prime Minister. In those days, whenever foreigners came to visit it had to be reported. There were some British in Kathmandu, and occasionally an American. We thought of them all as the same and called them all "Angrezi" (English). Only later, when more Americans came, we changed and began to call them all "Amrikani." It was very difficult in those days to invite an Angrezi home.

We were distant relations to the Prime Minister and my father, as a major in the army, used to work with the lower-ranking military personnel. But we had to go through channels for anything like this. You had to have connections, even within the Rana family, because some Ranas were against the government. Everyone was suspicious.

The ruling Ranas feared political discussions and suspected trouble from foreigners. The thing to remember is that in those days the Rana rulers were in trouble. But my father was not involved in politics. He didn't have any, and didn't talk of politics that I knew of. We were not rich Ranas, only average, and my father had difficulty affording to send me away to school. Even as a Rana, I was held back two years before I was allowed to go to school in Patna.

Our cooks and servants were, of course, Brahmins of the highest status. Only they could cook for us. It all had to do with Hindu ritual purity. We had a big house and my father put on a big party. Not a party in the sense that we invited many people, only our many family members. We all gathered downstairs, on the first floor, since strangers were not allowed upstairs near the kitchen. That was forbidden. Even after shaking hands with a *mlechha*, a foreigner, we Hindus had to take a bath, because we had touched someone of such low status.

It was very hard to get Father to the house, but we finally got permission. My father was very bold in that. It was Father Moran's first experience, his first dinner in a strict Hindu Nepalese house.

Life Under the Ranas

Life under the regime run by the richest Ranas catered mostly to immediate family members, their close relations, and a few other trusted elites. The ruling Rana lifestyle reflected a wealth and splendor gleaned from the sweat of the common people, and many Ranas accomplished little more than self aggrandizement and the enrichment of their own family fortunes on the backs of the peasants. They built themselves huge palaces punctuated with gaudy Baroque appointments and Victorian furnishings imported at great expense from Europe. They married much into the Indian nobility, with the sons and daughters of Rajput and Kshatriya *maharajas*. In Marshall's view, this was something of a blessing, for it brought new blood and new ideas. But no new ideas were acceptable if they threatened or interfered in any way with the power and prestige of the Rana leaders. Any persons in opposition to the ruling elite, the non-Rana monarchists as well as the scions of lesser Rana lineages by mixed marriage, were banished from the valley or exiled to India. Political and personal patronage was rife, fueling the revolution to come.

During their hundred year reign, the Ranas neglected virtually every department of government except tax collection. They ignored the mostly silent cries of the people for social justice and economic betterment.[6] In 1949, the Prime Minister also served as chief justice and his brother was commander-in-chief of the army. Their control was complete and repressive. With a few exceptions, the needs of the common people were neglected. Electricity was practically nil. The transport system was medieval. Water supply and sanitation, hospitals, most schools and virtually all other amenities were poor. There was no real concern for development or improvement, partly out of a fear that rapid change would undermine their own paramount position. And, as Fr John Locke later observed, "Education itself was a dangerous novelty." By 1951, only one hundred students in all of Nepal had finished high school.[7]

Those opposed to Rana rule felt that if change and progress were to come at all, it must come through revolution. No one could guess how much longer the Rana autocrats, with their policy of forced isolation from the outside and repression within the borders, would last. But there were many signs of disenchantment and decline. Revolution was in the air.

The education system was often talked about, but not much was done to improve it. The Durbar High School and Trichandra College were founded early in the twenty-eight year reign (1901-29) of Prime Minister Chandra S.J.B. Rana, but there had been little progress in education since then. In Marshall's view, "Nepal, like almost every princely state in India, was a backwater of educational oppression. Freedom of speech was almost nonexistent, the courts and all were dominated by the Rana family clique, all of whom were supposed to be loyal. There was only one real benefit—living was cheap. And if you were smart, with a modicum of learning, and if you were in the good graces of the family, you could prosper moderately. There was no great fluctuation in politics because there was practically no politics. There was no press, and Indian newspapers were closely watched and frequently banned from the kingdom. Indian films were not allowed because their tone was considered too patriotic, hence potentially dangerous. The college was a place open only to Rana favorites and was subsidized very much on a personal basis. The Prime Minister himself reviewed every student who applied for studies and he was very careful that only the most conservative professors were allowed to teach. It was an autocracy in the truest sense, the rule of one man, one family."[8]

A Royal Guest

In retrospect, Marshall wonders what they made of him, an outsider, a religious man and an educator whose whole lifestyle and philosophy reflected foreign ideas. During that month, no one spoke to him about his identity as a Catholic priest. Christianity, as a foreign doctrine, as foreign learning, was naturally suspect under the Ranas. There had been no missionaries of any sort in Hindu Nepal for nearly a century and a half. Marshall, however, made no secret of his identity and everyone with whom he dealt on an official level knew who he was and what he stood for.

"Later, I realized that while in Nepal I never once asked for liquor (forbidden to Hindus), although I did ask for lemon and orange squash for drinks. I brought with me a whole bottle of mass wine. Anyone at the guesthouse could see; I was not secretive about it. Each morning I arose early to say the mass, my private *puja* (worship). I'd go out into the guesthouse garden to say the rosary with my beads. And when I went off to the college each day, I'd leave my crucifix and the wine out in the room. The palace surely knew of it, but I acted no differently about the religious practice in Nepal than I had each day in Patna. Nothing different, no subterfuge, no chicanery. I wasn't hiding anything. I followed the same practice later when I returned to Kathmandu to open the school. If we are going to have a fight, I thought, let's have it out and be finished. I demand these freedoms, you see." But nothing happened. No one questioned or challenged him and he carried on his personal life as a priest quite normally, in private but not in secret.

One day at the college Marshall was asked to help grade an essay contest. "'Here are forty student papers for you to correct,' I was told. 'It is entirely voluntary.' Both Principal Pandey and Director-General Rana thought that I would be a neutral person, because I hadn't taught these boys. 'You don't know their names nor their backgrounds,' they said. 'You don't know their parents nor their families' positions. We've coded the papers with numbers instead of names, so you can't even guess, although you might assume that some are from Pandey or Rana families.'"

"Over the next few days I read the forty papers, weeding the stack down first to the ten best. I read those ten very carefully, checking for proper English grammar, syntax and spelling, for original ideas and imagination, for the work as a whole, the complete composition, whether it was printable and so forth. Finally, I tallied up the individual marks and handed them back. The best paper was on top, but I had no idea whose it was. I didn't know until much later the boy's identity."

"The following year, while negotiating to open the first Jesuit school in Nepal, in an idle moment, I asked Director-General Rana about it. 'Who won?' I asked. 'My own son,' he replied proudly. That bit of luck bolstered our respect and regard for one another during formal negotiations for the school."

Discovering Godavari

Marshall used every chance he could to discuss prospects for opening a boys' school in Nepal. Mrigendra Rana was keen on the idea, but he was cautious in discussing it. On Saturdays he arranged that one or another professor from the college would accompany Marshall on picnic trips out into the hills surrounding the Kathmandu Valley. On those occasions, Marshall would ask, "Can any of the boys write a proper paragraph when they first come to you in the college?"

"Well, now...," was their invariably hesitant reply. "No, they can't."

Then Marshall would press the point. "You know, of course, that they could learn these things in a good school," he said. "If they got good teaching in lower school and in high school, here in Nepal, and if they took better care and paid more attention, they could do these things well." Later, Marshall brought the subject up during his farewell audience with the Prime Minister.

Meanwhile, he used each weekend trip to look for a suitable site for such a school, should the Jesuits ever be invited to start one. The first Saturday he was accompanied by Jayendra Singh, one of the younger faculty members who later rose to become one of Nepal's finer diplomats. They trekked to Kakani, in the hills on the northwestern rim of the valley. After climbing eight miles to the top, they could see down into the Trisuli Valley towards Nuwakot, the hilltop fortress from which Prithvi Narayan, the first Shah king, led his Gorkhali soldiers on their successful invasion of the Kathmandu Valley in 1769.

The next week Marshall visited Nagarkot, at the northeastern end of the valley and, after that, Sundarijal, at the north. Each time a different professor accompanied him and each time they'd hike up the hills and have a picnic and hike back. Marshall enjoyed walking through the farm villages and seeing the rural people at work and observing some of their customs. It was all quite different from village life on the plains of north India. And each time he would comment quietly, tactfully, to his hosts about the need for a good school. But he also told them how difficult it would be to build a proper facility on such steep hillsides. "Students need some flat place for playing fields," he told them.

The month went by quickly and he was soon called back to the Prime Minister's office for a farewell audience before returning to India. By now he had become reasonably well acquainted with the Director-General and asked him candidly, "Should I say anything to your uncle, the Prime Minister, about a school?"

"Yes, please do," he was told encouragingly.

"When Mrigendra and I met the Prime Minister, he asked me bluntly: 'What do the Indians think about Nepal?' I answered him straightforwardly. I openly expressed what I knew about Nepal's image to the outside and my ideas about the need for better schools to help improve it. It seemed to me that his government was rather shy about trying to project a good image towards India."

Marshall asked him: "What is there ever in the Indian newspapers about your projects for the development of Nepal? And, when your students come to India to study without a good basic education here, they are greatly handicapped compared to Indian students. I know that the tutors here are good, but they are only available for a very few, select students, those from rich families, big families, your own family. But what about the average people? They have no chance to excel. How can the country develop? I tell my Nepalese boys attending school in Patna that when they return to Nepal, they should tell their parents, their uncles, their grandfathers, their government, how in India they have to learn to speak Hindi and how hot and dirty it is and how much at a disadvantage they are compared to Indian boys. Instead, they should study in their own language, here in Nepal, in a better climate, among their own people, and save money at the same time."

"You should consider this, Your Excellency," I said in conclusion. "Make an education plan for Nepal."

"Then I smiled and glanced at Mrigendra. He'd already been pushing the idea a little, apparently, because the Prime Minister responded positively."

"'Yes, yes,' he said. 'We'll have to think about this.' It was left at that, for the time being."

The next day Marshall went on a final hike and picnic into the hills, to Godavari, one of the Prime Minister's small summer estates. It was located in the valley, about eight miles south of the city, at the base of the north slopes of the Mahabharat hills.

Godavari —"chrysanthemum"—a place of flowers, forest and wildlife. Naturally ideal for a school, Marshall thought.

"At Godavari I immediately saw the potential. The possibilities for a school were the best there, out of all the places I'd visited. There was enough flat area for playing fields, good spring water and a very fine forest for Boy Scouts, especially, to hike and camp and do bird watching and study nature. It also had several good buildings that could easily be converted into classrooms and living quarters. And not least, Godavari was far enough away from the city and the politics and all the distractions of urban life that do not in any way help study and discipline. And the priests there would not always be the object of curiosity and suspicion. Out of sight, out of mind, I thought."

Back to India

A few days' later Marshall left Kathmandu to return over the mountains to India. He thought it strange that Mrigendra was not there to see him off. Perhaps he had been detained, or maybe the weather had something to do with it, he thought.

"There was a remarkable thing about my thirty days in Nepal. There was sunshine every day—not a drop of water, not a dark day, not a single cloud—until the last day. Then, as I was leaving, it all changed. There was a torrential rainstorm." The trail across the Mahabharat hills was slippery, but Marshall walked all the way out under a black umbrella, dressed in his black cassock, and arrived back in India without mishap.

The rain had also fallen at Patna, and after disembarking from the train at Sonepur station and crossing the Ganges, he had to call the school for a motorcar to come pick him up. Horses and buggies and rickshaws were out of the question in all the mud. A few days later he wrote to general Mrigendra, expressing his sorrow at leaving Nepal but hoping to return if formal arrangements could be made for him to start a school.

The reply came quickly. General Rana began with an apology for not seeing Marshall off from Kathmandu. He wrote that he had been stranded while on a family picnic in the hills at Kakani, cut off by a landslide that had obliterated the track. "His two-day picnic had been stretched to four because of all the difficulties caused by the storm that ushered me out of Nepal," says Marshall. "But he had some good news. He said he was pushing the idea of a Jesuit school with the Prime Minister."

Waiting for Word from Nepal

Over the next twelve months Marshall received occasional letters from Kathmandu, but no firm or final reply to his request to start a school. In discussing the possibility with Bishop Wildermuth and the Superior, Fr Welfle, Marshall found them eager to let him go to Nepal and willing to free him from his responsibilities in Patna. He had only to wait for Nepal's permission.

Finally, on November 1, 1950, Marshall was visited in Patna by General Mrigendra Rana who informed him personally that, indeed, the government was ready to allow the Jesuits to start a school at Godavari. Marshall remembers well the date. "It was the Feast of All Saints, and because I have the church calendar built into my memory, the date sticks."

Marshall had, all the while, been making long-range plans, but nothing concrete. Now he could put the final touches on his departure from Patna and his new assignment in Kathmandu.

Political events, however, conspired against it.

The Royal Conspiracy

Within a few days of receiving the go-ahead from Kathmandu, the Indian newspapers described far-reaching new events happening in Nepal. King Tribhuvan had gone into hiding inside the Indian Embassy and was seeking asylum in India. The revolt against the Ranas had come to a head and the King had made a bold move. The monarchists and anti-Rana factions in India were prepared to fight if the Ranas did not back down and allow the King to resume the full power of the throne under a new and more democratic, progressive system of government.

King Tribhuvan's move was designed to force the Ranas' hand, but it was not sudden. Rather, there had been considerable planning going on for some time in Kathmandu and also in Delhi within Nehru's government. The Indian ambassador to Nepal, C.P.N. Singh, was, in his way, a co-conspirator with the King. He had already alerted Delhi (it was later revealed) that something would happen in November. In preparation, he had secretly requested and received an additional contingent of Indian soldiers. They entered Nepal disguised as civilians while their uniforms, guns and other supplies were smuggled into the embassy grounds at Lainchaur, near the palace.

In preparation, on November 5, 1950, King Tribhuvan asked permission of the Ranas to go on an outing with his two wives, his sons Basundhara, Himalaya and Crown Prince Mahendra, and Mahendra's infant son Birendra who was about to turn five (b. December 28, 1945). Then, by prior arrangement, as they drove down the road north through Lainchaur away from the Narayanhiti Palace, the King's car suddenly swerved left and sped down a tree-lined lane and through the open gates of the Indian embassy compound.

The monarch's brashness and his conspiracy with the Indians took the Ranas by surprise. The Prime Minister considered Tribhuvan's defection tantamount to abdication, and reacted quickly. The Ranas so controlled the royal family that whenever the King left the palace grounds—strictly by permission only—one or more members of the royal family always remained behind. The hostage on this occasion was Tribhuvan's grandson, Gyanendra, the second son of Crown Prince Mahendra. Gyanendra (b. July 7, 1947) had only recently turned three years old. At the time of his birth, a court astrologer had informed his father, Mahendra, that this particular son would bring him bad luck, so the infant was sent away from the palace to live with his maternal grandmother. Now, the Ranas quickly brought the young boy to the palace and on November 7, 1950, they declared him King.[9]

In seeking asylum from the Indians, King Tribhuvan hoped to go to Delhi to convince the Indian government to force the Ranas to relinquish their grip on his country. To set the stage, Nehru sent airplanes from Patna to overfly Kathmandu, to demonstrate India's superiority in the matter. The planes dropped leaflets to the public, further fueling revolutionary fervor and inflaming enmity against the Ranas.

In Patna, meanwhile, Marshall had been tipped off by a local policeman of what was happening. "Go down to the airport", his informant said. "You'll see the planes."

A special plane was sent from Delhi on November 10th to shepherd King Tribhuvan and the royal entourage out of the country. The Ranas guaranteed their safe conduct and even allowed a cheering crowd to gather at Gaucher Field to see them off. He would return, King Tribhuvan told his people, only when he was reinstated as the monarch with full powers. The excited pro-king faction staged a huge demonstration as he left, but it quickly led to violence with police clubbing and some shooting in which many people were injured.

Following Tribhuvan's arrival in Delhi, negotiations began. Mohan Shamsher sent his brother, General Kaiser Shamsher, who served as the deputy commander-in-chief of the Nepal army, to India. At first they could not come to terms, and for weeks Prime Minister Nehru stage-managed the troubled talks between the King's party and the failing Ranas. The Ranas were determined to maintain power and thought that by acting as regents for Gyanendra, the infant they had installed as King, they could continue to rule. To keep control, they enforced a curfew in Kathmandu and sanctioned considerable repression of pro-king sentiment among the people. Meanwhile, with help from the Indians, the Nepal royalists fielded a small army against the Ranas from across the southern border. Compared with revolutions elsewhere, however, the events in Nepal that winter of 1950-51 were mild and relatively bloodless.

Return to Kathmandu
Meanwhile, Patna was being visited by the Jesuit provincial of Chicago, Fr Joseph M. Egan, the mission's formal link with Rome. It was he who would have final say over any expansion of mission schools into Nepal. On hearing of Marshall's plans, the provincial wanted to see the site and meet the appropriate Nepalese officials. Then Marshall made a very bold and potentially dangerous move. First, he contacted Mrigendra Rana in Kathmandu and told him they were coming. Next, he chartered a Beechcraft airplane and flew into Nepal with the provincial. They landed on the grassy Gaucher Field and spent the night at the royal guesthouse. Early the next morning, they drove out to Godavari to see the proposed school site. As Marshall later described it, "We came, we saw, and the Provincial and General Mrigendra agreed to go ahead with our plan."

It was still quite tentative, but while in Kathmandu, on January 7, 1951, Marshall was told that an armistice had just been signed, giving amnesty to the Nepalese revolutionaries. A new government would be formed immediately. On the morning of January 8th, it was announced in the Indian press. The new ten-man cabinet was a compromise of sorts. It included five liberals from the King's side and five trusted and experienced Ranas, some of them from lower-ranking Rana families who were relatively solid with the King. Mohan Shamsher remained as Prime Minister, but his power was greatly reduced. Plans were made for the imminent return of the king.

"Come at Once"

Back in Patna, Marshall carefully followed Nepalese events in the newspapers. He was anxious to move, despite the turmoil in Kathmandu; but he wisely decided to wait until the new cabinet was sworn in before formally raising, once again, the issue of a new school.

He timed his next move carefully. King Tribhuvan was to return to Kathmandu on February 16, 1951, an auspicious full moon day on the Hindu calendar, a day that became known thereafter as Democracy Day (*Praja Tantra Diwas*). One day earlier, Marshall sent a telegram to the newly appointed education minister, Nrip Jang Rana, a staunch supporter of the King and a social liberal. In it, Marshall reminded the minister that the Jesuits had already been given permission to start a school under the previous government and that now, under the new, more progressive, more democratic government, he hoped for the same level of encouragement and support.

On the afternoon of King Tribhuvan's return, Marshall received the answer by telegram. "It was one of the first decisions made by the new Government of Nepal and a good sign for the future. 'Come at once', it read. So, I came."

Notes to Chapter 9: Into Nepal

1. Thomas Hale, *Don't Let the Goats Eat the Loquat Trees* (1954, p.140).
2. Compared with one university in Moran's time, by 2010 there were eighteen colleges and universities in Bihar, covering general education as well as professional specializations in medicine, engineering, management, education and dentistry.
3. Prior to Fr Moran's first visit in 1949, the only sanctioned missionary activity in Nepal was by members of the Catholic Capuchin Order, during the 18th century (as described in Chapters 4 and 5). Several Jesuit missionary-explorers were also known to have visited the valley even earlier, however, though only passing through. Fr John Cabral came in 1628, the first recorded European visitor, and Frs John Grueber and Albert d'Orville passed through during the winter of 1661-62, from travels in Tibet. And, during the winter of 1721-22, Fr Ippolito Desideri, SJ, the last Jesuit to visit Nepal before Fr Moran, arrived from Lhasa. He stayed several weeks as a guest of the Capuchins before departing for India and Rome. The last Catholic priest of any order known to have been in Nepal before 1949 was the Capuchin Fr Carlo (Carlo Maria of Alatri) who lived there many years until his death in Kathmandu in November 1810 (Chapter 5).
4. The original government guesthouse complex was located on the northwest corner of Kathamndu's Tripureshwar intersection opposite what is now the national sports stadium. The old guesthouse had considerable historical importance. (Who knows all the famous folks who stayed there during Rana times?) Unfortunately for history's sake

and the interest of the chroniclers of Nepal's heritage, the one-storey red brick guesthouse buildings became the detritus of progress when they were torn down and replaced a few years ago by a huge, glittery shopping mall, the multi-storied United World Trade Center.
5. Pradyumna Rana's father's house is now called Mahendra Bhawan (after King Mahendra) and is currently used as a school.
6. This time in Nepal's social history is well documented by Fr Ludwig Stiller, SJ, and Dr Ram Prakash Yadav in *Planning for People: A Study of Nepal's Planning Experience* (1979). See also Stiller's *The Silent Cry* (1976).

   In a more recent and comprehensive account, historian Adrian Sever describes the pitiful situation of life in the kingdom under the Ranas: "The Rana family's monopoly of political power gave it a monopoly of economic power as well, and enabled it to exploit the nation's resources for its exclusive use... As a result, the major part of what the peasants of Nepal produced was appropriated by socio-economic groups that fulfilled no useful economic function, while the bulk of the population was left to eke out a living at subsistence level... The simple and inescapable fact is that the Ranas did not want extensive economic development of Nepal. As long as the economy produced enough to fulfill its primary purpose of catering to the wants of the ruling oligarchy, there was no point in interfering with the *status quo*..." The common people paid the price as the Ranas impoverished the land—"a legacy," Sever concludes, "that still bedevils the country to this day" (Sever, *Nepal Under the Ranas*, 1993, p.412).
7. John K. Locke, SJ, 'Fr. Marshall D. Moran, SJ.,' *Fiftieth Anniversary Book* (2001); online at http://nepaljesuits.org/nepal-jesuit-society/fr-marshall-d-moran-sj/.
8. For more discussion on the repression of literary expression in Nepal under the Ranas, for example, see the author's biography of one prominent intellectual of the time, in *Against the Current: The Life of Lain Singh Bangdel—Writer, Painter and Art Historian of Nepal* (2004, Chapter 5 *passim*).
9. Gyanendra Bir Bikram Shah Dev was the only King of Nepal who was crowned twice in his lifetime. His short first reign began in November 1950, when King Tribhuvan fled to New Delhi. It ended in January 1951, when the Ranas were deposed and Tribhuvan, Gyanendra's grandfather, returned to power from his brief asylum in India. During that short time, the Rana government minted coins in Gyanendra's name and established a special budget to support him, though the child king's first reign was never formally recognized internationally.

   Gyanendra's second reign began on June 4, 2001, following the Palace Massacre of June 1, 2001, which took the life of his elder brother Birendra and, ultimately, Birendra's son, Crown Prince Dipendra, who perpetrated it. King Gyanendra's reign ended on May 28, 2008, when the Hindu monarchy was abolished by the Nepalese Constituent Assembly and Nepal was declared a secular federal democratic republic.

10

Opening Godavari School

It was a great paradise for birds and animals. A little wild and isolated, perhaps, but all the better for teaching, undisturbed. The rhododendrons were in bloom when I got there and the orchids and other flowering trees and plants were beautiful. The local water was excellent, coming from a nearby spring that was sacred to devout Hindus.... The place had a wonderful, clean, quiet atmosphere. But I knew that I had a great deal of work ahead to put it into shape for a school.

Fr Moran, reflecting on his first days at Godavari.

Renovation and Renewal

A few weeks after receiving the "Come at once" telegram from Nepal, Marshall returned to Kathmandu. He flew for the second time, this time in a DC-3, landing on the converted cow pasture, Gaucher Field, east of the city. Air flights to Nepal were not such a novelty any more, after the revolution. It was March, the end of winter and the start of the hot, dry summer season that precedes the annual monsoon. This visit was a short one, for Marshall had to return soon to India to close off his relations with the Patna Mission.

Plans were to open the St Xavier's Godavari School on July 1, 1951. He was eager to begin.

In Kathmandu, Marshall hired a vintage car and driver to take him over the bumpy road nine miles (about fifteen kilometers) to Godavari. Along the way, and on every one of the countless drives over the decades since those first busy days, he admired the diligence of Newar Jyapu farmers plowing, sowing and reaping their fields. And in their villages along the way he observed the equally toilsome and arduous life of the Jyapu women around the houses and in the courtyards that lined crowded alleyways. He imagined it was something like what medieval Europe must have looked like.

The road itself, a simple rutted track, was very dusty when he first drove it in 1951, but he knew that when the rains came from June onwards that it would be a muddy quagmire. That meant that he had to have a very good vehicle to negotiate it, like a jeep with four-wheel drive. He would look into that possibility back in Patna.

As before, on his very first visit to Godavari in 1949, each time he reached the end of the road, up under Pulchowki hill, approaching the new school grounds, he was inspired and cheered. "I couldn't have hoped for a better site for the school," he told himself.

Marshall's first job was to renovate the former Prime Minister's summer palace, to turn it into a functioning boarding school with office space, classrooms and dormitories, bath house, kitchen and dining halls and a library, and a residence hall for priests and teachers. It would not be an easy task, for the old buildings were not well suited for a school. Godavari had once been a place of ostentatious leisure amidst extensive gardens, horse and elephant stables and riding paths, a country estate of courtly splendor where the elite were waited on by a crowd of servants. In 1951, however, since it hadn't been kept up in recent years, it all needed a great deal of repair. And it had to be done quickly if he was to recruit and enroll the first batch of students in time for opening day.

10. Fr Moran in a Godavari School classroom.

On one of his earliest trips hauling carpenter supplies and renovation equipment, he took time out to observe Godavari with the careful eye of a new school builder. He was pleased with the choice and undaunted by the task ahead. Godavari was away from the city, in a forest preserve. His first impressions were that "It was a great paradise for birds and animals. A little wild and isolated, perhaps, but all the better for teaching, undisturbed. The rhododendrons were in bloom when I got there and the orchids and other flowering trees and plants were beautiful. The local water was excellent, coming from a nearby spring that was sacred to devout Hindus. It flowed steadily, I was assured by local people, even during the dry season. The school site was at five thousand feet elevation, five hundred feet higher than the city, so there was no morning mists nor, later, the dirty smog that would cover the city."

To the north was a spectacular view across the Kathmandu valley, a vast expanse of terraced fields dotted with Jyapu farm villages, their ocher-colored houses topped with tiled or thatched roofs. And directly behind the school, at the south, was the nine thousand foot peak of Phulchowki, an eight mile (13 kilometer) trip by road or trail, straight up. Always on the lookout for opportunities to meet boys' physical and spiritual needs, he was pleased with Phulchowki so close at hand—"The boys would have great fun on hikes and campouts in the forest there."

As Marshall continued his solo tour of the Godavari compound that day, he took the time to study carefully the general condition of the buildings and the grounds. "The place had a wonderful, clean, quiet atmosphere. But I knew that I had a great deal of work ahead to put it into shape for a school."

He took pains to inspect each building of the neglected old estate. The prime ministers, he observed, had spent their summers here in cool luxury amidst native pines and rhododendrons and a number of exotic flowering trees and shrubs imported from abroad for the exclusive enjoyment of the ruling class. (The Ranas had declared that some varieties of exotic trees were reserved exclusively for their own properties, and prohibited commoners from planting or owning them.) Some of the most beautiful blooming trees and shrubs at Godavari are, in various seasons, the purple and pink blossomed jacaranda, bauhinia and bougainvillea, as well as Himalayan cherry, camellia, Himalayan ash, and jasmine. And there was a marvelous array of brightly colored birds that flitted about the gardens and forest. (Later, when bird watching became a popular passtime for Nepalese and expatriate birders in Kathmandu, the Godavari area and Phulchowki Hill became popular with ornithologists.)

But sented flowers and singing birds for a prime minister's pleasure are not the immediate needs of an educator and his students. The buildings and grounds that Marshall inspected were a long way from serving the needs of Nepal's first modern school. For starters, the main residence and servants' quarters would have to be remodeled. Later, he would have to see to the formidable task of converting the old horse and elephant stalls into more functional classrooms, dormitories and teacher quarters.

First, to establish a Jesuit identity to the place, he renamed the massive three-story central residence Xavier Hall. It had four very large rooms upstairs and four down, and a few smaller rooms here and there. It would serve as the central school building until others could be repaired or constructed.

Later, when classrooms were ready in other buildings, Xavier Hall came to house a small chapel; a wood working shop; the priests' private quarters, their dining room and library; and an infirmary where sick schoolboys could be looked after and Marshall could practice the basic medical skills he had learned. He eyed one small second floor room, next to his own quarters, for a future "ham shack"—thinking ahead to the day when he could go "on the air" broadcasting by amateur radio to all the world from the heart of the Himalayas. He had dabbled a bit with amateur radio from the high school in Patna during the few years since the war and hoped to continue from Nepal. (See Chapters 13-16.) But, for now, in 1951, and in the foreseeable future, that desire was only wishful thinking. He had years' worth of much more important concerns to keep him busy. He had a new school to administer.

Marshall walked through the expansive gardens in front of Xavier Hall, noting their general state of decline. They would take the skilled hand of a good gardener, he thought. In time, it could become a fine place for contemplation by priests and for inspiration, quiet study and play by their youthful charges. A succession of gardener-priests and Jesuit lay brothers eventually turned the weeds and overgrowth into an attractive and colorful landscape.

He stopped at the circular carriage drive to examine an oval-shaped fish pond with a central fountain spouting clear, fresh Godavari spring water. He estimated its diameter and its depth. Here, he thought, was an ideal small swimming pool for the boys, once the fish were removed and the scum and weeds were cleaned up.

He also visited the source of the spring, a few hundred yards uphill beyond the south wall. It was the site of a small but popular Hindu shrine. So pure is the water that it has never been chemically treated or purified. Only occasionally does the drinking water cause a little "constitutional loosening," as Marshall put it.

Outside the main compound, just below the old horse and elephant stalls, he marked out future playgrounds and sports fields for the boys. He jotted notes to have them leveled and outfitted with goal posts and the other accouterments of team sports like football (soccer), volleyball, and track.

On the east side of the compound, behind Xavier Hall, were the former servants' quarters and store rooms. With additional plumbing, they could be rebuilt to accommodate proper toilets, wash rooms and showers for the boys, as well as a kitchen and student dining hall.

In one out-building near a small back stream, he discovered a broken-down electric generator that had once supplied power to the estate. Marshall wrote a note to himself to hire a mechanic and electrician in Kathmandu who could put the generator back in order so the school could have lights. It might be a long time before a proper electrical line from town was installed to brighten this remote corner of the Kathmandu Valley. Electricity, in those days, was a rare and exotic utility in Nepal.

Between Xavier Hall and the old servants' quarters was a large courtyard that, with repairs and paving, could be converted for playing basketball and tennis and practicing drill. ("Tennis?" he thought. He hadn't played tennis since Florissant.) There was a lot to look after, to repair and rebuild, to rennovate and renew. It would take years to get it all done.

Returning to Kathmandu, Marshall hired a crew of carpenters, plumbers and electricians, and a foreman to watch over them. Then, when he saw them off to a good start at rebuilding the place, he flew back to India to wrap up his final responsibilities to the Patna Mission and to turn over his work to other men. The bishop had already appointed Fr Kevin Cleary to take Marshall's place as rector and local superior in Patna, and Fr Edward Niesen to serve as principal of the high school. (Fr Niesen later joined Moran at the school in Nepal.) The Patna school holidays began on the first of May, the hot season. A few days later, Marshall flew back to Nepal to continue rebuilding Godavari.

During the long wait of the previous year, he had drawn up a plan of action against the day when the sought-for permission to build the Godavari School came through. He intended to start with three classes of twenty boys each. "We'll begin with grades three, four and five. We'd start modestly," he decided, "then add more classes in future years." He knew that fresh schoolboys older than twelve or thirteen years of age would have accents and bad habits and would lack the necessary discipline. "I reasoned that we could get off to a quicker, easier start by thinking small and growing slowly, thoughtfully, carefully," he said.

"I would bring ten Nepalese boys from Patna with me, from the lower classes. They would form the nucleus of the new school, around which the systems and customs and habits and routines of our Jesuit school system would be carried over to this newest one at Godavari. Let those boys serve as captains and guides to the new ones, to help make the transition as painless and happy as possible. Pradyumna Rana, who had accompanied me to Kathmandu on my very first trip, was one of the first Godavari captains."

During all of May 1951, he was alone at Godavari, overseeing the renovation and new construction. The plumbers laid new pipes and made the connections for washrooms, showers, toilets and kitchen sinks. The carpenters repaired the doors, windows and window frames; and one group that he contracted from the city was busy making blackboards and book shelves and enough desks, chairs, beds and dining tables and benches to accommodate sixty boys. There was plenty of work to be done; but the painters had, perhaps, the greatest task, to clean, patch and paint the walls, floors and ceilings, in every room.

Help Arrives
On June 1, 1951, Marshall was in Patna once again, collecting the textbooks that had been delivered by train from the port of Calcutta. He bought special furniture and packed clothing and the personal effects of the first Jesuit teachers who were assigned to join him in Nepal. To transport all these items and much more, the largest of which was a new four-wheel drive Land Rover, he chartered a DC-3 Dakota, the most popular passenger and freight plane of that day.
The heavily loaded Dakota departed Patna on June 3. with Fr Moran, two other priests, Frs Francis Murphy and Ed Saxton, and over two tons of supplies. After bumping to a stop on the rough, grassy airfield in Kathmandu, they started the wearisome task of clearing Nepal Customs. It took five hours. "Then, our big job was to haul it all out over the rough track to Godavari. Our new Land Rover served us very well that day and for many years to come, running back and forth over the Godavari road, to and from our little corner of the valley."

Fr Moran was the school's first principal. He took responsibility for one class, and assigned one each to Frs Saxton and Murphy. Ed Saxton was a young priest who came as a volunteer for the first six months only. Frank Murphy was assigned to Nepal as the first Superior of the tiny new Nepal Jesuit community, a position he held until 1954. He taught English and served as the hostel prefect. He was a favorite teacher with the boys, well known for his talents as a musician and story-teller. For reasons of ill-health, however, he returned to Patna in 1961 and was eventually reassigned to the United States where he died a decade later.

One of the most formidable tasks in starting the new school in Nepal was processing the first batch of student applicants and enrolling the first sixty boys. Applications were received form the hopeful parents of three hundred boys. In a period of a few hours on June 25, at Singha Durbar, the central secretariat building in Kathmandu, the candidates were met and screened and final selections made with the help of several prominent Nepalese educators of that day. Fr Moran chose six individuials to help him, several of whom were closely involved in the founding of St Xavier's Godavari School. The interviewers that day were Rudra Raj Pandey, principal of Trichandra College; Netra Bahadur Thapa, Secretary of Education; Tara Man Singh, a member of the education department; and a Mr Burathoki from Trichandra College.[1]

School opened on schedule, on July 1, 1951. Everyone's spirits and expectations were high. On that day, primary education in Nepal took a giant leap from the medieval to the modern.

It is not surprising, when Marshall reminsced later about those early days at the very beginning of Godavari School, that his memory focused more on physical conditions and shortage of help than on the life of the boys or classroom events and activities. Over time, teaching and daily life became routinized, but the maintenance and improvement of the physical facilities were always with them, always big jobs, often with surprises when least expected or needed.

During the first few weeks and months, things went as smoothly as could be expected, despite inevitable breakdowns of equipment, sick (and homesick) boys, blood-sucking leeches and biting fleas in the school yard grass, and torrential monsoon rains that sometimes washed out the road or mired down the Land Rover in the ruts and effectively isolated boys and priests from Kathmandu for days at a time.

The monsoon laid off in September, heralding the cooler, drier fall and winter seasons. Nepalese winters are typically mild, with clear blue skies and fabulous views of the snow-capped peaks dominating the northern skyline beyond the near hills. The post-monsoon season was certainly welcome that first year, despite the chilly change it brought compared with what Marshall and the others had grown accustomed to on the plains of India. It reminded him of the cold time he had spent in the seminary at Kurseong twenty years earlier.

He used to take walks in the hills around Godavari, admiring the forest and the view of the Himalayas from the forest clearings. Sometimes a few boys would accompany him, and at times like that he never regretted selecting Godavari as the school site. The boys named one of the hills after Fr Moran; it was his favorite for hiking. Godavari had an idyllic beauty and restfullness about it, and was far enough out in the country to avoid the urban hassle of Patan and Kathmandu. Marshall was thankful that it was also far enough removed form the entangling political intrigues and changes that were a continual occurrence in the capital of the nation so newly emerged from its feudal past.

Fr Ed Saxton returned to India in December. In January 1952, he was replaced and the staff further enlarged by the arrival of Frs Bertrand Saubolle and Thomas M. Downing.

Fr Saubolle was an Indian born Frenchman who had lived many years in Darjeeling. He had learned to speak Nepali there and was eager to be involved in the start of the new school in Nepal. He petitioned directly to the Jesuit Father General in Rome for the job, and got it. As Fr John Locke puts it in the account of his life at Godavari, below, Fr Saubolle was "God's gift to the Nepal mission."

Looking Back
The Talents of Bertrand Saubolle, SJ
John K. Locke, SJ[2]

Fr Saubolle was born in 1904, in Orissa, of French and Irish parents. After attending Christian Brothers schools in Kurseong and Shillong, he went for his college studies to St. Xavier's College in Calcutta. From there he entered the Society in 1924. After novitiate and juniorate in Shambaganur, he went to Louvain for his philosophy. He returned after three years to regency at North Point in Darjeeling and theology at Kurseong. After theology, he served as parish priest in Hazaribag and then at St John's in Kurseong. From there he went to North Point College as minister and parish priest.

When the Nepal venture began in 1951, Fr Saubolle volunteered for work in Nepal. With his knowledge of Nepali and his multiple skills, he was God's gift to the Nepal mission. In 1952, he went to Godavari where he spent the rest of his life.

For ten years he served as Minister at Godavari and teacher in the school. As a teacher of Moral Science, he had a gift of enthralling the boys with his stories. A master of many trades, his teaching extended far beyond the classroom. He was a master photographer and a gardener. Mass wine was impossible to get In Nepal, so he took up the task of making it and produced a book on the subject.

He was a pioneer in the use of *gobar gas* (methane from cow dung) and built the first prototype plant in Nepal. When solar energy was first mooted, he made a prototype which provided hot water. He created an energy conserving stove and taught people how to use it. Early on in Nepal, he became interested in bee keeping as a science. He introduced the raising of rabbits for food and profit so that people in the village might increase their income. He wrote booklets on all these skills and distributed them to people. In his later years, the poet in him emerged and he wrote two small volumes of poetry.

Above all, he was a friend not only to the members of the community and the servants who worked for him, but to everyone in the villages around Godavari. Every afternoon he would take a walk through the villages. To this day, people around Godavari say, "Since Fr. Saubolle died nobody cares for us." What they mean is that nobody will take the time just to be with them, listen to their troubles, and share life with them. When he died in 1982, virtually the whole village came to pay their last respects.

Fr Saubolle had certain strong opinions about things and spoke out against what he thought was Marshall's heavy taskmaster demands on the first few priests to join him in Nepal. Marshall did not lay off, however, but later recalled about those times and about Fr Saubolle's concerns that "Our numbers were rather few and we were certainly overworked. In a gentle way, Fr Saubolle let us know that he thought we were being too audacious and daring to try to do so much with so few people. But, despite the work 'overload,' as he called it, we kept to our plans. The school facility continued to be improved. We were all quite pleased with the results."

Fr Saubolle worked unstintingly for thirty years at Godavari, until his death in 1982.

Fr Thomas Downing was from Cincinnati, Ohio. After he came to Nepal in 1951, he was responsible for the Godavari School accounts, and he supervised the hired help. He started right out in the Fifth Standard, a class he taught for the next thirty-five years until his death in 1987. Downing was a very popular teacher. His class plays and theatrical productions, especially 'Hansel and Gretel,' became very popular among the boys. Fr Locke later wrote of him: "Tom was truly a man in whom there was no guile. He said what he thought, a man of true honesty and simplicity. This was a quality which generations of Fifth Standard boys understood and appreciated. They feared him as a stern disciplinarian, but they also trusted him, confided in him, and tried to imitate him."[3]

Looking Back
On the Goodness of Fr Thomas Downing
Chiranjivi S.S. Thapa, Godavari Class of '58

I shall always remember Fr Downing because I was his first Hansel.

I remember Fr Downing as a teacher, among the best, as a magician, as a counselor on extra-curricular activities. He was a perfectionist in everything he did. He rose early, got the boys to wash, bathe, clean themselves, and to study, sing songs, and play games with good cheer, which was always infectious. But I remember him above all as a man who was good.

'Hansel and Gretal' was the young Godavarian's introduction to the eternal truth that ultimately good triumphs over evil. It has become fashionable to say evil is banal; it is more true to say that, like the witch, it is ugly. Goodness is a quality with its own intrinsic and exclusive virtue transcending all other qualities. Like the first star of the evening in the haze before dusk turns into night, the quality of being good has a unique and unmistakable brilliance which all others see as experience. Fr Downing's personality radiated this brilliance and shine of goodness.

Fr Downing was a priest, a Jesuit priest, operating in a non-Christian environment... Although (he) was a Catholic priest and we, his boys, were Hindus, he was one of us, ...blessed with the essential goodness that makes humans of us...

Over a thousand of those whom he taught will carry on, and will get thousands of others to carry on, the greatest message that he bequeathed, that being good is what we should all aim for, that aspiring for goodness represents the highest purpose of human existence, that others will follow us when we are good, and that we pledge to follow Fr Downing because he was above all good; he was good at all times, and he was good towards his Creator, towards his fellow human beings, and particularly towards his Jesuit colleagues, other teachers, and us his pupils of the Godavari community...

A good man is dead, but the good in him lives on forever.[4]

Marshall shared thirty-five years with Fr Downing. Fr Jim Dressman remembers that each man was a gifted and competitive story-teller. Each challenged the other, in sometimes uncomfortably close quarters. "To watch them in action was some fun," Fr Dressman once said. "At times Moran can be pretty tough on others with whom he doesn't see eye-to-eye, and since he and Downing had very different personalities and both were strong-willed individuals, they did not often agree on things." What impressed Dressman, however, was Downing's readiness to change and grow in his approach to life, to teaching and in interpersonal relations. After some years,

Fr Downing took a counseling course at a center in South India. He came back a changed man, and was given the job of spiritual director to the Nepal Jesuit community. "After that, Tom didn't take everything lying down. And that made it all the more interesting," Dressman said.

The New Year 1952 saw Godavari "full up" with the addition of new classes, more student recruits and the school's first Nepalese staff. The first three Nepalese were brought on to assist with classroom teaching. They were Krishna Prasad Pradhan, Aian Bahadur Shrestha, and Bishnu Prasad Jha. Mr Jha served as the boys' Nepali language instructor. In the pedagogical philosophy of Jesuit schooling, attention to the students' cultural heritage is an important responsibility. The students are Nepalese first and foremost, the future leaders of the country and the people, so their national and cultural identities must not be neglected.

Gradually, school operations were routinized and operations of the Jesuit House became familiar. "It was natural that when we had a small number of students and a small staff, we were a very happy, close knit family. Many of the boys of those early days, when they reminisce and look back on their classes and boarding experiences, speak about the close friendships and the family spirit that prevailed." And, as Marshall once said elsewhere, when looking back on his own youth, it was a time "when memories go deep."

The Jesuit Chronicles

Highlights of those early years at Godavari were recorded in the Nepal Jesuit *Vamsavali*, a Nepali word for a kind of historical chronicle of events.[5] The Jesuit Chronicles duly record the first Easter mass, for example, attended by nine Americans and British residents of Kathmandu, some of whom were Anglicans (Church of England). That event was an expression of Christian ecumenism espoused by Marshall and the others, and it provided a small glimpse of the future, just a few years away, when the popular Italian prelate, Angelo Roncalli, would preach worldwide Christian unity in his role as Pope John XXIII. It also previewed a time, not far off, when members of a new Protestant mission to Nepal would regularly join the Catholics in celebrating major Christian holy days together.

In May 1952, Fr Downing directed the first school production of 'Hansel and Gretel,' the first of what became a popular annual event, a Godavari tradition. May also saw the first boys' boxing match. The contestants were trained by Fr Murphy. The best fight was between Kabir Rana and Hira Kaji of fifth grade. Each was awarded a special prize, a Guatemala postage stamp. The Chronicles duly note, however, that Hira Kaji did not collect stamps, a fact that apparently did not diminish his enthusiasm as the victor.

In June, the volleyball court was completed. At about the same time, a nearby building called Nara Mahal was purchased with money donated by Marshall's Mennonite grandmother, Catharine O'Keefe. For years, Nara Mahal was used as a residence hall for Godavari school teachers.[6]

On July 1, 1952, the Jesuit Chronicles acknowledged the first anniversary of the opening of the school, with this note: "All members of staff (are) teaching every period plus other duties = duty from 6:30 AM to 8:30 PM seven days a week." A few days later work began to convert the former horse and elephant stables into more functional, usable space as classrooms. The renovation job took seven months and was completed in February 1953.

On December 30, 1952, the Jesuit community received its first Christmas card from the royal palace. It was signed by King Tribhuvan himself and sent by special messenger to Godavari—five days late, but greatly appreciated by the priests nonetheless. Four months later, Crown Prince Mahendra visited the school. This was a major event, for which everything was scrubbed, shined and polished (and the road out from Kathmandu repaired). It was the first of many royal visits.

School Life
Over the years, as more boys joined Godavari School, occasional clashes of culture were recorded in the Chronicles. For example: "Some boys refuse to take a bath as they say it is forbidden to take a bath in the afternoon if their parents are still alive." Some rather mundane activities had to be carefully planned and sensitively timed and dealt with, to avoid clashing with Nepalese cultural and Hindu or Buddhist social and religious predilections. Later, on trips back to America, Fr Moran was often interviewed about being a Christian missionary in a predominantly Hindu culture, and about the Jesuit mission's approach to religious teaching. Sometime American Catholics who heard or read what he had to say questioned his ecumenical liberalism and tolerance.

For example, Nepalese laws restricting the free choice of its citizens in religious matters always bothered Marshall. But "They've been without Christianity for two thousand years", he was once quoted as saying. "I don't think there's any need to hurry. God will make things easier if He wants." When this opinion was attributed to him in the popular *Chicago Catholic* magazine in 1986, it caused a flurry of concern and criticism among some readers.[7] He weathered the storm.

Another time he described his approach, the Jesuit approach, as being "like an open door—if people want to look in, to come in, then we'll talk with them." But, he disclaimed going out and dragging people in, especially using high-powered tactics for conversion. It was not his way. This approach, too, was questioned by some who thought he should be more forward with issues of conversion.

An early 1953 entry in the Chronicles noted that with the new year, the enrollment had jumped to 119 boys, in classes two through seven. As the school grew in size and prestige, Marshall paid considerable attention to recruiting new staff. He was quite successful at getting good teachers, including American Jesuits, Indian scholastics and Nepalese lay teachers. AS the school's image of quality education grew, so did his importance as its "contact man," as someone called him. He was a real diplomat in the sense of always striving to project a good personal image and school image, combined. Sometimes the two were hard to distinguish, and in the early years some Nepalese thought of Godavari and Fr Moran as one.

More New Priests

Among the teachers Marshall recruited to Nepal in the early 1950s were Frs Bob Mayer, who arrived in November 1952, and Ed Niesen, who came the following May. Fr Niesen had previously helped Moran establish St Xavier's School in Patna. In Nepal for the first time, he lasted less than a week, due to a severe asthma attack. Two years later he returned, and stayed on until 1968, working as "principal, rector, treasurer, builder, buyer, prefect of health, math teacher, and 'big shoulder' for so many for so long."[8] In 1968, however, his ill-health forced him back to Patna. He died there in 1974.

During his time in Nepal, Fr Niesen taught mathematics. He was also considered to have "moulded Godavari School into the fine educational institution, which it still remains today." partly in his role as "a master builder, remodelling and reshaping the odd buildings left from the Rana days to include a new kitchen, a library, a science lab, more classrooms, etc., and the Jesuit residence at Nara Mahal."

Fr Niesen was also "a great sportsman and with General Nara Shamsher (of the Nepal Sports Council) conducted the entire sports programme in Nepal that was organised to celebrate the coronation of King Mahendra in 1956."[9]

Looking Back
Fr Niesen's Contributions to Nepalese Sports
Hemanta Rana, Godavari, Class of '62

It was... in the year 1958 I believe, that I first had the good opportunity of meeting Fr Niesen, SJ. And curiously enough, I happened to meet him not at St Xavier's School where once I was a student, but at the National Stadium—in which field we were destined to meet more often with the very same purpose of conducting sports of all kinds. I had been sort of dragged towards the stadium that year, by my cousin Laxman Shah and brother Sagar Rana where they were participating in the athletic meet that the Royal Nepalese Army was organizing. (Fr Niesen)...was as usual a top official of the meet, whereas I was only a bewildered young kid who was watching with great awe and delight.

(That) inflamed my interest in sports, and Fr Niesen highly inspired me to work, organize, and devote myself in this field. Those days were still very vivid in my memory. I can still remember Fr Niesen... running about helping and supervising other officials of the meet; Fr Moran announcing cheerily from under the big dais, General Nara Shamsher standing commandingly at the finish-line, and S.P. (Superintendant of Police) Fateh Bahadur with pistol-in-hand at the starting-line... I simply cannot forget those days... It is certainly no exaggeration to say simply that Fr Niesen is one of the architects of Nepalese sports itself. To my mind he ranks immediately after General Nara Shamsher in giving sports a firm footing in Nepal.

Some years after he had gone back to India, Ed Niesen revisited Nepal. "It was at that time that his greatest gift became obvious as the teachers of the two schools, the carpenters, masons, and workers gathered round to greet him and recall the 'old days'."

Fr Niesen once said: "A school is not judged by the number of First Divisions (graduates). The best students will do well because of or in spite of the school. A school is judged by whether or not it can get ALL the students through the exam with good results, especially the poorer and the muddling students."[10]

Looking Back
'Fatherly' Fr Niesen
James J. Donnelly, SJ

If one were to put briefly the strongest impression that Fr Niesen made, I would say he was "fatherly" to everyone he met. He was a true father to the whole school family: students, staff, and workers... (Over the years) he built deep loyalties (such as with) Handyman Padma Chhetri, Blacksmith Ram Singh, Carpenters Sher Kazi and his brother Sain Bahadur; Gamesman Jackson, Bookbinder Gopal, plus the cooks, the painters, the masons, and our driver. The same loyalty grew up between him and shop-keepers in town...

He showed a special care for the reputation of the students. He would never allow any tale-bearing in public. His anger would flash, like the wrath of God Himself, if anyone would publicly criticize another. The person's reputation that was at stake was too precious to allow such talk.

The development of the spirit of the school is largely due to his influence. Father (Niesen) already was a seasoned "school man" when he arrived in Kathmandu. He brought with him a rich background of experience and success in the Senior Cambridge system of education, as a result of his 13 years at St Xavier's Patna...

He liked to have student competitions—both in the classroom and outside. He encouraged all sorts of contests and the more fun they involved, the better they were. He showed a deep interest in the school essay and story contests, in the class and school spelling contests, in mental arithmetic contests and, above all, in both the elocution contests and in dramatics. He appreciated the learning that came from student competitions. He liked self-expression and sense of perfection that the students learned from such activities.

As a teacher, Father was outstanding. He communicated very well with his students. He was orderly, interesting, and thought-provoking... Mathematics was his specialty. He knew his subject well, and he knew how to teach it...

(Father Niesen) took a lively interest in the whole development of the students. Academic excellence was always of great importance. But he also took great pains about their diet, about their recreation, such as games, cinemas, and other entertainment, and about their spiritual and emotional growth...

He seemed to show special affection for one in difficulties, for instance a boy in trouble with a teacher. He sat at his principal's desk, called the boy around to him, and talked soothingly face to face, while holding the boy around the waist with his gentle, supportive arms. Boys whose troubles Father shared remember the peace that he was able to restore to their troubled spirits. He gladly took up their burdens and in his gentle, kindly talking restored them to a sense of their own personal worth. Though Father was a very busy man with many problems (ill health) of his own, nothing stood in the way of his giving full attention and as much time as was needed to help such boys to have their problems ironed out. His tactfulness with persons with problems was truly outstanding. It was in such situations, I believe, that his fatherly love was most remarkably proved.

Visits to Town

Every week during those early years, when the number of boys enrolled was still low, Fr Moran took them on special trips into town to visit their families. He would load fifteen into the Land Rover and ten more in a special trailer attached behind. Off they'd go, bumping over the dirt road through dust or mud, depending on the season, through the villages and past the farms, a little over nine miles (15 kilometers) into town. Marshall and his charges made two trips in the morning and one or two in the afternoon, to different parts of the city.

As the numbers of students grew, the faithful Land Rover was not enough, so he rented an old British weapons carrier vehicle. "It had been carried into the valley by coolies and converted by enterprising owners into a bus, of sorts. Only after 1956, with the opening of the Tribhuvan Rajpath, the first road from India, were proper busses with seats and windows in the modern style seen in Kathmandu."

By periodically hauling the boys into town in this way, their parents were put at ease in the face of a lot of critical talk stirred up by the conservatives, or, as Marshall called them, "the 'super orthodox' who had never even spoken to foreigners and did not have a good opinion of scientific or modern education." Nor did some of them especially cherish the notion of Christian teachers instructing Nepal's Hindu youth. The Jesuits were reminded of the troubles the Capuchin Fathers had endured at the hands, and tongues, of the Hindu priests while living in Bhatgaon (Bhaktapur), Patan and Kathmandu, the valley's three city-states, two centuries earlier. Times and conditions had not changed greatly; Nepal was still a conservative society. But the Jesuits were thankful not to be too widely or wildly criticized or questioned, although an occasional rumor reached them about somebody's concern over their activities and the general goings-on at Godavari.

On some of those trips to town, Marshall would stop by at the customs house to negotiate release of vital equipment and supplies that had arrived from India. Importing the mass wine was always a problem, until he convinced customs officials to call it "grape juice" on official documents, thereby getting it through more easily. Otherwise, they paid dearly for it. Occasional comments in the Jesuit Chronicles of the early 1950s indicated the exorbitant fees levied against certain categories of imported goods. Once, the Chronicles noted a 125 percent customs duty on a new jeep for the mission. And, another time, "Mass wine costs Rs 50 per bottle: Rs 4 actual cost, Rs 1 freight, Rs 45 customs duty," an amount that the fledgling mission could not manage for long.[11]

Soon after that the innovative Fr Saubolle started making the mass wine himself, at much less expense. At first he did not know how to make wine, and Marshall's remark—"It's easy: just ferment some raisins"—did not help much. Then Fr Saubolle looked up the subject in an encyclopedia and taught himself. The first batch was served at mass during Holy Week, April 1952.

Some items in the Chronicles simply describe day-to-day circumstances of life at Godavari. The record reflects both the mundane and the monumental. Some examples:

> *February 7, 1953*—"First debate at Godavari School; participants classes 6 & 7."

> *February 8, 1953*—"New classrooms at the gate finally finished; Ft Moran paints the windows; classes held there today" (in the converted elephant stables).

In June, Edmund Hillary came to town following his successful summit assault on Mount Everest with Tenzing Norgay Sherpa. The 1953 British Mount Everest Expedition was led by John Hunt. The following brief entry appears in the Chronicles:

> *June 16, 1953*—"Sir John and Lady Hunt visit the school; he gives talk on the ascent of Everest." And, a week later—"Reception at the school for Sir Edmund Hillary."

These were big events for Godavari School, students and teachers, alike.

Early Visitors to Godavari

While the school prospered and grew, outside events began to impinge on it. Nepal was opening up to the world, after a century of stagnant isolation. Many international visitors—mountain climbers, diplomats, writers, and even Hollywood stars—began to visit the exotic city. On these occasions, Marshall and his fellow priests were invited to attend social functions and affairs of state in their roles as the first resident foreigners in the valley in modern times. They felt at times that they were on exhibit.

Many receptions were held at the Royal Hotel, a converted Rana palace located near the center of Kathmandu. The Royal was the closest to a modern hotel that Nepal had for many years. It was renowned for its busy bar and a chandeliered dining hall. The Royal was run by the White Russian expatriate-entrepreneur, Boris Lissanevitch.[12]

By many Nepalese, the priests were held in awe, unused as the locals were to having exotic foreigners, clergymen at that, living in their midst and unaccustomed to seeing men dressed in black cassocks with stiff white clerical collars. Foreign visitors, too, were impressed and considered the priests to be pioneers in what was, to their outsider eyes, a rather quaint, even primitive place to visit. Inevitably, at Marshall's insistence, many of these visitors were driven out to Godavari to meet the school boys. It was important, he felt, that the students be exposed to people and events of importance to the rest of the world.

Looking Back
Men of the Mountains
Fr Moran

I met Edmund Hillary of New Zealand for the first time in 1952, the year before his famous assault on Everest. He had come to climb in preparation for the British Mount Everest Expedition, which was planned for 1953. A Swiss expedition had the first chance at the peak in 1952, but they failed to get beyond 28,000 feet. The Sherpa, Tenzing Norgay, was a member of that expedition. I met him in Kathmandu afterwards and arranged for him to be admitted to Holy Family Hospital in Patna for treatment of malaria. He always appreciated that and became a good friend.

In 1953, we all met the English Expedition members, led by John Hunt. During the climb we eagerly followed their ascent of the peak from the daily reports that reached Kathmandu by runner. When the climbers finally returned from the mountain in June, we met them in a grand public reception held in the center of the city where thousands of Nepalese had gathered to cheer and congratulate them. They had reached the summit of Everest on May 29, my birthday. The announcement of their triumph reached Kathmandu and the world in early June, on the morning of Queen Elizabeth's Coronation in London (June 2). It was a momentous occasion all around. Hunt and Hillary were knighted for their successful exploits on Everest.

I also met an Indian named Goswami—his name means "master of the cow"—who claimed that he saw pictures of Mt Everest taken from an airplane two weeks after the summit assault by the British team. He said that he couldn't see any footprints, a revelation that cast doubt, but only temporarily, on the claims that Tenzing and Hillary had reached the top. It was a sad exhibition of anti-British animus and bad feeling. He even wrote a book about it; but it was eclipsed, of course, by Sir John Hunt's own account in *The Ascent of Everest*, later that year.

John Hunt and Edmund Hillary and others from the expedition came out to the school. On a blackboard set up in the gardens, they explained to the boys the expedition's time table, day by day to the top. We were pleased to be the first in the world to have this careful lecture and description, long before the rest of the world read about it.

Besides the Swiss and British expeditions, both of which visited the school, we also met members of a Japanese expedition to Manaslu, an Italian expedition to Langtang, and a Swiss expedition to Dhaulagiri. One sad event interrupted all these happy occasions when I arranged and conducted the funeral for the leader of an Argentinian expedition. He had been carried overland to Bir Hospital in Kathmandu, where he died of exposure and pneumonia.

It would be tedious to name all of the expeditions that we met in those first few years. The list is over a hundred, including Yugoslavians, Germans, Italians, Spanish, and others.

The Jesuit Chronicles continue:

August 17, 1953—"Fr Downing gets his visa renewed; new visa good 'as long as he remains at Godavari School'."

Fr Downing later moved away from Godavari to teach at the new school in town, but nobody seemed to notice.

August 28, 1953—"Airport closed for one week; too wet for planes to land."

June 23, 1954—"New cook hired for the kitchen; pay: Rs 20 per month plus rations."

September 27, 1954—"Barber hired: he is to cut all the boys twice a month for Rs 3 each time." (This was necessitated because of the steadily increasing number of school boys.)

September 30, 1954—"Holidays begin. All Godavari boys walk home; given lunch at Jawalakhel..." (Jawalakhel was the site of the new St Xavier's School in the city.)

Opening the Jawalakhel School

By 1954, the three-year old Godavari School was becoming overcrowded and the older boys needed a high school to continue their studies. After long discussions with the priests at Godavari, their superiors in Patna and the Nepalese authorities, Marshall prepared to open a second school closer to Kathmandu in order to accommodate the increase in day scholars and boarders and those ready to move on. He located a Rana palace in Jawalakhel, near the zoo, on the outskirts of the city of Patan. It was purchased on September 5, 1954, at a cost of 440,000 rupees (approximately $147,000 at the time.)

The first five grades were then moved into the city and Godavari was converted into a boarding high school.[13] The conversion of Godavari School into a proper high school was conducted by Fr Ed Niesen.

Marshall then moved into town and lost no time in opening the new St Xavier's Jawalakhel School. The event was heralded by this entry into the Jesuit Chronicles:

> *September 6, 1954—* "Move to Jawalakhel begins. Road completely breached below Harisiddhi (a village on the road to Kathmandu). Jeep can move only between Godavari and there. First lot of beds sent in with coolies who spend the night in Harisiddhi."
>
> *September 7, 1954—*"Fr Downing and ten boys move to the new school; everything has to be carried and everyone has to walk from Harisiddhi" (a distance of about five miles).

St Xavier's Jawalakhel School opened the following day after morning mass:

> *September 8, 1954—*"Third standard boys come in; all bedding, desks, chairs and boxes brought by coolies."

Kumar Khadga Bikram Shah (Class of '58) remembered the occasion. "We students were instrumental in setting up the Jawalakhel School. I remember well that sometimes Fr Moran was a very hard taskmaster. On Sundays, before lunch, he used to lead walks with the boys along what we called 'Father Moran's Hill,' northeast of Godavari. That prepared us. He timed one of our walks to help carry the furniture to town. We each carried small pieces, nothing very large, almost half the way from Godavari to Jawalakhel."

With expansion and rising enrollments, more priests and teachers were recruited from the Indian mission and from the United States. In the first decade, over twenty-five priests and lay brothers joined the staff, along with a dozen Nepalese teachers. Some of the priests stayed on for many years, forming the nucleus of the Nepal Jesuit community including, besides those already mentioned, Frs John Blanchard (who came in 1954), Eugene Watrin (1955), Joe Scharf (1956), Ludwig Stiller (1956), Bill Schock (1956), Jim Dressman (1956), John Locke (1958), Charles Law (1958), Casper 'Cap' Miller (1958), Tom Gafney (1959), Leo Cachat (1961), and Marty Coyne (1961). Fr Jim Donnelly came in 1961 and, except for a short absence in 1991, he remained in Nepal until his death in 2009. From 1981 to 1991 Fr Donnelly served as principal of the Godavari School.[14]

With all these new arrivals and expanded activity, the complexity and pace of life among the Nepal Jesuits increased. Marshall now lived at the Jawalakhel School (until 1968 when he moved back to Godavari). The new school was located on the outskirts of Patan, across the Bagmati River south of Kathmandu proper. Being in town brought Marshall into much closer contact with activities (and intrigues) of city life, including the politics and the social life, such as parties at the Royal Hotel, receptions at the British and American embassies, and the like. Many more foreigners sought him out, including Catholic tourists at Sunday mass.

Looking Back
Sundays in the 'Blue Room'
Fr Moran

My Sundays were of a rather uniform pattern for almost fifteen years after I moved to the city in 1954. I would go at seven o'clock with Fr Downing by motor to the Royal Hotel and stay with him until the end of his mass. I heard confessions and met many of the tourists who came. Then I drove out to the west side of Kathmandu, to Rabi Bhawan ("Rabi's Palace"), one of the former Rana palaces belonging to General Rabi Shamsher Jang Bahadur Rana. At nine o'clock I served mass in the "Blue Room," a big reception hall. The U.S. government had leased the palace for its development aid headquarters. They graciously let us and the Protestants hold services there; weddings, funerals, Sunday mass, prayer services and community-wide ecumenical services for expatriates at Easter and Christmas.

The altar in the blue room was made by the very talented son of one of the Protestant missionaries, a young man named David Alter—an altar by Alter. Our part of it included three back pieces that fit together to depict the four Gospels. We would assemble it before mass, then take it down afterward and store it for the week in a box underneath. The Protestants used the room for their services at ten o'clock.

For some years the resident Americans asked me to give an orientation talk, about twice a month, after the ten o'clock church service. First the Protestant group would have a prayer service, then I would give a lecture on Hinduism, Buddhism, or the history of Nepal. All highly appreciated.

After mass in the blue room, I was often invited to breakfast nearby with different families of the Americans from the AID group, or with tourists at the hotel. Lots of conversation and discussion of local or world issues. These were most interesting and enriching experiences.

In those days there was very little documentation about Nepal and, compared with the vast literature on Nepal available today and the number of good bookstores there are now in the city, Marshall thought it "unbelievable (then) how few books could be bought, how few had been written about Nepal. The bibliography in the early 1950s was perhaps five or ten books and they were not very valuable, as they were impressionistic and sometimes very biased in favor of the old Ranas who had been their patrons and promoters. The liberal point of view was not stressed and the need for reforms and development was almost totally ignored."

One of the most liberal reforms on Marshall's agenda, after the St Xavier's School at Jawalakhel was under way, was the opening of a school for Nepalese girls. He remembered how much of a hassle the building of the Patna Women's College had been. It had run against the grain of India's social conservatives. He hoped that the same sort of confrontation would not be repeated in Nepal. But with two boys' schools now operating in the valley, the demand for a proper girls' boarding school was being heard and was strongly supported. So the Jesuits set about to help get it started. The chronicle records the following actions:

> *November 22, 1954*—"Bishop Wildermuth arrives for first visit to Nepal with two IBMV sisters hoping to open a school here; sisters look at possible sites" (IBMV, Institute of the Blessed Virgin Mary).
>
> *December 17, 1954*—"Superior of Patna Mission, Fr Ed Mann, arrives from Patna for visitation. Sisters continue to look for school site..."

Founding St Mary's School for Girls

The founding of St Mary's School for girls was a major historical event for Nepal. After some searching, a building known as Thula Bhawan (literally "Big Palace") was made available at Dhobighat adjacent to the Jawalakhel boys' school. The Prime Minister himself had to sanction the purchase; the way was cleared in December 1954. Marshall played a major role in helping to secure the property and contracting for renovations. By then he had had plenty of experience in both. Mother Benigna became the first superior of the school.

St Mary's School opened on February 15, 1955, for the first fifteen girls. A month later the hostel was ready, to which twenty girls were assigned. By the end of the year there were fifty-six boarders. Thereafter, St Mary's School grew steadily in popularity and prestige, admitting thousands of Nepalese girls over the years.

St Mary's, like St Xavier's boys schools at Jawalakhel and Godavari, soon became well known for its superior scholastic achievement. The sisters at St Mary's have taught many of the daughters and nieces of the royal family and other young women from both elite and commoner families of Nepal. Many St Mary's graduates have gone on to become leading professional women in the life and society of the nation.

In January 1983, a second girls' school was opened by the sisters in the western mid-hills town of Pokhara. And soon after, two more were founded: St Mary's School at Sanepa in Lalitpur District near Kathmandu, and St Mary's in Gorkha, in the mid-hills west of Kathmandu.[15]

The Jesuit Chronicles continue:

> *February 2, 1955*—"Severe earthquake followed by tremors all day and the following day."
>
> *March 13, 1955*—"King Tribhuvan died in Switzerland."
>
> *March 14, 1955*—"King's body arrives from Switzerland, Fr Moran meets the body at the airport; three wreaths were placed..., one from each of the three schools" Then, following traditional Hindu mourning customs: "Nearly everyone in town has shaved his head for the king's funeral. All Nepal teachers take off for the entire mourning period of 13 days. No day scholars come to school for 13 days."
>
> *April 14, 1955*—"Interim cabinet dissolved, replaced by a Council of Royal Advisors."
>
> *April 28, 1955*—"The deed for the purchase of the Jawalakhel property was signed today."
>
> *August 20, 1955*—"Dhobi (laundryman) payments: Rs 2 per month per boy."
>
> *November 19, 1955*—"Fr Niesen came to town (from Godavari); had to walk in and back."

Wild Animals in the Night

The national zoo is just over the wall of the Jawalakhel School, creating occasional diversions for the naturally curious school boys. The natural wilds are just over the wall at Godavari, and sometimes forest animals, especially leopards, were brave enough in the early days of the school to enter the campus grounds and roam around the gardens and buildings. Nowadays they are rarely seen.

One dark night, Fr Niesen had an encounter at the Godavari School gate that tested his nerves. He had just gotten out of the car to open the gate to enter, when he saw a big cat standing in his way. At first he ignored it—just a big house cat from the village, he thought. Then he looked more closely, and those bright eyes told him otherwise. Leopard!

He jumped back into the car, slammed the door and honked loudly to scare it away and get someone's attention inside. Nobody came and the cat took its own good time before sauntering off into the night. Niesen did not sleep very well that night.

When the forest came down to the edge of the school yard, in the years before its decimation by woodcutters, the leopards and various other jungle animals were common visitors—far too common for some.

Looking Back
Leopards in the School Yard
Eugene L. Watrin, SJ

When I came to Godavari in 1965, I was vice-principal for seven years, and principal for another five. I have many memories of the place from those years. Among the most chilling things were the leopards.

In the winter, especially, we'd hear them almost every night. I used to live in the little bungalow across the fields down below the main gate. When I walked down there after dark, I often heard their distinctive coughing noise where they hung out by the little stream out back. I wasted little time getting indoors late at night.

Once we raised a pair of dachshunds that slept on the floor inside the back door to the dining hall in Xavier Hall, under the staircase. That part of the building was open to the outside and one night a leopard snatched away the female of the pair. The surviving male was so frightened it had a nervous breakdown and died.

On another occasion our big Labrador retriever disappeared while out walking in the forest with the boys. He certainly didn't get lost and the evidence was that he'd been snatched by a leopard. Our big sixty-two pound boxer was also caught and eaten by a rather daring leopard, right under a dormitory window. In those days there were no bars or screens on the windows. The dog slept on the porch outside and the boys slept just next to the wall inside. Suddenly the dog growled, then let out a scream. Fr Dressman got up and looked out to see the leopard standing over the dead dog on the grass in front of the building. The next morning we followed the tracks to where the leopard, carrying the dog, had gone up and over the high wall next to the guest house. We never found a trace of the poor dog.

On the Dogs of Godavari and St Mary's Schools

Over the years, priests and boys at Godavari and the sisters and girls at St Mary's School in town have taken great pleasure in their dogs. Certain Godavari and St Mary's School dogs have achieved something of a reputation among dog fanciers, including big Tibetan mastiffs brought down out of the mountains. One Tibetan mastiff from St Mary's was exported to the United States in the 1970s, to form part of the foundation stock for a new American breed.

Another dog, a cross between a Tibetan mastiff and a retriever, gained great fame and admiration at Godavari. Fr Watrin remembers how "the dog got his revenge on a pesky monkey that used to hang around the school taunting him from the tree branches. That monkey drove the poor dog wild with fury, until one day while bouncing up and down in the trees, a branch broke and the monkey fell. The dog was on the startled monkey like a shot, picked it up and shook it to death, breaking every bone in its body. End of monkey. For the rest of the day, that dog had a most satisfied look on its face!"

To Fr Watrin "that particular dog was the most wonderful hunter I've ever seen. He had a great sense of smell and superior eyesight and hearing. One day while I was out walking with him, he spotted a black koklas pheasant in a tree atop the marble quarry, a mile away."

With his interest in dogs whetted by experiences such as these, Fr Watrin went on to help found and charter the Nepal Kennel Club, the first dog club in Nepal. He continued to raise dogs for years, both pure-breds and mongrels, in the compound of the Godavari Alumni Association building where he lived for many years, in downtown Kathmandu.

The Godavari Marble Quarry

Godavari is famous for its cool, clear spring water that serves many purposes, both sacred and profane. It has long been a pilgrimage site for devout Hindus. Some years ago, a brewery was built nearby to take advantage of it. Godavari is also locally famous (but to environmentalists, rather infamous) for its marble quarry. Over the years, the quarry expanded in size in response to growing demand for the high quality marble for building purposes. Between the noise of blasting and hauling stone from the mountain and the thick fine dust that has settled on the forest, combined with increased cutting of the surrounding forest for firewood by the villagers, the wildlife and the quiet ambience of the once pristine Godavari forest gradually slipped away. The great bare scar of the quarry can be seen looking west from the school yard.

In the early 1950s, the quarrying was a relatively small scale, simple operation. The miners used a water wheel to cut the marble. Nowadays, the heavy duty blasting disturbs one and all. Fr Watrin remembered seeing a rock as big as a man's head that Fr Marty Coyne picked up in the school yard where it had fallen after a particularly large blast was set off in the quarry. School buildings nearest the west wall were often pelted with rock fragments. In recent years, the marble operators have been under pressure from environmentalists to clean up their act and reforest the damaged mountainside. Some conservationists have even advocated closing it down altogether and restoring the peace and calm that was once a hallmark of the Godavari forest. It would certainly make for quieter schooling. And, with reforestation, perhaps the old wildlife woulde once again haunt the school yard at night.[16]

As if to counterbalance the ugly scar of the marble quarry, the government established a beautiful botanical garden in the valley east of the school and established Nepal's now well known botanical and medical plants research center. The botanical gardens are a popular spot for townspeople to visit on weekends and holidays for picnics and outings. Parents of the boys often take their young sons there for walks while visiting the school on weekends.

Somehow, the comings and goings of leopards, pet dogs, the marble blasting and picnickers in the gardens never made it into the Jesuit Chronicles. But other school and national events often did:

> *January 23, 1956* (at the opening of the school year)—"Fees raised from Rs 75 to 90 for boarders plus deposit of Rs 200; day scholars Rs 15 per month."
>
> *January 27, 1956*—"New interim cabinet installed. Prime Minister: Tanka Prasad Acharya. Education Minister: Balchandra Sharma..."
>
> *April 16, 1956*—"Barber came, did 105 boys and three fathers for Rs 11.50."
>
> *September 20, 1956*—"Francis the horse arrives at Jawalakhel."
>
> *October 9, 1958*—"Death of Pope Pius XII..."

These few glimpses from the first decade of the St Xavier's schools in Nepal, and of the Godavari experience in particular, are indicative of the daily life and teaching that went on there in the mission's formative years. During those years and following, much was happening in the growing mission, too much to tell. Many priests and brothers came and went, too many to name individually. There were high points and low, as in all social enterprises, at all schools.

> *March 29, 1959* (a truly high point in the chronicle)—"Easter Sunday (Senior) Cambridge (examination) results—9 first (division), 4 second, 1 third. First Cambridge exams in Nepal."

These fine scores point up the school's success, after that first decade (almost) fulfilling the Jesuit quest for quality and high standards, for excellence in education.

And outside the schools, beyond Godavari and Jawalakhel campuses, the Jesuits observed, and duly recorded in their Chronicles, momentous events that set the pace for rapid social and political transformations in Nepal, in the affairs of state.

Notes to Chapter 10: Opening St Xavier's Godavari School

1. Several other individuals closely involved in the founding of Godavari School included Surya Prasad Upadhyay (Home Minister in 1951) and his brother, Sharada Prasad Upadhyay (Director of Education), along with Dr Jit Singh Malla (the school doctor) and Jyan Bahadur Pradhan (construction engineer). These men were especially honored in 1976 at the twenty-fifth anniversary of the founding of Godavari School as Fr Moran's main people, the school's co-founders.
2. The story of Fr Bertrand Saubolle's life is told in the *Nepal Region's 50th Anniversary Book* (2001), online at http://nepaljesuits.org/nepal-jesuit-society/jesuits-in-memory/fr-bertrand-saubolle-sj/.
3. The story of Fr Thomas Downing's life in Nepal is told more fully in the *Nepal Region's 50th Anniversary Book* (2001) (*ibid.*).
4. From a eulogy for Fr Thomas Downing, dated March 30, 1987.
5. John K. Locke, SJ, *Jesuits in Nepal, 1628-1985: A Vamsavali* (1986); the Jesuit Chronicles.
6. After 1978, under the leadership of Frs Leo Cachat, Bertrand Saubolle and Jim Dressman, Nara Mahal was converted into a retreat house, the Godavari Ashram, and reopened in 1981. It is most frequently utilized for retreats by Jesuit scholastics, brothers and priests, some from other dioceses as far away as Burma, Malaysia and Singapore. It is also a popular retreat among lay Christians, mostly Catholics, of the wider Nepal community.
7. The quote was attributed to Moran in an article entitled 'Don't push conversions, warns Nepal missionary', in *The Chicago Catholic* (January 24, 1986, p.32),
8. Anonymous, 'Teachers and staff members of St Xavier's Godavari School: 1951-1986' (n.d.).
9. *Ibid.*
10. The description of Fr Ed Niesen's contributions to the early development of Godavari School, and of St Xavier's School at Jawalakhel, in the city, is by John K. Locke, SJ, in the *Nepal Region's 50th Anniversary Book* (2001).
11. In those days three rupees equaled approximately one U.S. dollar, so that fifty rupee bottle of wine cost almost seventeen dollars, an excessive price at the time.
12. For the story of Boris of Kathmandu, see Michel Peissel, *Tiger for Breakfast* (1966).

13. With the opening of the new elementary school in 1954 at Jawalakhel, in the city, Godavari School served as a high school until 1968, when it reverted back to an elementary school and St Xavier's Jawalakhel became the high school (for day scholars).

    Three decades later, in 1996, the role of Godavari School was again examined and it was decided that Godavari would become (1) a neighborhood school (primarily for the benefit of children residing in the rural area), (2) co-educational (enrolling girls as well as boys), and (3) exclusively for day scholars (the boarding facility was phased out). Eventually, it would be modified once again to include high school classes.

14. Biographical information about many of the long-term Jesuits may be seen at <http://nepaljesuits.org>.

    Several of the Jesuit fathers became well known for their scholarship on Nepalese subjects. Among them were Frs John Locke, Ludwig Stiller and Casper Miller; and several earned their doctorates at Nepal's Tribhuvan University in Kathmandu.

    Fr John Locke (1933-2009) was a renowned Buddhist scholar who, when he taught at Tribhuvan University, was highly respected by students and faculty alike for his depth of knowledge and sympathetic insight into the religious beliefs and practices of Nepal. His two best known books are *Karunamaya: The Cult of Avalokitesvara□Matsyendranath in the Valley of Nepal* (1980) and *Buddhist Monasteries of Nepal: A Survey of the Bahas and Bahis of the Kathmandu Valley* (1985, 2009).

    Fr Ludwig Stiller (1928-2009) was a well known historian of Nepal to whom Professor Mahesh Chandra Regmi, the preeminent Nepalese economic historian, once said, "You have taught us to respect what is ours." Fr Stiller wrote: *The Rise of the House of Gorkha: A Study in the Unification of Nepal 1768-1816* (1973), *The Silent Cry: The People of Nepal 1816-1839* (1976), *Planning for People: A Study of Nepal's Planning Experience* (1979, co-authored by Ram Prakash Yadav), *Letters from Kathmandu: The Kot Massacre* (1981, as editor), and *Nepal: Growth of a Nation* (1993).

    On the passing of Reverends Locke and Stiller in 2009, with tributes to their remarkable scholarship, see Kanak Mani Dixit's eulogy, 'The passing of two Jesuit Nepali scholars' (*Nepali Times*, Kathmandu, 20-26 March). Their life histories are given online, in brief, at http://nepaljesuits.org.

    Among other notable priest-scholars in Nepal are: Reverend Casper ('Cap') Miller, SJ (1933-) who studied cultural anthropology and wrote *Faith-Healers in the Himalaya* (1987, revised in 1997), and *Decision Making in Village Nepal* (1990, based on his PhD dissertation), and Reverend Gregory Sharkey, SJ, who wrote *Buddhist Daily Ritual: The Nitya Puja in Kathmandu Valley Shrines* (2001).

15. More recently, the Nepal Jesuit Mission has opened several other schools including a boys' school in Jhapa District (southeastern Nepal) and St Xavier's College in Kathmandu. There are also several social service ministries. See http://nepaljesuits.org/ for more information.

16. In 1992, the quarry operators made an expansion plan to acquire the Godavari School site, far short of the end of the Jesuit's ninety-nine year lease. The issue went into litigation in the courts, led by several St Xavier "Old Boy" lawyers who strongly oppose the idea.

11

Affairs of State and High Society

Once when I was out driving the jeep broke down. As I got out to see what the trouble was, two Nepalese walked by. One of them pointed to me and said to the other: "He's a father moran." Father Moran had become a common noun!
  Fr Eugene Watrin, SJ, reminiscing on the 1950s

Fr Moran was at every party in those days. If a visitor didn't see Fr Moran in Kathmandu, his trip wasn't really complete.
  T.N. Upraity, pioneer Nepalese educator

In February 1955, Nepal's King Tribhuvan took gravely ill. Hoping save his life, the royal family flew him to Europe for treatment. Crown Prince Mahendra remained behind to serve as regent in his absence. A few weeks later, in mid-March, the King died and his body was returned to Kathmandu for the royal cremation on the banks of the Bagmati river at Pashupatinath Temple. On the morning of the funeral, Marshall was invited to bring several school boys to the airport to board a Dakota (DC-3) to fly over the river dropping flowers before the cremation.

On the very day that King Tribhuvan's death was announced, Mahendra Bir Bikram Shah Dev was enthroned, although the formal coronation event was delayed for a more propitious time, over a year later.

King Mahendra had very definite notions about governing his country and was concerned about political infighting and the difficulties his new Prime Minister, Matrika Prasad Koirala, was having in managing the affairs of state, the economy, and the society. Already, as regent, Crown Prince Mahendra had dissolved Koirala's Congress Party government. Ruling directly from the palace, the King formed a royal advisory council and sent an official commission into the countryside to assess the will of the people. These were the first moves in Mahendra's gradual re-shaping of the Nepal system

11. Fr Moran in front of Xavier Hall, Godavari School, with his Ham radio antennas on the roof.

of government. The effects of change and a further modernization of Nepal under Mahendra were felt almost immediately, both in public services and political structures.

In June 1955, for example, air service to the country was upgraded with the inauguration of new buildings and a new runway for the Kathmandu valley. The first aircraft to land in the valley had come in April 1949. The landing site, the old cow pasture (*gai charan*) after which "Gaucher Airport" was named, was located a few kilometers east of the city, on a plateau above the sacred Bagmati River. Today, a nine-hole golf course separates the more modern airport on the site from the cremation *ghat*s that line the river at Pashupathinath Temple.

One of the most historic first flights had occurred on November 10, 1950, when an Indian Air Force plane arrived at Gaucher Field to whisk King Tribhuvan and members of the royal family away on the brief, self-imposed exile in India. The next most notable landing was Tribhuvan's triumphant return, in February 1951. Fr Moran had also flown in twice to Gaucher Field, once in the month before the King's return, and once soon afterward. By then, the use of Gaucher field for flights of DC-3s and smaller craft was well established from north India.

Until 1955, however, Kathmandu's airport conditions were primitive—a bumpy grass runway, a few huts for ticketing and receiving passengers, and a siren to warn cow herders of the impending take-off or landing of a plane, the signal to chase their beasts off the field. With the improvements in 1955, and the renaming of the lowly cow pasture to Tribhuvan International Airport, services were much improved.[1]

Several other improvements to life in the kingdom heralded Nepal's full emergence into the world community of nations. In 1955, Nepal became a member of the United Nations. (An earlier attempt in 1949 was vetoed by the Soviet Union, probably at the insistence of the Indian Government, which opposed the Rana regime.) From 1956 onward, an office of resident representative of the United Nations was established in Kathmandu.

In January 1956, a new government was formed under Prime Minister Tanka Prasad Acharya. In April, Nepal's first modern financial institution, the Nepal Rastriya Bank, was commissioned. And, in May 1956, the Royal Coronation was held.

The Royal Coronation
King Mahendra's formal Coronation was held on May 2, 1956. This grand event attracted world attention and was attended by official

guests, distinguished world leaders and diplomats, and many newsmen from Asia, Europe and North America.

Looking Back
Preparations for the Coronation
Michel Peissel[2]

The coronation of King Mahendra was (an) event that rocked Nepal and attracted the attention of the world to the little-known Himalayan kingdom. No funds were spared to make it not only the biggest affair the kingdom had ever known, but also the first big step of Nepal in its progress away from isolation and toward modernity. Everything had to be done from scratch. The entire nation could muster in its two hotels, the Royal and the Snowview, accommodations for only about fifty people. All of a sudden, Boris[3] was asked to see to it that 112 foreign dignitaries and over 100 news correspondents be given the best in board and lodging.

The whole valley became the scene of feverish preparation, and the Royal Hotel the headquarters of operation. Every temple in Kathmandu was redecorated; roads were enlarged; the two miles of tarmac streets in the valley were lengthened to three miles with the aid of volunteers. For the great occasion, the Cow Field Airport had to be rebuilt; the thatched shed that had served as customs house and air terminal there was replaced by a true stone one. Boris was given charge of the government rest house and of five other palaces destined for distinguished guests.

Boris had suddenly become one of the key figures in Nepal. The small Himalayan kingdom had much to learn of Western ways, and Boris was incessantly called in for consultation on matters concerning the do's and don'ts of Western society.

At all costs, Nepal, in line with its traditional hospitality, wanted to give its guests the best of the amenities of the Western world. And despite the disadvantages of its centuries-old isolation, it succeeded not only in proving an excellent host but also in offering the foreign dignitaries one of the most beautiful and incredible spectacles imaginable.

Nations far and wide sent their representatives—including China, India, Bhutan and Tibet among the closest neighbors, and Japan, Great Britain, France, the United States and others from farther away. Marshall and the other priests played host during these exciting days to many of the visiting dignitaries, some of whom they already knew from previous occasions.

Japan sent Ambassador Sijiro Yoshizawa who looked after his country's Nepalese interests (mostly mountaineering) from the embassy of Japan in New Delhi. In the preceding years, Marshall had hosted Ambassador Yoshizawa and his wife at Godavari during occasional visits up from India. The ambassador told him many stories of life during World War II, and Marshall was fascinated by descriptions of life in Nazi Germany where Yoshizawa had been posted. "He and his very charming, even elegant, wife frequently visited the school to have lunch with us," Marshall recalled. "He was a very pleasant person with a great interest and affection for Nepal. And he was a Catholic."

The representative of the French Government was Count Stanislas Ostorog who was also on assignment to his nation's embassy in New Delhi. Count Ostorog's family was of Polish heritage, having earlier fled in exile to live in France. There, the count had risen to the position of a prominent diplomat. Count Ostorog always made it a point to visit the priests at Godavari and Jawalakhel. He, like the Japanese ambassador, was also a Catholic, and when visiting Nepal he attended mass and even served the mass to Fr Moran on several occasions. Both the Japanese and the French ambassadors knew Marshall better, and had more in common with him than any others in the coronation's foreign dignitaries.

President Eisenhower's official representatives were two prominent Americans: Dr Charles Mayo, MD, of the famous Mayo Clinic in Rochester, Minnesota, and Lowell Thomas, the well known newsman, film maker and international raconteur. Lowell Thomas had two agendas in Kathmandu. The official one was to represent the American president. Another was to make a Cinerama film, *Search for Paradise,* depicting an adventure in the Himalayas.

Arriving in Kathmandu a few days ahead of the coronation festivities, Lowell Thomas and his entourage camped in a tent city set up for them in the courtyard of one of the Rana palaces. His advance man was Dr Tom Gilliard, an ornithologist from the American Museum of Natural History in New York City and one of Thomas's colleagues in The Explorers' Club. Their official camp caterer was hired for this trip from one of India's finest restaurants, Gaylord's of New Delhi.

Thomas described the opulent gifts brought by attending delegates and put on display at the palace ahead of the coronation events. He was greatly impressed by those from China, especially the "rolls of exquisite rugs, superb Chinese screens and several huge Ming vases..." But the American delegation was somewhat embarrassed when they presented the American Government's not so ostentatious gift—a photograph of the US President.

Thomas and ornithologist Gilliard, however, saved the day and considerable face for the Americans "at the eleventh hour" as Thomas put it in his autobiography *So Long Until Tomorrow*. They had scoured the warehouse at the American Museum before coming and were able to present the palace with one hundred rare bird of paradise feathers, an essential feature in the royal crown. "When all the coronation presents went on display in the palace ballroom, by far the most spectacular was our stunning display of those plumes of the birds of paradise—plus the autographed picture of President Eisenhower!"[4]

Of the coronation itself, Lowell Thomas later wrote a brief and color description of the event.

Looking Back
An American at the Coronation
Lowell Thomas[5]

It was early when I reached the shrine courtyard where the ceremony was to be held. With Dr and Mrs Mayo and Virginia Bacon, I sat in the stands set up for the international delegations and the highest Nepalese nobles. In the middle of the courtyard was the throne, a large divan with metal snakes for a back and topped with a huge, golden-headed cobra. Hindu priests in robes were busy with their preparations. We had been promised royal cooperation for the ceremony, and we got it: The ponderous Cinerama camera was placed right next to the throne, as were the powerful, glaring motion pictures lights. Months later, Cinerama audiences would get a much better view of the proceedings than we had from the V.I.P. stands.

A salute of thirty-one guns was reverberating when the royal couple appeared, walking under royal umbrellas, proceeding towards the throne. The king, a frail-looking man who seemed much younger than his thirty-six years, was dressed in a simple suit of white cotton, and, as always, wore dark glasses. The queen wore a crimson sari, her long hair flowing free. Mahendra could have had many wives but preferred monogamy. When his previous queen had died, he simply married her sister.

The astrologers had calculated the exact moment for the act of bestowing the crown, 10:43 a.m. (May 2), and at that instant, following a series of arcane preliminaries, the rite was performed. A crown, studded with gems worth millions and set by generations of long-dead craftsmen, was placed on King Mahendra's head. Then, with the salute of cannon fire as a signal, the king and queen left the cobra throne and went into the palace. The throng in the stands poured out. The coronation was over.

Well, not *quite* over, for that same afternoon the crowds lining the streets of Kathmandu saw a splendiferous parade which included "...elephants, some two hundred of them, their swaying howdahs covered with gorgeous trappings of silver and gold. Most conspicuous of all was the royal elephant, the mightiest of his breed, laden with magnificent tapestries atop which rode Their Majesties in a howdah like a golden throne. Many of the elephants carried delegates from foreign countries, most of them in brilliant Oriental costume. The funniest were those of us from the West in our tail coats and top hats. I felt supremely ridiculous—imagine wearing a topper atop an elephant!"[6]

Cinerama's *Search for Paradise*
Shortly after his arrival in Kathmandu, Lowell Thomas invited Fr Moran to join him and his camera crew for lunch in their tented accommodations. There was a crew of fourteen photographers and assistants, including several cameramen assigned to operate their units simultaneously during the filming. Thomas asked suggestions and advice from Marshall and invited him to some of the places that were being filmed, both before and after the Coronation.

Thomas had certain scenes in mind for the film, including the old footpath up from the Tarai, the trail over which Marshall approached Kathmandu on his first trip in 1949. Marshall found an old Rolls Royce for them to use as a prop; it was stripped of its engine and wheels (to reduce the weight), then painted to look nice. A crew of sixty coolies was engaged and filming commenced to reenact carrying the vehicle up the steep mountain trails years earlier (as depicted in old *National Geographic* magazine photos).

Several actors were posed as if accompanying the car up the trail to attend the royal coronation. The fakery astonished Marshall, for by this time, 1956, the new Tribhuvan Rajpath (King Tribhuvan's "Royal Highway") had already been completed by the Indian Government with financial assistance from the Colombo Plan, and none of the coronation guests actually had to walk into the kingdom. The new motor road was a narrow and torturous eighty mile adventure. Those who drove it had to cross two high passes and negotiate miles of hairpin turns that, as an act of courage, would itself have made a good filming. But the more ancient approach to the valley, sweating coolies and all, was apparently considered far more romantic and picturesque for Cinerama purposes.

Film audiences are often subjected to such tricks to make a point or create a scene. One Cinerama sequence was filmed in the Tarai lowlands, depicting the old style tiger hunt from elephants. Marshall remembered it later: "You know, I told Lowell Thomas, that the elephants have wonderful bells that ring 'biiing, biiing', hanging from a long rope. The filming there had already been done, and Thomas said, 'I didn't get that sound'."

"'Well,' I told him, 'I'll make it for you.' And I went around and got some drinking glasses that rang with a similar sound when struck, and that's what they dubbed into the film," said Marshall.

When *Search for Paradise* premiered in Hollywood, Lowell Thomas remembered the assistance Fr Moran had given him. Marshall could not attend, so Thomas invited his mother, Bertha Moran, all the way from Chicago to help celebrate the event. "There she sat, next to Lowell Thomas and the stars of Hollywood, including the president of Paramount and Metro-Goldwyn-Mayer and other big-wigs of the movie industry. She was like a little fish in a big pond. She loved it." It was a topic of much conversation and reminiscing when Marshall's mother finally visited Nepal several years later.

Coronation Sports

Several priests from St Xavier's played prominent parts during the coronation, helping organize and present the national sports day events. The most prominently involved were Frs Niesen and Watrin. School boys, college students, the police and the army all participated in track and field games, including a long distance marathon run and a cycle race.

General Nara Shamsher J.B. Rana chaired the coronation's athletic program and asked the Catholic Fathers to assist him. Frs Watrin, Niesen and others worked hard on planning, starting and judging many of the sports events, keeping it all in motion and on time. Even Fr Moran had a part to play. By now he was well known around the city for his huge Ariel motorcycle and was assigned to drive it as pilot for the marathon runners and the bicycle races on their cross country route to and from the central stadium. These were the first real games and modern sports spectacles ever held in Kathmandu.

Looking Back
Coronation Sports Day
Eugene L. Watrin, SJ

In 1956, Fr Niesen was the principal of Godavari School, and I was his vice principal in charge of extra-curricular activities. When the Coronation Sports Day was announced, we both agreed to help.

But if anyone was in charge, it was Fr Niesen. He was a dedicated sports man, was good at scheduling, and was a famous referee, often asked to work soccer games in the new national stadium at Tripureshwar. (It's been enlarged several times since then.)

For Sports Day, our boys entered various races and the team competitions—basketball, football (soccer) and field hockey. Fr Niesen, who'd had experience in these sorts of 'Olympic style' sports at the Patna school, took charge of training and coaching. I coached basketball and played on the team selected from 9th class. That helped, I guess; we easily won and were each given a nice cup by the king. Our boys also won the 200 meter relay—they were always good at that race.

In field hockey, we lost to the North Point team from St Joseph's School in Darjeeling. North Point was Crown Prince Birendra's alma mater (he attended up through 5th class, before he went on to Eton in England), so he was proud of their good effort.

Fr Niesen was very keen on marching and drill and taught our boys the techniques. Their uniforms were very classy looking—white pants, sky blue shirts and blue and gray-striped ties. When the tournament began, each team was expected to go on parade in the stadium. Our boys had practiced very hard and followed the Nepal Army team in line. I think everyone agreed that the school boys marched better than either the army or the police team—or at least as good.

As they passed the reviewing stand carrying a flag, they performed 'eyes right' and everyone clapped. Fr Niesen had worked hard to drill them and was very proud. But when the announcer identified them as "Father Moran's boys", Niesen was a bit upset. He'd worked so hard, and Fr Moran wasn't even there to see the event; he was out on his motorcycle guiding the bicycle races and the 10,000 meter marathon.

We were often identified with Fr Moran. I guess it was only natural. We dressed alike, and to the Nepalese we Jesuits probably all looked alike in our white cassocks. Once when I was out driving the jeep broke down. As I got out to see what the trouble was, two Nepalese walked by. One of them pointed to me and said to the other, "He's a father moran." *Father Moran* had become a common noun!

More Affairs of State

Following the coronation, the king furthered his considerable power and authority over the development of the country. A number of events and actions were taken to distance the nation from its long period of isolation.

During November 1956, Nepal hosted the Fourth World Buddhist Conference, which Buddhist leaders from all the nations of Southeast Asia and Japan attended. On that occasion, Lumbini, in the Nepal lowlands adjacent to India, took its rightful place as one of the most important religious shrines and cultural centers of Nepal. An inscription on a stone pillar erected around 250 BC memorializes the pilgrimage of King Ashoka to the site, and testifies to its claim as the birthplace of Gautama Buddha six centuries BC.

In July 1957, after eighteen months in power, the king dismissed Prime Minister Thanka Prasad Acharya's government, and a new cabinet was formed under K.I. Singh. It lasted fewer than one hundred days. The king was discouraged with the way Nepal's new found democracy was functioning—or foundering. The infighting between parties was debilitating, he felt, and counterproductive to national growth and social progress. To rectify the situation, he commissioned a new constitution and set dates for general elections.

The elections were held from February to May 1959, soon after which a new government under B.P. Koirala (brother to M.P. Koirala, an earlier prime minister) took office. In little over six months, however, this government was also dissolved and the king stepped back in to manage by direct rule until an entirely new system of governance could be worked out. The nation's experience with party-oriented democracy was not working, he felt, and it was time to restructure. His decision marked the end to Nepal's first tryst with democracy. (It was thirty-one years later, in 1990, before multi-party democracy re-emerged in the nation.)

On January 5, 1961, King Mahendra's new 'Panchayat Raj' form of government was announced. Under this partyless system, the prime minister and ministerial cabinet sat at the top, directly accountable to the king. King Mahendra wielded supreme authority from his offices in the Narayanhiti palace at the center of Kathmandu. And, although some semblance of free elections was operating, the king held the ultimate reins of power. Below the king and his cabinet, the government functioned through a tiered system of elected assemblies (called *'panchayats'*). The top-most assembly was the national parliament (Rastriya Panchayat). Beneath that were the regional, district and village panchayats. (The Panchayat system lasted until 1990 when, after a popular people's uprising, Mahendra's son, King Birendra, reinstated a multi-party system of democracy.)

Boris and the Royal Hotel

Over the years and decades since King Tribhuvan's triumphant return to Nepal and the opening of the country to the rest of the world, many foreigners have come to live in Kathmandu as resident 'expats' (expatriates). Some came to escape personal problems or political persecution elsewhere. Others came as missionaries, aid workers, or volunteers; some as writers and artists; and, not a few, just to 'hang out' in the city's exotic ambience. They have come from India and China, eastern and western Europe, New Zealand, Australia and North America.

One of the most colorful to arrive soon after the reopening of Nepal in the early 1950s was a White Russian émigré entrepreneur named Boris Lissanevitch, with his Danish wife Inger.

Boris moved to Nepal from Calcutta in September 1951. His was already a life of storied variety and charm. As a talented and gregarious youth, he had fled in 1924 from the strangulating society of Red Russia. Then he joined the Ballet Russe and set out to tour the world as a ballet dancer. The Ballet Russe was the creation of the impresario genius, Sergei Diaghilev. Boris's life with Diaghilev and his internationally famous troupe took him dancing through Paris and Monte Carlo, Buenos Aires, Bombay, Shanghai, Saigon and, in time, Calcutta. At Calcutta, Boris left the ballet and struck out on his own. In 1936, he opened the '300 Club', which a few years later, during the war, became a popular night spot for Allied officers to unwind away from the Asian war fronts. But the club was not his only adventure. He also dabbled in caviar, operated a whiskey distillery, and helped establish Cathay Pacific Airlines.

And what was he doing in Kathmandu in the 1950s? Why, running the Royal Hotel, of course. There, in a refurbished old Rana palace, he held forth with stories of his wild and wide-ranging life, and lavishly entertained his guests, both millionaires and ordinaries, around the great central fireplace of his Yak and Yeti Bar. He also raised pigs and peacocks on the compound. Boris almost eclipsed King Mahendra at his coronation, in his appointed role in charge of handling many of the arrangements—bed and board—for the scores of special guests and Western visitors to the valley.

Boris's Royal Hotel, with its Yak and Yeti Bar, chandeliered dining hall and rather unkempt sprawling gardens, was a favorite hangout for the rich and the beautiful, those who would be called the "jet set" a decade later. They included Kathmandu's own elites, some of the wealthier Ranas and certain member of the royal family. It was here that Fr Moran, and other priests, would periodically drop in to rub shoulders with notable Nepalese and foreign celebrities. With its cosmopolitan flavor and rustic European ambience, the Royal was for years the 'in' meeting place of town.

About the only other Western style hotel in town was the Snowview, in Lazimpat up the road from the Royal. The Snowview was run by an Anglo-Indian entrepreneur, Tom Mendies and his

Canadian wife Betty. When it came to socializing, however, the Snowview was plain and quite 'tame' compared to the Royal.

Sometimes, in the early 1950s, King Tribhuvan would come to the Royal for a special event or just drop in at his whim from the palace across the street. On such occasions one or more of the three princes, Mahendra, Himalaya or Basundhara would accompany him. Prince Basundhara was the playboy of the royal family. An even more frequent visitor to Boris's hotel was His Highness Field Marshal Kaiser Shamsher Jung Bahadur Rana (who also lived across the street opposite the royal palace). The French explorer and writer, Michel Peissel, considered the Field Marshal to be "beyond doubt the most famous among them" and "one of the most colorful and enigmatic of Nepalese."[6]

Early on, the Swiss geologist and explorer Toni Hagen, "another true character of the valley,"[8] encamped at the Royal between treks in the Himalayas. Marshall Moran knew Toni Hagen well and was often there to meet him. Toni Hagen worked for the United Nations, and since a U.N. Representative was not appointed to Nepal until 1956, Marshall served in the interim as his contact and back-up person. "I worked hard for him for five or six years, arranging porters, sending money out to him when he needed it, handling his mail brought out by runners and his film for processing. I even wrote to his wife every two or three weeks to keep her calm and happy." In 1960, Toni Hagen published one of the first large format picture and adventure books of Nepal, entitled *Nepal: The Kingdom in the Himalayas*.

Hagen's compatriot, Werner Schulthess, also showed up on occasion, with huge rounds of smelly yak cheese for the hotel kitchen from one of the cheese factories he had established in the mountains. The Austrian mountaineers and explorers, Heinrich Harrer and Peter Aufschnaiter, of *Seven Years in Tibet* book fame, showed up off and on. Even Agatha Christie stayed at the Royal, although she was apparently not moved to write a mystery based on this location. Another writer, however, the Eurasian novelist Han Suyin, did use the Royal Hotel as a novel backdrop. Han Suyin spent part of a year at Boris's hotel writing scenes for *The Mountain is Young*, in which she revealed (and quite liberally invented) what many outsiders took to be the exotic life (and, in her book at least, some seamy affairs) of certain members of the Kathmandu expatriate community. Similarly, Michel Peissel also stayed here while researching and writing *Tiger for Breakfast*, his biography of Boris.[9]

During climbing seasons, in fall and in spring, many Himalayan expedition set up camp in the hotel gardens, and hotel guests often had to wend their way through crowds of Sherpas and porters packing up their basket loads in readiness for long overland treks east towards Everest, Cho Oyu, Makalu or Kanchenjunga, or west towards other peaks such as Annapurna or Dhaulagiri. Sometimes, Sir Edmund Hillary and his family flew in from New Zealand to make the hotel their home away from home between visits to the high Sherpa villages below Mount Everest. Some of the early Russian cosmonauts and American astronauts also visited the Yak and Yeti. Early in the 1960s, a few young American Peace Corps volunteers (the author among them), in town from the villages, could be found hanging out in the bar, sipping drinks (what few we could afford), trying to experience a bit of Kathmandu's remarkably exotic expatriate social life.

The Flemings, Nepal's First Medical Mission and Early Emergencies
The Methodist missionary, Robert ('Bob') Fleming Sr, was another of the early characters of Kathmandu, though not the sort to be seen cavorting much with the drinking crowd at the Royal hotel. Fleming first arrived in 1950, a year after Marshall's first trip. For awhile 'Dr Bob' Fleming, PhD, thought he was the first foreign expatriate to enter the valley in the twentieth century, until he met Fr Moran who set him straight. Fr Moran was not the first, either.

Bob Fleming was a Protestant missionary educator, who for some years had been headmaster of a Christian boarding school in the north Indian hill station of Mussoorie. His wife, 'Dr Bethel' Fleming, MD, was a missionary doctor. The Flemings had three missions in life—Bethel's medical work, Bob's education work, and his pioneering ornithology of the Himalayas.

Bob Fleming was a careful ornithologist; his first sojourn into the kingdom was a 1949 birding expedition to west Nepal, near Tansen, in Palpa District.

Two years later, Dr Bob came back with Dr Bethel to open the United Mission medical facility in Kathmandu, the first Protestant mission to the kingdom.[10] Their two children, Bob Jr and Mary Beth, came with them, and when not away at boarding school in Mussoorie or later at a university in America, they lived with their parents near the Shanta Bhawan Hospital outside of Patan city.

In 1953, the Flemings opened their first clinic, at Bhaktapur, a few miles east of Kathmandu. A few months later they opened a second clinic at Teku, in Kathmandu near the confluence of the Bishnumati and Bagmati rivers, at what had been the government's contagious disease isolation center (for patients suffering from cholera or smallpox). It was now expanded to take general medical patients and emergency cases.

Marshall associated with the Flemings in both of their roles—the medical and the ornithological. On the medical side, he took personal pride in bringing the first patient to Dr Bethel's clinic in Teku, on the day that it was officially opened. When the date was announced, the Flemings were informed that the prime minister would be out of town, and since he wanted to be present at the official opening, the ceremony had to be rescheduled for a week earlier. Prime Minister Matrika Prasad Koirala came with his Chief of Medical Services, Dr Jit Singh Malla. Others present at the ceremony besides the Flemings were Paul Rose, who directed the U.S. Operations Mission, along with Fr Moran, nurses and other staff.

After the ribbon cutting for the medical clinic at Teku, Marshall joined the Flemings and their guests for tea. "Then we politely each went our separate ways. Back at the school I found the headmaster from the nearby village waiting for me, in great distress. He said that his pregnant wife was having difficulty delivery and was 'about to die.' I told him, 'Go home and prepare her to go to town. I'll be right there to help.' Then I put a mattress in the back of the jeep and drove down into the village to get her. From there, I rushed her to Dr Bethel's new clinic. There was only a nurse present, and she objected that they wouldn't be open for patients for some days yet. 'I was told you had no mattresses yet for the beds, so I brought one,' I said. 'And besides, you and the doctor can do better than I because I have no experience in maternity cases.' Then I dashed off to find Dr Bethel—at supper with Paul Rose and his family in a house not far away. I took her directly to the clinic, left her to do what was necessary, and returned to Godavari."

The next day Marshall inquired about mother and child. Both were safe, he was told, but it had been difficult. The child should have been delivered by caesarean section; and since it was not, there was a considerable but successful struggle, he was told.

Two years later, the little Teku clinic was moved and upgraded to a proper hospital in an old Rana palace on the outskirts of Patan, It was called, appropriately, Shanta Bhawan; *shanta* means 'quiet', 'peaceful' or 'tranquil' (or loosely, 'holy'), and *bhawan* means 'mansion' (or loosely, 'palace'). An altogether appropriate name for a mission hospital.

The large new hospital needed many more staff, and soon other American medical missionaries arrived. Among them was the experienced couple, Doctors Edgar and Elizabeth Miller, MD. They had given up a lucrative practice to come from Wilmington, Delaware, where they had been personal physicians to the wealthy American industrialist family, the Duponts. Years before, as pious

Method mission-minded medical students, the Millers had wanted to work overseas. Now in their old age they found the chance; they sold their practice and moved to Nepal where they served for about a decade before finally retiring.

One Sunday after church services at Rabi Bhawan, a Nepalese man on a bicycle met Marshall at the school gates. He was frantic. In his stumbling English and Nepali he told Marshall that an American had been killed in a jeep accident, and there were some *"thulo manches"* (important people), and he must come at once.

"It sounded like a lot of people were involved, and when I had sorted out his story I had one of the other fathers phone immediately to Shanta Bhawan Hospital for an ambulance, to the government hospital for an ambulance, and to the military headquarters for help! Then I drove my jeep at high speed to the place the man had said, a place called Tika Bhairab on a mountain road over a ridge on the edge of the valley. I found the American, Freddy Moore of the Ford Foundation, alive but in very serious condition. In the jeep with him was a Mr Thapalia, Chief Magistrate of Lalitpur District (Patan) and his son, a Mr Upadhyaya and his wife and baby in arms, and some other important people, about ten altogether in that small vehicle. It had gone out of control down the mountainside. There were a number of broken bones and one fatality, Mrs Upadhyaya. But her baby had survived. Freddy More was the last person to be thrown from the jeep as it rolled, and he was moaning and groaning on the ground. The people said 'Take him first,' out of concern, I suppose, that a foreigner was so badly hurt."

"With great difficulty I turned my jeep around on the narrow mountain road, and put Moore on the floor with two or three others of the injured in the seats. Then I crawled—that's the only word for it—I crawled and crept down the mountain in first gear. After about two miles I met one of the ambulances and Dr Bethel Fleming, who took charge of the badly injured Moore. His pelvis was broken in two or three places, and the internal injuries were extensive. The ambulance ride took over two more hours of slow driving, because every jolt of the car gave him excruciating pain. At the hospital, a visiting missionary surgeon took over, treated his internal injuries and set the bones. The doctor didn't think Moore would survive. But he did, and not long after he moved back to his house to recover. Six weeks later, on a Sunday, the two of us, Moore on his motorcycle and I on mine—because we were both enthusiasts with motorcycles—held a reunion with all the doctors and nurses involved, to thank them."

Moran, the Motorcycle Priest

During the 1950s and 1960s, Marshall was well known in Nepal as the "motorcycle priest." He could be seen roaring along almost any day scattering chickens and children in his wake. He had ridden a motorcycle in Patna for years, a straight line four-cylinder Henderson with a sidecar that he dubbed "the bathtub." In Nepal he acquired a big red British Ariel with a 350cc engine. "It was a little on the heavy side," he said. "What was good about it was that I didn't have to worry about a battery. The lights ran off a magneto, and that saved me a lot of trouble."

When he moved from Jawalakhel back to Godavari in 1969, Marshall left the Ariel behind and got himself a smaller 100cc BSA, a British motorcycle manufactured by the Birmingham Small Arms Company. "Much lighter. Danced around on the road. Every bump was a leap in the air," he said. "But it was very economical, and the axle broke only three times on that bad road. When that happened, I had to make my own axles. I replaced the first one with a very poor Indian steel product from Calcutta. It didn't last long. The second time I went to one of the garages and got a good piece of steel and cut it down, taking the measurements from the old broken axle. The last one was made from a piece of American junk steel, which lasted the rest of my experiences in Nepal."

His last motorcycle was a Japanese Suzuki. "It had great shifting and a self starter, and excellent lights. The engine was 125cc and would go almost a hundred miles on one gallon of petrol. Very economical and very quiet. But, when I turned seventy-five, in 1981, there was a petition from my staff: 'Please do not ride the motorcycle. We worry too much about the old man on the motorcycle.'"

Back in the 1950s, Fr Moran could often be seen (and heard) roaring into the Shanta Bhawan Hospital compound to visit a patient or attend a hospital board meeting. Not long after the hospital was opened, the missionaries asked Marshall to serve on the board of directors. Marshall was often at the hospital, delivering, retrieving or visiting sick school boys or their family members, in the wards or accompanying them in for x-rays, or seeing that they got a proper setting of a broken arm or leg. When he had passengers to deliver, he used the school jeep; but, if alone, he came on his motorcycle.

In time, the United Mission also opened a nurses training program and much more recently the mission helped build and staff the more modern and efficient Patan Hospital complex. Then, old Shanta Bhawan Hospital was closed. (The building and grounds now serve as a private school, unassociated with the Protestant mission.) Over the years, the United Mission to Nepal also opened hospitals and several technical training schools in locations outside of the Kathmandu valley.

The Flemings' Contribution to Nepalese Ornithology

For many years while Dr Bethel was the head medical doctor at Shanta Bhawan Hospital, Dr Bob served as hospital administrator. Often, however, he was off birding in some remote corner of the kingdom. After their son, Robert Fleming Jr, earned his doctorate in Zoology. he joined his father's passion for Himalayan ornithology. They collected bird specimens exclusively for the Chicago Field Museum of Natural History, which soon prided itself on holding the most complete collection of Nepalese birds in the world.

When the Flemings first came to Nepal, only a few hundred Nepal birds were known by professional ornithologists. Most of them had been recorded by the scientist-diplomat Brian Hodgson, British Resident to the kingdom, in the early to mid-nineteenth century. In time, the two Bob Flemings, senior and junior, nearly doubled Hodgson's record to over eight hundred species. In 1976, together with the renowned Nepalese artist, Lain Singh Bangdel, and several assistants, they published *Birds of Nepal*, the first comprehensive field guide. It is still a standard reference work on the subject.[11]

Sometimes Fr Moran also joined Bob Sr as an avid bird watcher and collector.

Looking Back
Birds for the Boys
Fr Moran

One day Bob Fleming asked me why I didn't make a bird collection for the school. "Well," I said, "I'd need to know a little about preserving them." At that, Bob replied, "Let's go get a bird or two, and I'll show you." So off we went, Bob with a little air gun, very accurate, and me as the new student of ornithology. Our first bird was a scarlet minivet, a beautiful little creature. We opened it, cleaned out the innards and had only the skin and feathers left. Then we sprinkled it with alum and boric acid and a little salt, inside, as preservative, stuffed it with cotton and sewed it up. That's how I started. I soon had about sixty birds.

Nepalese boys are real marksmen with slingshots. When I started collecting with them I told them firmly, "Don't shoot every bird you see. Only shoot new ones for the collection. Do your practicing on trees or flowers or something, but don't shoot birds just for fun—that's forbidden."

One afternoon while driving the jeep up a little hill on a very rough road, bouncing along, one of the boys with me shouted, "We don't have that bird, Father!" And before I could stop he aimed his slingshot and shot at a bush about thirty feet away. The bird dropped dead before I could stop. What a shot!

We dressed it out and stuffed it, then tried to identify it to satisfy our curiosity. Bob Fleming was away in America, and we couldn't find the bird in any book. The boys and I were very eager to know its identification, so I took it to a Mrs Proud, a lady at the British Embassy who knew a lot about birds. It took her two or three days to find it in a book on Asian birds. I don't remember now just what species it was but I told her that since it was so rare to Nepal she could send it to the British Museum if she'd like.

I never thought what Bob Fleming would think, but after he returned and heard what I'd done, he scolded me. "I send my specimens to the Field Museum in Chicago, your own home town, your own museum," he said, "and you neglected to keep this rare one for me."

Frankly, I never thought of it.

The Mountain is Young

Among the scores of invitees to the 1956 Royal Coronation event was the young Eurasian novelist, Han Suyin, who had recently achieved notoriety for her book *A Many Splendoured Thing*. Han Suyin's novelist-eye 1956 view of the city of Kathmandu is revealing of at least some of the city's charm and medieval character and, not least, its expatriate social life. The book reflects considerable author's license, overwhelmed by the exotic and fueled by a vivid imagination.[12]

In *The Mountain is Young*, Han Suyin described her "Khatmandu" through the diary of a fictional Anne Ford, a "beautiful English girl... in search of herself." Miss Ford's personal view of the city (and Han Suyin's, too, no doubt) was heavily romanticized: "Khatmandu, word, peal of bells, sweet and grave bronze bells with a prodigious echo, calling among mountains... mountain bells, calling, lingering, tolling, reflected from slope to slope... This is real."

Miss Ford, in the story, feels a kind of "mountain exhilaration" on her arrival in Nepal, an elation that seizes her with an ecstasy that streams through the story line and pours out of the pages. She admits to being "mad already through echo of the name..., and here it is, the heart of spring itself, golden sunlight spilling off the tops of dark hills, softness in the air, as of petals much compounded, crushed with substance of air; like burning bushes of pink firebrands of almond and plum blossom, more luminous as evening grows blue and dark..."[13]

Han Suyin stayed several months in the kingdom, at the Royal

Hotel, gathering material for her love story. Persons familiar with the more exotic expatriates and elite Nepalese of the late 1950s will recognize some of them in the book, thinly veiled despite the author's disclaimer that it's fiction and that all "beings (in it)... are illusions of the mind."[14]

Among the book's most prominent characters are Vassili, the hotel manager, and his "Nordic goddess" wife Hilde (obviously Boris Lissanevitch and his Danish wife Inger). There is also The Field Marshall, described, not inaccurately, as "a philosopher" and "His Maharani..., the most beautiful woman in the world" (modeled after Field Marshall General Kaiser Shamsher Jang Bahadur Rana and his wife, his *rani*). "His Preciousness the Rampoche [sic] of Bongsor" (probably based on the Chinia Lama of Boudhnath monastery), is described as "an Asian Churchill (who) wore a zoot suit," but is then put down rather litigiously as "the biggest crook of the Himalayas." There are many other characters in the book, variously described as teachers, engineers, missionaries, a revolutionary, a scholar, a priest, et cetera, sometimes clearly and sometimes only vaguely recognizable as persons living in Kathmandu at the time.

Han Suyin's presentation of her Dr Fred Maltby as "Chief Medical Officer of the Hospital" and his wife Eudora Maltby as "a writer of inspirational music," seems to be the inverse of Bob Fleming and his wife, Dr Bethel. Noting the plot's pre-feminist revolution style, the author's characterization of the decidedly un-Fleming-like *Mal*tby, as a milque-toast like male missionary doctor, probably provided the author with a more plausible background character in light of the rest of her seamy tale.

Not least in her thinly veiled cast of characters is one Father MacCullough, described as "the inevitable, indestructible, knowledgeable priest." She has much to say, often by innuendo, of this fictional Jesuit striving (in her view) among the sinful of the valley. By far the most flattering comment about him, and the one that reveals, perhaps, her true respect for Fr Moran in real life is that "few men did more and better work in the Valley than Father MacCullough."[15]

Marshall's opinion of Han Suyin's racy novel: "I wish it were never written!"

Tibetan Refugee Relief Work

During the decade of the 1950s, Nepal had opened to the outside and Moran had built his school. By the early 1960s, Nepal was on the map, so to speak, and people were flooding to Kathmandu—diplomats, development workers, Peace Corps Volunteers (starting in 1962), mountaineers, and Western tourists. There were also thousands of destitute refugees arriving from Tibet. In 1950, Chinese troops had invaded Tibet, but it took until 1959 for local resentment to come dramatically to a head in an event that shook Lhasa and greatly affected its southern neighbors, India and Nepal.

In 1959, at the time of *Losar*, Tibetan New Year, a time when Lhasa was typically crowded with Tibetan pilgrims from the hinterlands, a rumor spread among the populace that the Chinese occupiers were about to remove the Dalai Lama to Peking. At that, faithful Tibetans by the thousands rallied to protect their beloved spiritual leader and created a considerable scene challenging the authority of the Chinese military occupation. One night, disguised as a commoner, the Dalai Lama was sneaked out of his summer estate, the Norbulingka, and over the course of the next two weeks was smuggled southward to safety in India.

In the wake of his secret and unexpected departure, life in Lhasa became extremely dangerous as Tibetans rose up with primitive arms against a vastly superior Chinese militia. The Chinese rapidly crushed the Lhasa uprising, an event that set off a mass exodus in the wake of their leader's escape. Many of the refugees were Buddhist monks, wealthy landowners, businessmen and the highest classes of elites, who considered their chances of survival under the repressive rule of the Chinese as slim. Many others were poor peasant farmers and yak herders whose fear of communism was also very real. Something close to eighty thousand Tibetans fled south and crossed the Himalayan passes into northern India, Nepal and Bhutan.[16] Of them, perhaps twenty-thousand arrived in Nepal. (The figure has been exaggerated higher, but no one ever counted them.)

A great many of them were nomads from western Tibet. Their conditions were pitiful, uprooted from their highland home, bringing only what they could carry on yaks to the border, and on their backs from there southward down into the Himalayan foothills. Sick and bedraggled, some settled in the mountains at places like Dhorpatan in the west and Chialsa in Solu Khumbu at the east, but many of them eventually found their way into the Pokhara and Kathmandu valleys. They fared badly, and tragically, in the lower altitudes, unaccustomed to the heat and unhealthy conditions of the lowlands. It was not long until the plight of those in Kathmandu, especially, came to the attention of the Nepalese authorities and some of the resident expatriates, including Fr Moran, who felt moved to help them. Fr Moran told many stories of those hectic days, some of which are recounted in *Settlements of Hope*, a 1989 book by Ann Forbes.[17]

News of the Dalai Lama's escape from Lhasa on the night of March 10, 1959, was quickly broadcast around the world. He had escaped the watchful eye of the Chinese, dressed in rough hewn clothes of a Tibetan militant, without his tell-tale spectacles. Twenty-one days later, weary from his flight on foot and horseback across the Himalayas, His Holiness (as he is popularly known to Tibetan Buddhists) crossed the southern border out of Tibet to freedom.

Ann Forbes wrote this of the events: "The world had its eyes riveted on the Dalai Lama and the refugees entering India; any donations of food, money, medicine, or clothing were sent immediately to the Dalai Lama, who subsequently settled in the hills north of Delhi, in Dharmsala. Meanwhile, the 20,000 refugees streaming across the border of Nepal were overlooked by the headlines and thus missed out on much of the aid. The Dalai Lama himself was overwhelmed with trying to organize assistance for the Tibetans flowing into India; even if he had had any provisions to offer, the communication between India and Nepal delayed word for some time on the refugees remaining in the Hindu country. Although the Nepal Government was willing to accept Tibetans, the monarchy did not have the resources or the international connections that India did, and could offer little material relief to the refugees."[18]

At that time in Nepal, there was only a small welfare organization, and as Fr Moran observed, for some time after the refugees began pouring into the country, nothing much was done. Forbes quotes him as saying, "There was no Red Cross or any other group helping the Tibetans. They were arriving by the hundreds and were under a tree here, under a tree there. They gravitated to Boudha and Swayambhu (Buddhist centers in the Kathmandu valley) with their dirty black tents. (Most) had never lived in a house in their lives; 90 percent were nomads. They were a menace to Kathmandu, diseased people and dirty, and they were dying; in the morning they would be found dead by the road."

Marshall knew that the Nepal Government was largely incapable of providing much help to the Tibetans; there was little money and little expertise to work with refugees whose conditions were so pitiful. He also knew that his combined knowledge of Nepal and its customs, his connection with government officials, and his close association with the few (at that time) international aid agencies in Kathmandu were probably the best around. He determined to do what he could to organize some sort of relief program with as much help as he could muster from both Nepalese and expatriate sources.

He began by forming the Nepal International Tibetan Refugee Relief Committee, sometimes known by the clumsy acronym

NITRRC—or, more often as "Father Moran's Committee." The committee was comprised of a number of prominent foreigners in the community. Ann Forbes reports that they held their first meeting in early April 1960 at Boris's Royal Hotel where, over pastries and tea, they set their goals. Those were, "to collect, administer, and disburse funds and relief on behalf of Tibetan refugees in Nepal." The first money-raising event was an Easter party sponsored by Americans living in Kathmandu.

Fr Moran's committee included some of the most prominent names in the social and diplomatic life of Kathmandu. Marshall was chairman. The treasurer was Mrs Elizabeth Clough, whose husband ran the British Council. Mrs Katherine Weatherall was secretary. Others included Boris and his wife, Inger, along with Dr Bob Fleming and Peter Aufschnaiter, a Tibetan-speaking Austrian who figures prominently in Heinrich Harrer's book *Seven Years in Tibet*. Heidi Schulthess, wife of a Swiss cheese maker, was involved and takes credit for encouraging the early development of the now lucrative Tibetan carpet weaving industry under the committee's auspices. Another active member was the Swiss geologist, Toni Hagen, who played a critical rule in securing funding for the committee. Some relief agencies that he approached on behalf of the committee did not fully appreciate the situation and, at first, their responses were negative and unsupportive. Part of the problem was an image of the refugees as mostly big landlords and lamas who were described in one report as "predominantly Charlatans."[19] A similarly negative viewpoint was written in 1960 by the author of a fact-finding mission from Switzerland representing the International Committee of the Red Cross.

Fr Moran told Ann Forbes that during the first year some problems and disagreements arose between the Tibetan leaders and some of the foreigners involved. In Marshall's words, "The Tibetans have tremendous aristocratic levels of who's who. The official types did not want to get their hands dirty, they wore fancy clothes, and they were not willing to cooperate with our committee." As a consequence, some reports received in Switzerland were distorted. Meanwhile, most of the refugees were living in extremely unhealthy conditions, and starving. A report to the United Nations High Commission for Refugees (UNHCR) described the situation like this: "Many, especially women and children, died on the way, or soon after arrival. Those who survived the grueling trek over the rugged 16,000 foot Himalayan passes were starving and utterly exhausted. None could speak the... language, nor could their hosts remember Tibetan... Unaccustomed to the hot climate and low altitude, the majority developed skin diseases and gastric disorders. All needed food and shelter, and most needed medical care."[20]

Working alone, Fr Moran's committee was simply unable to meet the great demand. Fortunately, with the help of Toni Hagen they soon began getting assistance from outside, from British, Australian and German sources.[21]

One of the main settlement areas in the Kathmandu Valley was close to St Xavier's Jawalakhel School. There, on an open stretch of flat land, the poor Tibetans set up their tents and tried to live according to the customs of many centuries in Tibet—sleeping in dark, heavy tents; wearing heavy woolen clothing that smelled like yak; subsisting on a diet of red meat hung to dry in the sun. In the heat and humidity of the valley, however, the people were sweaty and the meat was quickly rotten and stinking. In the high, cold climate of Tibet, they had suffered few health hazards; here in the lowlands, however, they suffered terribly from disease and ailments previously unknown to them. Their situation was unbearable, and posed major challenges to those who would help.

Fr Moran's committee also helped the refugees to construct cooler grass huts to live in. Some concerned Western women staged a bathing campaign at the water spigots, where they cut, washed and combed the long hair of the men, especially, to get rid of the resident vermin. They also instructed the Tibetans in the use of latrines, and they distributed rations—varieties of food that most Tibetans were unaccustomed to cooking or eating, like rice flour, onions, powdered milk and lentils. And because they disliked the flavor of the cooking oil they were given, they put it to alternative use fueling the oil lamps on the altars of their make-shift Buddhist shrines. Some of the oil also showed up for sale on the local market.

A major problem was providing adequate, light weight cotton clothing, to replace the heavy, smelly woolen garb brought down from the cold plateau of Tibet. The solution came from a very unexpected source. According to Ann Forbes, Boris Lissanevitch of the Royal Hotel had been planning a Chinese war movie, which he intended to film in Nepal's lowland. In his typical extravagant way, Boris borrowed two hundred elephants for the set, and built two villages of twenty to thirty huts to be burned in one scene. For the actors' costumes, he had hundreds of lightweight Tibetan robes sewn. When the movie scheme failed, Boris returned the elephants, abandoned the villages, and turned all the clothing over to Fr Moran's committee to distribute to Tibetans in real need!

All this work went reasonably well until November 1963, when disaster struck. Marshall received a call at the school in Jawalakhel from the local magistrate who gave him twenty-four hours to have all of the refugees out of the valley. Marshall was stunned. What? Why? Where would they go? What would they do? He could get no good answers. The official was adamant—the Tibetans must leave. As Marshall described it to Forbes, it was too late that day to contact any more sympathetic officials, so he had little choice but to obey the unexpected order. Without telling the refugees the real reason, he explained, instead, that they had to move temporarily in order to have their living area deloused. He urged them to pack up and move, tents and all.

Marshall recounted the events to Ann Forbes: "We made a big show of it and went through a lot of silly operations. I didn't dare tell them that the government said they had to get out." The group reassembled in the grassy area in front of Nepal's small zoo in Jawalakhel, then "The following morning I went to the King's secretary and said, 'This is empty land that they're staying on, no one was living there. We're doing you a favor and turning the refugees into law-abiding citizens. We're starting a new industry and bring(ing) in foreign exchange. Then this hyena comes in and kicks them out! He's not helping anything, and he gave them no new place to go. Will you have the King call him and say let those people go back?'"

That was Fr Moran's way: go straight to the top. "He was the kind of fellow," another of the priests once described him, "who would always try to get things done from the top down. That is the way it is done in Nepal. He knew a lot of people and was very much the diplomat."

In 1965, Fr Moran and his committee turned over responsibility for Tibetan refugee work to the International Committee of the Red Cross (whose work was later taken over in Nepal by the Swiss Government). Then, life settled back down to more normal proportions for awhile. Marshall never tired of reading about Tibetan religion, however, nor meeting and greeting famous foreign Tibetologists and high lamas when he had the chance. Among the former were Professor David Snellgrove of England and the Italian religious historian, Giuseppe Tucci. Among the latter was the Chinia Lama of Boudhnath temple in Kathmandu, another of the valley's characters of the 1950s and 1960s.

Over thirty years later, in 1986, Marshall was reminded of the refugee project of the 1960s while on a twelve day overland tour of Tibet, paid for by one of his Catholic friends in honor of his eightieth birthday. In a small way it was the finale to a long quest to see a few of the places where some of the seventeenth and eighteenth century

Jesuit explorers he had read about, such as Frs Cabral, Grueber, d'Orville, Cacella and Desideri, had been. Marshall was also curious to see where all the refugees had come from, and what the situation under Chinese rule was like. Frs Marshall Moran and Gene Watrin traveled together with a small tour group by bus from Kathmandu, up over the seventeen thousand foot Nyalam Pass and across the high plateau through Shigatse and Gyantse to Lhasa.

In Shigatse word got around that Fr Moran, who had worked with Tibetan refugees in Nepal, was in town. It was one of those occasions in Marshall's life when some event from the past caught up to him. Fr Watrin later described what happened. They had just settled in their hotel room after supper "when there was a knock at the door and a message that a visitor had come to see us. One of the Tibetans who used to work with Fr Moran on the Tibetan refugee program in the early '60s heard that we were in town and came with Lamdark Rinpoche, the personal representative of the Panchen Lama, to pay their respects. As he said, 'We are disgraced. You did so much to help our poor people in Nepal and now you are in our city and we haven't done anything for you. You must at least have a soft drink with us in the dining room.' After finding the key and getting the long-locked dining room open again, we sat and talked for a long time over Chinese coke. The Rinpoche spoke German, Tibetan and English, and was a most gentle and considerate person." Before they left, the Tibetans insisted that on their return from Lhasa, the two Fathers should visit the Panchen Lama's palace, but as they arrived back long after dark the following week they were unable to accept the invitation.

Fr Moran, never much of a writer, later printed the following brief, cryptic description of his Tibet trip on a picture postcard depicting the grand Potala Palace overlooking Lhasa:

LHASA – OCT 17, 1986. ARRIVED OCT. 12. BACK IN KAT. OCT, 20. OVERLAND BUS TRIP ALMOST AS RUGGED AS LEWIS & CLARK FOR SCENERY, GEOGRAPHY AND 5 PASSES OVER 15,000 FEET. DUSTY, PANORAMIC. DESERT AREAS, GLACIERS, MT. EVEREST GRAND FROM THE NORTH SIDE. DETAILS SOON FOR YOU. PILGRIMS (IN) UNENDING LINES. BUS TRAVEL SURPRISING, GOOD AS CAN (BE) EXPECTED. FARMING DEVELOPMENT EVIDENT. GOOD CLOTHES, CONSUMER GOODS, BUT FAR TO GO. WEATHER MILD WITH LIGHT SNOW – GONE IN A FEW HOURS. HIGH, SHOWY PEAKS ALL AROUND OUR 600 MILE BUS TRIP

BLESSING, (signed) Marshall SJ

Visitors and Watchers

Kathmandu has always held a particular fascination for visitors. Beginning with its opening up in the early 1950s, and particularly after it received world attention from the spectacular royal coronation events of 1956, travelers have made a special effort to come and see it. In the early days, as far back as the 1930s, Nepal merited only a few rare pictorial articles in magazines—the *National Geographic* for one—mostly because it was so tightly closed to outsiders and visitors were as rare as those bird of paradise feathers in the royal crown. Today, the charms of Nepal and the Himalayas are quite regular fare in travel gazettes, and in uncounted, full-color, large format coffee table books full of Sherpas and Gurkha soldiers, temples and medieval street scenes, mountain peaks and rural farm scenes all blended together to evoke a charm and an enchantment quite simply not found anywhere else in the world.

For many who came during the late 1950s and in the 1960s, Nepal—and Kathmandu in particular, for the vast majority saw only the Kathmandu Valley—fascinated visitors by its storybook-like charm, the atmosphere of an ancient Asian city encountered elsewhere only in romantic travelogues and explorers' journals. Before the noise and pollution brought on by hoards of smoke-belching cars, trucks and busses, and the sight of mis-matched electrical wires entangling centuries old shrines and monuments, before all the street junkies started crowding personal space peddling Tibetan carpets or Chinese Tiger Balm or rupees for dollars on the black market, and before so many new hotels offered so many modern conveniences (air conditioning and hot water showers, no less!), just feeling and smelling and seeing *old* Kathmandu and its sister cities of Patan and Bhaktapur were enchanting adventures.

Those early visitors were far more daring and stalwart, and far more imaginative, than today's jet-set varieties (the same ones you see exciting the very same looking busses at the Taj, the Great Sphinx, or the Acropolis). For the early ones, sauntering relatively unhassled and unhurried through the ancient streets and alleys of the city, observing the Nepalese way of life and age-old customs (unsullied, yet, by TV, the Internet, and globalization), their uncomprehending glimpses into forbidden courtyards and temple compounds, their ears assailed with the melodic but unintelligible sounds of the vernacular Nepali and Newari of the city dwellers and the rough dialects of Tamangs and Bhotia traders from the hills and mountains, combined with a feeling of "being watched" furtively by the kohl-lined eyes of shy women peering out from elaborately carved wooden windows overhead, were altogether a powerful experience.

It charged all the senses at once, overwhelmingly, and led to conjuring up all sorts of marvelous and mysterious notions, and not a few conspiracies, especially when reconsidered in light of the intriguing social life back at Boris's Royal hotel. Even, or perhaps especially, the resident expatriates and wealthy notables of the town seemed to fire the fancy of newsmen and writers, movie stars and diplomats and other luminaries and dignitaries, yesteryear's dreamers and seekers, today's "dharma dollies." And there were the watchers; the expats seemed always to be watched.

Occasionally during the 1950s and 1960s, one heard whispered speculations about who among the resident expats was a spy. A rumor circulated that Fr Moran was one. After all, didn't he have the connections in high places? And didn't he hang out with the society set? And wasn't his work among the anti-communist Tibetan refugees sure evidence of his real motives of intrigue? And (after he once again took up ham radio) didn't he have the technological means for communicating to the outside whatever it was he was thought to be spying on?

Marshall always put the notion that he was some sort of secret agent to rest with a hearty laugh, and his close Nepalese friends dismissed it as so much gossip-mongering by a few naturally suspicious individuals and speculating newsmen. As one prominent Nepalese official put it, "It is difficult to know who is a CIA man. But, one doesn't have to spot Fr Moran for that. We had a *real* CIA man back in those days and everybody knew who he was." (He was *not* Fr Moran.)

Years later, the author met the man "everyone knew" as the "CIA man" at a small reception for two Nepal Jesuits visiting America, at a private home in the rural suburbs outside of Washington DC. On arrival, I was introduced to a covey of "old Nepal hands," only few of whom (besides the two priests) I had met before. But I knew when I was introduced to the one "everyone knew" as a CIA agent. Marshall had once described him to me (in Kathmandu) as a good friend and a devout Catholic, whose affiliations with "The Agency" were no secret. One after another, that evening, I made my acquaintance with others in the room, and as we engaged in the idle conversation that receptions tend to invoke, I innocently inquired about what had taken each of them to Nepal. One after another, I was told that he or she had once been "on assignment" in the Kingdom.

Some people say that the ranks of the CIA are filled with members of the Church of Latter Day Saints (the Mormons). But it seems that a good many members of the Catholic faith have also worked for "The Firm"—along with Protestants, agnostics, atheists, and others of various ilk and inclination. What brought the members of that dinner party together that evening was not only their past familiarity with Nepal, where they had worked in various positions during the 1950s and early 1960s, but also their mutual personal allegiances to the Catholic Church. It was primarily as fellow Catholics, not so much as fellow spies, that they had come that night to greet the two reverends who were visiting from Kathmandu. I quickly realized that I was the only *non*-Catholic and, along with the two priests, one of the few *non*-CIA operatives present.

Marshall knew he was being watched during his first few decades of life in Nepal, especially by the Russians and the Chinese. Someone once told him that he had been written about in the Moscow publications *Isvestia* and *Pravda,* no less. Before Nepal, he had also been watched by various anti-American factions in India. When he first came to Nepal, the Korean War was on, and the American Ambassador to Delhi warned him that the reactionary Indian press was speculating on the American role in Asian affairs. Historically, he was in good company, for both the Capuchin friars and the Jesuit priest-explorers before him were also suspected of being foreign agents. At the time Fr Moran was preparing to go to Nepal, one Indian newspaper, the tabloid *Blitz*, named him and pointed out the dangers of an American, and a priest, going to Kathmandu. They implied that Nepal would become the next battle ground between the great powers. Given the hype, Marshall avoided publicity.

In the early 1950s, well before the road from India opened (in 1956), the American Ambassador, Chester Bowles, trekked up from India for a visit. Marshall hiked out along the trail above Thankot to greet him. "I was up at the top, on the pass above Thankot, when Mr Bowles arrived on a horse, and Mrs Bowles in a sedan chair. Some *Time/Life* magazine photographers were there taking pictures. They said 'Come on Father!' and motioned me into camera range. 'No,' I said. 'You want the Bowles-es, not me.' I could have been in the magazine."

Another time, while on an Asian tour, Eleanor Roosevelt arrived in Kathmandu and made a big thing of seeking out Fr Moran. "And a similar thing happened—the press was all around her." But Marshall was also careful not to get in any of those photographs. "I refused," he said, "because I know, I can prove, the Russians were on my trail. I could have fed them. Then they could have said, 'Look at this. He was in this picture. He was there. He had to see Bowles.,' Or, 'He was with Mrs Roosevelt.' I down-played publicity like that because I was very much aware, especially during those first ten years, that the publicity would embarrass the Nepal Government. I wasn't thinking of my own self, I was thinking of how it might jeopardize our school. And later, when Nepal took in the Tibetan refugees and I served on the refugee resettlement committee, we played hush-hush on that one, too. We had to."

Marshall was single-mindedly intent on providing nobody with the ammunition to concoct a conspiracy out of an innocent acquaintance that he or another priest might have with some well known public or international figure.

Not every American visitor to Nepal in those early days was as respectable as Eleanor Roosevelt. In January 1970, for example, U.S. Vice President Spiro Agnew showed up for a visit lasting twenty-two hours. Nepal was the fifth nation on his eleven-country Asian tour. The Associated Press reported that he was met at the airport by Nepal's Prime Minister Kirti Nidhi Bista and the American Ambassador Carol Laise, and that "Schoolgirls hung garlands of flowers on Agnew and his wife Judy as cannon of the Royal Nepal Army fired a 19-gun salute." One chronicler at the time described part of the scene as Agnew was driven into the city: "The crows cawed a welcome, [and] the sacred cows were herded off the road to avoid a confrontation with the motorcade..." A more recent blogger has noted that, "Clearly, those who saw Nepal struggling to emerge into the modern-day world under a system reminiscent of the Middle Ages were influenced more by its quaintness than its exclusiveness."[21]

It was on arrival at the airport that Agnew made a rather infamously embarrassing diplomatic gaff. It is said that as he alighted from the plane, he told the greeting crowd that he had "always wanted to visit this part of India" (or words to that effect)!

When Marshall was asked about the incident, he remarked: "What's the use of mentioning him? That's past history." He was very adroit at putting down those for whom he had low regard.

Marshall remembered many visitors with admiration, however, and occasionally with puzzlement. Sometimes they walked in on him unannounced, just to meet the "famous Father Moran of Kathmandu," or to ask for help.

Looking Back
The Lady and Her Hair Dresser
Fr Moran

Back in 1956, not long after King Mahendra's Coronation, in November I think, I was at my desk at the Jawalakhel School clearing up the day's work. It was early evening, and the lights were dim, as the electricity power was poor. Suddenly a very striking, flamboyant, or shall I say overdressed, lady walked into the room. I'll never forget her marvelous hair make-up. Without introduction she said: "The American Ambassador in Delhi suggested I meet you, Father. He said you could assist me to go into the mountains on a trip." She acted as if I knew who she was. When I asked, all she said was "I'm Mrs Selznik."

It meant nothing to me. And I didn't think much about it, since that name is not terribly extraordinary. But in my dullness, I thought that she, like many tourists who looked me up, would go in two minutes. To reply to her request, I said, "A trip into the mountains? Well, it depends on what you have in mind, how much time you have."

She had ten days, she said, and rather than go skiing in Switzerland or touring the same old places in Europe—she seemed to have grown bored of that—the said that she would like to get a horse and go out for a week or so in the Himalayas.

"Well," I said, "I would not recommend a horse," and explained neither the trails nor the horses were dependable. I'd never heard of anyone going into the mountains on a horse. And, as there were no tour agencies then as there are now, I offered to send one of my students and his sister to accompany her.

"Why?" she asked.

"Because they speak English, and the Sherpas and cooks and porters need someone to communicate to them exactly what you want. Otherwise they may take advantage of you. I don't want you to get into any trouble. I'd rather you go away with happy memories, so I insist that you have someone accompany you."

I told her that the easiest routes were up to Helambu or Langtang Valley north of Kathmandu. She had little time to go anywhere more distant. And there she could see a bit of the Tibetan Buddhist culture.

Then I said, "I'd like to know more about you. I've heard of a *David* Selznik who made films when I used to live in America. Would you know him?"

"He's my husband," she replied.

But that didn't help me much, either. She still hadn't told me her famous name. "That means that you are a Hollywood personality," I said. "Then you'd know John Huston who directed 'The Maltese Falcon', 'The Treasure of the Sierra Madre' and 'The African Queen'. He visited me here just a few months ago," I told her.

Then I asked, "Are you an actress?"

"Yes," she said. "My first film was 'Song of Bernadette'."

"You're *Jennifer Jones*!" I exclaimed. "Why didn't you tell me that in the beginning?"

For the first time, she smiled. Before that she was very much aware of her dignity, I believe, thinking that I must certainly know who she was. But when she realized that I had volunteered to help her, in total ignorance of who she was in the movies, she became more friendly.

I saw her off into the mountains the next day, along with the student and his sister. Before she left, she said I might be getting a telegram from David. She'd given him my name to contact in Kathmandu.

A telegram came the next day, and the next, and the next. "Send her back. Send her back," they said. To which I sent a reply, something in a light tone, to soothe him, something like: "Don't get excited, she's in safe hands."

And every day I was visited by a Japanese lady who told me she was Miss Jones's personal hair dresser and traveling companion. A Japanese hair dresser? Now that was exotic. She was worried about Miss Jones, and asked me every day: "What is the news? What is the news?"

After three or four days, Miss Jones was back, much earlier than expected. I expressed my surprise. It seems that the cook had gotten drunk one night and rolled down the hill! She thought that if the press found that out, they might make something embarrassing out of it. Poor publicity. I almost laughed. And although the cook was unhurt, and was up making breakfast the next morning, the publicity angle worried her. So she had to return.

She came back rather humbly, I thought, but graciously left me two big boxes of tinned goods, some of the fancy food she had rather extravagantly taken with her. Money was no object, and she had hired lots of porters to carry it all.

She thanked me for my help, then asked what I might like sent out from the States. I suggested some films for the boys to enjoy, and Fr Downing suggested classical music. A few months later two big boxes arrived. One was full of 16 mm films, like 'Goodbye, Mr Chips' and 'Mickey Mouse' and other Disney specials, and Shirley Temple's 'The Little Colonel' and some adventure stories. Perfect stuff for children.

The other box was full of 78 LP records, including some Mozart and Brahms and Beethoven's nine symphonies, and violin concertos played by Jascha Heifetz, and Artur Rubenstein playing the piano concertos of Chopin. And Wagner's 'Tannhauser'. I never liked Wagner. It was Downing's choice, not mine.

The air freight alone on all those heavy records was many times their purchase price. As I said, for her money was no object.

From 1979 to 1989, Marshall went once a month by plane to Biratnagar, in the southeastern corner of Nepal, then by jeep to Dharan where there was a British Gurkha military base, to conduct Sunday Mass. Both the Catholics and the Anglicans invited him.

Marshall liked going, in part to break up the routine of Kathmandu.[23] While starting out on one such trip in 1984, he met another famous movie star.

He was in the Kathmandu airport, about to board the flight to Biratnagar, the airfield closest to Dharan, when a travel agency friend rushed over to him. "There is someone here from the United States who would like to meet you, Father," she said. She led him to a knot of people waiting to board a flight to Mount Everest.

Marshall was preoccupied, as his flight had been called and he still had to pass through security and board. "I didn't have much time to spare, but I couldn't refuse, could I?"

His friend introduced him to someone named Redford. "Now, I should have known. But it made no sense to me, since I'd seen very few modern movies. I'd never seen him. He was a total stranger."

The ensuing brief conversation went something like this: "What do you do for a living?" Marshall asked, all innocence, uncomprehending.

"I'm a Hollywood actor. Robert Redford," he said with a big smile, unabashed.

Looking back on that embarrassing moment, Marshal wondered: "What could I say? They had called my flight for the last time, and I wanted to get on that plane! 'You know, I must catch my plane,' I said. 'You won't mind, I hope,' And I excused myself."

"I should have known that Robert Redford was *some*body. How many people had he met who didn't know that? What did he think?—that I was just ignorant? Or a joker? Or getting old and feeble? I usually did better at meeting famous people. But, you never know... I did better when one of the astronauts came to town."

Whenever any prominent mountaineers or well known scientists were in Kathmandu, Marshall went out of his way to invite them to the school to talk to the boys. One of the most famous and interesting to visit was the astronaut Stuart ('Stu') Roosa of Apollo 11 fame, along with William ('Bill') Pogue, of Skylab-II.

Looking Back
Hosting Astronaut Roosa
Fr Moran

One fellow whom the boys and I admired very much was astronaut Commander Stuart Roosa. We had kept close track in class of NASA's moon landings, and the boys and I knew who Roosa was, and of his fame as Commander of Apollo 11. Stu Roosa had been a professor of mathematics at the Air Force Academy in Colorado before being selected for the moon mission. After his famous trip—the first manned lunar landing in July 1969—he was sent by the U.S. Information Agency on a world tour, giving slide lectures and showing off moon rocks.

I met him one evening at a reception at the American Ambassador's residence. When I arrived, all sorts of government officials, ministers and other VIPs were in a crush around him. His wife sat alone on the sofa, so I went over to rescue her, I thought. "This won't go on all night," I said, "and if I didn't meet him on the way in, I'll certainly meet him on the way out."

I soon discovered that she was a pious Catholic, as he was, and that they had three teenage children back home in Houston, Texas. I explained that I was an amateur radio operator and asked for their home phone number, in case I got a chance to call them on a ham radio phone-patch. Then I invited them both out to Godavari to give a talk at the school.

Early the following morning, before breakfast, I contacted a ham operator in Texas, who put a call through to the Roosa house. When Stuart and his wife arrived at the school about nine o'clock, they were astounded that I had just talked with their children.

I had told them that their parents would be home on the weekend, on Saturday, and that I was sending them a little present. "Look," I said to them on the air, "I'm sending each of you a little rosary from Nepal." Stuart's wife protested when she saw the three rosaries I was giving her to carry back—"There should be five," she said!

"Alright," I said. "I'll give you enough for the entire family." And we all laughed. They were very pleasant people.

Those rosaries were nothing special, just cheap little plastic ones, I lose them so fast. They weren't even made in Nepal or India but, of course, they came from Nepal so were something special to the people to whom I occasionally gave them as gifts. And, if you knew how many of them are underground. Whenever I bury someone, I put one in the casket, so when you get to heaven you'll see people with them saying "This came from Nepal, you know!"

Commander Roosa gave a nice talk to the boys, describing the Apollo mission, rocketry and weightlessness, the works. I'd prepped them by describing a bit about what it was like in space without air pressure or gravity, eating out of squeeze tubes and drinking from containers that floated about the cabin if you let go of them.

So the boys were ready, and asked a lot of questions, like "How do you move about if you are floating in the air?" Commander Roosa replied that they had hooks to attach to about the cabin, and that it took lots of practice to manage. "We can be upside down," he said, "and it makes no difference. And we drink water by pumping it into our mouths."

About a week after they left Nepal for home, I tried contacting a ham radio operator in the Houston area again on the radio. "CQ Texas," I called on my amateur radio. No response. "CQ Oklahoma... New Mexico... Louisiana..." No response. I was ready to give up when a voice broke in: "I'm in Salt Lake City," he said. "Give me the number and I'll place the call for you." Now, I hadn't said anything about a phone number, but these fellows can guess when you want to get a message through. So the Salt Lake City ham phoned the Roosa house in Houston. They do this as a service, at their own expense, you know. Stu Roosa answered, and we chatted and reminisced about his brief visit to Nepal.

He was so moved by the contact with Nepal again that he sat down and wrote me a long letter saying something like, "This is a new dimension to me, a new idea. How did I miss ham radio?"

Then he paid the school and our boys a supreme compliment: "Of all the schools I've visited," he said, and he'd been all over Asia, "Godavari sticks out in my mind, not only because of the beautiful surroundings, but from the keenness of your boys and their intelligent questions."

Notes To Chapter 11: Affairs of State and High Society

1. The siren at the Kathmandu airport remained in service for many more years, warning people who were crossing the runway to hurry, and alerting the guards to chase off any stray dogs. Cows are no longer pastured there, the runway has long since been lengthened and paved, the entire site has been secured against wandering animals, and a modern new terminal building now serves international travelers.

    In a little known parody of the Kathmandu airport's stray animal problem of the 1950s and '60s, Art Buchwald, the American humorist and syndicated *Washington Post* newspaper columnist, once wrote a play called 'Sheep on the Runway.' (The fact that it was not sheep, but cows and dogs that had to be chased off the runway each time a plane landed was not important.) *Time* magazine labeled the play "a cartoon allegory" featuring "a group of bumbling, do-good-ing, fast-talking Americans [who] lead a small neutral Himalayan nation in Asia into a deadly heap of trouble." The main characters in the play are described by *Time*'s anonymous theater critic, as "walking labels: the Hawk (a syndicated Washington columnist), the Ambassador, the Pentagon Man, the C.I.A. Man, the A.I.D. Man, [and] the Local Prince." The play was directed by Gene Saks, and ran from January to June 1970 at Broadway's Helen Hayes Theater in New York City. (Anonymous, 'Theater: Laughter in the dark,' *Time* magazine, February 16, 1970; online at www.time.com/time/magazine/article/0,9171,904182,00.html.)

2. Michel Peissel, *Tiger for Breakfast* (1966, pp.209-210).

3. Boris Lissanevitch was a White Russian émigré and proprietor of the Royal hotel in Kathmandu. He is the subject of Michel Peissel's book, *Tiger for Breakfast* (1966).
4. Lowell Thomas, *So Long Until Tomorrow* (1977, pp.208-210).
5. *Ibid.* (pp.210-212).
6. *Ibid.* A 'topper' is a top hat; i.e., a tall cylindrical man's hat worn on formal occasions. It is a tall cylindrical hat with a narrow brim, typically black and made of silk.
7. Peissel, *Tiger for Breakfast* (1966, p.58).
8. *Ibid.* (p.56).
9. Among the famous visitors who stayed at the Royal Hotel in the 1950s and early 1960s, several wrote books. Besides Peissel's *Tiger for Breakfast* (1966), see Toni Hagen's *Nepal* (1960, 1992), Heinrich Harrer's *Seven Years in Tibet* (1954), and Han Suyin's novel, *The Mountain is Young* (1964).

    Among other expatriates occasionally seen hanging out in Boris's Yak and Yeti Bar in those days was the author of the book you are reading. I remember several winter evenings in the early 1960s, when I sat by the warm fire in the bar, listening to Boris tell ribald jokes and tall tales to me and my friends, and to other far more famous guests.
10. See Jonathan Lindell, *Nepal and the Gospel of God* (1979), and Grace Nies Fletcher, *The Fabulous Flemings of Kathmandu* (1964).
11. Robert L. Fleming Sr, Robert L. Fleming Jr and Lain Singh Bangdel, *Birds of Nepal* (1976).
12. Han Suyin's, *The Mountain is Young* (1958), was the first novel about expatriates enjoying the high life in Kathmandu. 'Han Suyin' was a pseudonym for the Chinese-born Eurasian writer (and physician) named Elizabeth Comber (born Rosalie Elisabeth Kuanghu Chow). Before coming to Nepal, she had already published several other novels, including *A Many Splendoured Thing* (1952), which was made into a popular movie. She also wrote non-fiction (biography and history).
13. Han Suyin, *The Mountain is Young* (1958, pp.42, 46).
14. *Ibid.* (Preface).
15. *Ibid.* (p.101).
16. Melvyn C. Goldstein, *A History of Modern Tibet* (1989, Postscript, p.825).
17. A novel, *Cairns* by Dan'l Taylor (2009), describes some of the conditions of upheaval among Tibetan refugees at this time.
18. This quotation, and all that follow from Ann Forbes' *Settlements of Hope* (1989), are from pp.23-44.
19. Forbes (*ibid.*, p.27), quoting a report on the situation by the resident representative of the Swiss organization Schweizer Auslanhilfe.
20. Quoted by Forbes (*ibid.*, 1989, pp.27-28, from a 1975 report to the U.N. High Commission for Refugees, the UNHCR).
21. Eventually, over twenty philanthropic and refugee relief organizations graciously helped fund Tibetan relief in Nepal during the early 1960s, including the Nepal Government, many bilateral and multilateral aid agencies, world church groups, foundations, and private citizens.

22. The sources of the descriptions of Spiro Agnew's 1970 visit to Kathmandu are an Associated Press release (dated January 5, 1970) and a commentary at nepalinetbook.blogspot.com (posted in March 2008).
23. It was during free time while on his regular trips to Dharan that he dictated into a pocket cassette recorder much of his life story that became the basis for this book.

12

Men to Serve Others

Live for God;
Lead for Nepal
Godavari School motto

The Daily Routine
Each morning during the 1980s, the decade before he died, Marshall arose regularly at 4:30 a.m. in his little room behind the ham shack on the second floor of Xavier Hall. After a quick wash-up, he began his day, like all the other priests at Godavari, by attending to personal prayer and a reading of the Breviary (the Divine Office) for about half an hour. At 5:15 a.m., the priests and brothers assembled quietly downstairs in the Fathers' community chapel to celebrate the mass. The role of chief celebrant was rotated among them day by day.

By 5:45 a.m., Marshall was at his radio and on the air to the rest of the world. The only times this routine was altered was when atmospheric conditions deteriorated, due to the interference of solar activity (usually solar flares), or when the combination of low sun spot count (which occurs on average every eleven years) and winter season coincided to produce difficult conditions for DX operation. During those times, Marshall had trouble reaching his radio friends beyond the immediate South Asian region.

Breakfast was served at 7:15 a.m. and was a quick affair. After someone said grace, all manner of conversation ensued, usually about school affairs. It was a far cry from the sometimes mandatory silence kept by Moran and his colleagues when they were theology students at St Mary's College in Kurseong, India, a half century earlier.

The Godavari cook of over twenty-five years, Habule Tamang, was rarely seen out of the kitchen. The bearer, Nati Tamang, a shy man who had been at Godavari since 1958, brought in the morning fare—the "corn flakes" Marshall often talked about on the radio. Marshall ate sparingly, "like a bird" someone once said. He prided himself on careful eating habits. At breakfast, "no eggs" he would say. "Too much fat and cholesterol. Not healthy." He smeared his

12. Fr Moran operating his ham radio rig.

toast thick with peanut butter, instead. "A rich source of protein. The body needs protein," he rationalized.

Immediately after eating, Marshall's first duty was to attend to any sick boys in the upstairs infirmary. He would already have taken their temperatures, sometimes twice—once at 5 a.m. and again just after signing off from the morning radio schedule. Now, at 7:30, he observed them more closely and doled out any medicines that were prescribed. Marshall, as the Infirmarian, was assisted by Panchaman Lama, a trained male nurse and one of Godavari's long time lay teachers.

During the first few months of each school season, Marshall met with newcomers to the school (those students who filled the few vacancies that occurred each year in classes two through six), to drill them in spoken English. These lessons usually lasted a half hour, from 8 to 8:30 a.m.

As the grand old man of Godavari School, Marshall took special pride in managing the student march-in each morning, Sunday through Friday, outside the main student assembly hall. The school schedule followed the national tradition—businesses and schools were open from Sunday through Friday; Saturday was a day off. Consequently, weekly church services were also conducted on Saturdays.

Marshall's life-long tinkerer's curiosity and gift for handling electrical and electronic equipment came in handy, as he set up the loud speakers and cassette player to broadcast the morning march. Then he would stand at the door to be sure the boys kept the proper beat. The boys remember him as a real stickler on this.

Some also remember the "thrashings" they infrequently got at his hand for doing something bad or mischievous. But they also remember that he would always come into the dormitory that same evening to see that the boy who'd been in trouble was alright and understood that the discipline was not in any way malicious or mean.

Moran timed school events to the minute. Morning assembly lasted no more than fifteen minutes, whereupon first class started. Fr Moran also taught each day, although his schedule was considerably reduced in the last years of his life. His primary and lasting responsibility was teaching Sixth Standard English, followed immediately on three days of the week with Special English for three other classes, either poetry or readings on tapes or unstructured conversation and listening, or some other special language activity. Since classes at Godavari and throughout the St Xavier's School system in Nepal are taught in English, every boy had to master it in order to succeed.

Starting in 1984, on one day each week, Marshall ran a computer class for class six boys. The computers, two of them, were old Commodore models with outdated CPM operating systems. They had been donated in bits and pieces by friends in England and the United States. They were loaded with programs for writing, music and games. He was barely literate in CPM—it had come along too late in his life and he was never inclined to upgrade the school's computer equipment to DOS, Windows or Apple operating systems, as they were unfamiliar to him. "Marsh learned a little bit about a lot of things," someone said of him, "enough to be able to talk about it, but if the conversation got beyond a certain point he'd change the subject." Fr Donnelly sometimes observed Marshall and the boys at the computer and once noted that "He was undoubtedly the first primary school computer teacher in Nepal, not counting Lincoln School run by the Americans, and he was at least one year ahead of the Buddhanilkantha School for Nepalese boys run by the British."

Promptly after computer class, or more precisely "at 10:05 a.m.," as Marshall pointed out, he made his almost daily drive into town. After 1984, he was accompanied one day a week for shopping by one or more of the Filipino Sisters of the RVM Order (Religious of the Virgin Mary) who taught at Godavari, and after 1991, by someone from the Sisters of St Joseph's of Cluny, from Kalimpong, India, who replaced the RVM sisters. Once a week he would deliver sick boys to a dentist, an eye doctor or a general practitioner. "To avoid too many trips, he had a formula—"three boys, five extractions." This cut the medical trips back to three per week on average.

In town, Marshall also had a fairly regular routine: check the mail at St Xavier's school in Jawalakhel; attend to messages left for him by friends (in his Jawalakhel School message box), often a fellow amateur radio friend or a friend of one, or anyone else of his large public of admirers; and, if he had time and not too many boys to shepherd around in the jeep, he would stop by the author's house for coffee. He loved rich, brewed-from-dark-roast-beans coffee, and would always manage to eat a few home-baked cookies from our kitchen, as well. (It was on these occasions that he told anecdotes about his experiences in Nepal and India, which initiated this biography.)

One year, Marshall also taught a course on current affairs in town at the Jesuit juniorate (college) located at Kamal Niwas on the outskirts of Patan. The dean of the juniorate was Fr Casper (Cap) Miller, who appreciated Marshall's little bit of assistance. The juniorate had capacity for sixteen young men each year under Fr Miller's tutelage. The juniors came from India, mostly, and had already completed a year of candidacy and two years of novitiate training. Over the years, some of them moved on up to fill positions gradually vacated by the aging American Jesuits in the Nepal mission.

Sometimes Marshall returned to Godavari from his trips to town, in time for lunch; and, sometimes not. Lunch is usually served at 11:40 a.m., to coincide with the school boys' lunch hour, although during winter and on holidays it would not begin until 12 noon. The boys ate their meal of rice, vegetables and meat or egg, and lentils, in a large dining hall behind Xavier Hall. The priests ate in a small private room on the lower level of Xavier Hall.

The priests' lunch typically started with soup, followed most days by rice, lentils and a choice of curries—meat or potato with vegetable—along with a salad and some fresh fruit or gelatin dessert. And all day long, for tea time or at any time, the table was laid with fresh bread and rolls, jams and peanut butter, some cake or cookies, and full thermos pots of hot water for making tea or instant coffee.

Fr Moran had no scheduled work after lunch during the later years. This was his rest time. If he was tired, he would retire for a short nap in his small room upstairs in Xavier Hall; or he would read. "The world was his apple," as Fr Donnelly once described it. "He read whatever he could." It was something he never neglected. The Father's Library was full of books, magazines and journals, and so was his ham shack and his private bedroom. The latter was a small, Spartan space with a bed, desk and cabinet for his clothes, and a curtained window looking out over the Godavari gardens. Among his favorite books were the fifteen volumes of *Theological Investigations*, by Fr Karl Rahner, SJ, and *Resurrection: A Biblical Study*, by Fr Francis-Xavier Durrwell, CSSR.[1]

From 1960 on, when he was back on the air with amateur radio, he would often tinker with his radio gear during the afternoon. He also spent long hours each week monitoring videos borrowed from friends, making copies for the school library. Before 1984, he showed 16mm films. Some were in the school's permanent collection, but most were borrowed from the American or British libraries in downtown Kathmandu. After 1984, when the school acquired video equipment, he started building up an impressive library of several hundred titles, "adventure shows for the older boys and cartoons for the little guys," as he put it.

Fridays, and evenings before the start of school holidays, were video time. The show room at the top of Xavier Hall was poorly ventilated and while video duty was always entertaining, in at least one respect it was a real challenge—all those smelly feet! Dozens of boys crowded into the room to watch a video show, after leaving their shoes at the door. Fr Moran made it a point to sit at the back of the room, near an open window, with *his* shoes *on*.

Moran regularly met his ham radio friends in the late afternoon, and again from 5:30 to 6:30 p.m. (morning hours in North America). Then, at 6:50 p.m., all of the Fathers gathered in the chapel for common prayer. Supper followed at 7 o'clock, after which the priests retired to the library to play cards. Marshall was sometimes late to the library because right after the dinner hour he might have to deal with boys complaining of headaches, stomach aches or other ailments. In the library, he'd join the other priests to play cards or engage in idle talk. There was always a thermos of tea or hot chocolate to drink and usually a tin of cookies that were baked up and sent out to the priests by the Sisters of St Mary's Convent of Kathmandu.

Sometimes he went back to the ham radio for a nighttime rendezvous; but more likely he went to bed. The next morning's 4:30 a.m. rising came early, and each school day was busy. Fr Moran's life of over forty years in Nepal was dedicated to the Jesuit educational apostolate: teaching boys and young men.

Men for Others
Jesuits wear many coats—as theologians and preachers, spiritual guides and confessors, school teachers and university professors, scientists, anthropologists, archeologists and historians, humanists, writers, and emissaries, and a few amateur radio operators, and more. But the role of teacher is at the heart of the Society. The St Xavier School system was founded in Nepal by Fr Moran for teaching, as an educational enterprise. It has maintained that primary focus over the years, although its activities have enlarged somewhat to include research and development work, and social services and counseling.

The educational role of the Jesuits dates from the very beginning of the Society, five centuries ago. The fundamental roots of the teaching apostolate are found in the ways that St Ignatius saw the world and its concerns, and how he addressed them. But much of the basic philosophy and structure of the Jesuit education system, both in the preparation of its own recruits and in the school it has established around the globe, dates to one of the earliest and strongest of the Jesuit Fathers General, Claudio Acquaviva, sometimes called the second founder of Jesuitism. Fr Acquaviva (1543-1615) was an Italian Jesuit priest who served as the Fifth Superior General of the Society of Jesus. He organized the first uniform curriculum of studies for Jesuits in training as well as for the schools in which Jesuits teach young men to serve others.

While Fr Acquaviva's original ideas have been subject to reinterpretation and changes over the years, the basic plan is still retained, its primary values and its basic goals readily lived out in the Jesuit schools and classrooms of Nepal. Two of the main values are found in the Jesuit notions about community and student; but other values, like freedom, growth, excellence, and justice are interwoven throughout.

A school, the Jesuits say, is fundamentally a community united in its vision, sharing the hopes, aspirations, experiences, successes and failures of each member—from the senior-most staff person to the youngest schoolboy. Virtually all activities are focused on this goal, from school uniforms to team sporting events to hikes and picnics and Parents' Day visits.

In Nepal, this school-community spirit is clear and easy to see. It began with the founding of Godavari and has continued through the years in school-community life at the St Xavier's Jawalakhel School campuses, at the Gorkha and Jhapa District schools, and at St Xavier's College in Kathmandu. The school spirit of community continues among the "old boys" even after graduation, through the Godavari Alumni Association, a strong society of civic-minded graduates. The GAA was founded in 1960 and has offices in central Kathmandu. It includes members from the St Xavier's boys' and St Mary's girls' schools, many of whom are active in social and civic affairs and in the formation of public opinion. The GAA sponsors public seminars and a lecture series, sports events, and various other public and alumni gatherings.

The spirit of the St Xavier's alumni is one that reflects their sense of responsibility and of shared experiences, past and present. Graduates consider it as important and as memorable to them as the more personal events of their family's lives and homes.

Another principle of the Jesuit education is the student-centered curriculum, sometimes called by the Latin term *cura personalis,* or "concern for the individual person as a person." The student focus goes well beyond the mere achievement of success and prestige. It seeks the development of an enlightened, creative, well rounded individual who can function with ease and worthiness in the larger society.

While scholastic excellence is, obviously, not the only goal of a Jesuit education—good sportsmanship is another—scholarship is nonetheless of utmost importance. To some degree, the measure of the Nepal Jesuit schools can be taken in the success of its students and graduates in their lives as adults functioning in a developing nation.

In 1991, after a decade serving as the principal of the Godavari school, Fr James Donnelly wrote of the hard questions that Jesuit educators must answer: "...what kind of product do we want?" he asked. "What does God want and what kind of person does Nepal need? That's a key toward our vision of the boy we want to get into the school." Fr Donnelly went on to point out that "We want boys who are happy to be back in their families, and boys who are eager to help out their country, and not to be all out only for #1 (themselves). God was leading me right... to ask questions about what kind of products are we to select? These questions are important. The answers are not easy..."[2]

Donnelly then wrote (with the "distinct advantage of freshness of recall," as he put it) about the principal's life, outlining some of the incredible detail that needs constant attention in the smooth operations of a school such as Godavari. The task is formidable. It requires dedication and strong leadership. Fr Donnelly's reminiscences provide an inside picture of the running of St Xavier's Godavari school.

Looking Back
On Running Godavari School
James J. Donnelly, SJ[3]

Concentrating on the main task of the school—educating the boys in their studies and training them to become 'men for others'—has been my main concern over these ten years. Our boys' overall development is worthy of the best efforts of each of the staff, and I feel at ease with myself that I have given this my best shot. I feel contented now that during my ten years I tried to be a second 'father' to the boys, as my practical way of showing to God my love of Him and my consecration to Him as one of His priests.

Myriad details of school and hostel administration kept crowding upon me daily over the ten years; helping the staff to stay contented and well-motivated; listening to their problems and needs; paying them what I considered a family living wage; drawing up for the boys properly balanced schedules and routines; overseeing the boys daily morning inspection, exercise, and drill; conducting the daily assembly for the staff and boys; approving of substitutions of the staff; record keeping of the boys' performances and achievements recorded in the 'Principal's Diary' and on the 'Principal's Long Sheets'; keeping records of various other details as well, such as the daily weather keeping; overseeing the perfecting and the teaching of the boys; book-keeping and key keeping; lending active support and encouragement in all the school's extra-curricular and co-curricular activities, such as sports and games;

Parents' Day and elocution contests; spelling and mental arithmetic contests; involving myself in regular though infrequent details such as the boys' weights and heights; Xavier Forums and seminars for the staff; checking regularly on bed wetters; banking and weekly shopping; overseeing the administration of the 'Donkey Stick' for speaking English at all times around the school; serving as Scout Patron for the Cub and Boy Scouts of Classes 5 and 6; supporting the weekly social service work on Tuesdays; finally, serving at all times as the 'goal tender' for settling boys' complaints about others who scrapped with them or bullied them. Through all these and many other similar involvements... I have felt trusting in God, self-assured, and confident that being at Godavari has held out tremendous meaning for me...

One of the chief reasons parents choose Godavari for their sons is that our school rule stresses the use of good correct English both inside and outside of the classroom. We give the boys a day-by-day opportunity, year after year, to grow in all four skills of English— *listening* with good comprehension to English spoken by expert English language users, who have mastered its use... (to) *speak... grammatically* correct English...(to) be able to *read easily* and with good comprehension in different registers of English.... Finally, we work on their *writing* skills, so that they can write fluently, correctly, intelligently, and with facility...

Marks Far Above Average

Frs Donnelly and Moran, their Jesuit colleagues and other teachers, often expressed great pride in the achievements and accomplishments of their former students and graduates throughout the nation. For years, the peak achievement of each high school graduating class was successful completion of the Senior Cambridge examinations, from Great Britain. The students of Nepal's St Xavier's Schools consistently did well on them, attracting wide attention, sometimes engendering (and enjoying) the envy of others outside of the St Xavier's School community.[4]

On his occasional visits to the United States, Marshall was often asked to talk about the meaning and accomplishments of the St Xavier's schools in Nepal, especially about Godavari school and his personal philosophy of education. In the late 1980s, for an audience in Washington DC, he reminisced on the start of the school nearly four decades earlier. Then he asked the audience, rhetorically, "How is it that from the very beginning of the school, our boys got such high marks, marks far above the average of India, some of the best marks in the world? What is the reason for this success? Here is where my philosophy comes out," he said. "These boys identify with the people of their country. There is unity and harmony between the various classes of people in Nepal. They feel for the children who can't go to school for economic reasons or for the fact that there aren't enough teachers or schools."

He went on to describe the daily regimen at Godavari and the necessity of keeping the boys busy. "When they're happy in the classroom and are kept busy outside the classroom, they don't get into trouble. It's the old saying: 'Idleness is the devil's workshop.' The boys work and play and study hard all day," he told his audience. Then, with a broad smile, he added—"And they never have insomnia!"

He described how the school boys compete on teams callec Bears, Tigers, Lions, and sop on, at the Primary, Intermediate and Senior levels, and how they operate on a system of merits and demerits that keeps each boy striving to improve himself and help his teammates. "You'd be surprised," he said, "Godavari is a school without litter." He was always proud to point out how each boy picked up after himself daily (and after holiday picnics with parents) so as not to get demerits that might keep him away from swimming, or Friday video, or the weekly visit to the store for sweets.

Basically, Marshall said, "We begin with reading, 'riting and 'rithmetic—the 3-Rs... I am an optimist. I know that every human being has a good side. You must reach that good side constructively and positively, and with trust—it takes a lot of trust. And you have to risk disappointments and perhaps failure..." Speaking as a Nepalese citizen, he concluded that "The most precious resource that we have are the brains, the hearts, the people of our country."

Nepal's Attempts at Educational Reform

One role that Jesuit educators tend not to shirk is involvement, when invited, in national educational planning and reform movements. Nepal has made several attempts to upgrade and improve its education system, with varying success. During the 1950s, Marshall became closely involved with the first educational reform movement in modern times, the Nepal National Education Planning Commission, which was convened in 1954.

During the early 1950s, King Tribhuvan, and King Mahendra after him, were keen to modernize the Nepalese system of education. Tribhuvan's first step in this direction was allowing the Jesuits to establish a foothold at Godavari in 1951, immediately after he returned from his brief exile in India and had formed his new government in Kathmandu. Both Tribhuvan and Mahendra encouraged an overall revamping and updating of the entire Nepalese education system. Marshall played a valuable part in that activity.

With the formation of the education commission, Fr Moran joined with several other reform-minded academics, including the leading Nepalese educator of the time, Trailokya Nath Upraity, and the American adviser, Dr Hugh (Barney) Wood. Upraity later earned his doctorate in education in the U.S. and went on to become Vice Chancellor of the Tribhuvan University system. His reminiscences outline the circumstances and consequences of Fr Moran's involvement and the importance of St Xavier's Godavari School as an example of modern education.

Looking Back
Fr Moran and Educational Reform
Trailokya Nath Upraity, PhD[5]

Father Moran played an important role in educational planning. In 1954, he was appointed to the first Nepal National Education Planning Commission, on which he served several years. He made very valuable contributions. We were talking about a new plan for education for Nepal, and while the commission had many members, some were not very knowledgeable about education problems. Moran was. Everyone knew that education was a valuable asset to the country, but planning it was something very new. We were always grateful for his involvement.

Fr Moran has always been one of the few people who could be invited to almost any important education function and activity. People respected him. The art of presentation was important to him, so people say that Fr Moran always has something significant to say.

During this time, too, many people visited Godavari to see what a modern school was all about. For many it was something new— the biggest school they had ever seen was the Durbar School (in downtown Kathmandu), but its premises were not really designed for a school. It didn't look much like one. Godavari School was much different, and it attracted a lot of attention.

Fr Moran's View of Educational Reform

Marshall's work on the National Education Planning Commission was important, but by no means easy nor entirely rewarding. His inspirations for planning and reform grew out of his earlier experience in India, from both its highlights and its frustrations. While working in Patna, "I was 'dragged' into an educational group in Bihar to help plan that province's basic education plan," he said. "Bihar's education system dated back to 1939, in association with the Gandhian educational reform movement, the so-called Wardha Scheme countrywide."

"First of all, Gandhi actually had little to do with it, with the details of it. He just gave his name in approbation, although in retrospect he may well have read it; he may have even drafted parts of it. In a nutshell, Gandhi saw the failure of the prevailing educational system of British India. He was convinced that it failed to meet the needs of village people. The Wardha Scheme was established to promote education for the rural masses. Gandhi pushed for studies and teachers to aim at practical and vocational skills. The best and the brightest, he thought, should not be drawn into the cities, but should return to dedicate their lives to the rural society—to bring literacy and practical improvements to farming, village handicrafts, sanitation, better housing and social justice. While this was fine, for some, I didn't think its rural focus could very well have addressed the future needs of a modernizing India."

"My approach was this: to ask that the Wardha Scheme not be imposed on the whole of Bihar Province, but rather to experiment with it in only two or three educational districts of a few hundred thousand people. Since there was no experience to guide us or help us, I knew that we would have to make our innovations and practical applications in order for it to work. I encouraged the Indian educators to try out new and practical ideas according to local needs and local context, but also to maintain good standards."

Marshall learned a great deal from working with the Gandhian approach, and from watching as it was abandoned during the war years of the 1940s. Its abandonment, he thought, may have been influenced by the British, who preferred not to encourage educational experimentation during those troublesome times. "But much of the influence came out of a conservatism on the part of those in the education departments, men who were basically opposed to change and improvement anyway. Our Bihar experiment was just too practical, too ambitious, and the conservatives were opposed to bringing in new ideas. Having experienced that in India, now I saw the same situation happening in Nepal."

Looking back on it, three decades later, Marshall went on to say: "Nepal's education system in the early 1950s, after the Ranas were gone and the new government under King Tribhuvan was in place, was very fragile and shaky. It was poorly organized, much along the lines of the old Indian system based on the British system of comprehensive final examinations. As one cynic put it, India's imitation of the British system was adopted by Nepal, thus making it twice-removed from the original. Unfortunately, the weaknesses of the Indian experience were being reiterated in Nepal, despite various attempts at making change. That was the case in 1954, and some of it remains the case today."

The work of Nepal's National Education Planning Commission in 1954 and onward was greatly influenced by old guard conservatives who were not very enamored with change, who defended the status quo dating back many years to the conceptual poverty of the Rana educational regime. Countering them were several true reformers among the Nepalese and their American advisers, some of whom were attracted to the philosophy of John Dewey, the contemporary American educator. In the early 1900s, from his post in Education at Columbia University, Professor Dewey espoused a kind of educational pragmatism based on a theory of instrumentalism by which he believed that education must equip students to deal with the practical problems of everyday life. Dewey held that educators must teach their students to confront changing conditions in society and to be able to respond with new solutions. Nonetheless, Marshall considered "Deweyism" to be a fad, and it held little attraction for him.

It was all well and good for American schools, he thought, but when it came to applying Dewey's approach to Nepal, "I was in total disagreement," he said. He was undoubtedly dissuaded by what he saw in it as far too much experimentation. Marshall and his Jesuit colleagues in Nepal tended to operate from a slightly more conservative basis, but of a conservatism different yet from that which they confronted in Nepal and India. Marshall's conservatism was always more along the lines of setting firm standards and holding to them in the classroom, on the campus, in the dormitories, for the preparation of young men to approach their adult lives solidly grounded in the principles of good behavior and positive social action.

Fr Donnelly's reminiscences expressed it well. The conservative standards of Jesuit pedagogy were reflected under his decade-long principalship at Godavari, for example, by insisting on daily exercise and drill for students and their mandatory attendance at school assemblies; by maintaining a dress code; by keeping accurate records of student performance and achievement; by good teaching; by holding contests; and by keeping the books and maintaining good discipline throughout. In short, Jesuit educational conservatism stresses establishing and upholding high moral standards among all involved—teachers, administrators and students, alike—while, at the same time, adapting to the inevitable changes that come along, with great care and sensitivity.

Jesuit pedagogues are not against progress; indeed, they are among the world's leaders in educational advancement. But they express serious reservations about the sorts of constant experimentation, re-thinking and re-organizing that Dewey and his followers espoused. Marshall felt that constant change tended to undermine established norms and standards. In his mind, this led inevitably to academic fragmentation and confused students, teachers and parents, alike. Better to establish and maintain firm guidelines for teaching and learning, and codes of behavior that reflect the needs and circumstances of the nation and the people than to fall for fads that were, in his mind, potentially disruptive.

This is what the St Xavier School system in Nepal tried to exemplify and was promoted by Moran since its start in 1951. To do otherwise, to exist in a constant state of flux, no matter how pragmatic, simply ran against the grain of Fr Moran's expression of Jesuit educational philosophy.

"Imposing too much Deweyism on top of Nepal's already weak educational system was not the way to reform it," he said. "The weaknesses of the traditional Nepalese system of education were the weaknesses I had witnessed in the Indian system. Our commission printed them in its report, a long litany about the poor standards of Nepalese education, as demonstrated by undisciplined teachers who were poorly trained and poorly paid, who didn't apply themselves, who didn't meet their classes on time, and so forth."

The government had difficulty admitting that Nepalese teachers were underpaid. "That admission would reflect badly on the system. Every department and every program—in health, forestry and agriculture, for example—was clamoring (and still is) for the limited finances that existed. Education, perhaps more than the others, had suffered badly under the mis-rule of the Ranas." As a result, he explained, Nepal's teachers were so poorly paid that they preferred tutoring students for the extra pay they could earn, over preparing for class and correcting papers. "There was also corruption in the examination system," he said. "Exam papers were leaked to students ahead of time, and there was indiscipline during exams, even violence against teachers and invigilators (examination proctors), just as I had seen in India. There was little difference, really. Poor is poor."

"All of this and more was discussed, and the commission tried to identify and root out the abuses," he went on. "Teaching, for example, was all lecture, as if boys age ten or twelve or fourteen were college students. Classes were excessively large, sometimes over a hundred students, sitting in dirty, rundown buildings. The teaching medium was Nepali; and this may sound incongruous, but English was being taught in Nepali! Teachers spent too much time on grammar, lecturing on parts of speech, nouns and pronouns, verbs and adverbs, for example, and not enough time tutoring students on how to use them to make sentences and form paragraphs. Nor were there any inspiring or stimulating stories from literature or history, or any poetry, to back it up. In most schools, what few good books existed were usually locked away by the teachers out of concern that they would be destroyed or lost by being used! Where textbooks featuring English prose and poetry were available, in the last two years of high school, they were greatly abused in an atmosphere of cramming for the inevitable exams."

"Everything depended on passing the final exams," he said, and it still does. "The teaching was so poor, and the learning also, that students resorted to memorizing the textbooks word for word, expecting to prove their 'comprehension' of it all on the exams, whose questions were often leaked to them in advance. And all of this—you can imagine!—was taught in a few hours or, at best, only a few days, just prior to the exams. You can also imagine who the most popular teachers were: those who prepared the students directly to pass the exams."

Over the years, Marshall heard Peace Corps Volunteer teachers assigned to Nepalese high schools express dismay, discouragement and frustration when—no matter how popular as teachers—they were inevitably abandoned by their students during the last few months before final exams. Even the brightest students preferred to cram under the tutelage of those teachers who taught them to pass the dreaded SLCs, the School Leaving Certificate exams, rather than study under more progressive teachers who could teach them how to *think*. Thinking the answers did not help on examination, only memorizing them did. Marshall blamed the problem on "weak, imperfect school systems, where the goal is to pass the examination, not to get real knowledge, *real* knowledge." Under such systems, memorizing is more important than thinking or learning.

Marshall's concerns about this poor system of education were clearly expressed during the commission meetings, by him and by others. But while their voices may have been heard, they were not much listened to. The problems were duly discussed by the group and were mentioned in the report, but little was changed. As he noted in 1991, with hindsight: "In the 1960s, the Nepal educational reformists faced it all over again, and to a large degree they still do. The next generation of planners admitted, in the 1960s, how poor and degraded the system remained, how little had changed since the revelations of 1954. In those days it was difficult to talk about and admit these things. The political and factional groupings, and the conservatism, made it difficult for a man like Professor Hugh

Wood (an American education specialist), and foreign advisers and volunteer teachers after him, to do their best, to do what was needed. To really get down to the essential needs, and to the truth, to teach inspirationally and creatively, to teach students *how to learn,* was considered too dangerous, especially for reform-minded Nepalese educators who had to get along in the system long after the high-minded advisers and volunteers were gone."

The 1954 education commission published its proceedings in a large book that was, in Marshall's thinking, "over inflated with cliché and jargon—and all too much 'Deweyism'. It was a lot of words, but not much that was practical. It didn't contain much with which to solve Nepal's educational problems, financial or political."

One of the biggest factional problems to beset educational reform came directly to Marshall's attention in a personal way through an encounter he had on the last day of the commission meetings. There was an attempt by a group of people from the lowland Tarai region of Nepal to try, at the last minute, to get the commission to adopt a second language policy. They wanted recognition of some of the border dialects as legitimate languages of instruction in Nepal, languages such as Hindi, Maithili, and Bojhpuri, very much related to north Indian languages. Marshall felt that Nepalese students already had to deal with two languages, Nepali and English; so that imposing another language would only have confounded the system even more.

It reminded him, regretfully, of the weakness he had seen in the Indian experience, where the medium of instruction was a bone of contention for years, reflected in great rivalries, open quarrels, and even violence among different language, ethnic and religious groups. "Nepal didn't need to repeat that experience then, nor does it now," he said. "Not that long ago, in Nepal's newly elected democratic parliament (in 1991), a similar issue was raised when one of the delegates from the (lowland) Tarai got up and spoke to the legislature in Hindi. The Nepali-speaking majority moved very quickly to impose a Nepali-only rule on the assembly. This created all sorts of animosity."

"Since the Tarai people outnumber the hill people, this is a red-hot issue. It works quite counter to national unity." To Marshall's way of thinking, "Unity should come through one language."

On the last day of the commission, he was approached by some Tarai people and asked to support their second language proposal. He bluntly told them, "In the name of national unity, I cannot think of adding yet another language to the over-burdened and badly taught children in your schools. Use your second or third language for commercial purposes, or whatever, but when it comes to education there should be one language, for national unity."

"I'm sure I didn't make many friends among them for saying that!" he concluded. "But I was worried about it and had to say what I believed."

School Admissions and Rejections

Marshall's colleague on the education commission, T.N. Upraity, had a son in Godavari school. He was one of the fortunate to have been enrolled, while hundreds of other applicants are turned away each year. The number of seats available is always limited and the standards are high. And while the tuition is not severe, it is out of bounds for many. (The St Xavier's Schools have liberal admission and scholarship policies, however, and the administration tries to balance enrollments by geography, ethnicity, and religious status, and to help boys out financially where it is required.) Upraity knew about the problems the priests encountered when they rejected some applicants.

"Naturally," Professor Upraity said, "people were interested in Godavari, and everyone who could afford it wanted his child admitted there, so one of the problems Godavari was facing was the problem of selection. They had a very rigorous admission test, but there were many pressures. Fr Moran knew very well that if he were to survive here he had to be accommodative of those pressures. Pressures from high officials and all that. So, I think of him as a diplomat."[6]

All the principals of the Godavari and Jawalakhel schools have to be diplomats. It comes with the calling. They have to be, in order to survive and continue to serve.

In those days, each knew well the pressures applied annually to enroll a certain son. Fr Donnelly spoke for all the priests in school administration in Nepal when he described "taking the heat" and still maintaining good relations with parents of unsuccessful applicants, some of whom were high officials in the government. "The biggest trial in my life (as school principal)...," he said, "was dealing with parents who tried unsuccessfully to get their boys into our school. We never consciously gave them a final *no*, but in practice a large percentage of those appealing for a place for their sons did not get them in. I continually found it uncanny how each family seemed to find their own individual reasons for requesting 'special consideration' for their sons. I always tried my best to listen sympathetically to their appeals. They were paying our school the supreme compliment of believing that Godavari offers the best all-round formation of our students, and that is precisely what they wanted for their sons."[7]

Marshall's Mother's Visit

One of the biggest events in Marshall's personal life over his many years in Nepal was the arrival of the only family member ever to visit him abroad, his mother, Bertha Moran. She came in November 1960, in part to join in celebrating the Silver Jubilee Day of his ordination as a priest, November 21. (She had been unable to attend his ordination at Kurseong twenty-five years earlier.) Her trip was an extra special event, since Bertha was already well into her eighties and such a long trip at that age was something of a challenge. Although she died within months of her return to the USA, during her Nepal visit she was quite fit and well up to it, according to several of the nuns who remember it and all the events she attended.

As a youth, Marshall had been especially close to his mother. He missed her terribly in the first years of his assignment in India. She, for her part, had worked hard over the years to raise funds to support his India work and, after that, the Nepal Mission. Now, on her trip, she saw some of the fruits of her own labors. He made the most of it, of course, and showed her as much as he could during her short stay.

Marshall met her in Calcutta. He had flown down from Kathmandu to meet her, and had arranged to drive back in a car that had been ordered and delivered to Calcutta for an American foreign service worker in Nepal. Marshall occasionally performed this special retrieval and delivery service of cars delivered to the Port of Calcutta that had been ordered by embassy and international development families. It gave him a good excuse to visit his old haunts in Bihar on the way through. The trip across West Bengal and Bihar to Nepal takes several days, and in this case, with his mother, slightly longer. They stopped in both Patna and Bettiah, where Marshall had spent so many years. "It was an adventurous experience," Bertha remarked to one of the St Mary's nuns when they finally arrived in Kathmandu. The nuns arranged for her to stay at St Mary's convent where Moran served as chaplain. It was adjacent to St Xavier's Jawalakhel school, where he was principal at the time.

During her visit a reception was held at the Jawalakhel school, where Bertha was especially honored and garlanded by the nuns and priests. Marshall's Silver Jubilee celebration was held on the 21st of November at St Mary's school. A special mass was said and a religious concert performed in his honor, attended by priests from the Jesuit mission, some nuns and girls from St Mary's, and a few friends from the general public.

One day Marshall drove his mother out to Godavari School where they enjoyed a short visit, including a tour of the gardens, lunch with the priests and a special program on her behalf in the boys' library room (the Rana Prime Minister's former gun room). On November 26, she attended the official opening of Xavier House near the old royal palace in downtown Kathmandu. Xavier House was established as a meeting hall for the Association of Old Boys, forerunner to the Godavari Alumni Association. Bertha was asked to cut the ribbon. According to the Jesuit Chronicles, about forty Godavari and Jawalakhel school "old boys" attended.

Where Have the 'Old Boys' Gone?
In November 1965, the Boy Scouts of Godavari celebrated the school's tenth anniversary of scouting. Nepal's Chief Scout, nineteen year old Crown Prince (later King) Birendra, was invited to preside over the celebration. During the afternoon, he witnessed demonstrations of scouting lore and skill by the boys, including a march past, first-aid, bridge-building, semaphore signaling, knot tying and other typical Boy Scout activities.At the end, as the crown prince was being escorted to his car to drive back to the palace, the principal, Fr Eugene Watrin, invited him to return at any time to spend more time with the boys. The Prince smiled and reminded his host that he was at all times accompanied by three Godavari old boys—his two *Aides-de-Camp,* Lieutenant Shanta Kumar Malla and Lieutenant Tara Bahadur Thapa, and by his political-cum-economic adviser, Chiran S.S. Thapa. As Prince Birendra entered his car, the boys of the school raised a cheer to their future monarch.[8]

Since its founding, Godavari School has prepared Nepalese boys and young men for exemplary service to royalty, to public affairs and to private enterprise. Kesari Raj Pandey, in his role as Director of Public Instruction and as Chief Guest at the 1965 Parents' Day celebrations, summed up the nation's appreciation for the school and its product.[9] "I know that the standard of education that Godavari school has been imparting to its students is high and appreciable," Pandey said. "The ardent desire of parents to get their children admitted into this school and the heavy rush for admission every year clearly prove the higher standard teaching and the popularity of this school... As the Chairman of the Selection Board for Scholarships in the Ministry of Education, I have had several opportunities to interview some of the applicants passing from this school; and, to my great satisfaction, I have found them smart in physique, well-informed in national and international outlook, and well-versed in English conversation. I cannot but appreciate and thank the teachers of this school for their very genuine and sincere efforts in laying a solid foundation for the future careers of so many students."

Fr Donnelly remarked with pride after hearing Mr Pandey's speech that "It is always appreciated to get such strong public support for the school's educational efforts." He also noted the outstanding results of the most recent (1964) Senior Cambridge exams: All passed, with fifty percent in First Division. "Joy abounded," he said.[10]

One of the best years for the Senior Cambridge occurred two years later, in 1967, when seventy-five percent of the students took First Division honors.

Sometimes alumni appreciation for their Godavari experience turned up unexpected results. Mr Panchaman Lama, a lay teacher at the school, once visited a nearby fish farm where he met the manager, a former Godavari student of some twenty-five years earlier. The man expressed his gratitude the following morning, with delivery of a big fish for the staff.[11]

And where else have St Xavier alumni gone in life? A good number have pursued higher education abroad and returned to serve Nepal in a variety of occupations. Those who stayed home did equally well. Both groups include men of virtually every caste and ethnic group in Nepal, from most regions and districts of the country. Over the years, the careers and accomplishments of St Xavier graduates have been highly varied, including: officials in the royal palace (*aides-de-damp,* a press secretary and counselors in various fields); gentlemen farmers; doctors of virtually every specialization; pharmacists; lawyers; economists; accountants; planners; politicians; educators at all levels in national and international academic institutions; architects; telecommunication engineers; nuclear scientists and physicists; chemical engineers; civil engineers and construction contractors; mechanical engineers; military officers in the Nepal Army, Indian Army, British Brigade of Gurkhas and on United Nations peace keeping missions abroad; police officers; journalists and editors; printers; administrators and public enterprise executives (for government); development specialists for national and international organizations; foreign service officers and diplomats; social workers; airline pilots; sports officials; bankers; industrialists; traders; and businessmen in travel and tourism promotion, real estate, fuel supply, food research and timber supply, garment making, carpet and textile manufacturing, tanning and shoe manufacturing, photography, restaurants and hotels..., and on and on.

Many Xavierians have served in a variety of high positions in civil society and public service, including officers in the Nepal Jaycees and Jaycees International; Public Service Commission; National Planning Commission; Nepal Mountaineering Association; Cancer Relief Society; and in the Lions, Rotary and other service clubs. An outstanding number of graduates have been honored with some of the highest national and international awards, including the nation's Mahendra Vidya Bhusan, several levels of Gorkha Dakshin Bahu and the Trisakti Patta, and the UK's Most Excellent Order of the British Empire (MBE).

The list grows year by year.

Celebrating a Godavari School Birthday

In October 1991, six months before Fr Moran passed away, the Nepal Jesuits celebrated their fortieth year since the founding of Godavari School in 1951. The occasion was jointly shared with the twenty-fifth anniversary of the Godavari Alumni Association (GAA). It was a large and festive event, held on the soccer field at Godavari under a large open-sided tent. Among the highlights were an awards ceremony, several speeches and a cultural show of skits and Nepalese music and dance presented by some very talented and well-rehearsed young schoolboys. It concluded with a reception for King Birendra and Queen Aishwarya, followed by a large celebratory *bojh*, a feast, in the school gardens.

As much as anything, it was an event commemorating the foresight and determination of Godavari's Father Founder, Marshall D. Moran, SJ, and of years of hard work by a host of priests, lay teachers, parents, alumni and Nepalese educators who worked with him. It was they, and not any single individual, who kept the spirit of St Xavier's Schools and of Jesuit education alive and well in Nepal for those forty years—and continuing on today—since that eventful day in 1951 when Fr Moran (in Patna, India) responded enthusiastically to the official call from Kathmandu to "Come at once."

The Chief Guests of the day were King Tribhuvan's grandson, King Birendra Bir Bikram Shah and Queen Aishwarya Rajya Laxmi Devi Shah. At the start of the afternoon's events, the royals were ushered to the place of honor at the front of the large crowd. There they presented service awards to some of Godavari's long-serving staff. Then they sat back to enjoy the show, smiling proudly as schoolboys performed skits and Nepalese dances. And they laughed at some of the anecdotes and tame jokes expressed at Fr Moran's expense as elder priest, educator and radio ham.

At one point, a small but symbolic event occurred. Several St Mary's alumni, dressed demurely in pastel saris, asked to speak informally with their former classmate, Queen Aishwarya. A few attentive bystanders who overheard their conversation were pleased, as the queen appeared to be, when these women spoke to her in the polite but more simple dialect of the common people, instead of the previously customary and stiffly honorific language of the Nepalese court. That seemingly slight change in protocol was subtly momentous, for it symbolized the new spirit in the land following the popular People's Movement of the previous year, 1990, when the King returned the nation to democracy. That simple act of speech reflected the true spirit of democracy and equality.[12]

The afternoon was salted with talk both serious and funny, with illustrious vignettes out of the past and ambitious plans for the future. During the speeches, Fr Jim Dressman, in the role of Father Rector of the Nepal Jesuits, spoke proudly of the past and optimistically of new plans for the expansion of the Godavari program. And A.V. Fr Mathew Assarikudy, Principal of Godavari School, spoke for all when he sais, "We, the Jesuits in Nepal, are proud of you, the alumni of the school... We are happy and satisfied when you are doing well in your life. We are happy when you appreciate our work and cooperate with us to continue the work we are doing to serve the people of Nepal. We have given you whatever we could, and our hope is that in turn you will continue to give to others whatever you can... We are sure that as alumni of Jesuit schools you are sharing the Jesuit *charism* (Jesuit spirit) with many others in your own particular life situations, working sincerely, standing for truth and justice, loving God and serving your neighbor, especially the poor, the needy, and the less privileged."[13]

As is customary for such celebrations, the alumni planning committee published a souvenir booklet. In it, several other priests and lay teachers wrote proudly of Godavari's academic history and achievements. Fr Leo Cachat, SJ, Superior of the Nepal Jesuit community, described the sometimes painful transition of St Xavier's from a school system based on the Cambridge Overseas Examination to full integration with the National Education System Plan during the 1970s. And Fr Eugene Watrin wrote of his pride as a sportsman about school athletic events that pitted boys against boys, and school teams against some of the best sports clubs in the country. "And sometimes the school boys won!" he said.

But it was a short piece by Fr Marty Coyne, Principal of St Xavier's Jawalakhel School at the time, that summed up the true spirit and meaning of the St Xavier's system of education in Nepal. He described the dedication of St Xavier's students, alumni, priests, teachers and parents alike, in the development of well rounded, well educated youth to serve their country.

Fr Coyne stated an elemental truth, that "no boy *happens* to become educated and grow up into a principled, energetic, positive addition to the population of Nepal. It simply does not happen by chance or luck. No one receives a gift like this out of the blue. No one can have it earned for him by someone else, any more than one could enjoy himself a delicious meal—eaten by someone else."

Instead, he said, that sort of education for life and for service "is a product of a lot of work by a number of people over quite a long time at some expense and through, perhaps, not a few difficulties... And what a wonderful thing it is when they all work together positively in the education of the boy-to-be-young-man... When they do work well, the product is indeed a thing of beauty and a joy forever, an Xavierian who lives for God and leads for Nepal. It does not just happen..."[14]

Note to Chapter 12: Men to Serve Others

1. CSSR is the *Congregatio Sanctissimi Redemptoris*, a Roman Catholic missionary order founded in the eighteenth century by Saint Alphonsus Ligouri.
2. James Donnelly, SJ, 'Ten years at Godavari, 1981-1991' (1991, p.19).

    In their *Framework for School Renewal*, Frs. Stephen Chethipuzha and Jose Murican wrote that the Jesuit school "aim is not so much to prepare a socio-economic elite as to educate real human persons who will be leaders in society in every field of service" (1989, p.11).
3. Donnelly, 'Ten Years...' (1991).
4. In 1976, Nepal adopted a new education plan and the Senior Cambridge was officially replaced by a nation-wide School Leaving Certificate (SLC) examination system at the St Xavier's and St Mary's Schools. (The SLC had been the standard in all other schools in the nation for many years.) For several years, however, though the Jesuits adopted the SLC system at St Xavier's, they continued to offer Senior Cambridge preparation to its SLC graduates who achieved first division scores. And for a long time the older teachers looked back with nostalgia on the "Cambridge years." They looked upon their former students' high scores on that internationally renowned examination with pride.
5. T.N. Upraity, interviewed in Kathmandu (May 23, 1987).
6. *Ibid.*
7. Donnelly, 'Ten Years...' (1991).8.   James Donnelly, SJ, '1965—Banner year at Godavari School' (1986, p.135).
8. *Ibid.* (p.137).
9. *Ibid.*
11. Panchaman Lama, reminiscing in James Donnelly, ed., *St Xavier's Godavari 1951-1986 Anniversary Souvenir* (1986. p.161).
12. In 1990, following a decade period of royal rule and extreme political discomfort culminating in popular demonstrations—the *Jana Andolan* or

'People's Movement'—lasting several months, King Birendra restored Multi-Party Democracy to Nepal. For months thereafter, the royals were not often seen in public. The events at Godavari in October 1991 represented, in a way, part of their "coming out" to show their public face once more to the nation.

On Friday, June 1, 2001, King Birendra and Queen Aishwarya were among those assassinated by Crown Prince Dipendra in the infamous Palace Massacre at the royal residence, Narayanhity Palace, in downtown Kathmandu. Dipendra, who suffered a gunshot wound to the head (some say by his own hand, but more likely by his own *Aide-de-camp*), died a few days later, whereupon his uncle, King Birendra's younger brother, Gyanendra, became king. Seven years later Gyanendra was deposed and the monarchy was abolished effective May 28, 2008, when Nepal's constituent assembly declared Nepal a Federal Democratic Republic.

13. Mathew Assarikudy, SJ, 'The Society of Jesus and Jesuits in Asia' (1991).
14. Marty Coyne, SJ, in GAA, ed., *Godavari Alumni Association (GAA) 25th Anniversary, St Xavier's School 40th Anniversary, 1951-1991* (1991, p.25).

HAM PRIEST OF THE HIMALAYAS

13. Fr Moran talking to school boys during the 40th anniversary celebration of the founding of Godavari School, 1991.

13

On the Air

> *He's the kind who loves everybody, loves to talk with people, loves to visit on the air. But, being a 'rare one' and the only ham over in Nepal it is pretty hard for the guys to get to 'work' him. When there is a big 'pile up' no one gets through.*
> A ham radio operator describing Fr Moran

On the Air

During the winter of 1959-1960 and thereafter, Marshall was back on the air as an amateur radio enthusiast. Despite his important role in Nepal as an educator-priest, Fr Moran was probably more famous to more people during those years as "The Voice of the Himalayas" than for anything else. In the course of time, many thousands of amateur radio buffs the world over chatted with him personally. Some of them kept in touch with him by radio almost every day.

The technical challenge, personal excitement and pure fun of radio first consumed Marshall's tireless interest as a teenager in Chicago. It was reinforced when he established a small amateur station as a science project in the Patna school, using surplus equipment left behind by the Allied forces stationed nearby during the Second World War. When Marshall moved up to Nepal in 1951, however, he left radio transmission behind. He had only a receiver on which he listened faithfully each day to the BBC news beamed from London. It was not until December 1959 that he once again took up amateur broadcasting, this time from Kathmandu to the rest of the world. By then, there were enough teachers on staff to help Marshall and the other pioneer priests of Godavari and Jawalakhel to share the heavy load of responsibilities. Between 1955 and 1960, many new priests arrived in Nepal, some of whose names are still closely associated today with Jesuit work in Nepal. Only then did Marshall feel free enough during early morning and evening hours to go back "on the air" as an amateur radio operator.

The Voice of "Mickey Mouse"

"CQ. CQ"—an amateur radio operator's call goes out to anyone who happens to be listening. Virtually any morning in Nepal, evening in the Western hemisphere, between 1960 and 1992, radio amateurs listened attentively through the static for a voice, virtually the *only* voice, from the Himalayas. "CQ. CQ-stateside," Marshall would say while "keying" the mike (microphone) and fine tuning his transmitter. His electric rotator dial was set to point a roof-mounted antenna due north across the Arctic pole. That is how he started his daily transmissions to North America.

In daily life, those who knew him well called him "Father Moran." On the airwaves, however, his friends shortened that to just "Father," although he was also known by the more distinctive radio nickname of "Mickey Mouse." And, far and wide among the great fraternity of amateur radio enthusiasts, he was singularly renowned as "The Ham Priest of the Himalayas." For years his was the only licensed ham in Nepal and the only priest on the air anywhere in the world's high attic, the Himalayas.

Marshall approached the radio amateur's hobby with his usual intensity and seriousness. It complemented his normal life as a priest and educator. As anyone who knew him well would say, the radio hobby, both as an intellectual and recreational outlet, was a good fit for such a high-spirited Jesuit intellectual.

If you asked Marshall, he would tell you that radio was an inextricable part of his life in service to others. It allowed a richness of human friendship that cut through the isolation of life in Nepal and provided intangible rewards fully in character with his life-long personal quest to promote unity among peoples of diverse faiths, persuasions, nationalities, and hobbies.

On any particular morning of the year, he was seated in his cluttered radio shack at Godavari, upstairs in Xavier hall, the former Rana Prime Minister's summer palace. School boys sometimes crowded around him listening in awe and anticipation of someone, somewhere in the world responding to the ham radio operator's ubiquitous CQ code ("calling any station"). Then using a variation of the international phonetic alphabet, he gave his official call sign, 9N1MM. "This is nine enn one Mexico Mexico," he'd say. "That's nine nancy one Mickey Mouse calling stateside and standing by..."

When Marshall applied for and received his official amateur radio operator's license in Nepal in 1960, the first two digits, 9N, identified it as a Nepalese station, and the number 1 narrowed his location to Kathmandu. The last two letters of a call sign are unique to the particular ham and, in Marshall's case the double M's were suggested by him to represent his full name: Marshall Moran. (Seldom, however, do hams have the privilege of selecting their own letters.) In the normal course of operations, when identifying himself on the air, he did as the law stipulates by announcing his call sign, using the international phonetic alphabet, so that "MM" became "Mexico Mexico," and soon "Mickey Mouse," and that's what he was known by for all the years that he operated from Nepal.

Amateur radio operators call themselves "hams" for short. On those mornings when Mickey Mouse came on the air, American hams would be awaiting his call, especially those who regularly seek contacts with hams located in rare places around the globe. They call themselves "DX-ers" (DX means "distance"). The CQ call is the signal to reply and, inevitably, scores of DX hams were waiting to join the usual noisy radio "pile-up" to reach him. Fr Moran of Kathmandu was on the air!

The typical response to Marshall's call began with a cacophony of jumbled noise as scores of enthusiastic operators vied for get his attention. To the uninitiated, this "pile-up," as it is called in the peculiar jargon of radio amateurs, sounds like so many bees buzzing around a busy hive. Gradually through the crackling static, one or another voice would come through stronger than all the others, first the call sign, then the "handle" or operators nickname, then a pleasant "Good morning, Father." Often it was his friend WB4NFO (Pradyumna Rana), the former Godavari school boy who first accompanied Fr Moran into Nepal in 1949. Rana was a regular contact, operating out of his home in Alexandria, Virginia. Sometimes it was K9LF, William (Bill) Brown, an international lawyer calling from Lake Forest, Illinois. Or W7HCH, Don Coleman, a retired telephone lineman in Seattle. Or W2GBC, Bill Conner, a federal district court judge operating from Dobbs Ferry, New York. Or any one of scores of others with whom Marshall regularly rendezvoused.

Contacts Worldwide

In the busy years after 1960, when Marshall first put his new station on the air in Nepal, he talked to the world virtually every day, except when away on trips. (And when traveling, he was usually not far from someone else's ham "shack." He sought them out in every city or country he visited.

Since the very start of his ham operations from Kathmandu, Marshall regularly kept two daily "scheds" (schedules): early mornings (evenings in America) transmitting north over the pole, and late afternoons conversing with fellow members of the SEANET, a mixed group of radio amateurs all across South, Southeast and

East Asia who regularly assist ships at sea with friendly chatter and emergency traffic. Operators in Europe or East Asia or Africa would often pick him up off the "back of the beam" (the back side of an antenna). He often called his radio friends in Europe on the weekends, when he knew they would be home.

Marshall's daily radio schedule was seldom interrupted, unless there was an ill school boy who demanded his attention, or for "corn flakes," his term for breakfast. As one of his regular American contacts once put it, "Every evening about 9:30 p.m. (7:15 a.m. in Nepal), Fr Moran tells us, 'I've got to go to corn flakes,' And when its breakfast time, he's gone. You're lucky to say 'So long, Father!' I once asked him, 'What sort of corn flakes, Father?' He laughed. They don't have corn flakes over there," the ham explained. "Their diet is boiled rice. It's his little joke."

Both kings and commoners were on Fr Moran's list of world radio contacts. His royal friends included King Juan Carlos of Spain and King Hussein of Jordan. Virtually all the others were commoners, such as an American electronics technician, a German school teacher, a Russian civil engineer, a Japanese businessman, and one particular Yugoslavian gentleman reputed to be the world's fastest CW (Morse code) operator. Marshall preferred voice communication over code. He talked regularly with men and women of virtually every religious faith and occupation, and on occasion to fellow clergymen. They all called him "Father," and when signing off he always wished them his standard "God Bless."

Virtually everyone in the DX amateur radio world knew about or had talked with "Father" in Nepal, when he was active on the air. But, they also knew him as "Mickey Mouse." His call sign was unique, as the amateur radio "Voice of the Himalayas" and one of only a few American expatriate operators on the whole of the Asian subcontinent. Even among Jesuits he was an uncommon contact, rivaled in his time only by HV2VO, Brother Edwin (Ed) Amram, who used to operate from the Pope's summer residence at the Vatican's astronomical observatory at Castel Gandolpho in the hills outside of Rome. Marshall also spoke occasionally with Jesuit mission hams as far away as Peru and the Caroline Island in the South Pacific.[1]

Over the years, various American operators performed special services for Marshall, usually at their own expense, as volunteers. He relied on ham friends whom he met on the air on a regular basis to pass on birthday and holiday greetings to his non-ham friends and relatives in the United States. Some contacts were especially helpful, by supplying him with essential equipment and radio parts when he needed them. But he was most dependent on and grateful to his QSL and list managers, all volunteers in the United States.

Marshall's QSL Manager
In the world of amateur radio, much is said and done in code, for expediency (and harking back to a time when radio broadcasting was done by tapping out messages in Morse code). Much of the code is in "Q-signals," three letter symbols beginning with the letter Q. The Q-signals were originally used with Morse code to save time and improve communications. Some examples are "QRS"—a request to "send slower"; "QTH"—give me your "location"; and "QSO"—a "ham conversation."

QSL is a common Q signal meaning "Can you acknowledge receipt?" or "I am acknowledging receipt." A QSL card is a postcard that serves to confirm communication between two hams. Given Fr Moran's location (remote) and the number of hams seeking to contact him (many), he needed help over the years to manage his on- and off-air radio business. The stateside list manager kept track of all Marshall's contacts and sent out Marshall's QSL cards. A QSL card is a souvenir, typically emblazoned with the operator's call sign and sometimes a photograph. They are collector's items among DX-ers, much as baseball cards are to American sports fans. For years, Marshall's personal QSL card featured a picture of him wearing a white cassock sitting in front of his ham "rig," surrounded by a covey of wide-eyed young schoolboys.

DX hams avidly collect QSL cards, and receiving one in the mail is proof of contact. Some hams collect contacts by call sign number, country or rarity, so Fr Moran's card, being a "rare one" in all respects was extremely popular. Among new operators, in particular, receiving a card from 9N1-Mickey Mouse was considered an enviable and proud achievement.

Marshall's own radio shack was plastered with over two hundred QSL cards received from hams he had talked to all over the world. Along with a lot of other amateur radio memorabilia, he had hundreds, perhaps thousands, of QSL cards stuffed away in boxes. He never counted them and did not work very hard to collect them, but they arrived regularly in the mail. From his side, he was sure each month to send his list of contacts to his QSL manager, who then sent Marshall's card to acknowledged contacts.

For many years Marshall's QSL manager was N7EB, Ed Blasczyk, a retired electronics engineer living in Sun City, Arizona. For one so popular as Marshall, who typically met up to several dozen new hams in a single short session on the air, managing and mailing the

QSL cards was both time-consuming and costly. As a priest, Marshall was sworn to poverty and was so busy most of each day in the school that keeping up was a virtually impossible task. That's where Ed Blasczyk helped him.

Ed's association with Fr Moran began in 1960, when he heard from a mutual friend that Marshall would soon be on the air from Nepal. Ed was living in Philadelphia at the time. (He retired to Arizona later.) Ed explained how he became Marshall's QSL manager like this: "My call sign was W3KVQ, and I was already involved as a QSL manager for 28 other DX stations, so I knew the crush on a DX station's time in responding to QSL requests. I also knew that for a little country like Nepal to have a radio station start operating after a hundred years of feudal isolation would be like QSO-ing (having a conversation with) the rarest of the rare. I realized that Father would be absolutely bombarded with QSL requests, so I wrote and volunteered my services."

Ed Blasczyk handled Marshall's QSL cards on a worldwide basis and paid for the printing and postage out of his own pocket. He asked only that Marshall periodically send a copy of his daily QSO log. "I would rather he spend what free time he had operating his station," Ed said, "rather than replying to all the QSL requests." Marshall accepted the offer and a week or two later the first page of his log copy arrived at Ed's house, a year's worth, dated January 1, 1961.

This arrangement went on for three decades, and Ed never lost enthusiasm for the job. "It's been great! Those other 28 DX stations that I managed have gone by the boards, but my file folders of 9N1MM logs continue to expand," he said in the 1980s, when Marshall was at a high point in his amateur radio career. The number of confirmed QSOs to whom cards were sent numbered well over one hundred thousand, to over two hundred countries. Marshall called Blasczyk "the best QSL manager in the world." He was certainly one of the busiest.

Marshall's List Manager

For years, another operator named Ed Konop, W2WGS, in Pittsburgth, Pennsylvania, was Marshall's list manager. A list manager's job is like that of a dispatcher, or traffic controller. He is the one who brings order to the often chaotic attempts by DX-ers to log a rare contact. The manager has to have a powerful rig.

There is a regular protocol for list managers and DX-ers to follow. A manager keeps a regular schedule—every Wednesday for Fr Moran. Ed Konop would take a list of that day's interested hams and after contact was made with Kathmandu, he'd insist that order prevail. After start-up greetings back and forth with Mickey Mouse, Ed called the names on the list one at a time and allowed each eager ham to talk just long enough to establish a *bone fide* QSO (contact). Each ham was requested to sign off quickly, to allow the next on the list to say hello.

Ed Konop described Marshall as "the kind who loves everybody, loves to talk with people, loves to visit on the air. But, being a 'rare one' and the only ham over in Nepal, it is pretty hard for the guys to get to 'work' him. When there is a big 'pile up' no one gets through."

He first began managing the list for Fr Moran one busy night in 1961. Marshall was virtually under siege on the air waves, having difficulty keeping all the contending operators sorted out. After listening to the frantic attempts by dozens of hams to make contact, Konop powered through the pileup and volunteered to help. After that they met regularly each Wednesday, starting about 0100 hrs GMT (6:45 a.m. in Nepal) on the 20 meter band (14 MHz).[2] Sometimes the list of DX-ers trying to speak with Fr Moran was fifty to sixty operators long for a single session. At one minute a contact, it took an hour. During such a "list operation," ham etiquette demanded that no one interrupt except for an emergency.

By systematically "working the list," Ed Konop could satisfy many amateur radio operators in a single session. "It was Father's desire to help the little guys, those who don't have big antennas or powerful rigs," Konop said. "The list operation is the only way that some of them are going to get through to talk to him."

Special Messages

Marshall frequently transmitted and received personal and emergency messages. Sometimes he relied on another ham's "phone patch," a telephone (or "land line" in ham jargon) linked to a radio rig, not unlike a modem in a modern computer.

One day when Marshall was listening to a conversation between some hams in California, he heard one say, "If you are in Orinda, would you mind giving a phone call to my friend Al?"

A few moments later came the reply. "I can't," the other ham said. "He's got an unlisted phone number."

Marshall interrupted them: "Break, break," he said following ham protocol.

"Who's the breaker?" the California amateur said back.

"Mickey Mouse in Kathmandu," Marshall replied, followed by his full call sign as the law requires.

"Father Moran. Welcome! Come on in. Join us. What can we do for you?"

"If that's Al Schoenhofer, the jeweler from Orinda, you're looking for," he guessed, "maybe I can help you. His phone number is—," and Marshall read it out of the little black address book he always carried.

To everyone's amazement he had guessed correctly and the California ham reached his friend Al in Orinda. For a long time after that hams in California would regularly announce over the air, "Get your phone numbers from Nepal!" Marshall knew Schoenhofer from two visits the Californian had made to Kathmandu.

Marshall's little black book and his phenomenal memory were well known. One frequent DX contact described him as having a memory like a proverbial elephant. "He never forgets a thing. He carries that little black book with him and can dig out the name and phone number of anybody he's visited, or anyone who may have visited him. It is the same with the radio schedule. If we are supposed to meet to talk at a certain time, Father is there. Even if I don't hear him because of poor band conditions, you can bet he's there trying to get through. He's very regular, very prompt, and always keeps his schedules."

One time when he was talking to a contact in northern New Jersey, Marshall said, "Say, I've got a friend near you in Pauling, New York. His first name is Lowell. Please give him a call. I've got a message to pass on from some friends in Nepal. Here's the number—."

When contact was made through the phone patch, a secretary answered. "He's not in," she said. Then, with some agitation, suspecting a prank, she said, "Who are you? And why do you want to talk to him?"

Marshall replied, "I'm a ham operator with a message from Kathmandu." At that, the secretary softened her tone and listened to Marshall's message: "Please tell Lowell that his friends, Boris and the American ambassador, send their regards. They are asking when he'll come visit them again."[3]

Before signing off, the ham who had made this phone patch expressed his curiosity. "Who is this Lowell fellow, anyway?" he asked.

"Lowell," said Marshall, "is a famous news broadcaster."

"Well!" the New Jersey ham shot back, "why didn't you say it was Lowell *Thomas*?"

Marshall bristled (in his mild-mannered way) and said firmly but politely: "Because I don't want every Tom, Dick and Harry to know his phone number. It is unlisted, and this *was* a private conversation."

Another time, he was talking to a British ham located near Farnham, in the UK. "Farnham?" Marshall inquired. "'I know

Farnham. That's near the headquarters of the British Army.' So I said to my contact, 'Would you mind phoning up Sir John Hunt? He climbed Mount Everest some years ago, and visited me here at Godavari right afterwards. Please give him my regards."

The ham agreed and Marshall waited for his return signal. About five minutes later he came back on the air. "He scolded me," said Marshall. "'You've wrong, Father,' he said. 'He's no longer *Sir* John Hunt. Now he's *Lord* Hunt.'"

Marshall's comeback was unexpected: "How dare he become a 'Lord' without my permission!" he told the ham in Farnham.

Calling King Mahendra
In May 1964, Nepal's King Mahendra went on an official state visit to Germany in the company of the German ambassador to Nepal, William Loer. When Marshall heard of the trip, he asked for and was given the King's itinerary.

On the day before the King's scheduled arrival in Berlin, Marshall contacted a German radio amateur friend named Walter. "I have a friend named Bill Loer coming to Berlin tomorrow, traveling with another good friend of mine, a V.I.P.," he said without revealing the King's identity. "Would you mind getting in touch? Tell Bill Loer that there is an important radio message from Kathmandu. He'll understand."

Walter agreed, and they set a time and frequency for contact on the following day.

At the scheduled time, Walter phone-patched Marshall through to the King's hotel suite. Loer answered and Marshall addressed him with caution and diplomacy. "Hello, Bill. How are you? And how is 'our friend' enjoying his visit?"

"Very well, thank you," the ambassador replied. "He's right here listening to you. When I told him you were going to call, he wouldn't stay away. You may talk with him, but be careful what you say."

Marshall's message was not a pleasant one. Avoiding even such identifying protocol as "Your Highness," he simply informed the King: "Sir, the prime minister of India, Jawaharlal Nehru, has died."

"Yes," King Mahendra replied. "We have just heard. Please tell the family that we are canceling the rest of the trip. We will return to Nepal a week early after attending the funeral in Delhi."

A few years later, while King Mahendra was hunting in Alaska, Marshall spoke with him by radio once again. Contacting an amateur operator friend in Kodiak, Marshall asked him to ring up the distinguished visitors at their hotel. Everyone in the tiny community of Kodiak knew who *they* were. General Sher Bahadur Malla, the

King's *Aide-de-Camp*, came on the line and was delighted to hear the familiar voice from Kathmandu. He told Marshall that the King had bagged a bear.

Marshall said, "Please give my best to—."

"Yes, yes," the general interrupted. "He's right here listening."

Later, when King Mahendra flew back to Kathmandu, Fr Moran was at the airport to greet him. He stood near the front of the crowd. As the King passed by he smiled and said discretely, so that only Marshall could hear, "It was good to talk with you, Father. That's two times now!"

Clubs, Nets and Public Service

Ham radio is a hobby that bridges national boundaries and continents, personal philosophies and life styles. It is a busy sort of pastime. A ham operator is sometimes described by friends and co-workers, neighbors, spouses and children, as a recluse, often shut away for too many hours, nights and mornings, in his radio shack (over ninety percent of all hams are male), talking to the world, tuning and retuning the transmitter, repairing the antenna, rewiring some circuitry, buying and selling equipment, and bragging to all who will listen over the air and over dinner, about the rig, its power output, a certain beam or dipole antenna, local atmospheric conditions and propagation, or the number of DX stations contacted, especially the rare ones like Marshall Moran. All the while, this stereotypical ham is ignoring the rest of the household just to be on the air...

Exaggeration? Yes. But true? Of course, to a degree. Many hams paper the walls of their radio shacks with hundreds of QSL cards and, maybe, a picture of mom and pop, or the wife and kids.

Marshall's ham shack at Godavari was small and cluttered. On a table against one wall was his latest rig, a Japanese Yaesu 100 watt transceiver, model FT-757GX. It was given to him in 1990 by members of the Sapporo Radio Club on the island of Hokaido.[4] Underneath, gathering dust on the floor, was some older gear including the archaic Hammerlund receiver he had brought up from Patna to Kathmandu in 1951, and a Viking transmitter that he first used in the 1960s. He didn't toss much out. There was a shelf cluttered with books about both religion and radio against the window wall. And out of that window ran a mess of wires to his antenna on the roof. Two other walls were pasted with QSL cards and autographed photographs depicting a world of friends. His picture wall included snaps of a Jesuit priest or two, a portrait of Jesus, a news photo of Fr Moran with King Birendra during a visit to Godavari school, and signed portraits from his fellow hams, Juan Carlos of Spain and Hussein of Jordan.

Marshall had a story to tell about virtually every one of the QSL cards that he put up. "I got the one from King Hussein in 1970. The first time I talked to him I didn't realize who he was. He said, 'Call me Hussein.' Since Hussein had no QSL card from Nepal, he was eager to talk. I said I would appreciate his card, also, since he was my first contact in Jordon. When I asked for his address, he said, 'Just send it to the palace in Amman.' Only then I realized who he was. We had many contacts after that."

Missing from his radio shack wall, however, were Marshall's many amateur radio certificates, honors and awards. They pleased him, of course, but because he was not an overly proud man (and wall space was limited), most of those items were stuffed away in a box in the corner. Among them were a dozen or more honorary memberships to local US radio clubs he had visited on his occasional trips back home to America. If you asked him for them, he would show you; otherwise few people around him knew they existed.

There was one award that he laughed about. On a trip to Boston one year, he was hosted by member of a ham club called the Sons of Boston. Just before departing on his trip back to Nepal, he was given an award certificate specially created for visiting hams who frequently "worked" (talked on air with) members of the Boston club. "Guess what?" Marshall said, holding up the certificate, "I'm now an official S.O.B.!"

The Ham as Loner, or Not

Some amateurs may start out as loners, but not Marshall Moran. Those who do, typically do not stay loners for long. Once a novice ham gets on the air, transmits his first call sign with the CQ code, an almost magical transformation begins. By the seemingly mysterious workings of a phenomenon known as a "skip" of the radio waves off the ionosphere, the answer may come from Russia, Germany, Ireland, Brazil, Spain, Malaysia, Alaska or Antarctica, from a man or woman, young or old, king or commoner, living thousands of miles away.

When the novice hears that first voice responding to his call, the change into an eager, outgoing, tech-savvy, happy sort of character begins. The simple pleasure of chatting with another amateur in his own shack somewhere out there in the wide world is well savored and frequently shared. With a simple "Break, break," any other amateur tuning in can join the conversation and share opinions of world affairs, news about home, a message to a distant relative, word of a flood, earthquake or other emergency, or just pass the time of day comparing equipment or propagation and reception conditions.

There are on air protocols about what *not* to discuss: politics and religion, for example.

Hams come in many technical stripes, also. Most operate purely by voice. That was Marshall's preference. But some prefer to operate CW and tap out or "key" their conversations with lightning speed using the radio world's well known system of dots and dashes, the di-dahs of Morse code, named after Samuel Morse who patented the telegraph in 1840. CW was the original means of amateur transmission and, until recently, novice hams were expected to pass a Morse code proficiency examination in the process of achieving a beginner's license. After a ham operator dies, whether a code or a voice operator, he is commonly referred to euphemistically as a "silent key."

Radio teletype (RTTY) was also once in vogue, but over time it was replaced by a computerized packet system, whereby operators communicate by keyboard, monitor and printer through special linkups for global radio-computer networks.

By convention, world radio authorities have dedicated certain frequencies for each of these specialist operations, and even distinguish between those who hold only beginners, or novice licenses, from those who have general or expert licenses. Several well-known American astronauts have been amateur radio aficionados. Colonel Edwin (Buzz) Aldrin, the second astronaut to walk on the moon, conducted a transmission to earthbound ham operators from space. (One early astronaut even went one step further, by experimenting with mental telepathy between space and earth.)

Special satellites have been placed in earth orbit to assist global ham operations, especially useful during emergencies when telephone lines are down. Many hams maintain backup battery packs and portable power supplies, or maintain mobile rigs in their automobiles, for just such emergencies.

It is activities like these and personal connections with a world full of amateur radio aficionados, that typically have remarkable impacts on a new ham's personality. Thus, as Fr Moran often pointed out, the singular image of the radio amateur as a loner is one-sided, incomplete, inadequate and probably unfair; for hamming is, above all, one of the most sociable, public-spirited and outgoing hobbies around. Its jargon and various codes may be arcane, but its overall message and its meaning, premises and purposes reflect the universal spirit of friendliness and public service.

Worldwide Recognition

After almost three decades as a world class amateur radio operator (and only four years before his death), Fr Moran's lifelong commitment to public service was recognized when he became the second person ever to be awarded the International Humanitarian Award (in 1987) by the quarter million member American Radio Relay League (ARRL). During the award presentation, held in 1988, the ARRL praised Fr Moran as one "who, through amateur radio, (is) devoted to promoting the welfare of mankind," and as a man with "an indomitable spirit to learn as well as teach." The award plaque shows two hands clasped above a map of the world with this simple inscription:

FRIENDSHIP—HELP—UNDERSTANDING—THROUGH AMATEUR RADIO.

The ARRL award was one of the few that Marshall hung on his wall. He was proud of it. Recognizing his accomplishments, the radio hobbyist's *QST* magazine heaped praise on Marshall at the time as one who "has assisted thousands of individuals and groups worldwide. His mission shack has issued news of climber rescues in the Himalayas, Indian border skirmishes and visits by international dignitaries to Kathmandu... His QSOs have generated such a spirit of benevolence on the part of amateurs the world over that many hams have donated unsolicited contributions to help fund mission programs... By his own estimate he has received more than 300,000 Christmas cards from amateurs and shortwave listeners around the world."[5]

In 2002, a decade after his death, Fr Moran was recognized once again by the amateur radio fraternity when he was inducted posthumously into the CQ Amateur Radio Hall of Fame. In winning this award, he was remembered as "a Jesuit priest who, for years, was the only active amateur in Nepal." The Amateur Radio Hall of Fame recognizes individuals who have "significantly affected the course of Amateur Radio" and whose professional activities have "had a significant impact on their professions or on world affairs."[6]

Ham radio is, above all, a shared enthusiasm of international dimensions and impacts, one that transcends boundaries and national interest, race or religion. Fr Moran epitomized its international spirit. And while at one level, ham jargon is quite unique, with its complicated Q-signals and esoteric terms, at another level it is a universal language used by thousands of men and women who share the accomplishment of putting a rig on the air and an interest in telecommunications with so many others out there on the radio waves.

It should come as no surprise that amateur radio enthusiasts form clubs. Some meet on the air at prearranged times and frequencies. Some are organized by mutual interest, among doctors, lawyers, ship captains, or mountaineers, for example. Some elaborate amateur nets have been established to perform public service function, as in medical emergencies, and others have been set up in support of missionaries and as church group functions. There are also international Boy Scout networks, police association nets, mobile emergency nets, armed services nets, hobbyist nets, and various public service and educational networks. The list is long, interest is high, and their various activities are popular among amateurs the world around.[7]

In 1964, Marshall helped found the special group of regional and sea-going amateurs called SEANET, the South East Asia Amateur Radio Network. The SEANET was formed in 1964 to help ships' captains in the sea lanes of Asia. Its stated objective "is to promote international understanding and fellowship among hams and to relay emergency, medical, urgent or priority traffic." It has been especially active assisting in emergencies at sea and during major disasters in the region. For years, SEANET-affiliated operators have met daily on the 20 meter band (14.320 MHz) at a regular time: 1200 GMT (1800 hours or 6:00 p.m. in Bangladesh; 5:45 p.m. in Nepal), and for awhile, Marshall was "net control" in charge of rotating discussion among ham members in all the countries involved and on ships at sea. Though he operated from a land-locked country far from the sea, the reason he was so actively involved was the typically good reception and broadcast propagation available from the Himalayas throughout the region. Today there are many SEANET members in countries all across Asia and on the Asian oceans, and hams on land and at sea keep regular contact with one another.[8]

Operating under emergency conditions is one of the hallmarks of the amateur radio world, and it is what many ham organizations and individual hams are recognized for doing well on short notice. Marshall had his fair share of excitement on the air, including assisting with medical emergencies in Nepal, evacuations from ships at sea, and relief to a storm-stricken expedition in Antarctica. While "working" an amateur radio operator located in Antarctica one year, he even delivered an Easter sermon on the air.

Looking Back
Emergency in Antarctica
Fr Moran

It's not uncommon to pick up signals from as far away as Antarctica. I remember in 1963 talking off and on to an Australian expedition operator who was transmitting from the edge of the continent, from a place called Mawson Base. His name was Ian, and he said his home was the island of Tasmania. We sometimes chatted about current news of a non-controversial nature, about personal affairs and about the scientific work of the expedition. Of course, radio etiquette and rules tell us we are not supposed to make obnoxious criticisms of nationalities, or countries or politics. Nor can we engage in financial transactions on the air.

Within these limits, Ian and I carried on long conversations, sometimes about our radios as most hams do, and the types of antennas and transmitters we had. I also told him about our school and the students. During these transmissions, the boys would crowd into my radio shack to listen. They enjoyed our conversations and learned a little geography in the process.

One afternoon, Ian told me they were in the midst of a severe snow storm, with the winds up over one hundred miles per hour. Great damage was being done, he said, and he asked that I be sure to tune in again the following day at the same time and frequency, in case there was trouble. The next day, after we had re-established contact, he passed on an emergency request. "This is official now," he said. "I have been authorized to ask you to inform the Australian government of our situation. The storm has destroyed our high towers, so that our normal links by radio-telegraph and radio-telephone are impossible. You, in Nepal, are the only operator we've heard and spoken to, the only contact we've had in the last twenty-four hours." Then he gave me the details of whom to contact in Australia. I told him to stay on frequency; he might hear me talking to Australia.

I immediately CQ'd Canberra. In a few moments I made contact with an Aussie ham. I asked him to pass the message from the expedition to the government telecommunications authorities, to send relief to Mawson Base.

All this time, Ian could hear my side of the conversation, but not the Canberra ham through whom I was passing his request. This is part of the short-wave peculiarity. The transmissions and propagations skip and jump from the ionosphere. Many areas close by that are silent can be heard, using the skip, in other parts of the world, often thousands of miles distant. Here I was, two continents away, far north of the equator, talking clearly with both Antarctica and Australia, while they, being so close, could not hear each other.

Sometime later, after Ian left Antarctica, he stopped by to visit me in Nepal on his way to England on holiday. We had a great time reminiscing about the events of that great Antarctic storm.

Another time I was in fairly regular contact with an American expedition located quite near the South Pole. It was their winter and they were under the snow, experiencing Antarctic storms for weeks and months at a time, waiting for the weather to improve, for summer to come. Their antennas were high enough, however, so that their transmission could reach me. We had established a fixed time on weekends to speak with each other. In a sense, I was their life-line to the outside world.

One day their operator said, "Our chaplain wants to talk to you and ask a favor." When the chaplain came on, he explained that he was not a Catholic but was a Baptist minister. "All that you say on the radio is being taped," he said. "We play it back at lunch table. It is very interesting to hear about Himalayan expeditions, about the people of Nepal and your experiences up there, and especially the current news that you pass on to us from the BBC in London and other broadcast stations. You keep us up to date when we can't hear them. Now my favor to ask is this," he said. "If you will give us a sermon, I will tape it and play it at our church service on Easter morning. Are you willing?"

Of course I was. "Let me prepare a few points," I said, "and tomorrow when we meet again at this time and frequency, I'll give you a short sermonette."

So the next day I gave my little talk, which was played for all to hear under the snow at the South Pole. That saved me a trip and all that plane fare and hardship of going to Antarctica! I went by voice, instead, all for their benefit, a special one on Easter Day.

I did the same thing once at the request of a ham operator in Gatlinburg, Tennessee. He taped me for play-back at his church, on another Easter Sunday.

So, I've preached to two far corners of the earth, without ever setting foot in either place.

With all of Fr Moran's activity and fame as one of the world's rarest hams, talking to the whole wide world from the Himalayas, we may well ask how he came to be that well known radio enthusiast and amateur operator. When and where did he get his first radio? And what did he do about his passion for radio all those years he was in India before settling in Nepal?

Notes To Chapter 13: On the Air
1. Caroline Island is also known as Caroline Atoll and, since 2000, as Millennium Island because it was one of the first points of land on Earth to see the sunrise at the start of the new millennium, January 1, 2000.
2. GMT means Greenwich Mean Time, named after Greenwich, England, which is astride the world's Prime Meridian (zero longitude). After 1986, GMT was replaced by UTC (Coordinated Universal Time) based on atomic measurements rather than the earth's rotation. In military and aviation contexts, and sometimes among ham radio operators, GMT or UTC is also called "zulu time."

0100 hrs GMT is the same as 9 o'clock p.m. EST (Eastern Standard Time in the USA), or 6:45 o'clock a.m. Nepal Time. 20 meters is a popular bandwidth for DX amateur radio.
3. For more about Boris Lissanevitch, the White Russian émigré of Kathmandu's Royal Hotel fame, see Chapter 11: Affairs of State and High Society. The American Ambassador was Madame Carol Laise.
4. During the 1970s-80s, Fr Moran broadcast using Drake Twins; i.e., a Drake TR-4 transmitter and a Drake R-4 receiver.
5. *QST* magazine (December 1987, pp.45-48). *QST* is the official journal of the American Radio Relay League, the U.S. national association for amateur radio (founded in 1914). *QST* means "Attention all amateurs," a term (code) traditionally used to indicate that an announcement or bulletin is at hand. Another popular ham radio magazine goes by the code letters *CQ*.
6. '*CQ* announces CQ Amateur Radio Hall of Fame Class of 2002', posted May 31, 2002, on the ARRL website (www.arrl.org/news/stories/2002/05/31/102/).
7. See www.arrl.org/FandES/field/nets/client/netsearch.html for a list of registered ham radio networks.
8. The SEANET maintains an information website at www.sabah.net.my/seanet/. See also www.s2dx.org/index.php/articles/60-cq-seanet. The SEANET may sound anachronistic in this age of instant communications via the cell phones and the Internet, but when Fr Moran was operating (pre-Internet) it was, and remains, a vital link during emergencies all across the Asia-Pacific region. And, even now, as one SEANET member has recently put it well, an amateur radio group like SEANET "is very very appropriate for disaster mitigation networks where you know for sure, absolutely sure, double sure, that the radio network is working fine and will work on the day that you will need it, it only requires a 12V cell battery to power up a radio transmitter/receiver in a manner to reach thousands of miles away your party who can send help or send messages" (*sic*) (Samudra, 2004, 'Amateur radio operators on disaster mitigation').

14

First Radio

Up in my room, papa and the stranger waited in expectation as I made the final adjustments and connections to the primitive radio set. I remember that it was the high-voltage line to the plates. Then I connected the antenna and turned it on. Nothing happened. Silence. For the moment, at least, this boy's first wireless receiver was embarassingly silent.

   Fr Moran, recounting his first experiment as a boy
   with a wireless radio set

Marshall Moran's fascination with radio dates to within a few decades of the very beginning wireless operations in America. It was 1918 and he was a twelve year old seventh grader when he first caught the "radio bug."

As a boy in Chicago Heights and later in Chicago proper, Marshall struck up friendships with two young radio enthusiasts, both named Ralph. The first was Ralph Gorrell, who lived near the Moran home in Chicago Heights, Illinois. He was at least five years older than Marshall and was preparing to enter college. For several years already, he had been making simple, primitive radios. He had read about them in magazines like *The Wireless Age* and *QST*. When Marshall expressed an interest, Ralph Gorrell began by teaching him radio theory and how to construct receivers. Ralph was one of the few thousand early young amateur radio operators, and in the spirit of the hobby he shared everything he knew with the neighbor boy named "Marsh."

Looking Back
First Radio
Fr Moran

In those days one of my greatest interests was using telegraphic code with the Morse alphabet, by continuous wave carrier, or CW as we call it today. Ralph Gorrell and I strung a wire between our houses in Chicago Heights and sent messages back and forth using buzzers and wires. We also experimented with wireless code transmission.

13. Fr Moran talking to school boys during the 40th anniversary celebration of the founding of Godavari School, 1991.

It was another year or so before we discovered broadcast radio. In the meantime we gave no thought to using voice transmission.

When our family moved into Chicago in 1919, I kept up my interest in radio by reading occasional columns on the subject in *Modern Electrics* magazine and some others. Sometimes the Chicago *Tribune* printed diagrams of radio circuits. They fascinated me.

About that time I also remember reading about a young radio experimenter named Edwin H. Armstrong who, just a few years earlier, in 1912, had invented a new feedback circuit called the "super-regenerative." This invention greatly enhanced the sensitivity of the signal received and raised the volume of the incoming sound over anything that had yet been achieved.[1]

Armstrong's new regenerative circuit was hailed as the most important discovery since the Englishman, John Fleming, invented the basic vacuum tube in 1904. Wireless telegraphy—or 'radio' as it came to be called in America about the time of the war[2]—was barely a quarter century old, dating to the inventions of Heinrich Hertz and Guglielmo Marconi in the 1880s and 1890s in Europe.

I was fascinated reading about all this. When we moved to Chicago I wondered how I could continue my hobby now that my friend Ralph Gorrell was not nearby to help. That's when I met Ralph Berger.

As I became acquainted with my new neighborhood, I kept a sharp look out for any house with an antenna on the roof. I knew that those wires up in the air would tell me where a radio hobbyist lived. I was on my bicycle after supper one evening when I saw an antenna about two blocks away on Monroe Street, near 43rd. I peddled over, found the house, rushed up onto the porch and knocked on the door. A lady opened it.

"There is an antenna on the roof," I said. "Is someone here interested in radio? I would like to talk with him."

This very kind lady, Mrs Berger, said to me, "You go right upstairs. My son Ralph is there. He'll be glad to see that *somebody* is interested. We think it is very—" but she didn't finish the sentence, some unkind thought about her son's fixation with the radio hobby, perhaps.

Ralph Berger was a young medical student, well on in school. I was only thirteen and he must have been about twenty-three. He was alone but welcomed me. He was just about to finish assembling a three-tube receiver set up on his workbench. I asked him what the two long copper wires were doing there.

"Here's the diagram," he said, handing me a piece of paper covered with lines and symbols. The lessons had begun.

"That is the six-volt line from the battery that makes the tube, or valve as the British call it, light up the filament. First it goes to a detector, then those same six volts light the two amplifier tubes."

He explained how each tube had a plate inside attached to a ninety-volt battery. In those days, they used large ninety-volt batteries made by the Burgess Company, to charge the plate circuits. He explained how to tune the antenna and how to use a variometer and variocoupler for tuning the receiver to stations on different frequencies. He also showed me how to listen through head phones and where to attach a speaker. In the simple circuitry of those days there were only about thirty components, as compared to several hundred now. All this took some time and I listened and watched with great attention.

"Now," he said after awhile, "you know a little something about radio. Why don't you try to make one like mine? It's not hard."

This was a heaven-sent opportunity for me, I thought. "How much will it cost?" I asked.

"About eighty-five or ninety dollars," he replied. Ninety dollars was a lot of money in those days.

Ralph gave me his hand-written receipts from the store so that I would know exactly what to buy. But where would I get the money to buy the components?

At home, that question caused some discussion. Eighty dollars! My father chided me and said, "Remember when Grandfather O'Keefe came back from China with a mahjong game? You didn't play mahjong very long. You lost your enthusiasm after a few weeks. Is the radio going to be like that?"

My answer must have sounded convincing, for in a few days my grandfather gave me a hundred dollar bill to begin. (That $100 bill of 1919 is worth over $1000 in today's buying power.)

The next Saturday morning I went downtown with the hundred dollars in my pocket to buy the parts at one of Chicago's first radio stores. I returned home carrying a soldering iron, solder, panels, coils, wires, condensers, turning devices, grid leaks, sockets to hold the detector and amplifier tubes, batteries and a bread board. The "bread board" was a thin piece of wood on which to fasten down the many parts. I started putting things together. In those days we used amplifier tubes; now, of course, we use transistors and don't need the tubes, nor such big batteries.

The family watched me cutting and soldering wires. And my younger brother kept asking "Do you think it'll work? Do you think it'll work?"

After three or four days my father asked, with a hint of impatience, "When *will* your radio receiver be ready, Marshall?"

"Tomorrow night, I hope," I replied.

The following evening a stranger joined us for supper. My father introduced him, but I've forgotten the name. There was no indication of his work, except that he was my father's friend. I found out his real purpose for being there only later, after eating. I was quite excited and rushed through supper. Then I asked to be excused from the table early.

"I'm going to my room now to put the finishing touches on the radio," I announced.

The stranger asked, "Do you mind if I come along? I'm interested in radios."

"Sure," I said.

Up in my room, papa and the stranger waited in expectation as I made the final adjustments and connections to the primitive radio set. I remember that it was the high-voltage line to the plates. Then I connected the antenna and turned it on. Nothing happened. Silence. For the moment, at least, this boy's first wireless receiver was embarassingly silent.

I turned everything off and after a few moments of reflection, I reversed the polarity, the positive and negative battery connections. When I turned it on again, it worked. I turned the dial of the receiver and was soon listening to an evening program of opera on KYW, Chicago's first radio station. I was thrilled!

The stranger smiled and turned to my father. "Frank," he said, "your son knows what he is doing. He doesn't need me here. I'll be going now." And he left.

After the man had gone, I looked at my father. "You didn't think I could do it?" I asked.

"I didn't want you to be disappointed," he replied. "It was only a question of helping you."

Papa was normally a quiet and inexpressive man and I appreciated his sincere interest. 'Thanks, papa," I said, smiling. "Thanks very much."

Marshall concluded telling this story with an observation. "Of course, I didn't know then what I know now, that after some seventy years the radio hobby still grips me. It is a wonderful hobby, not only to hear the radio and to transmit worldwide, but also to put one together and experiment with the antennas and all the components, the amplifiers and all the circuits."

Tuned In

Marshall's high school days seemed to go by very fast because of his new radio hobby. Every night, as soon as he finished his homework, he would retire to his room to listen to his homemade receiver and experiment with the circuitry, trying to improve reception.

When some of the neighbors heard Marshall's homemade radio receiver, they wanted one for themselves. He obliged them by starting a small business building simple tuners for sale. "For about ninety dollars and a day's work I could put together a radio. I added a making charge of ten dollars and sold my homemade radios for a hundred dollars each. That way I made a little extra for myself," he said.

World War I had just ended. During the war years all amateur radio transmitting in the U.S. and even listening to government transmissions was forbidden, although the prohibition was not very systematically controlled. In Chicago, it seems, nobody was very concerned. After the war, amateur radio began again, with a new respect that young amateurs had given it when they volunteered for radio service in the Navy, the Signal Corps or the Army Air Service. Important new advances in radio had been made during the war, many of which were inspired by private tinkerers and inventors.

Then a great thing happened. Public broadcasting began and listening to broadcast stations became a popular American pastime. At first, before early radio was adequately regulated, some amateurs entered broadcasting by playing phonograph records over their primitive transmitters. Marshall remembered hearing them on his homemade receiver.

When his high school science teacher learned of Marshall's keen interest in radio, he asked the boy to help maintain his own radio. The teacher, Fr John ('Buddy') Esmaker,[3] encouraged the boys in the class to learn all they could about radio, as wireless communication was becoming popularly known in America. He told the class that in his day, at the university while he was studying for a Master's degree in physics, little attention was paid to wireless. It took people a long time to realize its potential as a communication tool and as a means of entertainment. But once they did, the communications industry grew rapidly. Inventions and improvements came fast. It did not take long for Fr Esmaker to fire his students' imaginations and passions for radio by holding contests for hearing the most distant stations in class. They competed weekly to see who could tune in broadcast stations at home from the greatest distance.[4]

It was the practice at that time for stations in Chicago and across the state of Illinois to remain silent during certain evening hours so that interested listeners could tune in more distant stations. At these times the school boys listened intently on their primitive home receivers. Each Tuesday morning they would present to class the lists of stations they had heard. For a long time, a station in Denver, Colorado seemed to be the limit for long distance reception. Closer stations, like KDKA in Pittsburgh, Pennsylvania and WGY in Schenectedy, New York, were more common. When someone heard a station in Forth Worth, Texas, they got quite excited.

One Tuesday morning Marshall came to class claiming to have heard San Francisco, California. He was greeted by skepticism and incredulity. "Never! Unbelievable! How could he?" the other boys said, dismissing his claim.

Marshall's reputation was saved when Fr Esmaker spoke up and said that he, too, had heard the California station. "That made my claim believable, not bluff. I enjoyed a bit of the other boys' jealousy for awhile. In those days, we didn't know much about the effect of atmospheric conditions and sun spots on radio reception. We thought we were just lucky to hear stations from so far away."

Radio in India

After high school, during his year at Loyola University, Marshall found little time to pursue his passion for radio. And in 1924, when he entered the Jesuit Novitiate in Florissant, Missouri, he gave it up altogether. His time at school was spent concentrating on religious studies and his forthcoming assignment as a teacher in India. He resigned himself to the thought that he would most likely never return to the radio hobby.

After arriving in Patna in 1929, Marshall went for eight years without even hearing a radio. At Bettiah there was no electricity and battery-powered radios had not yet been well perfected. Instead, the responsibilities of school teaching and administration weighed heavily on him and took up most of his waking hours each day.

In January 1933, when he went to Kurseong to regain his health and study theology, the pressure of studies once again ruled out listening to radio, even if there had been one available for him, which there wasn't. He read, instead, anything that he thought had utility and value, especially books on history, travel, biography, philosophy and religion. He avoided novels, which to his thinking had little lasting merit. He kept abreast of the news by reading English and Hindi language Indian newspapers.

He missed many things during those years, but most of all he missed radio, both the news and the music, especially choirs and orchestras and opera broadcasts. Only in 1937, after his ordination, when he left Kurseong and returned to Patna, could he listen to the classics. A departing British civil servant had given the mission a set of 78 LP phonograph records (long playing vinyl discs that ran at 78 rpm). In Patna he also had access to the mission radio receiver, a second hand Philco, manufactured by the Philadelphia Storage Battery Company.

The Western world was heading towards war in those days, and while the news out of Europe was not always pleasant, it satisfied a craving to know what was happening. After the war started, Marshall was impressed by the great new developments taking place in both telecommunications and travel, especially the importance radio was having for airplane pilots and ships at sea.

In May 1940, while on a brief visit back to his seminary at Kurseong and to nearby Darjeeling and Kalimpong, Marshall was invited to visit the *Chogyal* (King) of Sikkim in his palace at Gangtok. While dinner was being prepared, they discussed the world news. Marshall noticed that the Chogyal had a Phillips radio receiver, a model larger than Marshall had ever seen.

"'You must be able to get the latest news every hour,' I said to him. But I was surprised when he said that he was dissatisfied with the radio. It didn't seem to be very good. I offered to show him some of the frequencies where he could hear the BBC all day long. He was pleased and surprised when I quickly found three stations, each broadcasting reports on war events in Europe. He appreciated this very much, although the news was bad. That very day, May 10th, was a fateful one for Europe: Hitler had invaded Belgium, The Netherlands and France."

While following the course of the war over the next months and years, Marshall kept track of the many changes in communication electronics. He was awed by improvements in the military radio equipment being sent out to India for the American forces. He sometimes visited a military aerodrome near Patna. On one visit he saw the latest model Hallicrafter and Hammerlund receivers, and on hearing them he felt the old exhilaration of his youthful love for wireless. When the Americans left India in 1945, after the war, Marshall bought a surplus Hammerlund receiver for the high school at the cost of only a few rupees. The Hammerlund trademark was reputed to be one of the best, and a far cry from the simple bread board tuners of his youth in Chicago.

St Xavier's Station, VU2SX, Patna

At first he listened mostly to the international news. His favorite station was the BBC, broadcasting from Bush House, in London. By 1947 he was tuning in amateur radio bands and listening to local Indian hams. He improved his antenna to hear them better, then wrote to one to find out how he, too, could become a licensed amateur radio operator.

The process was not difficult, he was told, only time-consuming. It necessitated his going to Delhi. During the next school vacation, in January 1948, Marshall took the train west to the capital to apply for his license in person. His first stop was an office in the Home Ministry that oversaw police and security matters. Radio licensing was considered to be a security matter, all the more so where a foreign national was involved. Marshall carried a letter from an Indian Army officer in Patna stating that he was not a security risk and that the Patna officials had no objection. That helped.

Then, carrying the requisite papers in hand from the ministry, he went to the national Post Office to get his license. The Indian Post Office, like its British counterpart, was charged with overseeing all telecommunications as well as letter and package delivery.

He was given a license good for two years. The call sign was VU2SX. The prefix 'VU' indicated that it was an Indian station. The number '2' designated the operating location in northeast India. The phonetic suffix 'SX' (which he specifically requested) stood for St Xavier, a reminder to any other radio operators listening in that it was the school's station and nothing more.

Back in Patna, Marshall installed a small rig in a room atop the flat roof of St Xavier's School. He strung a simple homemade wire antenna between two poles and was soon on the air. His power tube was known as a 6L6 that, together with a simple oscillator, gave the station a limited output of 10 watts, not strong enough for long distance transmissions, but a start.

"I was very careful," he said later. "I wanted to convince the authorities that I was not trying to become an international, as they called DX operators. The government had a suspicion of expatriates and I assumed that I would be monitored by the Indian Army. So, knowing that my equipment was poor and that I couldn't get good parts for improvement, I operated the rig mostly as a demonstration for science students at the school. It was a wonderful means of teaching physics and even history, about communications, about

Marconi the inventor, and the like. The contacts we made from the school were mostly with other nearby amateurs in northern India; that was the best we could do with our limited equipment. As a foreigner, I felt just plain lucky to have a license at all."

Sometimes when conditions were good, Marshall and his students heard American hams, but with their simple rooftop antenna those occasions were rare. During the hot, dry Indian summer from about mid-March to mid-June, ahead of the rainy monsoon, he closed the rig down altogether. On the subcontinent at that time of year, radio propagation, transmission and reception are notoriously bad. Intense heat, high winds and violent convention currents, and frequent thunder storms create great amounts of static and crackling in the ionosphere. "I didn't dare operate the rig from the school house roof during thunder storms!" To complicate matters, the electrical system in Patna city was inconsistent and generated considerable line noise.

One day, the high school science teacher asked Marshall to repair his commercial radio receiver. He liked listening to news and music programs broadcast by All India Radio, but the set was giving him trouble. "It's ironic," Marshall told the teacher as he took the set apart on his work bench searching for the problem, "but this takes me back to the time I fixed a receiver for my science teacher, Fr Esmaker, years ago at St Ignatius High School in Chicago." His interest and involvement in the radio hobby had come full circle. Strange, too, he thought, how opportunities open up when one least expects them.

Marshall was back to his childhood passion; and never in all the years after that was radio very far from him.

The Bombay Radio Club
Marshall was very careful to limit his amateur radio contacts to Indian stations. He knew very well the potential trouble that making foreign DX contacts might bring him from suspicious government officials. To increase his knowledge, he began talking to members of the Bombay Radio Club. The BRC was the first of its kind in India and its membership included Indian amateurs all across the newly independent nation.

"Father Moran in Patna" soon became a well known contact among BRC members. Once he became known, they offered him a complimentary life membership and invited him to participate in their annual conventions. Thus, in only a few months' time, the revival of his radio hobby had taken on new meaning. He was now a member of a fraternity of Indian broadcast amateurs, turning up regularly to operate from the radio shack atop Patna's St Xavier's High School. The school boys who joined him were as excited as he, as they shared in this captivating hobby. His handle, "Father," and his call sign, "VU2SX," became well known across the subcontinent.

One time Marshall was invited to inaugurate the opening of a radio club station at a Catholic boys school in the Bombay suburb of Bandra. Club members had asked to use the school site for their station, for which they offered to conduct classes in radio electronics to interested science students. On another occasion some years later, after he had settled in Nepal, he was invited back to Bombay to preside as the honorary chairman of the National Indian Radio Convention. He greatly enjoyed these gatherings with the elite of India's radio amateurs.

When Marshall first began "hamming" in India, local amateur operators were unable to import foreign equipment. Theirs were mostly homemade or war surplus rigs that, with time, became increasingly archaic and inefficient. In the beginning they, like all hams worldwide, transmitted and received on AM (amplitude modulated) band waves. But, with the steady increase of radio usage, the AM bands became overcrowded. Eventually, a new system called single sideband (SSB) was perfected in Europe and America, and as it became the preferred mode of operation Indian hams were left behind, unable to take advantage of it because of the law against importing the more modern foreign equipment.

At one of the meetings of the Bombay Radio Club, Marshall encouraged the club's officers to recommend a more liberal radio policy to the Indian government. They drew up a list and formally petitioned government officials to liberalize import restrictions, to provide more amateur frequencies and, in general, to allow more freedom of operation. They were pleased when the government agreed to most of their requests, especially the lifting of the ban on the important of foreign equipment. The new rules allowed a licensed radio amateur to import one transmitter and one receiver, or a combined rig called a "transceiver," once in two years. This had the effect of upgrading Indian amateur radio, and the new ability to operate SSB put Indian hams back into the world spotlight.

The BRC had an interesting membership, mostly professionals drawn from among the Hindu, Muslim, Parsi and Christian communities. Marshall was pleased to help them and was proud to be a member of "such a group of broad-minded amateurs, " as he put it. "They were my friends, a wonderful set of cooperative and trusting people."

All India Radio

Marshall's interest in radio in India was wide ranging. He not only enjoyed amateur operating and teaching schoolboys about it, but he repaired equipment, listened to short wave broadcasts, and participated in both local transceiving and limited DX-ing as a ham. Once he had re-established his interests in the hobby at Patna, he became well known and was asked to perform all sorts of public and private functions related to radio. Soon his interests and talents came to the attention of the authorities at All India Radio (AIR).

Not long after he had received his Indian amateur license, the government opened a public broadcast station for Bihar, in Patna. From there, AIR was better able to serve the outlying areas that could not always be reached by the older Calcutta station. Because of his knowledge of radio, Marshall was asked to join the Bihar state AIR advisory board. He agreed and although his role was small, there were occasions when his advice and suggestions were highly valued.

One such occasion came on the death by assassination of the saintly Mahatma Gandhi. On January 30, 1948, while on his way to prayers in Delhi, Gandhi-ji was shot by a Hindu extremist. When the news reached Patna, the Bihar station director called on Marshall for help. In those days public broadcasting in India was restricted to evening programs. Faced by this sudden emergency, the Bihar station director needed advice for memorial programming to replace the regular evening fare.

Marshall and the director made a list of state leaders to be asked to give eulogies, and they planned appropriate funereal music to broadcast. For the last item, Marshall suggested playing Gandhi's favorite English Christian hymn, one that the Mahatma had learned during his student days in London: 'Lead kindly light, amid the encircling gloom...'

"But we don't have that song," the station director told him.

"We will," said Marshall. "Just wait." And he dashed out the door to get it.

Marshall drove directly to the school where he quickly assembled some of the older boys in the auditorium and taught them to sing the song. Then he took them to the AIR station where they taped the hymn to be broadcast later.

The Bihar station's memorial service began on schedule that evening. It ended with the pre-recorded hymn. A short time later the national memorial service was broadcast from Delhi through all the affiliate AIR stations, countrywide. A solemn announcer said that before Prime Minister Jawaharlal Nehru spoke, they would play Gandhi's favorite hymn, 'Lead kindly light.' On hearing that, the Patna station director turned to Marshall with a broad grin and, despite the sad occasion, said, "Father, we scooped them! Delhi didn't tell me about their program plans, so we scooped them. It was your idea, Father. I'm going to write to ask that you be given a greater role in national programming."

Later, when his appointment to a national broadcast committee finally came through, the Indian Broadcasting Services offered him a position for planning and arranging speakers. They also requested his services in designing radio courses for teaching English to school children across India. But as much as it interested him, he had to decline. It was 1950, and by then he was making plans to move to Nepal.

Marshall thanked his Indian radio friends, but told them, with a mixture of disappointment and elation, "I'm going to Nepal soon, where things are much more primitive and where I think I can do a greater good. There is no radio there, no aerodrome, no cinema houses, no hotels, not even a motor road into the capital city from India. To get there I'll have to walk over the mountains," he said. "So, regretfully, I have to decline your offer."

In a few months he was off to Kathmandu, leaving India and many Indian friends behind. And once again, he left radio behind, but not for long. Radio was now firmly on his mind, an integral part of his persona and character, in his soul (so to speak). As an outlet for his indomitable spirit of public service, it was a way to meet the world beyond the geographical isolation of Nepal. He felt—no, he knew instinctively—that in due time, the opportunity would arise once again for him to indulge his love of radio.

Notes to Chapter 14: First Radio
1. Some years later Edwin Armstrong gained further fame as the inventor of a much more advanced radio circuitry known as FM, or "frequency modulation."
2. In the beginning it was called "wireless," but was soon popularized in America as "radio." Eventually, wireless became more narrowly associated with the British.
3. Fr Esmaker got his moniker "Buddy" from the name he called everybody else. He had a very long and distinguished career as science teacher at Chicago's St Ignatius school.
4. About the time that Marshall was in high school, long distance radio tuning became known as "DX," for "distance unknown," a term borrowed from telegraphy.

15

Voice of Nepal

> *Now there were two Disney cartoon characters operating from the heart of the Himalayas – 'Mickey Mouse' and 'Donald Duck.' This provided the Mount Everest Expedition with a certain unique, slightly humorous and certainly unforgettable identity, wherever in the world that amateur operators could hear us.*
>
> Fr Moran, on setting up radio receiver stations in Kathmandu for the American Mount Everest Expedition of 1963

In 1951, as Marshall Moran reentered Kathmandu valley to take up his new life, he thought he had left amateur radio behind. For many years it had been so, far away, part of an earlier time and place in his life. There was no precedent for amateur radio in Nepal, no government telecommunications office to issue a license, no equipment or parts for sale on the local market, no knowledge or interest by the local people. "Besides," he said, "I was too busy starting the school at Godavari to spend time on anything else."

Unlike his first eight years in India in the 1930s when he heard no radio whatsoever, in Nepal he had a radio receiver on which to listen to short wave broadcasts and the international news, and occasionally some classical music through the static.

Looking Back
Creating 9N1-"Mickey Mouse"
Fr Moran

When I came to Nepal, I had no amateur radio ambitions. I left all that behind me once again and didn't get back to it until the winter of 1959-1960. The break came when the Nepal government decided to install a nationwide single sideband radio telephone system so that government people and the public in emergencies could talk to Kathmandu from towns in the remote hills and lowlands. The installation was done by an American firm, Cook Electric of Chicago,

15. Fr Moran with school boys.

under contract to the United States Operations Mission, or USOM.[1] I got to know some of the contractors quite well, particularly a fellow named Sam Mazza. Sam was both a professional radio engineer and an amateur operator.

Working in Nepal was a real challenge for these fellows. There was virtually no internal communication system. I remember that there was one telephone line across the central hills, between Kathmandu and Pokhara, that was about a seven day walk. Now a bus can take you there, when the road is in good repair, in about six hours.

The telephone "wallahs," the operators along the line, used primitive handsets powered by dry cell batteries. Each station was about a half day's walk from the next. Getting messages through took a lot of shouting, especially with the usually bad line conditions.

Communications with the more remote areas of the country was mostly by "coolies" or runners going two weeks or more in one direction. It took months, sometimes, to get emergency messages in and out of the hills.

Even airline service was something new. The first airport was constructed in 1950 on Gaucher Field, a cow pasture near Kathmandu. After that, other airfields were gradually opened in the hills and the lowlands. With the coming of international development aid in the late 1950s and early 1960s, STOL airfields were built. The so-called Short-Take-Off-Landing light aircraft were quite popular for use under primitive conditions. The radio communications contractors from Cook Electric had to rely on these small planes and bush airfields to get to the remote work sites. Many places were easy, but some were difficult to fly into, like Jomsom and Jumla in the high mountains.

Tourism and trekking in the mountains were not yet popular, either. That came later. Nowadays, of course, the tourist industry is a major source of foreign currency for Nepal and facilities for travelers in the hills and mountains are found in even the most remote districts. But when Mazza and the other technicians went out, they found that they were the first Westerners ever to visit some places.

Besides Sam Mazza, there was another ham named Fred Vogel living in Nepal. Fred was also under contract to the USOM to build a modern lumber mill for the government at Hetauda, south of the Kathmandu valley. When I first met Sam and Fred in 1959, we got to talking, of course, about our mutual interest—amateur radio.

On hearing of their work around the country, I suggested that the radio installation team set up a base station in the government office at Kathmandu for communications with field stations. They could use the amateur bands for transmission until the new system was fully operating. We all thought that a temporary ham station would be useful to test and tune the new equipment. The technicians also needed to be able to order parts, send instructions to and from the remote stations, and so forth.

Mazza agreed with this and assumed that I would help out by operating a separate backup station, in case of emergency. He knew that I would be around on weekends and holidays when the government station was closed and off the air. Both Sam and Fred decided to put sets in their homes, too, so that we could all keep in contact and at the same time talk to the world as the first Himalayan hams.

Setting up our stations required special equipment. We decided that the best rig, given his project's needs and the conditions in Nepal, was a Heathkit Cheyenne, model HW-20. Hams called it the "Hot Water Twenty". It had an output of 50 watts AM—that's amplitude modulation—and was a fairly easy kit to assemble, even in Kathmandu. I still had my faithful old Hammerlund receiver from India days, so I needed only the transmitter and an antenna to get started.

We also needed licenses. The Nepal government authorities agreed with our plans and gave us special amateur call signs, the first in Nepal. The internationally established prefix for Nepal radio call signs is "9N1," or "Nine Nancy One" in the phonetic code that hams use. To make it easy, our suffix letters were our own initials: "SM" for Sam Mazza, "FV" for Fred Vogel, and "MM" for Marshal Moran. We then identified ourselves on the air phonetically as "Sugar Mexico," "Foxtrot Victor" and "Mexico Mexico." I had been watching too many Walt Disney films, I guess, for it wasn't very long after I'd got started that I substituted "Mickey Mouse" for the standard phonetic terms. The new name stuck.

I spent Christmas week of 1959 assembling the new transmitter, working on it a half hour here, an hour there, altogether about sixty hours' work. I logged every minute I spent on it in a notebook. Fred Vogel came by a few times to help me get on the air. For an antenna, I put up a wire dipole and a simple beam made from aluminum pipes.[2] At one time I even had what is called a folded dipole made with ribbon wire doubled back. Actually, I had a better antenna system than the other operators because I found more time to experiment with improvements than they did. I was living in town at the time, at the school in Jawalakhel on the edge of Patan, only a few minutes from Kathmandu. My antenna looked impressive up on top of the roof of that converted Rana palace.

The government radios were set with fixed crystals to operate on frequencies in the 40 and 60 meter bands, but our amateur frequencies were higher, at 15 and 20 meters. These higher frequencies get little interference from government, military or civilian radio. They work best during morning, afternoon and early evening hours.

After I got on the air, I met the contractors' schedule almost every day at 8 o'clock in the morning and 5 o'clock in the evening, before and after the normal work day. I handled traffic for them just as if I was in their office.

I could also transmit and receive other stations outside of Nepal. I was eager to do that, remembering the fun I'd had as an amateur in Patna.

Early Contacts

Marshall's first ham radio contact from Nepal was VU2IJ, Jimmy Mistry, in Bombay. "Jimmy was quite astounded at hearing me, all the more so when I told him I was the first amateur operator ever from Nepal." A few years later they met at an All India Radio Convention held at the Jawaharlal Nehru Scientific Center in Bombay. Another early Indian contact was VU2US, Lieutenant General K. Umrao Singh of the Indian Army.

Mickey Mouse Moran also talked in those first days on the air with a Russian ham located in Siberia at Novosibirsk, Russia's third largest city after Moscow and Saint Petersburg. The Russian ham's call sign was UA9KOG, and his name was Stanislaus. "Stan was a very friendly operator and we maintained contact off and on for many years until he was transferred to Lithuania. He must have been some sort of high party official in the Soviet government."

Reaching U.S. hams in those days was more difficult, unless the skip of the radio signal off the ionosphere was favorable. Occasionally, Marshall talked with hams in Great Britain, and he could contact hams located in closer locations like Singapore, Vietnam, Laos and Cambodia, for as long as American amateurs were operating there. He found, generally, that contacts within the eastern hemisphere were fairly easy. But because his Heathkit transmitter was weak compared with what some high-powered hams were using, and because his home-made antenna was of poor quality, the signal from Nepal was not often heard well elsewhere.

In 1960, when the Nepal telecommunications project was finished and the Cook Electric crew was packing to leave, Sam Mazza came out to Jawalakhel with an extra 20 meter beam antenna and told Marshall to keep both it and the project's Heathkit transmitter he had been using. The antenna was a great improvement for Marshall. The transmitter gave him permanence as a Himalayan ham.

"Friends often ask me how I got my first equipment. Now you know—mostly gifts, leftovers and surplus. But that is what hamming is all about, putting it all together, making it all work."

Traffic, Routine and Emergency

During those first days on the air from Kathmandu, whenever international amateur radio DX-ers heard Mickey Mouse Moran, there were two kinds of reactions. Those who had never heard of Nepal expressed surprise, curiosity and delight at the new contact (and immediately looked it up in an atlas). Or, if they had heard about this rare DX, they tried valiantly to power their way through the pile-up to make the coveted contact. During his first two or three years on the air, the demand for QSO (contact) with Fr Moran was so intense that he spoke to an estimated ten thousand stations a year. He quickly became known, and remained all his life, as one of the rarest DX ham QSOs in the world.

Because Marshall often had messages for family and friends in the United States, he maintained regular daily contact with certain hams who had a strong signal and kept a regular schedule. His principal contacts changed from time to time, but there were several who remained in touch for years. They were very special contacts and friends to him. During the mid-1960s he talked daily to K7KQ, Ken Hager, at home on Maury Island in Puget Sound, near Seattle, Washington. The schoolboys who listened in to this contact laughed when Ken said he lived on Maury Island; to them it sounded like *mauri,* the Nepali word for honey bee.[3] The buzzing sound of a "pile up" of operators trying to get through to Moran on the airwaves convinced them.

Ken's wife, Elsie, was an avid listener to all of Ken's contacts around the world, especially Fr Moran. Many of the wives of his predominately male ham contacts listened in when Fr Moran was on the air. "We bring a little diversion and pleasant distraction into the homes of many people like that," Marshall once said. "They often show their appreciation by sending books and cassette tapes for our boys to enjoy. It helps improve the school library."

Around 1970, Marshall met W2GBC, Judge William (Bill) Conner, on the air. Bill operated out of Dobbs Ferry, New York. When his son joined the Peace Corps in Nepal, the judge took up ham radio just to keep in touch, through Fr Moran.

For many years Marshall maintained regular contact with K9AWK, Bert Gaidostik, of Lombard, Illinois, near Chicago, in order to send messages back and forth to the Jesuit mission's Chicago Province office and to relatives and friends in Illinois. When his fellow priest, Fr James Donnelly, went to Chicago for heart surgery in the summer of 1986, Marshall kept a regular schedule with Bert in order to stay abreast of Donnelly's operation and recovery. K9LP,

Bill Brown, of nearby Lake Forest, Illinois, was also a frequent and faithful radio friend.

For over twenty years, 9V101, Reese (Bud) Whitney of Singapore was a very important and dependable contact for Marshall. By relaying messages through Bud, Marshall was able to respond to emergency requests on more than one occasion. Bud was a regular contact on the SEANET, which he and Marshall helped found. Once, working together on the air, they helped save the life of a young Nepalese school boy.

Looking Back
A Medical Emergency
Fr Moran

I had just powered up my rig at Godavari one evening when a jeep roared into the circle drive in front of Xavier Hall. It was the American Peace Corps doctor. He needed help. A volunteer had just come into town from Banepa, east of Kathmandu, with a Nepalese schoolboy who was suffering from a serious heart condition. The boy needed immediate surgery to survive, but at that time medical services in Kathmandu were not good for something so serious. On a chance, the doctor decided to come out to Godavari to see if I could contact his colleagues at St Mary's Hospital in Los Angeles. Perhaps they could take him.

"Can you reach Los Angeles?" the doctor asked after describing the situation to me.

"I'll try," I said, "but radio propagation conditions are not good right now and the chances of getting through are slim."

My best chance was a relay through Bud Whitney in Singapore. Tuning the dial to Bud's usual frequency hang out, I heard him talking to a California ham. But I could only hear Bud's side of the conversation. "Break, break, Bud," I said, without hesitating. "This is 9N1-Mickey Mouse in Kathmandu. I've got an emergency for your California friend. Over."

Bud's voice came back immediately. "We've got a breaker, California. Please stay on the frequency. Father Moran has an emergency for you from Nepal."

Then, to me he said, "I'll turn my antenna to hear you better, Father. Standby..."

As he turned his antenna toward Nepal, our contact improved and I was soon explaining the situation over the air. I gave Bud the telephone number of the hospital and the name of the heart surgeon to contact. Then Bud turned his antenna back to relay this vital information to the stateside ham, who placed the call by phone patch. Within minutes, we heard back through Singapore, "The surgeon is on the line in California," said Bud. "And, yes, the hospital can take the patient. They need only the date and time of arrival in Los Angeles."

Almost overnight, the Kathmandu Rotary Club and the boy's family and friends raised enough money to send him and a Nepalese doctor to the states. They were gone within the week and, on landing in Los Angeles, were met and whisked away to the hospital by ambulance.

The operation was a success. The boy recovered and returned to school in Banepa with the promise of a sound and healthy life ahead of him.

Stories like this are commonplace among hams. Radio amateurs are always ready for emergencies. When they occur, they take immediate precedence over the mundane chit-chat that usually crams the airwaves. The familiar "Break, break," when heard on the air, is like a police or ambulance siren. It is always and immediately given a clear pathway by everyone within listening distance.

Americans on Everest

An early highlight in Marshall's Nepal-based radio career came in 1963 with his involvement in the first American Mount Everest Expedition, the AMEE. Edmund Hillary and Tenzing Norgay with the British Mount Everest Expedition had summited Everest for the first time in 1953. They were followed in 1956 by the Swiss, and in 1960 by the Chinese. In 1963, an American team of climbers felt it was their turn to try for the top.

The AMEE team also decided to set up radio communications in support of the expedition. When they approached the Nepal government for permission to operate temporary radio stations at Base Camp on the Khumbu Glacier and in Kathmandu, Marshall helped secure the necessary clearances and licenses. The expedition team leader, Norman Dyhrenfurth, then asked the American embassy's military attaché, Colonel William (Bill) Gresham, to serve as the expedition's principal Kathmandu operator. Fr Moran became Colonel Gresham's backup.

After the stations were installed, Marshall listened to all the regular transmissions from Base Camp and handled emergency and other traffic whenever Colonel Gresham was away or otherwise off the air. Marshall still had the small Heathkit transmitter he had gotten from Sam Mazza and his old Hammerlund receiver. Colonel Gresham operated with a more modern and more powerful Johnson Viking rig.

The AMEE Base Camp radio license was registered with the Nepal government as 9N1ME, for Mount Everest. At Marshall's request, Colonel Gresham's station was given the suffix 'DD,' phonetically 'Delta Delta,' but soon known as 'Donald Duck.' "Now there were two Disney cartoon characters operating from the heart of the Himalayas—Mickey Mouse and Donald Duck. This provided the Mount Everest expedition with a certain unique, slightly humorous and unforgettable identity, wherever in the world that amateur operators could hear us," Marshall said.

The expedition's radio schedule was fixed for 5 o'clock each afternoon. On some days, a morning schedule was also kept. The AMEE equipment was set to operate on 40 meters (7 MHz), a noisy band wave that Marshall would have preferred to avoid. Most days when Colonel Gresham was operating, the call would go out on schedule. "9N1ME. Calling 9N1ME. This is 9N1DD-9N1DD-calling 9N1ME-9N1ME. This is 9N1DD calling, with 9N1MM standing by."[4]

Al Auten served as the AMEE Base Camp radio operator, but just as often others on the team would respond to the daily call from Kathmandu, climbers such as Barry Prather, Dan Doody, Maynard Miller, Jim Whittaker, or Normam Dyhrenfurth himself. The first contact between AMEE Base Camp and Kathmandu was made at 1700 hours (5 o'clock pm) local time on the afternoon of March 20, 1963. James Ramsey Ullman, the expedition historian and author, was present in Gresham's Kathmandu station. He wrote about it in the expedition book, *Americans on Everest*. After some time, at last, "There was Al, loud and clear from the Khumbu Glacier. It was a great event, and there were many 'rogers,' much give and take of both important messages and just plain satisfying gab."[5]

At the Kathmandu end, on some days the ham shack was crowded with people, including Ullman and several expedition wives—Sally Dyhrenfurth, Sally Richardson, Marian Ullman, Lila Bishop and Jolene Unsoeld. Sometimes the four Unsoeld children would also show up to listen. They would cycle over from their big house near the Chinese Embassy. Their father, Willi, a famous climber, was Deputy Director of the American Peace Corps in Nepal, on leave to make the climb.

Ullman also described a typical scene in Gresham's radio shack: "Ambassador and Mrs Stebbins often dropped by, as did Bob Bates of the Peace Corps and other Embassy people. Sometimes Base Camp was frustratingly shy of information as to what was happening up the hill. More often it had the latest news and passed it on. And on a few memorable occasions we were able, by what hams call a 'duplex operation' on the Base radio, to talk directly to the walkie-talkies at Advance Base or above. It was an exciting exercise in the imagination to try to visualize the speakers in their snow-and-ice world 18,000 to 20,000 feet above our heads."[6]

The usual traffic included expedition progress up the mountain, news of the scientific research being conducted and various expedition incidents and accidents. Sometimes letters from home would be answered over the air. There were expedition mail runners, of course, but they took about three weeks to carry the mail sack round trip from Kathmandu to Base Camp. Ham radio was much faster.

All went well with the expedition until March 24, when Base Camp failed to meet the schedule. Only the next day was the sad news announced, the mountain had claimed its first (and only) American expedition member, Jake Breitenbach. He died while negotiating the dangerous Khumbu Icefall.

Better news came as the weeks passed. "On April 17, in particular, there were a few moments of chilling tension when Al Auten said quietly, "I have an official expedition announcement... that Lute Jerstad and Dick Pownall had, the day before, reached the South Col, and chill turned to joy in Bill Gresham's shack." And, "...On April 29 Al Auten had word for us that the first assault team had reached the col. On April 30 that it had reached Camp VI..."[7]

Fr Moran, Colonel Gresham, Ullman and the others in Kathmandu, including government authorities monitoring the climb, had known for some time that May 1 was the day on which the team would make its first summit attempt. At the evening schedule that day, they all waited eagerly to hear what had happened. But it was not until the next evening, May 2, that word came down from the mountain. It was not what anyone expected, nor was it easy to receive.

Nothing about Mount Everest is easy, it seems, including radio communications from Base Camp. Propagation that evening on the 40 meter band was especially bad. To get through to Kathmandu, the expedition operator had to talk through a relay station in Ceylon (Sri Lanka), nearly a thousand miles away in the southern Indian ocean.

Nor was the message that arrived easily interpreted by the radio operators, climbers' wives, government officials and member of the press corps who waited anxiously in Kathmandu. "Two runners left at 1300 hours May One," was all it said.[8] Norman Dyhrenfurth, the expedition leader, was being secretive. Decoded, the cryptic message meant that two climbers had reached the top at 1 p.m. on May 1. But even knowing that, it was still anybody's guess (outside of Base Camp) just *who* those first summiteers were.

As Fr Moran later told the story, "Mysteriously, their names were not given. Everyone asked, 'Who are they?' It was very embarrassing to have to tell the Nepalese officials that, yes, two

Americans had reached the summit; but, no, the team leader would not release their names."

"In a guarded and tactful way, I tried to explain to the Nepalese and the press that the team was determined to stress teamwork between the American and Sherpa climbers and to down play individual achievement. Everyone remembered the diplomatic storm when the 1953 British expedition announced that Hillary had been the first on top, with the help of Tenzing Sherpa. Only later did they correct it to say that Tenzing and Hillary had reached the top *together*."

The annoying delay in announcing the climbers' names continued until Marshall told Norman Dyhrenfurth at Base Camp that Nepal government officials were becoming impatient, were guessing the identity of the climbers and were about to make a public announcement. After days of silence on the matter, Dyhrenfurth finally identified Nawang Gombu Sherpa and Jim Whittaker as the summiteers. He stressed that their success was the whole team's success, for without the help of the camp managers, cooks, porters, other climbers, and especially the Sherpas who hauled oxygen and supplies to the high camps, and even the mail runners, he said, no one would have made the top.

Ian Wollen, the British ham in Ceylon who relayed the messages from Base Camp to Kathmandu, later recalled with excitement the whole affair of coded messages passing back and forth across the full length of the subcontinent. He had helped the expedition in this way several times already, but the events surrounding the summit assault messages were special. "Because propagation on 40 metres was not so good," he said, "I'd use the 20 metre band, somewhere near 14320 kHz, and was able to relay messages between Base Camp and the Embassy, and also Fr Moran. In fact, this was how the message that the American climbers had reached the summit was passed to the outside world, first to the King of Nepal, then the *National Geographic*, then the London *Times* and the rest of the news agencies."[9]

After all the excitement of May 1, there was a lull in expedition activities while the climbers recouped their strength. A second assault on the summit was being planned. It involved two two-man teams of climbers simultaneously. One team would attempt the previously untried and dangerous West Ridge, while another team would climb up from the well-established South Col route to meet them on the top. This time it was announced ahead of time who was climbing: Willi Unsoeld and Tom Hornbein from the west and Barry Bishop and Lute Jerstad from the south.

It was the third week in May before the second two teams were in place to try for the top. Then, on the morning of May 22, a message came from Base Camp that the two teams were going for the summit that day. More information would come during the evening schedule.

During the afternoon, anxious listeners at Base Camp heard by walkie-talkie from the two climbers on the West Ridge route that they had experienced some difficulty crossing the so-called yellow band, a streak of tawny-colored rotten rock made up of clay interspersed with sandstone. It did not make for easy climbing, and when they finally reached the top of the band, some eight hundred feet below the summit, it was already 3 o'clock in the afternoon, very late by anybody's standards to go for the summit. But Unsoeld and Hornbein had no alternative. They could only continue upward; they had passed a point of no return. It was impossible, too dangerous, they told Base Camp, to return back down the difficult route they had just ascended. They were out of time, the route was too treacherous to descend and they had made up their minds not to turn back at any cost.

The plan was that the West Ridge team would try to join up with Lute Jerstad and Barry Bishop, who were approaching the summit simultaneously along the South Col route. Then, together, all four would descend to the safety of the South Col camp for the night. The West Ridge team had no choice but to carry out this plan and continue upward, despite the late hour. What Unsoeld and Hornbein did not know that afternoon was that Bishop and Jerstad had already reached the top well ahead of them and, not finding their colleagues and unable to raise them by walkie-talkie, they had already started down, late, worried and alone.

That evening Base Camp radio announced only that both teams were high on the peak. Nothing more. Marshall said he would try to make contact later in the night but failed. Ian Wollen tried from Ceylon. Another ham tried from as far away as South Korea. But all attempts were unsuccessful. As night progressed, all that was known in Kathmandu was that four climbers were somewhere high on the mountain. It seemed too late for any of them to have reached the safety of the South Col camp. They were almost certainly out of oxygen, tentless and without sleeping bags, the minimum requirements for survival out at those heights.

Marshall told the rest of story many times: "The West Ridge route had never before been climbed," he began, "so it was a very scary and daring ascent for Unsoeld and Hornbein. When they finally reached the top, it was already near dusk. There they saw the flag left three weeks before by Gombu and Whittaker and the fresh footprints that Bishop and Jerstad had made a few hours earlier. Of course, we in Kathmandu didn't know any of this until later."

"Seeing the hour, they started on toward the col, following the tracks in the snow."

"Meanwhile, in the radio shack with me at Bill Gresham's—Bill was away from Kathmandu at the time and I was operating—were Unsoeld's wife, Jolene, and Bishop's wife, Lila.[10] I was quite frank with them. We knew from talking with Base Camp that the South Col team had not left the summit until after 4 o'clock p.m. and that they had seen no sign of the West Ridge team. I told the two women that it seemed quite unlikely that either team could make it back down to the safety of camp on the South Col before dark. It was clear that they would have to spend the night out on the mountain."

"We sat in the shack for an hour after the disturbing no-news from Base Camp. Everyone was anxious and very nervous. We had all heard about the typical high velocity night winds on the summit and that they were the climbers' greatest threat. I said we'd all better go home and pray that there would be no wind this night, knowing that windless nights on the peak in that season were very rare. At our benediction service with the Jesuit Fathers at the school late that evening, I prayed for the safety of the climbers. I prayed that the winds would cease, if only for this one night."

Father Moran's story picks up again on the following day, May 23: "At 9 o'clock the next morning we heard some good news from Base Camp, that for the first time in weeks the mountain winds had been still!"

"We also heard that Unsoeld and Hornbein had reached the top the evening before. They had contacted Base Camp from the summit by walkie-talkie. But beyond that there was no further news. Nobody knew where any of the climbers were during the night and there had been no contact with them yet that morning."

Over the next few days the story came out about the history-making bivouac by the four climbers at twenty-eight thousand feet, the highest ever. Marshall and the others who stayed close to the radio were the first people outside of the expedition party at Base Camp to hear. Unsoeld and Hornbein had reached the top shortly after 6 o'clock p.m., May 22.[11] After a quick walkie-talkie communication to Base Camp confirming their success, and a few hurried photographs, they set out to follow the tracks of Bishop and Jerstad down to the safety of the South Col. But fatigue and darkness overcame both teams. By calling out through the darkness they eventually met up on the steep snow-covered slope. The four men then tried to descend further, knowing that their very survival depended on reaching camp. But, uncertain of the safest route, out of oxygen and with only one dim flashlight between them, they had to stop and find a safe place to bivouac. They found a ledge on which to huddle together a short ways below the ridge along which they were descending.

It was frigid cold and the exhausted climbers' feet and hands began to freeze. Willi massaged and warmed Hornbein's feet against his belly, while his own toes froze solid.

At first light the four men continued downward and soon arrived at Camp 7, the South Col, where other members of the team were anxiously waiting. Word of their arrival was relayed to Base Camp, then transmitted on the next schedule with Kathmandu. All four climbers had survived the night out and were now safe, though each was severely frostbitten.

Months later, Willi Unsoeld recounted his version of the harrowing hours that dark night at the top of the world to Fr Moran, the author and several other friends over supper one evening in Kathmandu. With a bit of wonder and awe, he reminded us all that without Marshall's intercession they might all have perished in the wind. During the afternoon, he estimated that wind gusts on the peak had reached seventy miles per hour. Then, inexplicably, he said, the summit's typical high velocity winds stopped for the night.

Marshall asked us all—*Was* it really so unexpected, so strange? After all, he subtly reminded his listeners, hadn't he prayed for just that? To which one true skeptic, a newsperson at the table with us, muttered, "Now, *really,* you don't *believe* that!?"

By the evening of May 3rd, after their horrendous overnight bivouac on the peak, the four American Everest summiteers were safe in the warmth of tents and sleeping bags at Camp 2 on the ice of the Western Cwm. The frostbite took its toll, however, and two climbers, Unsoeld and Bishop, had to be carried the rest of the way down to Base Camp and out of the mountains to safety and medical treatment. They had suffered the most from the cold, and later they lost various toes and fingers as testimony to their exploits. (Nine of Unsoeld's ten toes were later amputated, and Bishop lost all of his toes and tips of his little fingers.)

A few days later, Marshall got a message that the team was breaking camp and would be back on the air only from Namche Bazaar, the main Sherpa town two days' trek down the Khumbu valley. The strongest Sherpas were engaged to carry Unsoeld and Bishop that far. Marshall arranged a helicopter to airlift them off the ridge above Namche to the Shanta Bhawan Hospital in Kathmandu. He had phoned the American Embassy to set the dramatic rescue in motion.

"That ended almost ninety days of radio contact." Then, with a bit of well-earned pride, he said: "It was our little contribution to the successful American Mount Everest Expedition of 1963."

Epilogue

On April 9, 1992, as the 85-year old Fr Moran lay dying at Patan Hospital in Kathmandu, Jolene Unsoeld sent him the following message from her office in the U.S. House of Representatives in Washington DC. It poignantly brought back memories of the part he had played in the miraculous events on Mount Everest during the night of May 22-23, 1963:

> TO FATHER MORAN–9N1MM.
> I PRAY THAT THE LOVE AND GOODNESS YOU HAVE BROUGHT INTO THIS WORLD WILL CAUSE THE WIND TO CEASE WHEN YOU TRAVERSE THE SUMMIT TO YOUR NEXT ADVENTURE.
> MY LOVE TO YOU, FATHER MORAN.
> (SIGNED) JOLENE

On August 14, 1992, Father Marshall Moran was flown from Kathmandu to India for treatment. He passed away that evening at New Delhi's Holy Family Hospital (see Epilogue).

Notes to Chapter 15: Voice of Nepal

1. The United States Operations Mission (USOM) was an arm of the American government overseas, and predecessor to the U.S. Agency for International Development (USAID).
2. A dipole (or doublet) antenna is simply a wire strung between two poles, with the lead to the radio coming off the center of the wire. A beam antenna is usually constructed of aluminum pipe in the shape of a grid, mounted on a post (usually on top of a roof or a tower) so that it can be turned to tune radio waves.
3. Ken Hager and his wife, Elsie, were close friends of the author. Elsie was the author's godmother, and it was from Ken's ham shack in the mid-1960s that I first heard Fr Moran on the air, although I had already met him in person in Nepal, in 1964, while serving as an American Peace Corps Volunteer. A few years later I talked with Marshal Moran through a relay in Laos while operating my own small ham rig from Auke Bay, Alaska.
4. James Ramsey Ullman, *Americans on Everest* (1964, p.146).
5. *Ibid.* (p.100).
6. *Ibid.* (p.147). The American Ambassador was Henry Stebbins, and Bob Bates was the Peace Corps Director in Nepal.
7. *Ibid.* (pp.147, 193).
8. *Ibid.* (p.195).
9. The National Geographic Society was among the first to hear, after the King of Nepal, because of its major sponsorship of the expedition.
10. Also present in the ham shack with Fr Moran that evening was James Ramsey Ullman and Colonel Charles Wylie, the British embassy

military attaché. Colonel Wylie was a close personal friend of Willi and Jolene Unsoeld. He had been a member of the successful 1953 British Mount Everest Expedition with John Hunt, Edmund Hillary and others, and had spent many hours with Willi before the American expedition, pouring over pictures of the mountain, helping to plan the challenging West Ridge assault route. Wylie was therefore especially interested and anxious to listen in on the radio transmissions from the AMEE Base Camp that momentous day.

11. Unsoeld and Hornbein stayed for twenty minutes on top before beginning their descent towards the South Col in what would become the first traverse of Everest, west to east. During their brief walkie-talkie communication with Base Camp from the summit, Willi quoted a Robert Frost poem, apropos of the moment—"...*And I have promises to keep / And miles to go before we sleep / And miles to go before we sleep.*"

Willi's "promises" were to his wife, Jolene. After Everest, he told her, he would go on no more major mountaineering expeditions. The lines quoted were from Robert Frost's lyric poem 'Stopping by Woods on a Snowy Evening'; but Unsoeld changed the last two lines from *I* sleep to *we* sleep, to include Tom Hornbein.

After the expedition, Willi gave many lectures describing the climb. During one of them, someone in the audience suggested that because he and Hornbein had pioneered an entirely new route to the top, thus making mountaineering history, he could also have quoted the last three lines of another well known Frost poem, 'The Road Not Taken', which reads: "...*I took the one less traveled by / And that has made all the difference.*"

16

Friends Around the World

Amateur Radio: One World, One Language
Make Today Count
Peace to All Who Enter Here
   Mottos pasted on Fr Moran's radio shack door

A few months after the Mount Everest Expedition team had left Nepal, Colonel Gresham was transferred to the American Embassy in Argentina. Before leaving Kathmandu he gave Marshall his radio equipment. But he kept his call sign suffix, and talked to the world from Buenos Aires and other assignments as "Donald Duck" for several more years before he retired.

New Gear, Better QSOs

Gresham's single sideband equipment was a huge improvement for Marshall. Now he had the world at his fingertips, as close as the mike and the radio dial. His ability to talk regularly and clearly with hams on land and sea throughout Asia and the world was greatly improved. He was especially active in meeting sea captains while they crossed the Indian Ocean. Some skippered crude oil tankers from the Middle East bound for Pacific ports; others commanded freighters laden with produce and industrial goods. With the new, compact and sophisticated single sideband equipment that was available, a ship's captain could run a small amateur transceiver from his cabin, while his maritime radio officer carried on with official ship's traffic from the radio room.

During 1963, Marshall met many Asian hams and ships captains on the air. They talked regularly with one another, and it was out of such contacts that the SEANET was formed.

One such sea bound contact was Captain Bill Mulholland, whom Marshall later met in person on his twenty thousand ton tanker, off-loading American wheat in Bombay. Another was Captain Rusty Higginson, who hauled crude oil from Ra's Tannurah, Saudi Arabia, to the Philippines. Marshall talked to these fellows at about 4 p.m. Nepal time each day. That would be a few hours earlier in the Persian

Gulf. As Marshall described it, "Sailing east, when Rusty passed Ceylon and south India, we'd be on about the same time zone—though India and Nepal time are slightly off with the system of the rest of the world. Then, from Singapore, we'd be about two hours off, and from Manila, about three. We tried to meet on the air every day. I would make contact after classes were out each afternoon. Then, the school boys would crowd around and listen. We'd do this regularly, day after day."[1]

"One day," Marshall said, "Rusty told me he was going all the way to Hawaii and wanted to see if he could maintain contact every day. It was a challenge, something to shoot for. I knew it could only be accomplished with the best equipment under exceptionally good atmospheric conditions. We tried, and we did it."

As Rusty and his ship approached Hawaii, local radio amateurs in the islands began to pick up Marshall's signal and started pursuing a QSO with him. Contacts with ships at sea were *passé* for many Hawaiian hams, but a contact in the Himalayas was something special. They wanted to talk to what was, for them, a newly discovered station in Kathmandu.

One Hawaiian ham was very enthusiastic, so one day Marshall made a suggestion. "Let's surprise the tanker captain. Did you know that when he's in port he can't get off his ship to go to a hotel or out to a restaurant? He has to unload and turn around for the Gulf immediately. The poor guy. Why don't you take your wife and kids and some hamburgers and weenies down to the harbor and meet him? He'll be surprised, and you'll have a nice picnic and enjoy talking to each other."

They did it. Rusty was very pleased. "That's one way we hams can have a little fun," Marshall said.

After getting to know one another on the radio, the maritime mobiles and their land-based ham friends in Asia decided to form the SEANET—the South East Asia Network of Amateur Radio Operators (described in Chapter 13). Its purpose was to help out in case of emergencies and to keep each other company, especially the maritime mobiles who spend long weeks and months at a time on their lonely ships at sea.

As a co-founder and one of the eldest members, Marshall was given an honorary life membership. Then, to further improve his output, the SEANET members joined together to buy him a complete Drake radio station. When the R.L. Drake Company heard of it, they cut the price in half, probably thinking it was good advertisement. That was Marshall's first transceiver, a combination unit that transmits and receives on the same frequency. It was a marvelous improvement, one that allowed him even more power and clarity on the 15 and 20 meter bands (21 and 14 MHz, respectively).

The association with SEANET was one of Marshall's most cherished radio activities. He spent thousands of hours on the air with his friends and acquaintances at sea, speaking almost daily with the captains of the sea-going behemoths, from his tiny shack at Godavari School, in one of the most landlocked QTHs (locations) in the world.

Looking Back
The SEANET and Maritime Mobile Radio
Fr Moran

Our maritime mobile operations go like this. The ship captains each have US licenses with an MM, for Maritime Mobile, after their call sign. But this is only while they are out to sea. In port and anytime they are within three miles of shore, they have to ask permission from that country to operate as a portable unit—Portable-VU, for India, Portable-HS for Thailand, -JA for Japan, -DU for the Philippines, and so forth. Whether at sea or in port, they all try to meet our schedule each evening.

From the beginning, over twenty-five years ago, there has always been a big gang of land and sea hams to join in the club chatter each day. We meet regularly at 1200 hours UTC. Soon after we started, some British operators in Hong Kong got involved. Their call sign is VS6-, or Victor Sugar Six. Then came hams from Singapore, Malaysia, Indonesia and Ceylon. Even the Aussies and New Zealanders joined in. There used to be some good American hams operating from Vietnam, Laos and Cambodia, and in time we were joined by Americans living as far away as Afghanistan. Now, of course, the Indochina circuits and Afghanistan are gone and we are a geographically smaller group.[2]

We talk regularly with the maritime mobiles, the ships' captains, and from time to time we help them out with special information about wrecks, transportation news, emergencies, and just regular things. "I'm going to reach Singapore with some time off," one might say to a club friend on shore. "Will you be at home? Can you have a room ready? Let's have dinner together..." They are a friendly bunch.

Or we might hear of an emergency, a broken arm or leg or a cracked head from an accident aboard ship. "We need a doctor. Have an ambulance ready," followed by their estimated time of arrival in port. Once I picked up a "May Day" distress call from a small ship near Singapore that was being attacked by pirates. I told a Singapore ham to inform the Marine Police who did a quick rescue.

The early to mid-60s, when the SEANET got going, was a busy time for me. The SEANET is still going strong, although many of the old timers are gone. Through the SEANET I've made contact with an interesting medley of radio operators and ships' captains, some from as far away as Britain and Scandinavia, and throughout Southeast and East Asia. The Japanese are especially active in the net, but we've never held a convention in Japan. We're hoping one day to get an invitation from them.

The Net's first convention was in 1963. In the years since then we've met at Penang, Bangkok, Kuala Lampur, Singapore, Jakarta and Manila. I'm always invited. The members buy my tickets and provide great hospitality. I've stayed with some very warm-hearted, interesting people over the years, and have seen most of Asia for free. I owe these great amateur radio operators a great deal.

I especially remember one convention in the 1970s at Bangkok. The SEANET president was my host, a Thai army general in charge of his country's radio and television stations. He also ran a company making receivers and transmitters for the army. Radio engineering was his heart and soul.

He met me at the airport and took me in his car to the hotel. The car was outfitted with a portable transceiver. On the way through the traffic we talked to the SEANET-in-charge, or "net control" as we called him, to report my arrival.

The convention started out at 10 o'clock the following morning with technical talks and reports of various experiments by members. I spoke to them about the more than two dozen types of antennae I'd experimented with and various changes I'd made to the "specs" given in radio journal articles. It was all complicated technical talk, such things as a log periodic antenna, and broad band and directional antennas, and lead-ins to match the antenna to the transmitter and V-beams and verticals, and so forth. I had a good audience and got lots of questions. They were especially interested in how I overcame the unique transmission problems I'd encountered in Nepal by making modifications to my gear.

During the day we were given a tour of the Thai radio and television studios. And that evening we attended a grand banquet and heard a speech by the Thai government official in charge of all telecommunications. After that, as the eldest member and from one of the greatest distances and probably the operator farthest from the sea, I was asked to talk about interesting contacts I'd made over the air.

A Convention radio station had been installed to transmit at our regularly schedules time. When it started operating, I was given the mike to make the honorary first contacts with amateurs listening all over Southeast Asia. Those whom we contacted that evening were glad to get the special QSL card marked with the convention station call sign, HS0/SEA. It was a unique card to add to the collections of enthusiasts who like to plaster their walls with souvenirs from all the countries they've talked to.

The radio room was crowded and, after about twenty minutes with all the smoking and the heat, I passed the mike along to my Thai friend, Kamchai Chotikul, and made my escape to another room where there was an air conditioner. While sitting there I was surprised to hear Chopin waltzes and mazurkas coming from around the corner. I investigated and found a young Japanese radio operator playing a piano in a perfect classical style. I asked him to play some of Brahm's *Hungarian Dances*. He did, followed by something Japanese. But he was shy and must not have been prepared for that. "Let me play something Japanese for *you*," I said. "This is a tune we sang at my school when the crown prince and princess of Japan visited Nepal in 1975 for King Birendra's Coronation."

As I rippled through my little improvisation on the piano, he could see that my fingering was not exactly what they teach you in conservatories. He recognized the tune, though, and I asked if he knew the words. "No," he said. So I sang it for him as well, in Japanese. I had recorded the words in my little black notebook. He was delighted and we laughed together at the good fun of it.

Later that evening, when each country's hams were asked to dance or sing something from home, this same Japanese ham asked me for help. While my young friend played the piano, his compatriots and I sang the words out of my notebook to the great surprise, amusement and thundering applause of the crowd.

At Christmas, he wrote to thank me for helping the Japanese contingent save face that evening in Bangkok.

Help from 'Round the World

Marshall operated for several years with his Drake transceiver, but in the long run it was a problem for him. Modern transceivers depend on transistors that are, by nature, sensitive to power fluctuations. They don't do well in Nepal, where power surges, brown-outs and outages are all too common. The frequent power surges damaged the sensitive circuitry and when he had to fix a part, it required pulling an entire circuit board to send back to the manufacturer. That effectively put him off the air for weeks and months at a time. He had not had the Drake transceiver very long before he had to send a circuit board in for repairs, along with a letter explaining his problems with the poor electricity service. In return, the Drake Company sent back an older model that operated on the more reliable vacuum tubes. For his purposes it was a better rig.

He called this rig his Drake Twins, a model TR-4 transmitter and an R-4 receiver. "After that I stuck with the more old-fashioned tubes.

With tubes I could remove a burned out resistor, find the problem and repair it myself. And the wiring was bigger and easier to see and work with. While some operators will argue that the advantage of the transistorized gear is its small size and weight and all that, you really pay for it when you have trouble. If you can't fix it yourself, you've got to send it to the factory. Then they soak you twenty or thirty dollars an hour for labor and take weeks before they get it back to you."

Later, when hams from Sapporo, Japan, gave him a more modern transistorized Yaesu transceiver, he solved the line fluctuation problem by installing a voltage stabilizer and surge protector between it and the main circuit. "The Yaesu is small, powerful and convenient," he said after it was installed; but he still spoke with pride about his accomplishments with the Drake Twins.

Besides the transmitter, antennas are a key factor in radio transmission. Over the years, Marshall put up many different antennas, first in India and later in Nepal on the school at Jawalakhel and atop Xavier Hall at Godavari. He made most of them himself, except for the best one of all.

One evening Marshall contacted a Dutch ham, 7Z3AB, Henry Volkerts, operating from Saudi Arabia. Henry worked on contract there, in charge of all telecommunications for ARAMCO, the Arabian American Oil Company. Marshall talked to him almost every day for awhile.

Henry belonged to the local Arabian Knights club, a (k)night-time amateur network. It was he who had first introduced Marshall to a fellow club member, King Hussein of Jordan. Henry also had a bit of a sense of humor. One evening he challenged Marshall over the air: "I'm going to test you, Father," he said. "How does my signal sound?"

Marshall listened, then replied, "You are coming in two points louder than usual. What have you got, a new amplifier or a new antenna?"

"You're pretty sharp. You do watch your meter needles," said Henry. "I've got a new antenna. It's a six-element, three-band "trap antenna," the so-called "Thunderbird-6" model made by Telerex of Omaha, Nebraska. To reward you and because Christmas is coming, I am going to buy one for you, Father! So, now, how do I ship it out to Nepal?"

Marshall was taken aback, but he didn't protest Henry's generosity too loudly. "Look, Henry," he said, after he'd thought about it for a few minutes, "don't buy it from the factory. Order it from a dealer in San Francisco, instead. I've got a ham friend there who is coming out soon to Nepal to visit me. He can bring it to me direct."

Marshall's friend and Henry's gift arrived a few weeks later. It was held up in customs, but he retrieved it and the customs official saved face by noting that, after all, it was "just a bunch of aluminum pipes." Marshall installed it immediately, and began transmitting all the better.

Henry was not the only one to send him equipment. American hams were also very generous, and Marshall was not bashful when he needed something. Nor was he unthankful. When someone helped him out, it was soon well known among all those amateur operators who kept regularly in touch. For a long time the Drake Company supplied him with spare parts, until they went out of the radio business after the competition from Japan became too strong.

Many other friends around the world helped him whenever he needed something. They knew that as a priest he had no financial means of his own for buying new parts or replacing worn out equipment. One time a California DX club sent him a new microphone. Someone else sent him a new antenna rotator; they seemed to burn out more often than usual in the poor electrical conditions of Nepal.

School Boys on the Air

Marshall's hams shack was always open to curious boys from the school. And, if the door happened to be shut, they would knock politely and he let them in. For the school boys, the radio became a highly stimulating educational tool. The excitement his radio generated in the school is demonstrated by the photograph on Marshall's QSL card, of Marshall sitting at his rig, surrounded by a group of eager, bright-faced, smiling school boys.

"The boys learn a great deal from watching and listening," Marshall said. "Occasionally they join me to participate in radio contests and other events. Sometimes our contacts with other boys around the world stimulate them to exchange letters, postcards, photographs, drawings, paintings and cassette tapes filled with Nepalese folk music. Some of their artwork and stories about St Xavier's Godavari School has been featured in magazines in Germany, Britain, America, and Japan. I was very surprised one time when visiting a ham friend in Kyoto, Japan. He took me to a local school where I saw a whole wall, about twenty feet by twelve, completely covered with our boys' drawings. It was quite an exhibition!"

One year, the Godavari boys developed an especially close relationship with school boys in the German city of Tübingen. Their German school teacher was DJ9KR, Ulrich (Uli) Bihlmayer, a regular weekend contact for Marshall. Uli and his wife, Renate, even visited Kathmandu, three times. Uli's students periodically published a small magazine in English, which often featured Nepal and Nepalese pen friends.

Among his students, however, Marshall noted that their regular pen pals were not as well remembered and did not impress them as much as the friends they made by radio. "I think it is because of the characteristic of voice, the instantaneous exchange of ideas that radio allows, and the frequent good humor that takes place. The boys seem to remember and appreciate their radio friends more than those to whom they write and must wait weeks to hear back from."

Marshal gave this example: "One time some of my boys were listening to a group of Boy Scouts broadcasting from the Seychelles Islands. During that exchange, one of the Seychelles boys bragged how his islands were the 'Pearls of the Indian Ocean.' Promptly, one of our boys, whose name was Jwala, fired back that we in Nepal have the Himalayas—'The Diamonds of the World,' he said. To which the Seychelles scoutmaster said, '*Touché*! You win. You really outdid us on that exchange of boasting.' Jwala lived up to his name, which in Nepali means 'fire.' That boy was a real sparkler—very witty, very quick on the draw. It is such exchanges and such sharp boys that are best remembered by all."

Every year the Boy Scouts of the world hold a Jamboree on the Air. The purpose is to bring together scout radio operators and troops from around the world to talk with one another. Each Jamboree includes a contest where the young operators have to make as many contacts for their troop from as many nations as possible within a prescribed period of time.

The first time Marshall and students participated in it, he brought together Boy Scouts from St Xavier's High School and Girl Guides from St Mary's School. At the end of the day-long contest, they were among the top scorers, having talked with Asian scouts in Japan, The Philippines, Sri Lanka, India and Australia, and European scouts in England, The Netherlands, Norway and Sweden.

Ham Friends and Visitors

Marshall's radio contacts and special friends were not all from other countries. His Nepalese friends, many of them in the electronics business, were also among his closest associates and most frequent visitors. Many were "old boys," past graduates of St Xavier's Godavari and Jawalakhel Schools. Others were the parents and relatives of school boys. Some of his former students are still living in Kathmandu, but many are also scattered around the world, some of whom first learned about radio in Marshall's ham shack. Among them are several who gave him considerable help with his ham gear over the years, although in Nepal they could not officially operate as hams themselves.

One good Nepalese friend was Heramba Prasad Upadhyaya, who, as former Director of Telecommunications, helped Marshall get his first license. Heramba appreciated amateur radio and had some experience seeing hams operate. (Some of his superiors in the agency, however, being unaware of the true nature of the hobby, were generally unfavorable and negative towards it.) Since the beginning of ham radio in Nepal, starting with Mickey Mouse and friends after 1959, Marshall was virtually the only operator, expatriate or Nepalese, allowed to operate for any length of time under government license.

Once, during a formal reception, the King asked Marshall how his radio hobby was going. Marshall told him frankly, "Not well. My new license has been held up in the bureaucracy." The King promptly awarded him a license for life. "That solved *that* problem," said Marshall.

Another Nepalese, who was especially interested in amateur radio and assisted Marshall from time to time, was Krishna Khatri. As the Chief Engineer and Director for Radio Nepal, Krishna helped Marshall with repairs to a burned-out transformer and other parts.

Hari Saran Shrestha of Kathmandu was also quite gifted in electronics. Marshall met Hari through American friends with the U.S. Agency for International Development (USAID), when it was erecting a ropeway to haul freight from the lowlands over the mountains into the Kathmandu Valley. Hari expressed a strong interest in Marshall's radio and taught himself to read circuits and track down circuitry troubles, using an ARRL (American Radio Relay League) manual for guidance. Hari took up the radio listening hobby in the early 1960s. He quickly advanced far beyond Marshall in DX receiving. He also experimented with homemade dish antennas and satellite receivers.

The foremost radio amateur among Marshall's students was Pradyumna S. Rana, WB4NFO, who lived for many years in Alexandria, Virginia. "Rana, as he was called on the air, was one of the first boys I brought from Patna to help me open Godavari School."[3] He used to sit for hours at my elbow to listen and learn, read and study. He once put a Heathkit receiver together from a kit and then advanced far beyond his master. After going to the United States to study electronics, he stayed on to work for the telephone company in Washington DC."

Whenever Pradyumna came back to Nepal to visit his family, he would stop by "to chat with Father," as he put it. And, he regularly hosted Marshall during his periodic tours of ham clubs in America.

Bhakta S. Rana was one of Marshall's students who also went into electronics as a profession. He worked six years in Germany for Siemens, a prominent German industrial firm. When he returned to live in Nepal, he was put in charge of overseas circuits for his country's telephone and teletype operations. Later, he returned to Europe and traveled for the United Nations, setting up satellite receiving stations in Africa and training operators. He, too, always looked up Fr Moran when he was back in Nepal visiting family.

Ham visitors to Godavari came from all over the globe, representing almost every continent. At least ten or twelve times a year, operators visited Moran, radio friends with whom he talked on the air but had never seen. His most frequent radio visitors were from the United States. But many also came from European countries, including Germany and England, Spain and Italy.

They usually came one at a time. But, occasionally, Marshall entertained quite a crowd of hams. "One day the American ham, K9LF, Bill Brown, and his wife arrived in Kathmandu and came to see me. About the time they arrived, I was preparing to go to the airport to greet another radio amateur, Max Grossman, a tanker captain and one of my SEANET friends. When we all got back to the school, a German and a Swiss operator and their wives were waiting to see me. They had driven up from Delhi. Then an invitation arrived to join a Spanish ham from Madrid, EA3JC, José Cangas, for dinner in Kathmandu. We *all* went to dinner. The nine of us held a mini-convention of international dimensions that evening at a downtown hotel, brought together from around the world through amateur radio."

Sometimes his radio visitors joined Marshall as guest operators in the ham shack. "I've had guest operators from at least six countries, like Australia and Japan, from South and North America, several from Poland, and a few from other countries in Eastern Europe. One, an American named Thomas Warren, visited Godavari during a worldwide contest and logged over a thousand contacts in one twenty-four hour period. Tom didn't get much sleep. But, I'm not that avid," said Marshall. "I'm not so dedicated to sacrifice my sleep and my time to make that many contacts. The strain is too much for me."

The Yugoslavian Morse code champion, Tom Dugec, operated CW from Godavari one time while visiting Fr Moran during a Yugoslavian mountaineering expedition. Marshall had great admiration for Dugec's patience and stamina and referred to him, jokingly, as "that CW-nut."[4]

Marshall operated exclusively by voice, never by CW using Morse code. His reasons reveal something of his feelings and his approach to people. "You can't tell the other fellow's character, or tone of voice, on CW," he pointed out. "You can't tell whether he is pleased or smiling or what. CW is a machine operation, mechanical, like talking to a robot. And it's so slow. I can have a station a minute by voice, you see. You can't do that on CW. The other thing is, on CW you don't know if Bill or Joe, or whoever, is fat or thin or what! But, I can tell a lot from their voices—I can even tell their ages."

"I told a Russian once, when we had a good contact—now this is a good story, about a Russian ham operator named Willi—I said: 'Willi, you're seventeen years old.' And he said, 'Yes, I am.' Then I said, 'You're in engineering college.' 'Yes, Father. I am!' he said with some excitement. And how did I know all this? By listening. You learn a lot about people over the years just by listening. Now Willi is a professor in that same college and he loves talking to me."

Marshall described Willi as one of the first Russian operators to "melt," as hams put it; to become mellow, that is, and friendly, able to talk about his family and life in Russia. It took some Western hams a long time to warm up to the Russians, however, even to the so-called "melted" ones.

Back in the 1960s, when the first few Russian hams got their licenses, their signals were quite messy (unclear) and many hams did not want to talk with them, complaining that their English was bad, their signals were weak, they drifted around the band, or they lacked good manners on the air. In short, the Russians were perceived as not conforming well to amateur radio etiquette. But even before glasnost and perestroika, some of the Russian hams began putting out better signals. "They're among the best on the air now," Marshall once said, in the late 1980s. "I know, because I am one who talks often with the Russians. They've improved their image tremendously."

Part of the change was based on the great accomplishments of the former USSR in space science and the fact that the officials gave some of the geniuses of that program considerable latitude for self-expression. Ham radio is one form of self-expression, and it has been all to the good of the hobby. Marshall came to think of the Russians as "perfect gentlemen. But it took time. I've read some of their technical books on antennas. They are really excellent. Beautiful research and nice fellows to meet on the air."

"Ham radio is more than just a personal hobby. It is a means of international friendship and a valuable service to Hindu, Buddhist, Christian, Marxist, atheist, agnostic, Jew, Muslim, and even royalty. All republics of the former Soviet Union speak to us as friends and wish us their Merry Christmas and Easter greetings and let us talk of their families. One friend recently remembered my birthday and recalled that his last chat with me was seventeen years ago. Then he spoke of his wife and child and said I was one of his oldest friends from student days when he was a teenager. Is this not daily ecumenism?"

"You get to know people pretty well on ham radio," Marshall said in one of his reflective moments, "even when you never see them face-to-face. Just listening. It's what makes amateur radio so fascinating. It brings people together."

Then, he paused and asked: "Do you see that sign on my door? Someone sent it in the mail. That sign says it all: *Amateur Radio: One World, One Language.*"

The motto reflected Fr Marshall Moran's passion for ecumenism, oneness or unity, among all the people of the world. Ham radio fostered his personal expression of it. There were also other signs on the door. One read *Make Today Count* and another said *Peace to All Who Enter Here.*

And, next to them was a stuffed Mickey Mouse doll someone sent him. Taken together, all this radio shack graffiti reflected the complex character that was Marshall Moran. He was both a spiritual man and a man infatuated with the people of the world. He was serious but not without a spark of joy and a rich sense of humor. Ham operators remember him as an avid DX radio amateur, as the "Radio Amateur Voice of Nepal" and "Ham Priest of the Himalayas." On the air, he was one of the world's most famous DX amateur radio operators who, since 1992, is referred to, respectfully, by international hams, as a "silent key."

Notes to Chapter 16: Friends Around the World
1, Standard time in India is one half hour off the regular time zone (GMT + 5:30), while Nepal operates 45 minutes off (GMT + 5:45), putting it 15 minutes ahead of India. It has something to do with national pride.
2. Marshall was referring here to the late 1980s.
3. As a boy, it was Pradyumna Rana who accompanied Marshall on his first trek into Kathmandu in 1949 and was in the first batch of Nepalese school boys to enroll at Godavari. When Godavari School opened on July 1, 1951, Fr Moran selected Pradyumna Rana as one of the first school captains because he knew the routine and the rules from his previous schooling at the Jesuit school in Patna. His roll number, used for billing purposes and sewn on his clothing and other items of boarding school kit, was 'Number 1.'
4. Besides Moran's guest operators, a number of Japanese hams and a few of other nationalities were allowed to broadcast from the Nepal Boy

Scout headquarters in downtown Kathmandu, courtesy of Krishna Khatri of the Nepal Telecommunication Secretariat (in affiliation with the International Telecommunications Union of the United Nations).

Epilogue

The incommunicable part of us is the pasture of God.
Teilhard de Chardin, SJ

All things work together unto good for those who love God
Fr Moran's working motto, Romans 8.28

The Last Days
Fr Marshall Denis Moran, SJ, died at age eighty-five on the evening of Tuesday, April 14, 1992, at Holy Family Hospital, New Delhi.

He had been feeling unwell for several weeks, with occasional breathlessness as early as the previous Christmas. In the interim he was seen by two Nepalese doctors, one of whom had been a Godavari students. By April 4, his condition had worsened. It was Saturday, the Nepal Jesuit's Sabbath (Sundays being a normal school day in Nepal), and after mass Fr Jim Dressman gave Marshall the Sacrament of the Sick, then drove him to the Patan Hospital for medical observation and treatment. He was put under the care of one American and several Nepalese doctors, and was watched after round the clock. Jesuit Fathers and Brothers took turns staying with him.

This time of personal crisis for Marshall was also a time of national crisis for Nepal. For several days, as if to commemorate the second anniversary of the April 1990 Movement to Restore Democracy (Nepal's democratic revolution, the *Jana Andolan* or People's Movement), the streets of Kathmandu and Patan were alive again with riot police and angry young men agitating against what they perceived to be inequities in the new democratic order and in support of a variety of alternative political agendas. Several demonstrators were killed and some of the most severely wounded were brought to the Patan Hospital for treatment. They were placed in rooms quite near where Fr Moran was resting. A strict nighttime curfew was announced and visiting the hospital was difficult.

One afternoon, the supreme leader of the ruling Congress Party, Mr Ganesh Man Singh, paid a visit to the hospital to console those wounded in the demonstrations. When he heard that Fr Moran was in a room just down the hall, he went in and asked to speak to the ailing priest. Fr Moran recognized the distinguished visitor and took his hand. Then, Ganesh Man Singh told Marshall what many people felt: "Thank you, Father, for all that you have done for our country."

After several days without improvement, the medical staff advised the Nepal Jesuits that Marshall should be taken to India for further evaluation and treatment of his illness. On Tuesday morning, April 14, he was flown to New Delhi and was admitted about midday to the Holy Family Hospital Accompanying him from Kathmandu were Fr Jim Dressman and Sister Lisa Perekkatt. The evening of that same day he died of congestive heart failure, following acute symptoms of an internal malignancy. After simple rites, he was cremated and his ashes returned to Nepal.[1]

Life's Coincidences and Connections

Marshall's life and his death were full of coincidences and connections.

In March 1942, two young Catholic Euro-Indian boys, Alan and Darryl de Lastic, appeared at the doors of Patna's St Xavier's School seeking admission. They were war refugees and had just arrived in India after fleeing their home in Burma, which was being invaded by the imperial army of Japan. The Jesuit priests promptly enrolled both of the boys in Class VII. Alan remembers meeting Fr Moran at the school shortly after he arrived. "Father Moran struck me as being very kind and... very efficient because the school was well organized and maintained strict discipline," he later said. Years afterward he heard that Fr Moran had left India for Nepal.

Shortly after noon on the day of Marshall's death, the Archbishop of the Delhi Diocese, Most Reverend Alan de Lastic, visited Holy Family Hospital When he heard that Fr Moran had just arrived from Nepal and was being treated for an illness, he went to the room. The Father Superior was there with him and said to Fr Moran, "The Archbishop of Delhi has come to see you," to which Moran replied in a surprisingly loud and clear voice, "What a privilege!"

Archbishop de Lastic recalls that "These were the last words I heard from him. I then gave him a blessing and he crossed himself with profound respect. I was sorry to hear that he passed on a few hours later. I had not seen him for forty years."[2]

On February 3, 1966, a premature baby boy was born at the Shanta Bhawan Hospital in Kathmandu to an Indian Christian couple from Kerala. The father, Joseph Thomas, was a teacher at St Xavier's Jawalakhel School where Fr Moran was principal. The birth was difficult and there was concern throughout the Catholic community that both mother and baby might not survive. The child was placed in an incubator and watched over day and night. Fr Moran and other priests and teachers from the school came by often to see and bless the mother, and to pray for the life of the premature baby whom they had baptized Thomas Sachdev Prakash. Mother and son survived but shortly thereafter the family moved back to India.

In the early evening of April 14, 1992, the young twenty-six year old Dr Thomas S. Prakash, MD, was making his rounds of Holy Family Hospital. He looked at the chart for Fr Moran's room and recognized the name immediately. He knew of Fr Moran, he said later, because his father "used to talk a lot about him, his mission and the ham radio. I went to his room around 5:30 p.m. I told the persons around him of how I had heard about Fr Moran from my father. They tried to tell Fr Moran that. I don't know if he understood, but he held my hands in a gesture of blessing and said "God bless you, Doctor."

"Around 9 p.m. I went up to see him again. A senior doctor and staff nuns were around him. Fr Moran was gasping. Soon he had a cardiac arrest. I initiated a cardiac massage..., but despite our efforts he died. A mass was said soon after, beside his body. I was sad. Here was Father who had prayed so that I would live, and here was I, writing out his death certificate."[3]

Memorial Service

Six days later, on the Monday evening after Easter, April 20, 1992, a memorial service was held in Kathmandu on the spacious grounds of St Xavier's Jawalakhel School, which Marshall Moran had founded 38 years before. Nearly a thousand of Marshall's friends and devotees attended—Christians, Hindus and Buddhists alike. Eight hundred signed the condolence book, testimony to Fr Moran's respect and fame.

Fr Marty Coyne, Principal of Jawalakhel School, arranged the ceremony. He had the handball courts painted as the backdrop to the altar, set up the altar and accouterments and provided an amplifier system. Students from the school's leadership training program, guided by Br Jim Gates, managed parking for the overflow crowd. Fr Jim Dressman provided the coffin in which the urn with Fr Moran's ashes was placed.

The memorial ceremonies were presided over by Monsignor Antu Sharma, SJ, who gave the homily and led the service, some parts in Nepali, some in English. A small parish choir sang hymns. Eighteen priests, forming a semi-circle around the altar, concelebrated the funeral mass in its full Roman Catholic form, including blessings, prayers and Holly Communion. For the many non-Catholics present, a *Prasad* (gift of rose petals) was offered. As Fr Jim Donnelly noted, "Something was there for everyone." During the service scores of people silently approached the coffin to lay flowers, and several

Tibetans among them draped it with traditional white silk ceremonial *khata* scarves of greeting and departure.

Following the mass, Fr John Locke, the Acting President of the Nepal Jesuits, spoke on behalf of the Nepal Jesuit Society to thank everyone for attending and showing their respects. A formal condolence card from the royal palace was acknowledged and two letters were read aloud to the audience, one from the Honorable Prime Minister, Mr Girija Prasad Koirala, and one from the Congress Party's leader, Ganesh Man Singh. Some people quietly noted that the king had not come, his absence was conspicuous but not unexpected. Despite his lifelong friendship with Fr Moran, the king, as a Hindu monarch and someone considered sacred by millions of his subjects, was constrained by ancient custom to avoid association with death pollution, and contact with persons in mourning outside of the royal family was strictly prohibited.

Several prominent persons who were closely associated with the history of Nepal's St Xavier's Schools spoke to the mourners. Mr Panchaman Lama, who had worked for so many years beside Fr Moran at the Jawalakhel and Godavari schools, remembered him on behalf of the school community. He described Fr Moran as everyone knew him—a walking encyclopedia of the history of Nepal and a dictionary of names related to it. He also told how Fr Moran never seemed to run out of jokes and puns, and had a way of keeping people smiling all the time. Then a former student from the first batch at Godavari in 1951, the Nepalese movie actor, Mr Himalaya Lohani (previously known to his classmates as Surendra Lohani), gave a moving personal recollection. He spoke of occasions, both serious and funny, when Fr Moran's compassionate concern and good cheer saved the day. Like the time one boy was badly burned and Marshall rushed him to the hospital in town, and the time they were all hiking up Pulchowki Hill behind the school when a violent thunder and hail storm assailed them. His response was a bevy of his inevitable jokes, to calm the younger boys and take the fear out of their eyes.

Then Fr Dressman greeted the audience and announced that final interment of the Nepal Jesuit Mission's Father Founder would be held at Godavari Ashram out at Godavari School later in the evening. When it was time to go, a steady stream of cars, mini-buses, vans and motorcycles, over 150 people in all, drove solemnly south along the same road to Godavari that Fr Moran first took in search of a school site on a sunny Saturday in October 1949.

Marshall Denis Moran rests there now, in the gardens of Godavari School, in that "great paradise for birds...," as he called it. "A little wild and isolated, perhaps, but all the better for teaching, undisturbed..."

Notes to the Epilogue

1. I last saw Fr Moran sleeping peacefully in the Patan Hospital, in Nepal, a few hours before his departure for New Delhi, India. I was unable, however, to attend his memorial service the following week (I was away from Kathmandu at the time). The events of his last day and of the funeral were told to me by Frs Jim Donnelly and John Locke, and by my wife Kareen and daughter Liesl. The Most Reverent Alan de Lastic, Archbishop of Delhi, and Dr Thomas Prakash, MD, of Holy Family Hospital in New Delhi, filled in some of the details of Fr Moran's last hours. I thank them all for their consideration and help.
2. Most Reverend Alan de Lastic, Archibishop of Delhi, personal communication, 1992.
3. Dr Thomas S. Prakash, MD, Holy Family Hospital, New Delhi, personal communication, 1992.

Bibliography

Allen, Charles, 1983, *A Mountain in Tibet: The Search for Mount Kailas and the Sources of the Great Rivers of India*, London: Futura/Macdonald and Co.

Allen, Charles, 2008, *The Buddha and Dr Führer: An Archaeological Scandal*, London: Haus Publishing.

Anonymous, n.d., 'Teachers and staff members of St Xavier's Godavari School: 1951-1986', Kathmandu: Nepal Jesuit Society (unpublished mimeograph).

Anonymous, 1970, 'Theater: Laughter in the dark' (a review of 'Sheep on the runway,' a stage play by Art Buchwald), *Time* magazine, February 16, 1970; online at www.time.com/time/magazine/article/0,9171,904182,00.html.

ARRL, 2002, '*CQ* [magazine] announces CQ Amateur Radio Hall of Fame Class of 2002', ARRL (American Radio Relay League) online; online at www.arrl.org/news/stories/2002/05/31/102/.

Assarikudy, A.V. Mathew, SJ, 1991, 'The Society of Jesus and Jesuits in Asia.' An unpublished speech presented on October 4, at Godavari School on the occasion of the 40th anniversary of Godavari and 25th anniversary of the Godavari Alumni Association.

Bangert, William V., SJ, 1972, *A History of the Society of Jesus*, St Louis, Missouri: Institute of Jesuit Sources.

Barthel, Manfred, 1931, *Jesuits: History and Legend of the Society of Jesus*, translated and adapted by Mark Howson, New York: William Morrow.

Bell, Sir Charles, 1931, *The Religions of Tibet*, Oxford, UK: Clarendon Press.

Buchwald, Art, 1970, 'Sheep on the runway' (stage play); see Anonymous (1970).

Chethipuzha, Stephen, SJ and Jose Murican, SJ, 1989, *A Framework for School Renewal: Based on the Characteristics of Jesuit Education*, New Delhi: Jesuit Educational Association of India.

Coyne, Marty, SJ, 1991, p.25 in GAA, *Godavari Alumni Association (GAA) 25th Anniversary, St Xavier's School 40th Anniversary, 1951-1991*, Kathmandu: St Xavier's School.

Cuthbert, R.P., 1930, *The Capuchins*, London: Sheed and Ward.

Desideri, Ippolito, SJ, 1932, *An Account of Tibet: The Travels of Ippolito Desideri of Pistoia, SJ, 1712-1727*, edited by Filippo de Filippi, London: George Routledge & Sons.

Diwaker, R.R., 1969, *Saga of Satyagraha*, New Delhi: Gandhi Peace Foundation, and Bombay: Bharatiya Vidya Bhavani.

Dixit, Kanak Mani, 2009, 'The passing of two Jesuit Nepali scholars', *Nepali Times* (Kathmandu), No. 443 (20-26 March); online at www.nepalitimes.com.np/issue/2009/03/20/Tribute/15781.

Donnelly, James J., SJ, 1991, 'Ten years at Godavari, 1981-1991,' pp.19-23 in GAA, ed., *Godavari Alumni Association (GAA) 25th Anniversary, St Xavier's School 40th Anniversary, 1951-1991*, Kathmandu: St Xavier's School.

Donnelly, James J., SJ, 1986, '1965—Banner year at Godavari School', in *St Xavier's Godavari 1951-1986 Anniversary Souvenir*, Kathmandu: St Xavier's Godavari School.

Durrwell, Francis-Xavier, CSSR, 1960, *The Resurrection: A Biblical Study*, translated (from *Ressurection de Jesus: Mysteire de Salut*) by Rosemary Sheed, New York: Sheed and Ward.

Eliot, T.S., 1963, 'Little Gidding' ('Four Quartets' [1943]) pp.200-209 in *Collected Poems, 1909-1962*, New York: Harcourt, Brace.

Fisher, Louis, ed., 1963, *The Essential Gandhi: An Anthology*, London: George Allen & Unwin.

Fleming, Robert L., Sr., Robert L. Fleming, Jr and Lain Singh Bangdel, 1976, *Birds of Nepal*, Kathmandu: Avalok.

Fletcher, Grace Nies, 1964, *The Fabulous Flemings of Kathmandu: The Story of Two Doctors in Nepal*, New York: E.P. Dutton.

Forbes, Ann A., 1989, *Settlements of Hope: An Account of Tibetan Refugees in Nepal*, Boston: Cultural Survival, Inc.

GAA, 1991, *Godavari Alumni Association (GAA) 25th Anniversary, St Xavier's School 40th Anniversary, 1951-1991*, Kathmandu: St Xavier's School.

Gandhi, Mohandas K., 1927, *An Autobiography: The Story of My Experiments with Truth*, translated from the Gujarati original by Mahadev Desai, Ahmedabad, India: Navajivan Publishing House.

Gandhi, Mohandas K., 1932, *Speeches and Writings of Mahatma Gandhi*, Madras, India: Natesan.

Gandhi, Mohandas K., 1962, *The Teaching of the Gita* (edited and published by Anand T. Hingorani), Bombay: Bharatiya Vidya Bhavan.

Gandhi, Mohandas K., 1919-31, *Young India* (a periodical in 13 volumes), Ahmedabad, India.

Ganss, George E., SJ, 1970, 'Commentary and Introduction' to *The Constitutions of the Society of Jesus* by St Ignatius of Loyola, St Louis, Missouri: Institute of Jesuit Sources.

Garraghan, Gilbert J., SJ, 1938, *The Jesuits of the Middle United States*, vol.3, New York: America Press.

Gilson, Etienne, 1924, *The Philosophy of St Thomas Aquinas*, Cambridge, UK: W. Heffer & Sons.

Giuseppe, Father, Prefect of the Roman Mission (communicated by John Shore, Esq.), 1801, 'Account of the Kingdom of Nepal: Being an account of the consolidation of power within the Cat'hmandu Valley by Prit'hwinarayan, founder of the Shah Dynasty during the years 1767-1771,' *Asiatic Researches* (Journal of the Asiatic Society), vol.2.

Goldstein, Melvyn C., 1989, *A History of Modern Tibet, 1913-1951*, Berkeley: University of California Press.

Govinda, Lama Anagarika, 1966, *The Way of the White Clouds*, London: Hutchinson.

Gschwend, Joseph A., SJ., 1925, *The Patna Mission, India: In Charge of the Jesuit Fathers of the Missouri Province*, St Louis, Missouri: St Louis University.

Guinness, Alec, 1985, *Blessings in Disguise*, London: Hamish Hamilton.

Hagen, Toni, 1960, *Nepal: The Kingdom of the Himalayas*, Berne, Switzerland: Kummerley and Frey.

Hale, Thomas, 1954, *Don't Let the Goats Eat the Loquat Trees: Adventures of an American Surgeon in Nepal*, Grand Rapids, Michigan, Zondervan Books.

Halsall, Paul, editor, 2009, *Internet Medieval Sourcebook*, Fordham University, Bronx, New York; online at www.fordham.edu/halsall/source/aug-city2.html.

Han, Suyin, 1958, *The Mountain is Young*, New York: Putnam.

Harrer, Heinrich, 1954, *Seven Years in Tibet*, New York: E.P. Dutton.

Huc, M. L'Abbé, 1873, *Christianity in China, Tartary and Thibet*, 2 vols., New York and Montreal: D. & J. Sadlier & Co.

Hunt, John, 1953, *The Ascent of Everest*, London: Hodder & Stoughton.

Huxley, Aldous, 1944, *The Perennial Philosophy*, New York: Harper & Bros.

Jinpa, Geshe Gelek, Charles Ramble and Carroll Dunham, with photographs by Thomas L. Kelly, 2005, *Sacred Landscape and Pilgrimage in Tibet: In Search of the Lost Kingdom of Bön*, New York and London: Abbeville Press.

Lahiri, Manosi, 2007, *Here Be Yaks: Travels in Far West Tibet*, Branford, CT.: The Intrepid Traveler (first published in India by Stellar Publishers, 2006).

Levi, Sylvain, 1905, *Le Nepal: Etude Historique d'un Royaume Hindou*, 3 vols. Paris: E. Leroux.

Lindell, Jonathan, 1979, *Nepal and the Gospel of God*, New Delhi: Masihi Sahitya Sanstha.

Locke, John K., SJ, 1980, *Karunamaya: The Cult of Avalokitesvara–Matsyendranath in the Valley of Nepal*, Kathmandu: Sahayogi Prakash, for the Research Center for Nepal and Asian Studies, Tribhuvan University.

Locke, John K., SJ, 1986, *Jesuits in Nepal, 1628-1985: A Vamsavali* (Chronology), Kathmandu: Nepal Jesuit Society (revised, mimeographed).

Locke, John K., SJ, 2001, 'Fr. Marshall D. Moran, SJ.', *Fiftieth Anniversary Book*; online at http://nepaljesuits.org/nepal-jesuit-society/fr-marshall-d-moran-sj/.

Locke, John K., SJ, 2009 (1985), *Buddhist Monasteries of Nepal: A Survey of the Bahas and Bahis of the Kathmandu Valley*, Bangkok: Orchid Press/

Loyola, St Ignatius of, 1970, *The Constitutions of the Society of Jesus*, translated with commentary and introduction by George E. Ganss, SJ, St Louis, Missouri: Institute of Jesuit Sources (first published in 1609).

MacGregor, John, 1970, *Tibet: A Chronicle of Exploration*, London: Routledge.

Malhotra, Inder, 1975, 'Indifference to history: Painful lesson of the Advani-Jinnah episode', *The Tribune*, June 17 (Chandigarh, India); online at www.tribuneindia.com/2005/20050617/edit.htm#top.

Maritain, Jacques, 1933, *St Thomas Aquinas* (trans. J.F. Scanlan), London: Sheed & Ward.

Maritain, Jacques, 1958, *St Thomas Aquinas* (trans. J.W. Evans and P. O'Reilly), New York: Meridian Books.

Martin, Malachi, 1987, The Jesuits, New York: Simon and Shuster.

Messerschmidt, Don, 2004, *Against the Current: The Life of Lain Singh Bangdel — Writer, Painter and Art Historian of Nepal*, Bangkok: Orchid Books.

Miller, Casper, SJ, 1979, *Faith-Healers in the Himalaya*, Kathmandu: Centre for Nepal and Asian Studies, Tribhuvan University (rev. ed., 1997, Delhi: Book Faith India).

Miller, Casper, SJ, 1990, *Decision Making in Village Nepal*, Kathmandu: Sahayogi Press.

Nehru, Jawaharlal, 1936, *An Autobiography*, London: John Lane.

Nigg, Walter, 1959, *Warriors of God: The Great Religious Orders and Their Founders*, translated and edited by Mary Ilford, New York: Knopf.

Nikhilananda, Swami, translator, 1944, *The Bhagavad Gita: Translated from the Sanskrit, with Notes, Comments, and Introduction*, New York: Ramakrishna-Vivekananda Center.

Oiz, Henry Pascual, SJ, 1991, *Blessed of the Lord: A History of the Patna Jesuits, 1921-1981*, Patna, Bihar, India: Patna Jesuit Society.

Outler, Albert C., translator and editor, 1955, *Augustine: Confessions*, Philadelphia: Westminster Press; online at www.fordham.edu/halsall/basis/confessions-bod.html.

Pallen, Conde and John Wynne, editors, 1929, *The New Catholic Dictionary: A Complete Reference on Every Subject*, New York: Universal Knowledge Foundation.

Pandey, Kumar, 1998, 'A life worth remembering' (a review of *Moran of Kathmandu* by Donald A. Messerschmidt, 1997), *The Nepal Digest*; online at www.thenepaldigest.org/archive/the-nepal-digest-july-2-1998.html.

Peissel, Michel, 1966, *Tiger for Breakfast: The Story of Boris of Kathmandu—Adventurer, Big Game Hunter, and Host of Nepal's Famous Royal Hotel*, London: Hodder and Stoughton, and New York: E.P. Dutton.

Petech, Luciano, 1952-56, *I Missionari Italiani nel Tibet e nel Nepal*, in series Il Nuovo Ramusio II, 7 vols., Rome: Istituto Italiano per il Medio ed Estremo Oriente (IsMEO).

Prabhavananda, Swami and Christopher Isherwood, translator, 1945, *Bhagavad Gita: The Song of God*, Hollywood, California: The Marcell Rodd Co.

Pradhan, Kumar, 1991, *The Gorkha Conquests: The Process and Consequences of the Unification of Nepal with Particular Reference to Eastern Nepal*, Calcutta: Oxford University Press.

Radhakrishnan, S., 1953, *Bhagavadgita*, London: George Allen & Unwin.

Rahner, Karl, SJ, 1961, *Theological Investigations* (translated from *Schriften zur Theologie*) by Cornelius Ernst, Baltimore: Helicon Press.

Riccardi, Theodore, 1990, 'The Nevars of Chuhari', in Paolo Daffina ed., *Indo-Sino-Tibetica: Studi in Onore di Luciano Petech*, Studi Orientali, v.9, pp.291-303, Rome: Bardi Editore.

Samudra (N3RDX and S21X), 2004, 'South East Asia amateur radio operators on disaster mitigation: Amateur radio operators on disaster mitigation,' posted on the *Net Gold Listserv List*, December 28, 2004; online at listserv.temple.edu/cgi-bin/wa?A2=ind0412&L=net-gold&T=0&P=83492.

St Xavier's Alumni Association, 1990, *St Xavier's High School Patna: 50th Anniversary, 1940-1990, Golden Jubilee Souvenir*, Patna, Bihar, India: St Xavier's Alumni Association.

Sever, Adrian, 1993, *Nepal Under the Ranas*, New Delhi: Oxford & IBH.

Scheen, Fulton J., 1967, 'The hound of heaven' in G. Krishnamurti, editor, *The Hound of Heaven: A Commemorative Volume*, London: The Francis Thompson Society.

Sharkey, Gregory, SJ, 2001, *Buddhist Daily Ritual: The Nitya Puja in Kathmandu Valley Shrines*, Bangkok: Orchid Press.

Society of Jesus/Oregon Province, 2009, 'The Spiritual Exercises of St. Ignatius'; online at www.nwjesuits.org/JesuitSpirituality/SpiritualExercises.html.

Staal, Frits, 1986, 'In the realm of the Buddha,' *Natural History* magazine (USA), vol.85, no.7 (July), pp.34-35.

Stiller, Ludwig F., SJ, 1970, 'A letter of Fr Giuseppe da Roveto, December 29, 1769', *Tribhuvan University Journal* (Kathmandu), vol.5, no.1 (June).

Stiller, Ludwig F., SJ, 1973, *The Rise of the House of Gorkha: A Study in the Unification of Nepal 1768-1816* (Bibliotheca Himalayica, Series 14, Volume 15), New Delhi: Manjushri Publishing House

Stiller, Ludwig F., SJ, 1976, *The Silent Cry: The People of Nepal 1816-1839*, Kathmandu: Sahayogi Prakashan.

Stiller, Ludwig F., SJ, and Ram Prakash Yadav, 1979, *Planning for People: A Study of Nepal's Planning Experience*, Kathmandu: Sahayogi Prakashan for the Research Centre for Nepal and Asian Studies, Tribhuvan University.

Stiller, Ludwig F., SJ, editor, 1981, *Letters from Kathmandu: The Kot Massacre*, Kathmandu: Research Centre for Nepal and Asian Studies, Tribhuvan University.

Stiller, Ludwig F., SJ, 1993, *Nepal: Growth of a Nation*, Kathmandu: Human Resources Development Research Center.

Taylor, Dan'l, 2009, *Cairns—A Novel of Tibet: The People and Splendid Place*, Franklin, WV: For Words Press (www.forwordspress.com).

Thomas, Lowell, 1977, *So Long Until Tomorrow: From Quaker Hill to Kathmandu*, New York: William Morrow and Co.

Ullman, James Ramsey, 1964, *Americans on Everest: The Official Account of the Ascent Led by Norman G. Dyhrenfurth*, Philadelphia, Pennsylvania: J.B. Lippincott.

Vannini, Fulgentius, OFM, Cap., 1966, *Bishop Hartman* (new edition), Allahabad, Uttar Pradesh, India: St Paul's Publications.

Vannini, Fulgentius, OFM, Cap., 1977, *Christian Settlements in Nepal During the Eighteenth Century*, New Delhi: Devarsons.

Wefle, Richard A., SJ, 1963, *Pieces of India*, Chicago: Loyola University Press.

Wessels, Cornelius, SJ, 1932, 'Introduction' to *An Account of Tibet* by Ippolito Desideri, London: George Routledge & Sons.

Wessels, Cornelius, SJ, 1924, *Early Jesuit Travellers in Central Asia, 1603-1722*, The Hague: Martinus Nijhoff.

Whelpton, John, 2005, *A History of Nepal*, Cambridge, UK: Cambridge University Press.

Index

A
Account of Tibet (Desideri) 73, 83n, 84n, 100n, 186
Acharya, Tanka Prasad 223, 229, 236
Acquaviva, Claudio 268
African Queen 256
Agnew, Spiro 255
Aida 17
Aishwarya, Queen
   see Shah, Aishwarya
Akbar the Great 64, 69, 115
Alacoque, St Margaret Mary 55
Alban, Heraclitis 122
Aldrin, Edwin ('Buzz') 300
Alexander the Great 169
Alexander, Calvert 41
All India Radio (AIR) 169, 314, 316-17, 322
Allen, Charles 61n, 75, 84n
Alter, David 218
amateur ('ham') radio
   see radio
America (magazine) 138
American Mount Everest Expedition (AMEE)
   see Everest; radio, mountaineering
amoebic dysentery 124, 126
Amram, Edwin 292
Andrade (Andrada), Antony 75-81, 84n
Angelo, Kevin 111, 131
Apollo-11 258-59
Apostolic Carmelite Sisters 159
Arabian American Oil Company (ARAMCO) 166, 339
Archbishop of Calcutta
   see Perier
Archbishop of Cleveland 15
Archbishop of Delhi
   see de Lastic
Armstrong, Edwin H. 307, 317n
Ascent of Everest (Hunt) 215
Ashoka 60, 236
Assarikudy, A.V. Mathew 284, 286n
astronauts 258-60, 300
Aufschnaiter, Peter 238, 248
Auten, Al 326ff
Autobiography (Gandhi) 170n
Autobiography (Nehru) 170n
Azevedo, Francisco de 80

B
Ballet Russes 237

Bangdel, Lain Singh 197n, 243, 261n
Bangert, W.V. 69, 82n, 83n
Barthel, Manfred 146n
Bates, Robert 326, 332n
Batson, Marion 42, 151
Bell, Charles 86, 89, 100n
Benedict de Goes ('Br Bento') 75
Benigna, Mother Superior, St Mary's School, Kathmandu 219
Berger, Ralph 307-08
Bettiah, India 40, 71. 72. 93, 97, 99, Ch. 6 *passim*, 126, 131, 137, 139, 140, 148, 162, 163, 179, 180, 185, 280, 311
Bhagavad Gita 138, 147, 152-55, 170n, 171n,
    Bhagavad Gita, The (Sankaracharya) 171n
    Bhagavad Gita: The Song of God (Prabhavananda and Isherwood, trans.) 171n
    Bhagavadgita (Radhakrishnan) 171n
    see also *Gita, the Light of Asia*
Bhatgaon (Bhaktapur), Nepal 78, 90-91, 93, 94, 96, 99, 213
Bhotia (Bhote)
    see Tibetans
Bible 130, 134, 152, 154
Bihar, India xiii, 40, 46n, 59, 61n, 64-66, 70ff, 86, 97, 99, 105, 108, 113, 114, 125n, 128, 156, 157, 159ff, 175, 196n, 273, 274, 280, 316
Bihlmayer, Ulrich ('Uli') (DJ9KR) 340
birding, bird watching
    see ornithology
Birds of Nepal (Fleming *et al*) 243, 261n
Birendra, King
    see Nepal, Kings
    see Shah, Birendra
Birendra, Samuel 171n
Bishop, Barry viii, 328, 329
Bishop, Lila 326, 330
Bishop Hartmann (Vannini) 83n
Bishop's House, Patna 72, Ch. 6 *passim*, 145, 148, 160
Bishop of Allahabad
    see Gramaigna
Bishop of Patna 40, 46n, 72, 118, 119
    see also Hoeck
Blanchard, John 217
Blackwell, Fritz xiii
Blasczyk, Ed (W3KVQ, N7EB) 293, 294
Blessed by the Lord: A History of the Patna Jesuits (Oiz) 83n, 124n
Blitz (Indian newspaper) 254
Blue Room, Kathmandu 218
Board of Secondary Education (BSE, Bihar, India) 168
Bodh Gaya 116, 117
Bombay 50, 56, 57-59, 105, 108, 112, 138, 156, 166, 169, 314-15, 322, 334
Bombay Radio Club 314-15
    see also radio, India
Bonnot, Charles 49, 53, 55, 61n, 176
Book of Cases 132,
Book of Numbers 152
Boris
    see Lissanovitch

Bowles, Chester 254
Breitenbach, Jake viii, 327
Brennan, John 111, 113, 151
Bridges, Reverend 169
British Arab Petroleum Company (BAPCO) 166
Brown, William ('Bill') (K9LF) 291, 324, 343
Buddha 60, 72, 92. 117, 236
Buddhanilkantha School, Nepal 266
Buddhist, Buddhism 6, 60, 77-80, 82n, 88, 89, 116, 117, 138, 186, 209, 218, 235, 246, 247, 249, 256, 344
    see also Lumbini
Buchwald, Art 260n
Burathoki, Mr 204

C
Cabral, João (John) 81, 82, 88, 196n, 251
Cacella, Estevo 81, 251,
Cachat, Leo 217, 224n, 284
Cangas, Jose 343
Capuchin, Catholic Order Chs 4-5 *passim*, 105, 196n, 213, 254
The Capuchins (Cuthbert) 100n
Carlo
    see Maria, Carlo
Carlos, Juan, King of Spain 292, 299
Carnation Milk Co., Chicago 20, 21
Cathedral of St John, New York 12
Catholic explorers Chs 4-5
Catholic World (magazine) 138
Central Intelligence Agency (CIA) 253-54
Chaknee, school (in India) 120
Chamberlain, Cecil 162
Chardin, Teilhard de 347
Chethipuzha, Stephen 285n
Chhetri, Padma 211
Chicago Catholic (magazine) 209, 224n
Chicago vii, ix, xii, Ch. 1 *passim*, 27, 30, 31, 105, 109, 167, 306, 307, 310
    see also Jesuits, Chicago
Chinia Lama of Boudhanath (Kathmandu) 245, 250
Chogyal, King of Sikkim 312
Chotikul, Kamchai 338
Choudhury, Ranjit Roy 158
Christian Brothers 4, 148, 205
    see also Christian Brothers' School, Patna
Christian Settlements in Nepal (Vannini) 83n, 87, 96, 100n, 102n
Christian missions to the Himalayas Chs 4-5
Christensen, Harold xvi
Christianity in China, Tartary and Thibet (Huc) 73, 76, 83n, 84n
Christie, Agatha 238
Chuhari, India 72, 83n, 97, 99, 102n, 148
CIA
    see Central Intelligence Agency
Cinerama 231-233
City of God (St Augustine) 46n
Clergy Monthly, The (magazine; now called *Vidyajyoti*) 128

Cleary, Kevin 111, 158, 202
Clough, Elizabeth 163, 248
Confessions (St Augustine) 46n
Coleman, Don (W2GBC) 291
College of the Sacred Heart, India 110
'Come at once' telegram 196, 198
Commonweal (magazine) 138
communism 137, 246,
Congregatio Sanctissimi Redemptoris (CSSR) 267, 285n
Congress Party, India 152, 160, 161, 164
Congress Party, Nepal 227, 347
Conner, Bill (W2GBC) 291, 323
Constitutions (Jesuit) 36-38, 46n, 64, 69, 151
contagious hepatitis (jaundice) 124, 126
Coronation of King Mahendra 229-33ff
Coronation Sports Day 234
corrupt officials 140
Coughlin, Charles Edward 137
Coyne, Marty 217, 222, 284, 285, 286n, 349
Cripps Mission to India 164
Cripps, Sir Stafford 164

D
d'Orville, Albert 88, 196n, 251
Dalai Lama 77, 78, 84n, 88, 89, 246, 247
Darjeeling, India 71, 124, 127, 129, 141, 205, 235, 312
Darsie, Bonnie xiii
Dasain (Dassahra) Hindu festival 183
David Copperfield 17
de Lastic, Alan, Archbishop of Delhi xiii, 348, 351n
dengue fever (breakbone fever) 124
Depression, Great 5, 48, 54, 156, 171n
    see also Stock Market Crash
Dertinger, George 48, 49, 53, 55, 61n, 176
Desideri, Ippolito Chs 4-5 *passim*, 183, 196n, 251
Dewey, John 275, 276
Dharan, Nepal 257, 258, 262n
Diaghilev, Sergei 237
Dinapur, India 107, 124, 126, 127, 147, 148
Diwaker, R.R. 133, 146n
dogs 221, 222
Dominicans 68, 74
Donnelly, James J. ii, xiii, 211, 217, 266, 267, 270, 271, 279, 282, 285n, 323, 349, 351n
Don't Let the Goats Eat the Loquat Trees (Hale) 175, 196n
Doody, Dan 326
Downing, Thomas M. 26, 205-08, 216-18, 224n, 257
Dressman, James 207, 208, 217, 221, 224n, 284, 347-50
Dugec, Tom 343
Durbar High School, Kathmandu 177, 178, 186, 188
Durrwell, F.X. 267
DX
    see radio
Dyhrenfurth, Norman 325ff
Dyhrenfurth, Sally 326

INDEX

E
Early Jesuit Travellers in Central Asia (Wessels) 83n
East India Company 95, 97
Egan, Joseph M. 195
Eisenhower, Dwight D. 232
Eline, William I. 72, 107, 127
Eliot, T.S. 3
Epistles of Paul 153
Esmaker, John ('Buddy') 310, 311, 314, 317n
Essential Gandhi (Fisher) 171n
Everest, Mount ix, x, 3, 129, 214, 215, 239, 258, 297, 318, 325-27, 331, 332, 333n

F
Fabulous Flemings of Kathmandu (Fletcher) 261n
Far East (magazine) 40
Farrell, Felix 41, 42, 151
Felix, Joseph, of Morro 90
filariasis (elephantiasis) 124
Filipino Sisters of the RVM (Religious of the Virgin Mary) 266
Fisher, Louis 171n
Fleming, Robert ('Bob') and family 239, 243ff, 248, 261n
Fleming, John 307
Fletcher, Grace 261n
Florissant, Missouri Ch. 2 *passim*, 49, 72, 147, 311
Fonteboa, Bartolomeo 81
Forbes, Ann A. 246ff, 261n
Foster, Leon 42
Framework for School Renewal (Chethipuzha and Murican) 285n
Francis, John of Fossombrone 90
Franciscans 68, 85
Frape, Chris xvi
Freyre, Fr 88

G
Gafney, Thomas 217
Gaidostik, 'Bert' (K9AWK) 323
Gandhi, Kasturba 152
Gandhi, Mohandas ('Mahatma') 133, 151ff, 158, 160ff, 170n, 171n, 274, 316
Ganss, George E. 36, 37, 46n
Garraghan, Gilbert J. 83n
Gates, Jim 349
Gaucher Airport (Tribhuvan International Airport), Nepal 194, 195, 198, 229, 330
Genicot, Joseph 128
Gilliard, Tom 231, 232
Gita, the Light of Asia 153
    see also *Bhagavad Gita*
Giuseppe of Roveto 83n, 95, 96, 97, 100n, 101n
Giuseppe of San Marcello 97
Goa, India 64, 68ff, 75, 79, 80, 92, 112, 131
Godavari, Nepal school
    see St Xavier's Schools, Godavari
    marble quarry 222, 223, 226n
Godavari Alumni Association (GAA) 222, 269, 281, 283, 286n

Goldstein, Melvyn C. 261n
Goodbye, Mr Chips (film) 257
Gopal (bookbinder) 211
Gorkha Dakshin Bahu 283
Gorrell, Ralph 306, 307
Goshen, Indiana 12, 32, 35
Govinda, Anagarika 84n
Gramaigna, P. 71
Gresham, Col William ('Bill') (9N1DD) viii, 325ff, 334
Grossman, Max 343
Grueber, John 82, 88, 196n, 251
Gschwend, Joseph A. 118, 125n
Guesthouse, Royal (Kathmandu)
    see Nepal, Royal Guesthouse
Gugé (Tibetan kingdom) 77, 79, 80, 81
    see also Tsaparong
Guinness, Sir Alec 3

H
Hagen, Toni 238, 248, 249, 261n
Hager, Ken and Elsie 323, 332n
Hale, Thomas 175, 196n
Hamlet 175
Hansel and Gretal 115, 206, 207, 208
Harijan (periodical) 171n
Harrer, Heinrich 238, 248, 261n
Hartmann, Bishop 70, 71
Hartnett, Robert 30, 41
Heras, Fr 58, 59
Here Be Yaks (Lahiri) 84n
Hertz, Heinrich 307
Higgenbotham, Sam 163
Higginson, Rusty 334
Hillary, Sir Edmund 3, 214, 215, 239, 325, 328, 333n
Hindu, Hindus, Hinduism 6, 32, 60, 64, 71, 75ff, 90, 91, 105ff, 113, 116ff, 125n,
    138, 153, 154, 156, 161, 164ff, 170n, 180, 183, 187, 189, 196, 200, 201, 207, 209,
    213, 218, 220, 222, 232, 315, 316, 344, 349
Hindu-Muslim riots 164, 165
History of Modern Tibet, A (Goldstein) 261n
History of the Society of Jesus, A (Bangert) 82n
Hodgson, Brian 243
Hoeck, Louis Van 40, 46n, 72, 118, 119
Holy Family Hospital, Delhi 332, 347, 348, 349, 351n
Holy Family Hospital, Patna 161, 175, 215
Horace, Francis, of Pennabilli 90, 94, 99
Hornbein, Tom viii, 328-331, 333n
Hound of Heaven (Thompson) 17, 27
Huc, L'Abbe 73, 76, 78, 83n, 84n
Hunt, Sir John 214, 215, 297, 333n
Hussein, King of Jordon 292, 299, 339
Huxley, Aldous 154, 155, 171n

I
I Missionari Italiani nel Tibet e nel Nepal (Petech) 83n, 102n

Indian Embassy, Kathmandu 193
Indian Independence movement 161, 164
    see also 'Quit India' Movement
influenza epidemic of 1918-19 13
Institute of the Blessed Virgin Mary (BMV) 219
Isherwood, Christopher 171n
Ismail, Sir Mirza, Diwan of Travancore 157
Ivanhoe 17

J
Jackson, Gamesman 211
Jerstad, Lute viii, 327ff
Jana Andolan
    see 'People's Movement' (Nepal)
Jesuit, Jesuits, Society of Jesus *passim*
    see also Nepal Jesuit Society Chicago Province
    charism (Jesuit spirit) 284
    Chronicles (Nepal) 208ff, 224n, 281
    early missions to India Ch. 4
    early missions to Tibet and Nepal Chs 4-5
    Goa Province 68, 69, 75
    martyrs 51, 52
    Missouri Province xiii, 71, 72
    Missouri Province Archives xiii
    on spirituality 37, 38
    organization and administration *passim*, 147, 148
    priesthood 39ff
    Superior 155, 193, 203, 219, 268, 284, 348
Jesuit Missions (magazine) 40, 41
Jesuits (Barthel) 146n
Jesuits (Martin) 146n
Jesuits in Nepal (Locke) 100n, 224n
Jesuits of the Middle United States (Garraghan) 83n
Jha, Bishnu Prasad 208
Jinnah, Mohammed Ali 165, 166, 172n
Jinpa, Geshi Gelek 84n
John III, King of Portugal 67
Jones, Jennifer 256, 257

K
Kaji, Hira 208, 209
Kamal Niwas, Kathmandu 266
Kaur, Amrit 152
Kazi, Sher (Godavari School carpenter) 211
Khatri, Krishna 242, 246n
Khrist Raja (Christ the King) High School, Bettiah, India 113, 114, 121, 162
Kingston, Richard xiii
Kinloch, British military expedition (to Nepal) 95
Klein, Fr 111
Koirala, B.P. 236
Koirala, G.P. 350
Koirala, M.P. 227, 236, 240
Konop, Ed (W2WGS) 294, 295
Kot Massacre, The (Stiller) 102n

Kurseong, India
    see St Mary's Seminary

L
Lahiri, Manosi 84n
Laise, Carol 255, 305n
Lalitpur, Nepal
    see Patan
Lama, Panchaman 265, 282, 285n, 350
Lamentations of Jeremiah 141
Landon, Perceval 183
Lastic
    see de Lastic
Law, Charles 217
Le Nepal (Levi) 77ff, 84n, 100n
leishmaniasis (black fever) 124
leopards 220, 221, 223
lepers, leprosy 124
Levi, Sylvain 77ff, 84n, 88, 99, 100n
Lhasa, Tibet 77, 81, 82, 85ff, 94, 183, 196n, 246ff, 251
Liberation Theology 134
Lincoln School, Kathmandu 266
Lindbergh, Charles 41
Lindell, Jonathan 83n, 85, 98, 101n, 192n, 261n
Lisieux, Therese of 44, 46, 53, 55
Lissanevitch, Boris 214, 237, 245, 249, 261n, 305n
Lissanevitch, Inger 237, 245, 248
Little Colonel, The (film) 257
Little Tibet (Nepal) 64, 73, 74, 85
Life (magazine) 254
Locke, John ii, xiii, 83n, 99, 100n, 101n, 102n, 124n, 188, 197n, 205, 206, 217, 224n, 225n, 350, 351n
Loer, William 297
Loesch, Frank 155ff, 160
Lohani, Himalaya (Surendra Lohani) 350
London, England 35, 50-54, 316
Lost Christians in Tibet 74ff, 77
Lourdes, Notre Dame de 44
Loyola University, Chicago Ch. 2 *passim*, 311
Lumbini, Nepal (Buddha's birthplace) 60, 61n, 236

M
McCormick, Col Robert 137
Mckinley Public School, Chicago 9
McMenamy, Francis X. 42, 43
Madame Butterfly (operatic aria) 17, 21
Madras, India 110
Mahabharata 170n
Majowlia village and school, India 117, 118, 120
Malla Kings
    see Nepal, Kings
Malla, Gen Sher Bahadur 297
Malla, Jit Singh 224n, 240
Malla, Lft Shanta Kumar 281

Malpichi, Stanislao 80
Maltese Falcon, The (film) 256
Mann, Ed 219
Mann, Joseph 41
Many Splendoured Thing (Suyin) 244, 261n
Marble Arch, London 51
Marconi, Guglielmo 307, 314
Maria, Carlo, of Alatri 97, 196n
Marquard, Walter E. 122
Marques, Manuel 75, 80ff, 84n
Martin, Malachi 146n
Maryknoll (magazine) 40
Mayer, Bob 210
Mazza, Sam 320-22, 325
Medical Missionary Sisters 108, 161
Mehren, Richard 49, 53, 61n, 176
Mendies, Tom and Betty 237
Mennonites 6, 34, 44, 209
Merchant of Venice, The (stage play) 29
Merz, Nancy xiii
Messerschmidt, Kareen xiii, 351n
Messerschmidt, Liesl xiii, 351n
Messerschmidt, Hans xvi
Metzler, Edgar xv
Michelangelo, Fr 95, 102n
Mickey Mouse 257
Miller, Casper J. ('Cap') 217, 225n, 266
Miller, Edgar and Elizabeth 240, 241
Miller, Fr (of the Bettiah mission) 118
Miller, Maynard 326
Mishra, Amar 158, 171n
Missionaries of Charity 108
    see also Mother Teresa
Mistry, Jimmy (VU2IJ) 322
Modern Electrics (magazine) 307
Moore, Freddy 241
Moran, Family Ch. 1
    Bertha Inez Ch. 1 *passim*, 28, 35, 43-45, 234, 280, 281
        pilgrimage to France 43-45
        visit to Nepal 280-281
Moran, Marshall D.
    Award 171
    biographical interviews xii, xiii
    death and funeral xii, 332, 348ff
    Epilogue xii, xiii, 348-50
    'ham' radio operator Chs 13-16
    'Mickey Mouse' (N91MM) xi, Chs 13-16
    pilgrimage to England and France 50-56
    reflections on Aldous Huxley's philosophy 154-55
    reflections on Gandhi's philosophy 151-55
    reflections on Gandhi's approach to education 163, 273-74
    reflections on the *Bhagavad Gita* 151-55
    reflections on moral and liberal philosophy 132-35
    'silent key' 300, 345

trip to Tibet 250-51
in America
  childhood and youth 3ff
  departure for India 48-50
  first radio 19, Ch. 14
  first trip home from India 167-68
  home life in Chicago 3ff
  preparing for India 42
  student life in Chicago and St. Louis Chs 1-2 *passim*
  visiting the Canadian Rockies 45-46
in India Chs 3, 6, 7, 8
  arrival Ch. 3 *passim*
  building schools and hospitals 147ff
  civic responsibilities 168-70
  day in the life 120ff
  illness 126ff
  life in Bettiah Ch. 6
  life in Kurseong 127ff
  language lessons 114, 131, 132, 144
  meeting Gandhi 161-64
  meeting Nehru 165ff
  religious studies 109ff, 126ff, 150-52
    ordination 127, 141-43
  teacher 117-20
  tertianship retreat 150-52
in Nepal Chs 9, 10, 11, 12, 15, 16
  40th anniversary celebration 286n, 288, 307
  arrival in Nepal 175ff
  audience with Prime Minister Mohan Shamsher 185
  'Come at once' telegram 196, 198
  common noun 227
  critique of education 272ff
  founding St Mary's School 219-20
  discovering Godavari 190-92
  day in the life 263-68
  first view of Nepal 116-17
  'motorcycle priest' 242
  opening Jawalakhel School 216-17
  proctoring exams 178ff
  return to Kathmandu 195
  teacher Chs 9, 10, 12 *passim*
More, Joseph 111, 131, 132, 144, 145
Morrison, Bruce xiii
Morrison, John A. 41, Ch. 3 *passim*
Mother Teresa 108
Mount Everest
  see Everest
  radio, mountaineering
Mountain in Tibet, A (Allen) 84n
Mountain is Young, The (Suyin) 238, 244, 261n
Mountbatten, Viceroy of India 166, 172n
movie stars
  see Jones, Jennifer
  see Redford, Robert

Mulholland, Bill 334
Mullen, Raymond 112
Mumbai
    see Bombay
Murican, Jose 285n
Murphy, Frank 203, 208

N
Naidu, Sarojini 152
National Geographic (magazine) 183, 233, 252, 328
Nehru, Jawaharlal 138, 151ff, 158ff, 165-67, 170n, 171n, 194, 195, 297, 316
Nepal
    see also Moran, in Nepal
    Federal Democratic Republic (since 2008) 101n, 286n
    Kings
        Birendra Bir Bikram 197n, 236, 283, 286n, 298, 338
            as Crown Prince 194, 235, 281
            coronation 338
        Dipendra, Crown Prince 197n, 286n
        Gyanendra 194, 195, 197n, 286n
        Mahendra Bir Bikram 210, 229ff, 237, 255, 272, 297-98
            as Crown Prince 194, 209, 227, 238
            coronation 210, 230-35, 237, 255
        Malla Dynasty 90ff
        Pratap Singh Shah 95, 97, 102n
        Prithvi Narayan Shah 95ff, 101n, 191
        Shah Dynasty 97-99
        Tribhuvan Bir Bikram 99, 193ff, 209, 220, 227, 238, 272
            into exile 197n, 229
            return to Kathmandu 197n, 229, 236
    Multi-Party Democracy 286n
    National Education Plan 272-73, 275
    Palace Massacre (of 2001) 286n
    Royal Guesthouse 183-85, 196n
    sports, Sports Council 202, 210-11, 234-35, 269, 270
Nepal (Hagen) 238, 261n
Nepal and the Gospel of God (Lindell) 83n, 85, 101n, 102n, 261n
Nepal Digest, The (journal) xv
Nepal Jesuit Society 350
Nepal Under the Ranas (Sever) 197n
Nestorians (in Tibet) 83n
New Catholic Dictionary 170n
New Testament 114, 124, 130, 131, 135, 152-54
Niesen, Edward 158, 202, 210-12ff, 216, 220, 221, 224n, 234-35ff
Nigg, Walter 100n
Norgay, Sherpa Tenzing 3, 214, 215, 325
nostalgia 145, 285n
Notre Dame de Lourdes
    see Lourdes

O
O'Keefe, Denis and Catharine Ch. 1 *passim*, 28, 34, 35, 53, 209, 308
Oiz, H.M. 83n, 124n
Olenroth, George and Margaret 21, 22, 34, 35

Oliveira, João 80
opera, grand 19, 21
ornithology 239, 243
Ostorog, Stanislas 231

P
Palace Massacre (of 2001)
    see Nepal, Kings, Palace Massacre
Palestrina, Giovanni Pierluigi da 146n
Pandey, Kesari Raj 281
Pandey, Kumar xv
Pandey, Rudra Raj 184, 190, 204
Pandit, Vijaya Lakshmi 152, 158
Pant, Dipak Raj 102n
Pascal, Lazarus 114, 121
Pashupatinath temple, Kathmandu 227
Pataliputra, of ancient India 71, 72, 106, 169
Patan (Lalitpur), Nepal 78, 90, 91, 93, 94, 96, 99, 183, 205, 213, 216, 217, 239ff
Patel, Bulabhai 163
Patna, India xii, xiii, 7, 8, 40, 42, 46n, 58ff, Ch. 6
    Cathedral 70, 71, 83n, 98, 105, 107-08
        bell inscribed to Prithvi Narayan 98
    Diocese 40, 71, Ch. 6 *passim*, 143, 147, 148, 159
    University 155, 169-70, 175, 176, 178-79
    Women's College 159-61, 175, 219
Patna Mission, India (Gschwend) 125n
Peissel, Michel 224n, 230 238, 260n, 261n
People's Movement (Nepal; *Jana Andolan*) 285n
Perekkatt, Lisa 348
Perennial Philosophy (Huxley) 154, 155, 171n
Perier, Archbishop of Calcutta 141, 143
Petech, Luciano 83n, 102n
Pettit, Fr 118
Pias, John 117, 122
Pieces of India (Welfle) 61n, 105, 125n
pilgrimage, Catholic retreat 150-52
Pinto, David 111, 113
Planning for People (Stiller and Yadav) 197n, 225n
Pogue, William ('Bill') 258
Popes
    Benedict XIV 94
    John XXIII 208
    Paul III 67, 142
    Pius XII 223
POSH (port out, starboard home) 56
Pownall, Dick 327
Prabhavananda, Swami 171n
Pradhan, Jyan Bahadur 224n
Pradhan, Krishna Prasad 208
Prakash, Thomas S., MD 349, 351n
Prasad, Jamuna 179
Prasad, Rajendra 160, 162, 163
Prather, Barry 326

probabilism 132, 135
Pütz, Joseph 128, 129, 131, 135

Q
QST (magazine) 301, 305n, 306
'Quit India' Movement 158, 164
Quran 153

R
Racism 31-32
Radhakrishnan, S. 171n
radio, amateur ('ham')
    call signs
        7Z3AB (Henry Volkerts) 339
        9N1DD ('Donald Duck', Bill Gresham) viii, 326, 327, 334
        9N1ME (Mount Everest) 325ff
            see also radio, mountaineering
        9N1MM ('Mickey Mouse', Marshall Moran Chs 15, 16
        9N1SM (Sam Mazza) 320, 321, 322, 325
        9N1FV (Fred Vogel) 320, 321
        9V101 ('Bud', Reese Whitney) 324
        DJ9KR ('Uli', Ulrich Bihlmayer) 340
        EA3JC (Jos Cangas) 343
        HV2VO ('Ed', Edwin Amram) 292
        K7KQ (Ken Hager) 323, 332n
        K9AWK ('Bert' Gaidostik) 323
        K9LF ('Bill', William Brown) 291, 324, 343
        N7EB (Ed Blasczyk) 293, 294
        UA9KOG ('Stan' Stanislaus) 322
        VU2IJ (Jimmy Mistry) 322
        VU2SX (St Xavier's School, Patna) 313ff
            see also radio, India
        VU2US (K. Umrao Singh) 322
        W2GBC (Bill Conner) 291, 323
        W2WGS (Ed Konop) 294
        W3KVQ (Ed Blasczyk) 294
        W7HCH (Don Coleman) 291
        WB4NFO ('Rana', Pradyumna Rana) 291, 342
            see also Rana
    Catholic operators 292
    clubs 298-300
    CQ Amateur Radio Hall of Fame 301, 305n
    'Donald Duck' (9N1DD) 318, 326ff
        see also Gresham, Col William ('Bill')
    DX (long distance) xiii, 19, 263, 291ff, 298, 305n, 313, 314, 316, 317n, 323, 340, 342, 345
        Antarctica 302-04
    India 169, 311-17, 322
    mountaineering vii-x, 325ff
    Nepal Chs 15, 16
        see also Mazza
        see also Vogel
        creating 'Mickey Mouse' (9N1MM) 318-22
        'ham shack', Xavier Hall (Godavari School) 202, 289, 324-25

        school boys 289, 324, 340-41
    Moran's
        awards 301
        first radio 289, Ch. 14 *passim*
        list manager 294
        QSL manager 293-94
        radio public service 298ff
            messages, emergency and personal 259-60, 293ff
    networks
        SEANET 291, 302, 305n, 324, 334, 336-38, 343
        marine mobile 335, 336-38
    'silent key' 300, 345
    Thailand 336
radio, broadcast
    All India Radio (AIR) 169, 314, 316-17
    BBC (British Broadcasting Corporation) 289, 304, 312, 313
    early broadcast radio in America 306, 311
    early wireless 306ff, 317n
Rahner, Karl 267
Rana rulers of Nepal Ch. 9 *passim*
    life under 187ff, 197n, 200
Rana, Bhakta S. 343
Rana, Chandra Shamsher Jang Bahadur 188
Rana, Gen Babar Shamsher Jang Bahadur 185
Rana, Gen Kaiser Shamsher Jang Bahadur 195, 238, 245
Rana, Gen Mohan Shamsher Jang Bahadur 177, 184, 185, 195
Rana, Gen Mrigendra Shamsher Jang Bahadur 177, 178, 185, 190ff, 195
Rana, Gen Nara Shamsher Jang Bahadur 210, 211, 234
Rana, Hemanta 210-11
Rana, Jang Bahadur Kunwar 98, 102n, 176
Rana, Maj Mahendra 180
Rana, Nrip Jang 196
Rana, Pradyumna (WB4NFO) 180, 181-82, 183, 184, 187, 197n, 203, 291, 342, 345n
    malaria 180-82
Ranchi, India 46n, 129, 130, 148, 150-51, 155
Ravel, Fr 111
Red Cross 8, 169, 247, 248, 250
Redford, Robert 258
Religions of Tibet (Bell) 100n
Resurrection (Durrwell) 267
Richardson, Sally 326
Rise of the House of Gorkha (Stiller) 83n, 101n, 102n, 225n
Roosa, Stuart ('Stu') 258-60
Roosevelt, Eleanor 254, 255
Roosevelt, Franklin Delano 54, 137
rosaries 259
Rose, Paul 240
Roveto, Giuseppe of
    see Giuseppe of Roveto
Royal Hotel, Kathmandu 214. 218, 230, 236ff, 248, 249, 261n, 305n

S

Sacred Landscape and Pilgrimage in Tibet (Jinpa) 84n
Saga of Satyagraha (Diwaker) 146n

Sain Bahadur 211
Singha Durbar, Kathmandu 185, 204
St Alphonsus Ligouri 133, 285n
St Augustine 43, 46n, 111, 121, 135
St Francis of Assisi 37, 85
St Francis Xavier *passim*
St Ignatius High School (St Ignatius Academy), Chicago 4, 14, 22, 27, 28, 314
St Ignatius Loyola *passim*
St Louis University, Missouri Ch. 2 *passim*, 49, 58, 72, 142
St Louis, Missouri xiii, 15, Ch. 2 *passim*, 105, 109
St Mary's Schools, Nepal 219-21, 269, 280, 283, 285n, 341
St Mary's Seminary (St Mary's Academy), Kurseong, India 73, 124, Ch. 7 *passim*, 263
St Mel's Church, Chicago 19
St Mel's High School, Chicago 4
St Michael's High School, Patna 148
St Patrick's Cathedral, New York 12
St Peter's Basilica, Rome, Italy 44
St Stanislaus Novitiate, Florissant, Missouri Ch. 2 *passim*, 49, 72, 147, 311
St Therese
    see Lisieux
St Thomas Aquinas 111, 121, 124n
St Xavier's College, Kathmandu 225n, 269
St Xavier's Godavari 1951-1986 Anniversary (Lama) 285n
St Xavier's High School for Boys, Patna, India xii, 73, 111, 155-57, 158, 162, 168, 170, 171n, 175, 177, 212, 313
St Xavier's High School Patna (SXAA) 171n
St Xavier's Schools, Nepal
    Godavari vii, Chs 10, 12, 16 *passim*
        alumni 281ff
            see also Godavari Alumni Association
        founding 190-92
        school motto 263
        Xavier Hall xi, 126, 149, 201, 221, 228, 263, 267, 324, 339
    Jawalakhel vii, xiii, 216-20ff, 223, 224n, 225n, 249, Ch. 12 *passim*, 339, 341, 348, 349
Sankaracharya 154, 171n
satyagraha (passive resistance) 133-34, 146n
    see also Gandhi
Saubolle, Bertrand 205-06, 213, 224n
Saxton, Ed 203, 205
Scharf, Joseph 217
Schock, Bill 217
Schulthess, Heidi 248
Schultess, Werner 238
Schweizer Auslanhilfe 261n
SEANET (South East Asia Network)
    see radio, networks
Search for Paradise (film) 231, 233-34
Selznik, Mrs David
    see Jones, Jennifer
Sermon on the Mount 152-53
Settlements of Hope (Forbes) 246, 261n
Seven Years in Tibet (Harrer) 238, 248, 261n

Sever, Adrian 197n
Shah
   see also Nepal, Kings
   Aishwarya Rajya Lakshmi Devi, Queen of Nepal 283, 286n
   Bahadur 97, 98
   Basundhara 194, 238
   Birendra
      see Nepal, Kings
   Gyanendra
      see Nepal, Kings
   Himalaya 194, 238
   Kumar Khadga 217
   Mahendra
      see Nepal, Kings
   Tribhuvan
      see Nepal, Kings
Shambaganur, India 110-12
Shanta Bhawan Hospital 186, 239ff, 331, 348
Sharkey, Gregory xvi, 225n
Sharma, Antu 349
Sharma, Balchandra 223
Shaw, Mary K. xiii
Sheen, Fulton J. 33
Sheep on the Runway (stage play) 260n
Sherpa, Nawang Gombu viii, 328ff
Sherpa, Tenzing
   see Norgay
Shigatse, Tibet 81-82
Shimkhada, Deepak 100n,
Shrestha, Aian Bahadur 208
Shrestha, Hari Saran 342
Sign (magazine) 138
Silent Cry, The (Stiller) 102n, 197n, 225n
Singh, C.P.N. 193
Singh, Ganesh Man 347, 348, 350
Singh, Ram 211
Singh, Tara Man 204
Sinha, Anuragh 168
Sinha, Sarangdhar 179
Sisters of St Joseph's of Cluny 266
Skylab-II 258
Sloan, John G. 112, 113, 166, 167
Snellgrove, David 250
Snowview Hotel, Kathmandu 230, 237, 238
So Long Until Tomorrow (Thomas) 232, 261n
Song of Bernadette (film) 256
Sons of Boston 299
Sontag, Peter 110, 118
Speeches and Writings (Gandhi) 171n
Spiritual Exercises (St Ignatius) 37, 46n, 67, 130
Spitzer, Alice xiii
Staal, Fritz 84n
Starace, Cyrus ('Ciro') 132

State Mutual Book & Periodical Services Ltd. xv
Stiller, Ludwig F. ii, 83n, 100n, 101n, 102n, 197n, 217, 225n
Stock Market Crash 54ff, 61n
Sullivan, Bernard J., Bishop of Patna 72, 106, 118, 155-57
Suyin, Han 238, 244, 261n
Swiss Order of the Holy Cross 115

T
Taj Mahal 35, 60
Tamang, Habule 263
Tamang, Nati 263
Teaching of the Gita, The (Gandhi) 153, 170n, 171n
Tenzing Sherpa
 see Norgay
Teresa
 see Mother Teresa
tertianship retreat 39, 143, 150-52, 155
Thapa, Chiranjivi S.S. 207, 281
Thapa, Lft Tara Bahadur 281
Thapa, Netra Bahadur 204
Theological Quarterly 142
Theological Investigations (Rahner) 267
Theology Digest 142
Tiger for Breakfast (Peissel) 224n, 238, 260n, 261n
Thomas, Joseph 348
Thomas, Lowell 231ff, 261n, 296
Thompson, Francis 17, 27
Tibet Chs 4, 5 *passim*
Tibetan, Tibetans 245ff, 261n
 refugees, refugee relief (Nepal) 247, 250-51, 253, 255, 261n
  see also Forbes
 Tibetan Refugee Relief Committee 247, 248
  see also UNHCR
Time (magazine) 254, 260n
Times, The (London newspaper) 328
Treasure of the Sierra Madre (film) 256
Treaty of Sagauli 101n, 180
Tribune (Chicago newspaper) 19, 25n, 137, 307
Trichandra College, Kathmandu 170, Ch. 9 *passim*, 204
Tsaparang, Tibet 77ff, 84n, 86, 88, 89, 90
Tucci, Giuseppe 250
Turmes, Fr 138
Twain, Mark 108

U
Ullman, James Ramsey viii, 326ff, 332n
Ullman, Marian 326
UNHCR (UN High Commission for Refugees) 248, 261n
 see also Tibetan, refugees
United World Trade Center, Kathmandu 197n
Unsoeld, Jolene vii-x, 326, 330, 332, 333n
Unsoeld, William F. ('Willi') vii-x, 326ff, 333n
Upadhyay, Sharada Prasad 224n,

Upadhyay, Surya Prasad 224n
Upadhyaya, Heramba Prasad 342
Upraity, Trailokya Nath 227, 273, 279, 285n
USAID (United States Agency for International Development) 218, 320, 332n, 342
USOM (United States Operations Mission)
    see USAID
USIA (United States Information Agency) 259

V
Vamsavali
    see Jesuit, chronicles
Vannini, Fulgentius 83n, 87, 96, 100n, 102n
Varma, Badri 163
Vedas 138,
Verbum Dei 142
Vidyajyoti 128
Vogel, Fred 320, 321
Volkerts, Henry 339

W
Wall Street
    see Stock Market Crash
war
    Great War (WWI) 10, 13, 57, 130, 132, 137, 310
    Second War (WWII) 4, 169, 158, 171n, 231, 289
Wardha Scheme (education system)
    see Gandhi
Warren, Thomas 343
Warriors of God (Nigg) 100n
Watrin, Eugene L. 217, 221, 222, 227, 234, 251, 281, 284
Way of the White Clouds (Govinda) 84n
Weatherall, Katherine 248
Welfle, Richard Ch. 3 *passim*, 105, 122, 123, 125n, 131, 176, 193
Welzmiller, Francis 147, 151
Wessels, Cornelius Ch. 4 *passim*
Westminster Abbey, London 51
Westminster Cathedral, London 52, 61n
Whitney, Reese ('Bud') (9V101) 324
Whittaker, Jim viii, 326ff
Wildermuth, Augustine ('Gus') 42, 118, 132, 151, 162, 193, 219
Wireless Age (magazine) 306
Wollen, Ian 328, 329
Wood, Hugh ('Barney') 273, 278
Wroblewski, Joseph 158
Wylie, Col Charles 332n

Y
Yadav, Ram Prakash 197n, 225n
Yoshizawa, Sijiro 230, 231
Young India (Gandhi) 171n

www.ingramcontent.com/pod-product-compliance
Lightning Source LLC
Chambersburg PA
CBHW030517230426
43665CB00010B/652